A Good Life in Old Age?

MONITORING AND IMPROVING QUALITY IN LONG-TERM CARE

BETTER POLICIES FOR BETTER LIVES

This work is published on the responsibility of the Secretary-General of the OECD. The opinions expressed and arguments employed herein do not necessarily reflect the official views of the Organisation or of the governments of its member countries.

This document and any map included herein are without prejudice to the status of or sovereignty over any territory, to the delimitation of international frontiers and boundaries and to the name of any territory, city or area.

Please cite this publication as:
OECD/European Commission (2013), *A Good Life in Old Age? Monitoring and Improving Quality in Long-term Care*, OECD Health Policy Studies, OECD Publishing.
http://dx.doi.org/10.1787/9789264194564-en

ISBN 978-92-64-19452-6 (print)
ISBN 978-92-64-19456-4 (PDF)

Series: OECD Health Policy Studies
ISSN 2074-3181
ISSN 2074-319X

European Union

Catalogue number: KE-31-13-667-EN-C (print)
Catalogue number: KE-31-13-667-EN-N (PDF)

ISBN 978-92-79-28944-6 (print)
ISBN 978-92-79-28943-9 (PDF)

The statistical data for Israel are supplied by and under the responsability of the relevant Israeli authorities. The use of such data by the OECD is without prejudice to the status of the Golan Heights, East Jerusalem and Israeli settlements in the West Bank under the terms of international law.

Photo credits: Cover © valeriya_sh/Shutterstock.com; © vladis_studio/Shutterstock.com; © Zern Liew/Shutterstock.com; © Leremy/Shutterstock.com.

Corrigenda to OECD publications may be found on line at: *www.oecd.org/publishing/corrigenda*.

© OECD/European Union, 2013

Foreword

More and more people reach an age where they have to live with declining functional and cognitive abilities and thus become dependent on the help of others in their daily life. Protecting the right to a life in dignity of frail older people is thus becoming a major policy challenge.

This report is about how countries are addressing this challenge by developing measures to ensure a high quality of long-term care – care that is safe, effective, and centred around the needs and abilities of the care recipients themselves. In most respects, endeavours to improve long-term care quality lag behind comparable efforts in the health care sector, but there are some excellent initiatives in some countries which combine measurement of clinical effectiveness with patient-centred approaches to improve the quality of life of people in need of care. Such new initiatives to stimulate quality improvement have gained ground alongside traditional regulatory approaches. There are interesting examples of public reporting of quality performance of care-providers which enable older people and their families to make informed choices, and quality grading systems which encourage providers to compete on care outcomes.

This report is the outcome of a two-year collaboration between the OECD Health Division and the Directorate General for Employment, Social Affairs and Inclusion of the European Commission. The report discusses the importance of developing metrics for measuring safe, effective and responsive long-term care services, and looks at on-going country initiatives to improve the quality of life of frail elderly, as well as the technical and broader challenges to measurement and improvement.

Providing a life in dignity in old age is not only a moral imperative. It also makes good economic sense if it is achieved by assuring that older citizens can maximise their potential for independent living, thus reducing their dependence on others to a minimum. Empowering older people in such a way also enhances their protection against the risks of abuse or inadequate care. The OECD and the European Commission will continue to work closely together to explore how future long-term care needs can be met in ways that protect older people and their dignity, notably by delivering high-quality care services and promoting healthy and active ageing.

<table>
<tr><td align="center">**Mark Pearson**</td><td align="center">**Ralf Jacob**</td></tr>
<tr><td align="center">Head of the OECD Health Division</td><td align="center">Head of the Unit for Active Ageing, Pensions, Healthcare and Social Services at the European Commission</td></tr>
</table>

Acknowledgements

This book reflects the efforts of many officials and experts from the OECD, the European Commission and from countries, who worked collaboratively over a two-year period.

The report was principally developed by Francesca Colombo, who led the project, and Yuki Murakami, from the OECD Secretariat. It contains written contributions from experts and academics from countries across Europe, Canada and the United States, without which this book would not have been possible. In particular, chapters have been written by Iain Carpenter from the Royal College of Physicians in the United Kingdom and John P. Hirdes from University of Waterloo in Ontario, Canada; David Stevenson from the Harvard Medical School and Jeffrey Bramson from the Harvard Law School Class of 2012 in the United States; Henk Nies from Vilans, Utrecht and VU University, Amsterdam, Roelf van der Veen from Vilans in the Netherlands and Kai Leichsenring from the European Centre for Social Welfare Policy and Research in Vienna, Austria.

The report benefited from invaluable encouragement and suggestions from Mark Pearson at OECD and from Ralph Jacob, Fritz Von-Nordheim and Sven Matzke from the European Commission (Directorate General for Employment, Social Affairs and Inclusion). Many thanks also to Marlène Mohier, Nathalie Bienvenue, Josefa Palacios and Tracey Strange for her editorial contribution in preparing the document for publication.

The project would not have been possible without the help of country experts and delegates, including representatives from Health and Social Policy Ministries in EU and OECD countries, who provided technical input, background information, and feedback. An expert meeting discussed the draft report on 14 November 2012 in Paris. Comments on the report were also received from the World Health Organization, the Business and Industry Advisory Committee to the OECD (BIAC), researchers at the London School of Economics and the European Centre for Social Welfare Policy and Research in Vienna, and other experts.

The project was supported by a grant from the Directorate General for Employment, Social Affairs and Inclusion of the European Commission. It benefited from voluntary contributions from Belgium and Japan.

Table of contents

Part I

Measuring quality in long-term care

Part II

Policies to drive quality in long-term care

Part III
Case studies: Europe and the United States

Tables

Figures

Glossary

Accreditation: A voluntary or compulsory method to regulate the market entry and standards of any service provider. Service requirements are defined by specific regulations and compliance is assessed by inspection.

Activities of daily living (ADL): Include bathing, dressing, eating, getting in and out of bed or chair, moving around and using the bathroom. Often they are referred to as personal care.

Adverse (clinical) events: Any unintended and undesirable experience occurs to person receiving treatment and care as a result of inappropriate use of medication or medical treatment.

Care co-ordination and integration: The degree to which health and social care are interconnected and transitions between health and social care are harmonised.

Care effectiveness (Clinical effectiveness): Describes the degree to which the provision of care delivers the best possible health and social care to achieve best functional outcomes and prevent patients' conditions from worsening more rapidly than otherwise expected.

Care setting: The place where users of care services live, such as nursing home, assisted living facilities/sheltered housing or private homes, care at home and in the community.

Casemix: Classification systems that provide information about the overall resource needs of health care service recipients. Resource Utilisation Groups (RUGs) is an example of classification system to determine the relative cost of caring and used to determine in payment systems to reimburse costs.

Cash (or cash-for-care) benefits: Include cash transfers to the care recipient, the household or the family caregiver, to pay for, purchase or obtain care services. Cash benefits can also include payments directed to carers.

Dementia: A loss of brain function that affects mental function related to memory impairment, low level of consciousness and executive function. The most common form of dementia is Alzheimer's disease.

Elder abuse: Refers to actions, occurring within any relationship which causes harm or distress to an older person.

Family carers or caregivers: Include individuals providing LTC services on a regular basis often on an unpaid basis and without contract, for example spouses/partners, family members, as well as neighbours or friends.

In-kind benefits: Are those provided to long-term care recipients as goods, commodities, or services, rather than money. They may include care provided by nurses, psychologists, social workers and physiotherapists, domestic help or assistance, or special aids and equipment. They might also include assistance to family caregivers such as respite care.

Instrumental activities of daily living (IADL): Include help with housework, meals, shopping and transportation. They can also be referred to as *domestic care or home help*.

Long-term care (LTC): Is defined as a range of services required by persons with a reduced degree of functional capacity, physical or cognitive, and who are consequently dependent for an extended period of time on help with basic activities of daily living (ADL). This *personal care* component is frequently provided in combination with help with basic medical services such as *nursing care* (help with wound dressing, pain management, medication, health monitoring), as well as prevention, rehabilitation or services of palliative care. Long-term care services can also be combined with lower-level care related to *domestic help* or help with instrumental activities of daily living (IADL).

(LTC) at home: Is provided to people with functional restrictions who mainly reside in their own home. It also applies to the use of institutions on a temporary basis to support continued living at home – such as in the case of community care and day care centres and in the case of respite care. Home care also includes specially designed, *assisted or adapted living arrangements* for persons who require help on a regular basis while guaranteeing a high degree of autonomy and self-control.

(LTC) institutions: Refers to nursing and residential care facilities (other than hospitals) which provide accommodation and long-term care as a package to people requiring ongoing health and nursing care due to chronic impairments and a reduced degree of independence in activities of daily living (ADL). These establishments provide residential care combined with either nursing, supervision or other types of personal care as required by the residents. LTC institutions include specially designed institutions where the predominant service component is long-term care and the services are provided for people with moderate to severe functional restrictions.

(LTC) quality: Refers to effectiveness and care safety, patient-centredness and responsiveness and care co-ordinaton which relate to technical quality as well as experience that LTC users will have and the way care is harmonised across setting. Structural quality refers to staffing and management, care environment, and information and communication technology (ICT) and non-ICT assistive technologies that are instrumental to LTC quality.

(LTC) recipients (or care recipients): People receiving long-term care in institutions or at home, including recipients of cash benefits.

Patient-centredness: A dimension of LTC quality whereby LTC users are placed at the centre of LTC delivery. It refers to users' being are actively involved in their care, that their expectations are met and their care experience is pleasant.

Standardised assessment systems: A systematic tool or process to collect information on the needs of LTC users, based on a set of pre-defined concepts and data categorisation to guide care planning. These tools are typically used by clinicians or trained professionals to evaluate the physical, cognitive and functional needs of LTC users and rank their level of impairment. Resident assessment instrument (RAI) is one example.

User safety: Refers to the safeguarding aspect of care provision to avoid, prevent and ameliorate adverse outcomes or injuries caused from the processes of provision of LTC.

Executive summary

*Delivering high-quality care services has become
a policy priority*

With the ageing populations and growing costs, ensuring and improving the quality of long-term care (LTC) services has become an important policy priority across OECD countries. The share of those aged 80 years and over is expected to increase from 4% in 2010 to nearly 10% in 2050, while in 2010 OECD countries allocated 1.6% of GDP to public spending on LTC, on average. The goal of good quality care is to maintain or, when feasible, to improve the functional and health outcomes of frail elderly, the chronically ill and the physically disabled, whether they receive care in nursing homes, assisted living facilities, community-based or home care settings. This report focuses on three aspects generally accepted as critical to quality care: *effectiveness and care safety*, *patient-centredness and responsiveness* and *care co-ordination*.

*Monitoring LTC quality has been growing
in importance but needs further development*

LTC quality measurement lags behind developments in health care. Only a few OECD countries have well-established information systems for care quality. Four-fifths of countries have indicators of inputs, such as staffing and care environment, but only a handful of OECD and EU countries systematically collect information on quality. Over time work on quality measurement has come to encompass both clinical quality (care effectiveness and safety), user-experience (user centredness and care co-ordination), and quality of life.

While the collection of LTC quality data poses a number of challenges, there is a potential for harmonising data collection on LTC quality at the international level. The OECD measures health quality indicators such as avoidable hospitalisations for older people. Another system widely used in LTC, the interRAI system for assessment of care needs, aggregates person-level data, recorded for the purpose of care planning and provision of care, to compare quality of care and efficiency of services.

*External regulatory controls are the most
developed quality assurance approach
but enforcement might be lenient*

The most common policy approach to safeguard and control quality in OECD and EU countries focuses on controlling inputs (labour, infrastructure) by setting minimum acceptable standards and then enforcing compliance. In two-thirds of the OECD countries reviewed, certification or accreditation of facilities is either compulsory, a condition for reimbursement, or common practice. Australia, Japan, Germany, Portugal, the United States,

England, France have accreditation for home care providers. Outcomes, quality of life, choice and human dignity are the quality dimensions most often included in accreditation and standards. Specific regulatory protection mechanisms designed to prevent elder abuse range from ombudsman to adult guardianship systems and complaint mechanisms.

Despite regulation, compliance and enforcement may not be strong enough. There are still questions regarding the effectiveness of fines, warnings and threat of closure. Too much of it can stifle innovation or discourage providers from going beyond minimum requirements.

Setting standards for "doing the right things"
based on best practices is not widely in practice

Standardisation of practice is one way to find more effective solutions for driving care processes towards a desired level of care quality. All OECD countries use comprehensive care needs assessment to measure the level of disability of LTC recipients and determine eligibility for benefits. A growing number of OECD and EU countries use standardised tools and scales to guide care decisions and resource allocation, and develop quality indicators.

Conversely, standards of practice are not widely adopted yet due to the relatively low qualification levels of LTC workers, fewer peer-learning opportunities, lack of guidelines to respond to complex conditions of the frail elderly, and the difficulty of turning clinical guidelines often developed around specific diseases to cover the multiple, complex conditions of frail elderly. Canada, France, Sweden, and Germany, among others, have clinical guidelines around dementia care.

Market-based and care co-ordination approaches
are an appealing option to incentivise consumers,
providers and payers

Financial incentives and performance measures encourage competition among care providers and give consumers a basis for informed decision making. Two-thirds of OECD countries (primarily in Europe) have implemented cash-for-care, voucher or consumer-directed benefits delivering high satisfaction among LTC users although they may or may not make a difference to health or functional outcomes. Consumer-centred approaches and quality-rating systems assume frail disabled people can make informed choices, therefore the quality and simplicity of the information for comparing options is a key factor affecting their ability to choose. Offering providers financial rewards for delivering good outcomes in long-term care show potential but are limited to a handful of countries (e.g., Korea, the United States, Germany) and evidence on improvement in quality is not robust enough as yet. The need to address fragmentation of care is well understood.

While more complex conditions of the elderly require a higher degree of integration (multidisciplinary teams, organisational collaboration, joint care planning), it has proven difficult to collect systematic country examples for evaluation. Good case management, primary-care co-ordinators, integrated information systems linking data through portable records, multidisciplinary assessments teams and single-entry points have all been identified as potentially quality-enhancing.

Quality assurance schemes vary greatly: Cases
from Europe and the United States

Case studies in a selection of European countries and the United States show that current approaches to long-term care quality assurance focus on three key areas: the standards for provider participation; the monitoring and enforcement of compliance; and public reporting and other market-based approaches to improving quality. The present quality assurance system boasts a complex interplay of national, regional, local and voluntary rules, which can raise challenges for effective and efficient monitoring and enforcement of regulatory standards. While heavy regulation of LTC services, particularly institutional care services, has presented high administrative burdens for providers, the transition of quality assurance to outcomes-based measures should be supported by robust data infrastructure and clear guidance. There is potential for using market-based approaches to improve LTC quality, but incentives to spur desired behaviours must be trade off against possible unintended consequences.

Assessment and recommendations

Francesca Colombo *and* Yuki Murakami,
OECD Health Division

With population ageing, delivering quality care services is a priority across the OECD

There are good reasons why quality assurance for long-term care is on the policy agenda in many OECD countries. First, users of care services *demand more voice* and control over their lives. Expectations towards the quality of care of "baby boomers" are higher than those of their parents. Most recipients expect to live in a single room to maintain their privacy or expect care services to reflect their own individual needs and preferences. Quality LTC services can help frail and dependent persons being more autonomous and continue to take part in society, despite their conditions. Maintaining independence, autonomy and privacy have been shown to prevent depression and loss of interest in life.

Second, given the growing cost of care, LTC services are under *pressure to improve accountability* for money spent. OECD countries allocated 1.6% of GDP to public spending on LTC, on average, in 2010, but demographic changes are pushing long-term care expenditures and resource use to at least double by 2050. In Europe, about 60% of people aged 75 years and over have limitations in their daily activities. Across the OECD, the share of those aged 80 years and over is expected to increase from 4% in 2010 to nearly 10% in 2050. Though still relatively small, public LTC expenditure has shown a faster upward trend in per capita terms than health care spending, an annual average of over 9% across 25 OECD countries, compared to 4% for total public expenditure on health (between 2000 and 2010). Little is known about the extent to which cost increases correspond to improvements in quality of care, partly because of the difficulties of measuring outcome improvements for frail or dependent elderly, for whom physical and cognitive capabilities are inevitably set to worsen. In addition, monitoring of LTC quality is in its infancy, and rarely linked to measures of resource utilisation or expenditure.

Third, governments have a role and responsibility to play in *protecting vulnerable older people*. For example, WHO Europe estimates that at least 4 million people aged 60 years and over experience abuse or maltreatment in any one year in Europe. High-quality LTC services protect frail vulnerable persons and caregivers from potential abuses.

There is still insufficient measurement of care quality

It is fortunate that there has been a move towards better measurement of quality and better evidence-based approaches to LTC quality improvement. These efforts will help to benchmark performance over time and across geographical areas in setting targets for quality improvement, in encouraging competition between providers on the basis of the quality of service that they provide, or in helping LTC recipients make informed choices.

Traditionally, approaches to measuring the quality of long-term care have centred on measuring inputs such as staff to care-recipient ratios, but recognition that outcomes make a better basis for measurement has grown over time. More recently, pressure has grown to embrace quality of life and person-centredness as the appropriate focus of measurement. There are also questions regarding whose outcomes should be considered – those of the LTC recipient only, or also those of the family carers and LTC workers. Nevertheless, there remains some way to go before outcome or output measures of care quality are widely available. Depending on the indicator, between two-thirds and four-fifths of OECD countries have indicators of inputs, such as the LTC recipient-nurse ratios, the number of beds in nursing homes or the number of skilled LTC workers. Many countries do not collect measures of outputs. Information on diagnosis, functional status, and medical complexity is generally not available.

The measurement of long-term care quality is slowly developing

Developing information on LTC quality benefits providers, purchasers, consumers, and regulators in several important ways:

- It helps providers manage care services and workers.
- It helps care workers where they may wish to work.
- It offers consumers information for choosing among different care providers.
- It helps purchasers make informed resource-allocation decisions.
- It helps policy maker setting benchmarks for providers.
- It enables cross-national comparisons of performance.

However, quality measurement in LTC lags behind developments in health care. There are few countries that do not have some sort of national strategy for measuring the quality of health care provided. In contrast, quality measures for long-term care are often still in development. There are a number of challenges related to measurement that might explain this. Measuring quality raises definitional and methodological challenges. As the autonomy of most LTC-dependent people is likely to worsen with age, the main focus of quality in LTC settings is not so much on improving overall health status, but rather assisting dependent people in maintaining control over their condition and, where possible, reduce dependency and disability. Care is ongoing, which makes it difficult to choose a starting and end point for measurement. LTC is a complex mix of social and clinical care services. People need to navigate across care settings, and use different professionals with diverse qualifications. Practices are less standardised, and different forms of care provision coexist.

Despite the challenges, there are notable country exceptions. Some countries are collecting and reporting quality indicators on care effectiveness and safety at the national level (e.g., Finland, the United States, Canada, Korea and Portugal). Japan regards structural inputs, in particular the living environment and staffing, as key items worthy of measurement and reporting. Some countries take a wider perspective, by incorporating clients' perspectives and investigating social aspects or user experiences, such as the Netherlands, England or the United States. Australia and Spain have quality indicator development plans in the pipeline. The choice of indicators is at present still influenced by what data is available. In practice, sources of data for LTC quality reports are quite varied:

- *Standardised assessment results.* Canada, Finland and the United States use information from standardised assessment instruments (such as the Resident Assessment Instrument, RAI) to measure LTC-user needs and then generate indicators of the quality of care.

- *Administrative databases.* These are generated from claim data, inspections, or mandatory reporting of a minimum set of data from providers (e.g., Korea, United States, Portugal, England). Audits and inspections contain useful information on structural inputs, staffing, as well as care effectiveness and safety in some cases.

- *Registers.* A few OECD countries have registries for LTC users. Sweden has a set of well-developed registries in a number of clinical areas or specific conditions, such as the *Senior Alert* registry that gathers individual data on falls, pressure sores and malnutrition; the *palliative* registry and the *dementia* registry. Norway national registry of statistics for nursing and care services includes indicators on the use of restraints of nursing home residents and is used to inform decisions regarding the planning of services.

- *Ad-hoc surveys* of facility or individuals. In some cases, questionnaires include topics related to quality for specific conditions monitored in the study, mostly dementia, end-of-life care and elderly abuse (e.g., the Health Quality Council of Alberta, Canada).

Measures of care quality have focused on clinical aspects but many believe the right metrics ought to be quality of life

The analytical frameworks most often used to describe quality in LTC link quality with *structure, process and outcomes of care.* Indicators such as the characteristics of facilities, the level and training of staff, the safety and appropriateness of the environment, and information and communication technology (ICT) and other assistive technologies can be indirectly linked to good quality of care and can help reduce adverse events such as falls. While these structural and process measures are clearly important to good care, they are only indirect measures of outcomes. Rather, changes in health status, physical and cognitive functions attributable to care are the outcomes that are ultimately of most relevance. This has been recognised in many of the most advanced quality frameworks that are used to assess LTC nationally – LTC policy frameworks in Australia, Canada (Ontario), England, Finland, the Netherlands, and the United States all identify clinical-quality outcomes (care effectiveness and safety) as well as user-experience outcomes (user centredness and care co-ordination) as being the main dimensions of LTC quality. Quality of life, which is often identified as a main dimension of LTC quality, can be regarded as the overarching goal of LTC quality initiatives.

Clinical quality

Indicators of clinical quality help providers and administrations identify quality problems and point to adverse events in the provision of care or unmet needs. A review of country experiences and research projects revealed convergence around a small selection of six clinical quality indicators related to care effectiveness and user safety, most commonly identified as feasible to collect and as being appropriate measures of LTC quality:

- prevalence of stage 1-4 pressure ulcers;
- incidence of falls and fall-related fractures;
- incidence of use of physical restraint;
- incidence of residents using over medications and medication errors;
- prevalence of unplanned weight loss;
- incidence of depression.

However, a pilot based on nine most-advanced countries in systematic LTC-quality reporting (Ontario, Canada; Finland; Germany; Korea; Iceland; Netherlands; Norway; Portugal; and the United States) shows that data are mostly available only for pressure ulcers and the use of physical restraints (seven out of eight countries), followed by falls in five countries. Just half of the countries that reported data are able to report on medication use, weight loss and depression, which can be explained by lack of consensus regarding their relevance to care effectiveness and measurement difficulties. There is greater data availability in institutions than in home care and only Finland reported data on all six quality indicators for both nursing homes and home-care services. The coverage of data and the availability of time series differ significantly from country to country and are mostly limited.

This limited availability of LTC quality measures, even in countries that can be regarded as more advanced in care quality measurement, is indicative of the challenges faced. For other countries, the main reason for unavailability of data is that efforts to collect such indicators either do not exist, or, they remain the initiative of few providers but are not aggregated in national data collections. Where countries are still formalising and expanding LTC coverage and services, there has been little policy impetus for the development of quality indicators, and national database collecting LTC quality indicators do not exist.

The few available data offer nonetheless a useful indication of trends to individual countries. As to cross-country comparisons, a significant variation across countries is likely to reflect methodological and definitional issues. There are lessons that could be learnt from the development of quality of health care indicators, for example regarding criteria for inclusion of indicators (e.g., the indicator should reflect technical quality rather than a consumer perspectives; focused on quality and not utilisation; be built on a single item, not on a multi-item scale; be used for quality assessment at the health care system level, rather than the provider level; be constructed from administrative data using uniform or standardised coding systems; and focus on an important performance aspect).

Responsiveness and care co-ordination

While various policies seek to make care services more attuned with individual wants and needs (for example, by increasingly the scope for choice of service provider and over patters of care), measures of responsiveness are not collected on a regular basis across OECD countries. However, waiting times offer an indicator of poor access. Reasons for waiting times in the sphere of long-term care include inadequate capacity in nursing homes or home-care services, or the lack of facilities serving specific populations. According to a 2012 survey, 13 out of 14 OECD countries show growing concern about waiting times for LTC services and about half collect data on waiting times to access long-term care.

There is hardly any measure of care co-ordination. Indicators, commonly used in health care, such avoidable hospital admission for chronic obstructive pulmonary disease (COPD), can point to the effectiveness in the management of the condition by primary care and LTC systems. However, the indicators collected are not disaggregated enough to help identifying whether the patient was a frail elderly using LTC services or not.

Quality of life (QoL)

In a large number of OECD countries, staff-centred approaches or medical models have dominated the thinking around LTC quality measurement and quality assurance.

This reflected the fact that, beyond family carers, nursing homes were the main providers of LTC services. However, LTC policies in most OECD countries have shifted emphasis from being provider-centred to being person-centred, from focussing on institutional care to encouraging ageing in place and home care, and from providing solely benefits in kind to the use of cash benefits and self-directed care mechanisms. This has led to criticisms that measurement of LTC quality had focussed too much on medical or clinical quality, devoting little attention to the quality of life for people in need of care.

While hard to define, this "quality of life" concept can capture both the objective and subjective dimensions of quality and relate to LTC recipients' ability to live at their highest physical, mental, emotional and social potential. Quality of life seeks to capture "intangible" factors such as consumer choice, autonomy, dignity, individuality, comfort, well-being and security, relationships and meaningful social activity. Thus, quality of care, responsiveness and care co-ordination can be all regarded as contributors or determinants of quality of life.

Operationalising the concept of quality of life into metrics or indicators has proven hard. However, efforts to incorporate QoL into national reporting systems have started to emerge in a selection of OECD countries. Data are usually collected through surveys involving interviews with users or their legal representatives. Indicators have focussed on user experience or satisfaction, as well as social aspects of the care experience. For example, Denmark, Spain, the Netherlands, England, and the United States survey patient and user experience. In England, a National Adult Social Care Survey has used ASCOT to survey all LTC users. ASCOT is a tool designed to capture information about LTC outcomes from the perspective of the LTC recipients, which focuses on items such as cleanliness and comfort, good nutrition, safety, control over daily life, social interaction, occupation, accommodation and dignity. Denmark, Austria, Finland, and the Netherlands are starting to use ASCOT, too. In the Netherlands, legislation requires all LTC facilities to carry out surveys of users' experience based on the national quality framework for "responsible care".

Measurement of quality of life is to date less developed than clinical aspects of effectiveness and safety of care, which are themselves less well developed than measurement in health care. Besides challenges common to those encountered when deriving indicators of clinical quality of care (such as validity, reliability, comparability, bias, and relevance), the distinction between subjective views and objective assessment is sometimes hard to draw and there is no consensus around specific indicators to use. Many have argued in favour of a shift in focus from being medical-centred, to instead measure the extent to which LTC recipients' can self-direct care. However, even this risks missing important aspects of LTC quality. Given the complex nature of care, the most promising approach is an eclectic one, integrating both clinical aspects and user experiences.

Measurement of long-term care quality faces significant difficulties

Even supposing there was a consensus on what it would be useful to measure, turning such a decision into a practical indicator is fraught with methodological and implementation difficulties. LTC is a different type of service than acute care. Acute-care quality can be measured by focusing on achieving specific health outcomes and eliminating medical errors. However, the degenerative nature of LTC and the combination of multiple care settings involving medical, social, and housing domains makes it difficult to specify expected outcomes or set benchmarks for outcome improvement.

Despite the significant volume of academic debate about the appropriate focus for measuring LTC quality, in practice few OECD countries have well-established LTC information systems that cover issues of quality. Most of the other countries have not yet reached a national consensus about whether to collect data at a national level, and if so, which indicators ought to be collected and reported regularly. Part of the reason for the scarcity of information is, naturally, due to the lack of systematic data collection from reliable sources. However, in itself this is not the full story. For example, although a significant number of OECD countries use assessment instruments to evaluate LTC-users' needs and decide entitlement to benefits, few countries have used them to derive nationally representative quality indicators. At provider level, a number of nursing homes record information on LTC recipients, so providing useful information to managers of LTC services. Similarly, several OECD countries have clinical registries (e.g., on falls, use of restraints, medication) that include LTC users, so it would be possible to derive safety and care effectiveness measures for regular monitoring. Hence there is more data "out there" than has yet been used for purposes of monitoring the quality of LTC.

That said, there are weaknesses in the available data. Efforts to develop IT infrastructure have focused on acute care, with LTC or rehabilitation settings receiving a lower priority. An important barrier to improving measurement are split responsibilities between health and social care, fragmentation of service points, and differences in coverage of data. Concerns have also grown around data protection and privacy issues, including potential misuse of personal information from needs assessments, which have led to specific patient protection legislation in some countries (e.g., *Protection for Persons in Care Act* in Alberta and *Protection of Persons in Care Act* in Nova Scotia, Canada, several European countries, the United States).

What approach to driving quality improvements in long-term care?

In an ideal world, nursing homes and home care providers should have an incentive to develop measures of quality themselves – as in other areas of the service sector. In practice, the informational asymmetries that bedevil health care are strong in the area of LTC too. Evidence of elderly abuse, has called into question the ability of care providers' self-regulation to drive appropriate care. While many providers will seek to deliver high-quality care even in the absence of monitoring of LTC quality, others might deliver low-quality services to ill-informed care recipients. Although simplifying a rather complex picture, it is not misleading to say that most countries started by attempting to eliminate the worst cases of abuse and exploitation by monitoring the process of care, only later moving on to a wider objective of quality of care provided by a broader spectrum of providers, with the intention to promote the quality of life of LTC recipients.

Hence, typically OECD countries first introduced legislation in the sector to encourage safety and care effectiveness, and strengthened regulatory oversight of clinical quality of care. More recently they have sought to empower users to choose providers and services based on some measure of care quality. However, as will be shown, there has been little experimentation and even less evaluation of such experimentation, so what ought to be the most appropriate policy approach to drive quality in LTC remains an open question.

Policies and instruments to drive quality in LTC can be broadly classified into three groups. The first step to overcome poor incentives or failures of providers to self-regulate is to impose external regulatory controls to safeguard and control quality, which are typically focused on controlling input (labour, infrastructure) by setting minimum acceptable standards and enforcing compliance. A second approach is to develop standards seeking to normalise care practice in desirable ways, and then monitor quality indicators to ensure that care outcomes match desired objectives. And a final approach is to stimulate quality improvement through the use of market-based incentives directed at providers and at users, including by setting financial incentives and encouraging care providers' competition bases on some measure of performance. Table 4.1 (Chapter 4) provides a summary.

Regulatory standards remain the dominant approach to improve quality

Regulatory oversight involves setting external controls over nursing homes and, in some cases, home care and assisted living facilities. Such oversight focuses to begin with on the regulation of physical and human resources employed in the care process. This can be accompanied by standards prescribing structural and procedural requirements that however do not interfere with care providers' decisions or choices regarding care practices, processes and approaches. The assumption is that because providers are accredited and licensed to practise, they will in their practice meet the terms of the requirements. Compliance can be audited and the public can be informed about the fact that providers meet set standards. However, details of the assessment and inspection processes are typically kept confidential by regulators and not necessarily diffused publicly.

The set of requirements and procedures tends to be similar across countries, even if the term used varies: licence, accreditation, registration, certification or contract. The development of minimum standards, licensure or accreditation of facilities, and training requirements for workers are, in a way, the starting point of quality assurance in long-term care. In addition to official recognition, it is not uncommon for regulators to require additional quality conditions to be met by institutions, for example via accreditation or other regulatory means. This chapter simplifies the various names of the official acknowledgement and uses the term "accreditation". Many OECD countries, Australia, the United States (see Chapter 8 on "Long-term care quality assurance in the United States" by David Stevenson and Jeffrey Bramson for further details), England, the Netherlands to mention a few, set standards for structural inputs and care process, and reward providers with licensing and public reimbursement for a share of the cost incurred. Some countries, most notable Japan, have emphasised educational and workforce standards as the principal quality-assurance mechanism. Austria, Germany, Italy, Luxembourg and Slovenia have developed quality management systems for organisations. Most have created external assessment bodies to oversee quality of care. Across OECD countries, the focus of regulation has mainly been on settings minimum standards for residential settings. The quality of home care and assisted living facilities remains less regulated.

Legislative frameworks to oversee care focus on rights for care recipients and often include standards for inputs

A review of 25 OECD countries showed that they all have legislation setting overarching principles of adequate and safe care. Legislation aims to ensure that older people have the right to access quality care, receive appropriate care, and enjoy choice and control over care arrangements. While ultimately, the main goal of regulation is to guarantee accountability for resources invested in care processes, generally speaking governments seek to achieve three main objectives:

- guide providers and facilities on how to improve quality and safety of services;

- inform service users and their families as to what they can reasonably expect from a service; and

- inform regulators on various aspects of care provision, helping to identify gaps.

The central government is the principle regulator of LTC quality, but many OECD countries and non-OEDC European countries assign decentralised bodies, sub-national governments, or arm's length organisations the responsibility for implementing quality control and monitoring compliance. Almost a third of OECD countries have decentralised governance of LTC to state, regional or local level parties, which are responsible for supervising quality of providers (e.g. Canada, Finland, Korea, Switzerland) (Table 4.2 in Chapter 4).

Specific regulatory protection mechanisms to prevent elderly abuse have been embedded in bills of rights and legislation that elucidate the role and responsibilities of individuals and organisations in addressing cases of abuses (e.g., Alberta, Ontario and Nova Scotia, Canada, Germany and Norway, US states and federal government, the Netherlands, Japan, England and Scotland). Such legislation encourages public disclosure of cases and includes ombudsman and adult guardianship systems, as well as complaint mechanisms. With growing incidence of dementia and Alzheimer, some OECD countries have enacted dementia acts, which usually include principles of safeguard of safety and effectiveness of care.

Certification, accreditation and standards are commonly used to assure quality in LTC institutions

The main instruments to regulate LTC quality in institutional settings are licensure, accreditation and standard settings (Table 4.3 in Chapter 4; also see complementary discussion in Chapter 7 on "Quality measurement and improvement in long-term care in Europe" by Henk Nies et al.). Nearly all OECD countries require LTC institutions to be licensed. Generally, licensure tends to be based on minimum requirements to lessen the risk that nursing homes operate in unsafe or underperforming conditions. In additional, it is not uncommon for regulators to require additional quality conditions to be met by institutions. In more than two-third of 27 OECD countries reviewed, accreditation or certification of facilities is either compulsory (e.g., England, Spain, Ireland and France), a condition for reimbursement or contracting (e.g., Australia Germany, Spain, Ireland, England, and Portugal, the United States), or common practice (e.g., Switzerland). In all these countries, a large number of publicly funded LTC institutions are accredited or certified. Countries without such requirements face difficulties in enforcing accreditation among providers.

Accreditation recognises that an LTC facility meets certain criteria and is fit to operate. Accreditation is an evaluation process that assesses quality of care and services provided in LTC institutions, and sometimes assisted living facilities, and gives recognition that providers are competent, comply with the regulation and meet quality standards in their services. The purpose of accreditation is to encourage quality and safety through a mix of compliance and quality elements, which can extend to continuous quality improvement. The accreditation process usually involves self-assessment by care providers, review of performance against certain standards set by the accreditation body, and monitoring of ongoing performance against such standards. National accreditation bodies are often independent authorities, and can be private (e.g., Australia), although most often they are public bodies.

Typically, accreditation requirements involve benchmarks for structure, workforce and safety. Staffing levels are included in quality standards or initiatives in nearly all countries. Over time, quality dimensions built in accreditation and standards have evolved from inputs (e.g., ratio of skilled workers per LTC users) to processes of care (e.g., management of medication, records keeping and management, infection controls), and, more recently, outcomes, quality of life, choice and human dignity, as demonstrated in the case of Germany, Australia, Ireland, England, Canada and the Netherlands. In the United States, the inspection of nursing homes in order to oversee the quality of inputs has been in place since 1987. Process of care and outcome measures have been monitored from early 2000. Re-accreditation and inspection are not always compulsory and frequency varies across countries. Standards and accreditation might be imposed at national level. However, inspections and supervision usually takes place at sub-national level. Variation in accreditation and inspection across sub-national jurisdictions is a concern in some countries.

Besides accreditation, Germany, Spain, Slovenia, Austria and France require the use of quality-management systems at organisational level (such as ISO or E-Qulin) as part of minimum standards. These are internal quality-assurance mechanisms to measure quality at organisational level. Well-known quality-management systems include EFQM, ISO 9000, Qualicert, E-Qalin, AFNOR, Total Quality Management, and the Balanced Score Card, but which specific system should be used is often not mandated. Quality systems seek to engage organisations in ongoing monitoring with the aim of enhancing care processes and improve care outcomes. Larger organisations may adopt such mechanisms to comply with external requests for transparency and as a competition tool. However, these systems can require expensive paper work, and long time spent in writing reviews, carrying out surveys, training staff, recording outcomes and describing processed, which lead to higher costs for service providers.

Accreditation and standards for home care and community-based care services are less common and regulated. Examples include the United States (home-care agencies certification by state is a precondition for public funding), Spain, France (for commercial agencies), Australia (Community Care Quality Reporting Programme) and the Netherlands, where the national quality organisation (NZA) monitors competition in the home-based nursing sector. Criteria for care provided at home differ markedly from those set for institutional care. These broadly seek to regulate the extent a dependent person's home is adapted to their needs and the main areas covered are safety and staffing ratios. Frequency of inspections and evaluations varies (from every two years in Korea to every five years in France).

Minimum standards have increasingly extended to quality of life and management of dementia

Minimum standards – referred to as quality standards, expert standards or, simply, standards – have been used to ensure quality in LTC institutions or residential homes, although they are not compulsorily enforced by all countries. Such standards are often but not always key elements of evaluation criteria for accreditation or authorisation to practise, and can be found in many OECD countries (England, the United States, Ireland, the Netherlands, Australia, Japan, Germany, Spain, Slovenia, Austria and Portugal). They are designed to ensure safety and effective care through a number of criteria. England,

Australia, Japan and the United States have minimum standards or national license for managers.

The depth of information covered in standards varies, but there are common requirements across OECD countries. The ratio of LTC workers (nurses and/or personal carers) to LTC recipients and the number of qualified skilled workers are often included as a proxy for physical safety. Living-environment standards are set to prevent accidents. Other aspects covered are administrative matters and governance of care provision. More recently, elements have been added to address the quality of life of recipients, basic human rights as well as human dignity (the Netherlands, England, and the United States, Ireland and England), individualised care planning processes and reporting systems for adverse incidents and complaints (Ireland, United States, Ireland and England). Standards specific for dementia care are getting more attention, for example in Ireland and England.

Qualification and certification requirements for care workers do not extend to continuous education and ongoing monitoring often enough

The main approach to regulate the quality of care workers seen in most countries is through education and training for personal care workers and setting staffing ratio requirements for institutional care. Educational requirements set the minimum hours of theoretical and practical training for personal care workers. The hours, settings, modules, and final certification process vary significantly across countries, ranging from around 75 hours in the United States to 430 hours in Australia, and from 75 weeks of total training in Denmark to three years training for certified care workers in Japan (Table 4.4 in Chapter 4). Staffing ratios and the skill mix (e.g., number of nurses versus personal carers) in residential settings are also far from being uniform.

Although most care recipients receive care in their homes, qualification requirements are less stringent and less strongly enforced in domestic and assisted living settings. Where qualifications' requirements for workers in home settings are set, procedures to monitor that they are enforced during the processes of recruitment tend to be weak, especially where there are shortages of workers or difficulties in recruitment and job retention. Conversely, in LTC institutions, minimal qualifications, staffing ratios and skill mixes are regulated in most OECD countries, and monitored during processes of certification or accreditation.

Efforts to improve quality by focusing on reducing staff turnover, improving care planning, and users satisfaction have been developed in may OECD countries. However, only the United States has continuing education requirements for LTC workers and Japan offers financial incentives for providers to hire more certified care workers and to provide them with continuous training opportunities. In addition, in a majority of countries, much of the effort is placed on pre-employment checks rather than post-employment improvement of standards. Once a worker is hired, there is less guidance regarding how best to train, continuously educate and monitor existing employees to drive quality. There is also hardly information on processes to monitor whether an active employee commits a fault that would have prohibited them from working during their background check prior to employment.

Regulatory enforcement has been lenient

Surveys and inspections are the main mechanisms for monitoring compliance with set standards for providers subject to official registration. By checking adherence to desired quality levels, inspections can be powerful tools to encourage quality and counter elderly abuse. Although inspections can be part of accreditation process or continuous process to be accredited, they can cover wider topics than the minimum standards (e.g., review of medical records and interviews with residents and their families, and respect of human rights). Similar to accreditation procedures, the government sets rules and regulations for inspections, while independent agencies or regional governments often have responsibilities for supervising procedures and protocols. Quality dimensions range from structural issues and satisfaction of recipients, to safeguarding resident rights, and accountability. Inspections usually take place annually (e.g., Germany, Luxembourg, Portugal, Ontario Canada), between one and two years (United States, Korea), over a longer time such as three years (Australia), five/seven years (France), or upon request following complaints and inspection (Finland, Sweden).

For cases of poor quality and non-compliance with standards and regulation, there are several ways to inform and encourage providers to act on existing deficiencies, ranging from notification of non-compliance, to consultations and re-inspection, and sanctions, such as fees, temporary banning from admitting new residents, termination of services and closure of facilities.

However, there is uncertainty regarding the most appropriate targeting and improve-ment strategy for facilities that perform poorly. Despite regulation and standards, compliance and enforcement may not be strong or enforced enough. While in the most blatant cases of shortcomings, termination of services or cuts in public payments is enforced, for other less serious cases, enforcement of standards on the basis of audits and inspections can be harder. Closure of nursing homes is rarely imposed (e.g., the Netherlands, Germany). Inspections are costly for public or regulatory authorities, while adherence to norms and protocols can be expensive for providers. Providers complain about the time and expense involved in regulation leading to already scarce resources being directed away from actual provision of care. In the United States, for example, there is evidence that enforcement of federal standards has been lenient and the stringency of the audit process varies across states. Strict regulation has additional limits, for example it can stifle innovative initiatives and management creativity, and providers might focus only on what is regulated, rather than on quality improvement more broadly.

In some countries with decentralised governance, the split responsibility for setting and monitoring standards between different levels of governments can result in cross-state differences in the enforcement of quality monitoring and improvement. In addition, evidence of relationship between minimum standards, accreditation or workforce standards on quality of care improvement is not robust. This suggests that processes of care, such as the way staff is employed in care activities, their role and responsibilities, may have greater impact on quality than regulatory requirements.

There is potential for greater standardisation of care processes

One of the methods for making LTC delivery safe and effective is by setting standards for "doing things" that reflect best medical and nursing knowledge. The intention is to move beyond mere setting of minimum requirements that institutional providers and workers need to follow. Standardisation of practice is a way to find more effective – and possibly more efficient – solutions for driving care processes towards a desired level of care quality. As standards for needs assessment and practice are set, monitoring or external-oversight policies enable policy makers and providers to measure deviations from agreed benchmarks before taking corrective measures. This also provides feedback to citizens on whether LTC users' needs are being met.

Needs assessments are increasingly standardised, but the use of protocols to standardise care processes is not widespread

All OECD countries have needs assessment policies to measure the level of disability of LTC users and determine eligibility to benefits. Needs assessment helps governments target care needs but can also help providers develop care plans and identify potential areas of concern and risk. While there is no universal assessment tool, there are similarities in items measured to determine functional and cognitive capacities, such as need for help with daily living activities or medical need. Professionals involved in the assessments can be a multidisciplinary team (e.g., Belgium, Canada, France, Germany, Ireland, Portugal, and Japan). Care assessment is well developed for home-based care in Japan, Portugal, Germany and the United States, and often the same assessment tool as for residential care is applied.

A growing number of OECD countries have adopted standardised assessment tools (Table 5.1 in Chapter 5). Clinicians use these tools to appraise the physical, cognitive and functional needs of LTC users and rank their level of impairment into scales. They enable to record basic physical, functional and psychosocial information about LTC users' needs and their evolution (e.g., the Resident Assessment Instrument (RAI) in Canada, Finland, Iceland, Italy, the United States, and Spain; the AGGIR scale (autonomie, gérontologie, groupe iso-ressources) in France; KATZ and RAI in Belgium). Indices and scales help care providers prepare care plans and can support co-ordination of care across settings. These tolls present several advantages:

- They facilitate normalisation of care processes and can help drive them towards desired benchmarks or level of quality, for example through the application of practice guidelines or protocols of good practice.

- They can be used to prepare tailored care plans (e.g., Spain, the United States (Medicaid), Japan and Canada). Care plans specify appropriate care interventions, promote consistency in care and minimise variations in care provision. They can prevent adverse events, such as inappropriate prescription of medication for patients with multiple morbidities and have been used to identify persons at risks and to track improvement in physical and cognitive conditions.

- Standardisation of assessment also facilitates the planning of continuity of care across different care settings. For example, the RAI instruments have extended from nursing homes to home care, mental health, palliative care, and post-acute care. Care plans facilitate co-ordinated care across medical and social care workers.

There are nevertheless a number of challenges that have emerged and remain to be addressed.

First, there are questions regarding how to strike the right balance between standardisation of assessment and tailoring of care to individual needs and circumstances, especially as concepts such as quality of life and patient centredness gain momentum. While in some countries decisions about benefit entitlement take into account individual circumstances regarding social or family support of LTC recipients, a strength of standardisation instruments is that there is little room for subjectivity in the process of assessing nursing needs. This means that standardised assessment instruments are not incompatible with tailoring of care services to the unique circumstances of LTC users or regional differences. Many OECD countries using standardised assessment distinguish clearly between the (standardised) process of assessment which ensures equity in assessment of need, and the (tailored) process of drawing a care plan, which can be adjusted to individual needs and circumstances (e.g., Japan, Sweden, Spain, England's proposal under the 2012 White Paper "Caring for Our Future").

Second, while needs assessment processes seem to be well developed across OECD countries, they are often used for deriving eligibility to public funding and support prioritisation and resource allocation decisions. They have not consistently been employed at their highest potential to develop standards of practice, draw comparisons between individual data and practice standards, or guide nursing-staff clinical decisions. Few countries link assessment tools to clinical guidelines and protocols. Where protocols, guidelines and expert standards are used, they provide useful recommendations for the management of users' conditions and interdisciplinary teamwork (Programme of All-Inclusive Care for the Elderly; PACE programme, the United States). Guidelines could be especially helpful for the care of frail elderly because of the complexity of their needs and multiple vulnerabilities. However, while there is a tradition of development and use of clinical guidelines in medical care, there is comparatively less use of clinical guidelines to standardise *nursing care* in LTC settings. Some countries have guidelines that reflect useful care practices rather than clinical practice per se (e.g., Spain, France, Japan). Part of the challenge is that traditional clinical guidelines have been developed based on randomised clinical trials that exclude elderly patients, or have been developed around specific diseases, making it hard to adapt to multiple complex conditions of frail elderly. Thus far, few practice guidelines and care protocols that cut across care settings have been implemented.

Third, and critically, there is a need for developing better guidance for the care of people with complex neurodegenerative conditions such as dementia. Assessment tools still do not address well the complex need of people with dementia and the assessment of cognitive impairment remains therefore under-diagnosed. A positive development is the development of clinical guidelines around dementia care (e.g., Canada, France, Sweden, and Germany). Some OECD countries – e.g., Belgium, Denmark, France, the Netherlands, Norway, Sweden, England and Scotland – have national dementia strategies that stress the importance of specific care guidance for LTC providers.

Public reporting of LTC quality has grown in importance

Tracking users' functional or cognitive outcomes, self-assessment reports, the use of satisfaction surveys, peer reviews and external evaluation of indicators of quality, are all tools for monitoring – on a more or less regular basis – that LTC quality does not deviate from set or agreed quality objectives or practice standards. In parallel, some OECD countries (Germany, Netherlands, some Canadian provinces) are developing policies for measuring LTC user satisfaction. As quality of life is increasingly seen as an important metric to measure LTC quality, its objective monitoring becomes desirable.

While systematic recording of quality measures in LTC is still developing in most countries, as in the case of health care tools for monitoring LTC quality can take different forms, which can be seen along a continuum going from reliance on self-assessed reports by individual provider to external evaluations and public reporting:

- *Self-assessment reports.* Self-assessment is an internal evaluation that providers can make, often following instructions or guidelines specifying performance items. Self-assessment has been incorporated in accreditation procedures in Australia and Japan; however no country relies solely on self-assessed information in their quality-monitoring process.

- *Peer reviews.* Peer reviews give an opportunity to providers to benchmark and compare services with other providers. The assessment is done by a peer, on the basis of commonly understood or internal criteria. Recommendations for improvements remain confidential and shared between peers. To date, there is relatively little evidence of use of peer reviews in long-term care.

- *User experience and satisfaction surveys.* Some OECD countries (Canada, Spain, the Netherlands, Germany, England and the United States) have developed policies to monitor LTC user satisfaction or experience, however only a few monitor regularly this aspect of care and results are not consistently published. These surveys record the view of LTC users on different aspects of care and facilitate the identification of problem areas, offering an opportunity for users to voice their opinions. Information collected in surveys can range from quality of overall services to specific aspects on quality of life. There are efforts underway to standardise the measurement of LTC users' experiences to overcome subjectivity bias.

- *External evaluation* by external oversight body (such as rating agencies and independent third agency (e.g., England, Australia) and government agencies (e.g., Japan) provide an independent, objective assessment based in a set of evaluation criteria and standards. They are often used within licensing, accreditation and auditing processes.

Evidence on using information and public reporting to encourage performance improvement is inconclusive

A significant number of countries monitor care providers' performance through inspections and audit reports or governments' accountability reports, and make information available to the public (Australia, Canada, England, Finland, Germany, Ireland, Japan, Korea, the Netherlands, Sweden, and the United States; there are demonstration projects in Austria and in Catalonia, Spain) (Table 6.1 in Chapter 6). The results of inspections and audits furnish important information regarding gaps in care services. Common shortfalls reported through audits, surveys and inspections are safety and suitability of premises (e.g. infection control, fire hazard, safety), quality of care services and management (e.g. inadequate medication management and records), inadequate staff and inadequate training of the staff, including low understanding by care workers of safety and quality policies and procedures. Other shortfalls relate to users' quality of life and the lack of regular re-assessment of users' needs and autonomy level.

Public reporting is mandatory in the United States, Japan, England, Germany, Portugal and the Netherlands, and Ontario, Canada while it remains voluntary in Finland and in Austria. In many cases, reports can be accessed on the web or in a visible location at facilities. The frequency of reporting varies between a few months (e.g., the United States) and a year (e.g., Korea, Japan, and Germany). Information provided include administrative information (e.g., the number of staff, beds and services, as in Japan), but also inspection results highlighting deficits and history of noncompliance (e.g., Japan, Ireland), indicators of care effectiveness and safety (the Netherlands, United States), or user experiences (e.g., the Netherlands).

In England, the United States, Japan, the Netherlands, Germany and Sweden, reports are available at individual provider level. The rationale is that giving information on providers' performance relative to others peers may encourage poor performers to undertake improvements efforts. The issue has become relevant as a large number of OECD countries implement policies to encourage choice across LTC providers, including through the use of personal budgets or cash-for-care benefits and voucher systems.

This has led to interest in understanding how LTC providers and users respond to aggregate measures as well as provider-level ratings. Although monitoring of LTC quality and user experiences has grown in importance, there is little sign of correlation between public reporting of LTC outcomes and quality improvement responses by care providers or organisations. There is some evidence from the United States and Korea that reporting on performance have led providers to make some quality improvement effort, including on communications and responsiveness. However, there are other reports pointing to the contrary from Germany and Portugal, for example.

A possible explanation is that providers might need a long time to correct deficiencies on some of the outcome measures. There is concern that public reporting of LTC quality might lead providers to a focus only on the items being reported or to up-code LTC recipients' profiles to more complex care needs to demonstrate improvement. Providers might be more sensitive to reports on some care quality indicators where fear of adverse public reaction is higher (e.g., pain and the use of physical restraints). As evidence on quality improvement from reporting is inclusive, this seems to suggest that neither regulation alone, nor policies to standardise care practices and report deviations are individually most effective drivers of LTC quality improvement, and that a combination of policy approaches might be desirable.

Driving system improvement by creating an environment for consumer choice and incentives for providers

The review of policies to drive LTC quality improvement has revealed that regulatory processes are clearly important, but enforcement of regulation can be challenging and regulation of some care settings, notably home care, is lagging behind institutional care in most OECD countries. Seeking ways to standardise care processes appears to be desirable. The care sector lags behind developments in health care, but there can be technical and institutional barriers to overcome. Many OECD countries are now looking at ways to change providers and users' behaviours in order to create a quality "culture", by strengthening incentives for quality improvement. Such incentives can be internal, such as administrative and financial sticks and carrots; or they can be linked to market-based approaches that provide greater user choice, or leverage on public recognition.

Incentives for consumers can be good for quality of life but evidence of impact on clinical quality is not robust

Using market-based approaches to stimulate quality improvement is an appealing option. The idea is that LTC recipients can act as informed consumers, shopping across providers, searching for the care option that best fits their individual circumstances. The possibility to choose among care pathways and to place the needs of care users at the centre is increasingly recognised as a fundamental dimension of care quality. Two-thirds of OECD countries have implemented policies to provide LTC recipients with choice over the care they need, through cash-for-care or consumer-directed benefits. Many have consumer protection policies aimed at giving LTC recipients a "voice" and ability to address complaints. Some countries have introduced public reporting using star-rating systems to help direct LTC recipients to the best performing care providers.

Choice and consumer direction

Broadening choice across providers and settings is the first and the most common initiative that countries have taken to tailor care to consumer preferences. A number of OECD countries offer LTC recipients the possibility to choose across providers (e.g., Portugal, Spain, Japan), or between cash benefits and personal budgets and in-kind services (e.g., the Netherlands, Germany, the US Cash and Counselling programmes) (Table 6.1). The choice usually takes place at care-entry points, typically at the end of needs assessment processes. Consumer-direction mechanisms, including cash-entitlements, empower users and their families to make decisions on the care they need and value the most, and have now been introduced in nearly two-thirds of the OECD countries.

Cash-for-care is often associated with higher satisfaction among users. But the challenges to manage such schemes efficiently are also huge. Having choice does not automatically enable LTC users to use benefits without supervision. Unregulated use of cash benefits can be counterproductive for the quality of care, for example when there is little oversight regarding the standards for LTC workers that are paid through these benefits, or regarding the modalities for using the cash. A cash-benefit system with little regulation can discourage formal LTC labour markets if informal or unregulated markets emerge as in some southern and central European countries. Critically, there is no robust evidence regarding the impact of consumer direction mechanisms on care effectiveness and safety. Some evidence from Italy and the United States points to undesirable outcomes resulting from instances of poor or little regulation of consumer-directed systems.

Offering frail elderly a voice

Another approach to encourage care responsiveness and quality has been through mechanisms to empower LTC users and their families against cases of abuse and complaints. Legislation and regulations lay out the means and procedures to protect against abuses, such as mandatory reporting of neglect or improper care (e.g., in Israel; Ireland; Ontario, Canada), as well as measures to encourage disclosure of cases by frail elderly or rules to guarantee standards of workers (e.g., mandatory criminal reference checks as in Canadian provinces, training requirements). National-level campaigns (e.g., Ireland, United States), training for professionals on recognising and responding to elder abuse and access points where frail elderly can report experiences of abuse have been broadly successful (Ireland, Canada, Israel, the United States). Ombudsmen programmes acting as advocates of old people have been translated into specific action plans in some countries, for example the establishment of protective offices, improved communication services such as tool-free phone lines, improved use of multidisciplinary teams, trained to prevent and intervene or education programmes for elderly and their families. These programmes teach providers and LTC recipients to recognise symptoms of elderly maltreatment, be aware of their rights, and provide training to professionals and social workers. While these are powerful instruments to counter elderly abuses, they work on the assumptions, which cannot always be met, that frail elderly people (or their representatives) are wholly able to express themselves and their complaints.

Choice and quality grading systems

A handful of OECD countries (Germany, Korea, Sweden and the United States) publish reports on LTC providers along with grading of their performance (conversely, England has recently discontinued a star rating). For governments, grading systems can help increasing accountability and transparency. As to providers, they stimulate efficiency through incentives for competing. Quality indicators are the basis for ranking in all the countries, although ranks are calculated differently. There is encouraging evidence that public reporting through Nursing Home Compare in the United States has led to more informed decision making among LTC users. However, some evidence from England suggests that only one in six users were aware of public reporting and very few used this information to make their choices. As to the impact of the rating systems on providers, the main criticism is that different aspects of quality receive the same weight in ratings, with the result that deficiencies in one aspect (e.g., wound care or the prevention of pressure ulcers) can be compensated by good rating in others (e.g., nice surroundings, nicely decorated rooms).

On balance, all consumer-centred approaches – and especially quality-rating systems – are based on assumptions that frail disabled people can make informed choices. The quality and easiness of the information they receive for comparing options is a key factor affecting their ability to choose. However, there are questions regarding the methodology of the ranking and about how to address lower-performing providers. To date, it is unclear that rating systems have led to improved quality outcomes and high user satisfaction.

Paying providers for higher quality needs more evaluation and experimentation

Another way to encourage quality improvement is by offering providers financial rewards for good outcomes. These schemes aim to improve clinical quality of care, and encourage providers to implement processes that can lead to higher quality, such as generic prescription, improved care co-ordination, or electronic reporting of clinical information.

While performance payments seem to be gaining attention as a potential means to reward better performance and influence provider practice, few countries have initiated P4P incentives schemes to improve LTC quality. In Korea, the Value Incentive Programme (VIP) for long-term care hospitals links evaluation results with fee payments. In the United States, some states have started to implement a value-based purchasing model for nursing homes since 2009. In Japan, since 2009 a financial incentive scheme pays a bonus to nursing homes and community-based services that have been successful at improving recipients' functional status or at returning them home. Based on evidence available to date, it is not possible to draw direct causality between the use of payment incentives such as pay for performance and outcome improvement. These initiatives show potential – for example, changing behaviours around specific outcome items, stimulating greater reporting of data and greater use of assessment systems – but evidence on improvement in quality must be strengthened before they can be recommended more generally.

To encourage care co-ordination and integration, a mix of incentives for providers and payers is required

The need to improve quality of care by reducing fragmentation and fostering care co-ordination is widely understood. People needing LTC services are more likely to have chronic conditions or multiple morbidities. Poor care integration (or co-ordination) is a main cause of unsatisfactory quality in all its dimensions – safety, responsiveness, effectiveness – and can lead to preventable hospital (re)admissions. Ensuring seamless transitions across care settings is not only important for good quality of life of LTC users, but it is also necessity if harm to patients and cost to LTC services is to be minimised.

There is a continuum of approaches to integration by degree or intensity and complexity, ranging from integration of information (e.g., electronic records, transfer of LTC users' information into interoperable formats that can be shared across setting), to clinical integration (e.g., standardised diagnostic and comprehensive needs assessment), service integration (e.g., single-entry systems, management of transitions and of discharges from hospital to LTC and vice-versa), and organisational integration (e.g., bundled payments, integrated health and social care under a single management).

While there is some agreement that more complex patients and conditions might require a higher degree of integration (multidisciplinary teams, organisations merge, etc.) than in the case of most LTC recipients with simpler care needs (for whom referral and ongoing follow-up might be enough), it has proven difficult to collect country examples and evaluate them. Good case management or primary-care co-ordinators, availability of integrated information system linking data through the continuum of care, multidisciplinary assessments teams, single-entry points and the use of portable electronic health have been identified as improving quality, however there is scope for more systematic assessment of country experiences.

Conclusions

The main findings from the OECD study on monitoring and improving quality in long-term care (LTC) can be summarised as follow:

● LTC quality measurement still lags behind developments in health care. A majority of countries do not systematically collect information of quality, and if they do, their efforts are limited to collection of information on structural inputs such as staffing and the care environment. This is due to definitional challenges (e.g., whether the right focus of measurement should be inputs and processes or outcomes; whether the focus should be clinical aspects or responsiveness and quality of life), methodological challenges (e.g., the fact that outcomes for frail care recipients deteriorate over time regardless of how good is the care received), and implementation challenges (e.g. there are split responsibilities between health and social care, fragmentation of service points, and differences in coverage of data; data management requires significant financing and technical capacity; concerns have also grown around data protection and privacy issues).

● There are nonetheless examples from a handful of countries with advanced data monitoring systems for clinical effectiveness, care safety, and, increasingly, user satisfaction or social aspects of care. Experiences from the countries with advanced data systems suggest that relying on providers voluntarily providing information on quality may not be sufficient, and mandatory data collection might be necessary.

Initiatives to drive quality improvement on LTC have comprised of three main approaches.

● *External regulatory controls.* These are the most developed quality assurance approach but have been applied more often to institutional care than to home care or assisted living facilities. In two-thirds of OECD countries reviewed, accreditation, certification or minimum standards for institutions are mandatory or a condition for reimbursement. Qualification requirements for LTC workers are low, are even lower in home care, and do not extend to continuous education or ongoing monitoring. A main challenge of regulation is that enforcement has not been rigorous.

● *Normalising care processes and reporting on deviations.* In contrast to health care, there is little standardisation of care and monitoring of deviations from the care norm in LTC (with a few country exemptions). There is a potential for greater use of standardised assessment tools for monitoring LTC quality and developing protocols or guidelines for nursing care. Monitoring of LTC quality has been growing in importance, but evidence on the impact of public reporting on encouraging better purchasing of care, or informed choice by LTC recipients, is inconclusive.

● *Driving system improvement and creating an environment for consumer choice.* There is no robust evidence regarding the impact of consumer centred approaches (choice, grading, voice) on quality. Paying providers for higher quality has an appeal, but needs more evaluation and experimentation. Encouraging co-ordination and integration with health care is necessary, but there is little systematic assessment of experience.

PART I

Measuring quality
in long-term care

PART I

Chapter 1

Why the quality of long-term care matters

by

Yuki Murakami

and
Francesca Colombo,
OECD Health Division

Long-term care recipients are demanding greater flexibility, more choice, more autonomy and better service quality. These demands and public stories of inadequate standards of care pressure governments to increase transparency over the quality of care delivered to frail and disabled elderly. This chapter provides definitions and a framework for looking at long-term care quality in this report. Three key domains that are generally accepted as being critical factors underpinning care quality are considered: i) effectiveness and care safety; ii) patient-centredness and responsiveness; iii) care co-ordination. Three structural outcomes instrumental to delivering good quality care are also identified, namely: i) staffing and management; ii) care environment; iii) information and communication technology and other assistive devices.

With the ageing of populations, delivering high-quality care services has become a policy priority

Policy makers across OECD countries are faced with ever-increasing expectations from current and future long-term care (LTC)* recipients to make high-quality long-term care services available. Ensuring and improving the quality of long-term care services was ranked as the second most important policy priority (after ensuring fiscal and financial sustainability) across 28 OECD countries in 2009-10 (Colombo et al., 2011). Indeed, over the past five years, several countries have implemented policies to deliver better LTC services and improve accountability.

This report examines policy initiatives and indicators on LTC quality across a selection of OECD countries. In addition to examining the reasons why LTC quality has risen on the agenda of many OECD countries, this chapter provides definitions and a framework for looking at LTC quality that will be referred to throughout this report.

The rest of the report is structured in two main parts. First, Chapter 2 focuses on what data are currently collected and what indicators are used to assess quality in LTC. The second part of this report examines policies to monitor and improve quality in LTC, specifically focusing on structural inputs to ensure safe care, caring environments and skilled workforces (Chapter 3); initiatives and programmes to monitor quality and standardise practices (Chapter 4); and policies and programmes to drive improvement (Chapter 5).

Quality assurance for long-term care is important

LTC services support those who need them, on a continuing basis and often complement the efforts of family or friends. Quality LTC services help people maintain their health and functional status for as long as possible. In addition to this broad objective, there are at least three other important reasons why high-quality LTC services are an important policy concern for ageing societies: users of care services demand a greater voice and more control over their lives; there is a need to increase accountability for public spending on care given the growing costs of care; and governments have a role and responsibility to play in protecting vulnerable older people.

Users of care services demand a greater voice and more control over their lives

The expectations of "baby boomers" that the quality of LTC systems be higher than those of previous generations is certainly to be expected. In most OECD countries today, most individuals expect to occupy a single room, expect to be able to maintain their privacy, and expect care services to reflect their own individual needs and preferences. Individuals demand more choice, more responsive services and improved quality of life. As

---

* Long-term care (LTC): is defined as a range of services required by persons with a reduced degree of functional capacity, physical or cognitive, and who are consequently dependent for an extended period of time on help with basic activities of daily living (ADL). This "personal care" component is frequently provided in combination with help with basic medical services such as "nursing care" (help with wound dressing, pain management, medication, health monitoring), as well as prevention, rehabilitation or services of palliative care. Long-term care services can also be combined with lower-level care related to "domestic help" or help with instrumental activities of daily living (IADL).

the collective share of total income held by seniors grows, the population over 65 also has a greater voice and can put pressure on governments to respond. LTC users, their families and carers are better informed as to the range of services available, and often have strongly held opinions on quality. The high cost of care, particularly co-payments for institutional care, contributes to an expectation of receiving the best care available.

Linked to the demand for greater choice and quality services are demands for independence, autonomy and privacy. For an individual, becoming dependent can have significant repercussions on the ability to conduct a "normal" life. For someone who enters a long-term care facility, adjustment to life in a new environment is a radical change (Williams et al., 2003). Quality LTC services can help frail and dependent persons retain or improve their autonomy and continue to take part in society, despite their existing conditions. LTC services enable dependent persons to maintain control over their lives which in turn can prevent depression and loss of interest in life (Fiske et al., 2009). Supporting autonomy also involves the ability of a person to choose or to take part in the decisions affecting his/her life.

Given the growing cost of care, accountability for public spending on care must improve

Long-term care expenditure is set to double or even triple between now and 2050, as the share of older people in need of long-term care across OECD countries increases (Colombo et al., 2011). An obvious driver of this is longer life expectancy across the OECD. In 2010, people aged 65 years in OECD countries could be expected to live for another 21 years on average for women and 17 years for men (Figures 1.1 and 1.2). Across the OECD, the

Figure 1.1. **Life expectancy at age 65, 2010 (or nearest year)**

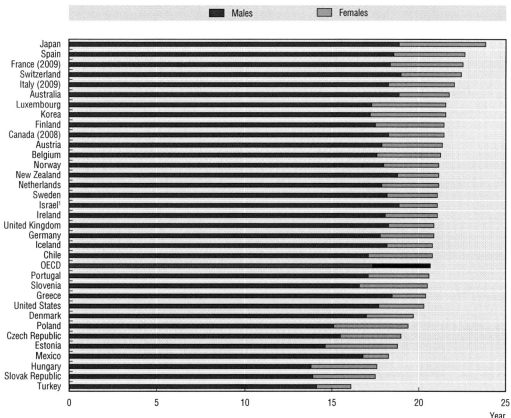

1. Information on data for Israel: *http://dx/doi.org/10.1787/888932315602.*
Source: OECD Health Data 2012.

Figure 1.2. **Life expectancy at age 80, 2010 (or nearest year)**

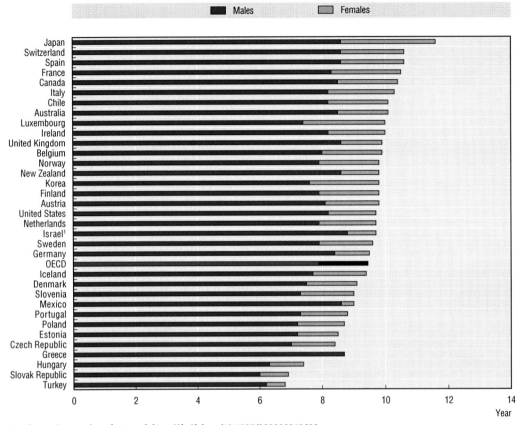

1. Information on data for Israel: *http://dx/doi.org/10.1787/888932315602*.
Source: OECD Health Data 2012.

share of those aged 80 years and over is expected to increase from 4% in 2010 to nearly 10% in 2050. Despite uncertainties regarding disability trends among elderly populations, based on the EU Survey of Income and Living Conditions, about 60% of Europeans aged 75 years and over reported that they had limitations in daily activities due to a health problem (Lafortune and Balestat, 2007; OECD, 2011a; Figure 1.3). As the share of people aged over 65 and 80 years grows, so the overall number of those needing care is expected to increase.

Demographic changes are pushing increases in long-term care expenditure and resource use. OECD countries allocated 1.56% of GDP to public spending on LTC, on average in 2010 (OECD, 2012; Figure 1.4). When private expenditures are considered, LTC systems across the OECD absorb around another 0.67% of GDP. Though still relatively small, LTC expenditure – particularly public LTC spending – has shown a faster upward trend in per capita terms than health care spending, an annual average of over 9% across 25 OECD countries, compared to 4% for total public expenditure on health (OECD, 2012; Figure 1.5). This trend is expected to continue.

Figure 1.3. **Limitations in daily activities, population aged 75 years and over, 2009**

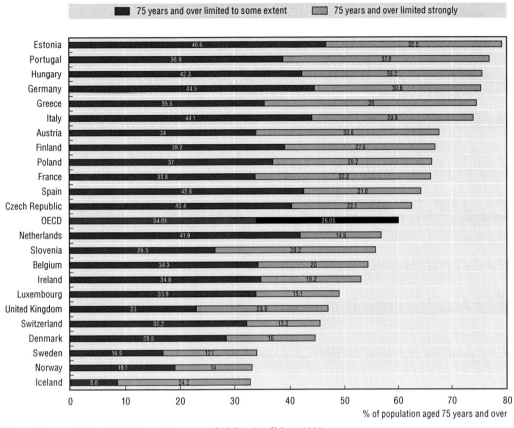

■ 75 years and over limited to some extent   ▨ 75 years and over limited strongly

	75 years and over limited to some extent	75 years and over limited strongly
Estonia	46.6	32.5
Portugal	38.9	37.9
Hungary	42.3	33.2
Germany	44.5	30.8
Greece	35.5	39
Italy	44.1	29.3
Austria	34	33.6
Finland	39.2	27.6
Poland	37	29.2
France	33.8	32.2
Spain	42.6	21.6
Czech Republic	40.4	22.1
OECD	34.01	26.05
Netherlands	41.9	14.9
Slovenia	26.5	29.2
Belgium	34.3	20
Ireland	34.8	18.2
Luxembourg	33.9	15.1
United Kingdom	23	23.6
Switzerland	32.2	13.2
Denmark	28.5	16
Sweden	16.9	17.1
Norway	19.1	14
Iceland	8.6	24.2

% of population aged 75 years and over

Source: European Union Statistics on Income and Living Conditions 2009.

As public expenditure on LTC continues to grow, there is pressure for LTC services to improve accountability for the money spent. However, little is known about the extent to which cost increases correspond to improvements in quality of care, partly because of the difficulties of measuring outcome improvements for frail or dependent elderly, for whom physical and cognitive capabilities are, by their nature, inevitably set to worsen. In addition, monitoring of LTC quality is in its infancy, and rarely linked to measures of resource utilisation or expenditure.

Governments have the responsibility to protect vulnerable older people

There are good reasons to be worried about elderly abuse. The US National Ombudsman Reporting System data, for example, shows that 7% of all complaints regarding institutional LTC facilities were regarding abuse, (gross) neglect, or exploitation (Administration on Aging, 2011). The World Health Organization European Region estimates that at least 4 million people aged 60 years and over experience abuse or maltreatment in any one year in Europe (WHO/Europe, 2011). Incidences of elder abuse have also been reported in a number of Québec's reports (Gouvernement du Québec, 2012).

Figure 1.4. **Public long-term care expenditure (health and social components), as a share of GDP, 2010 (or nearest year)**

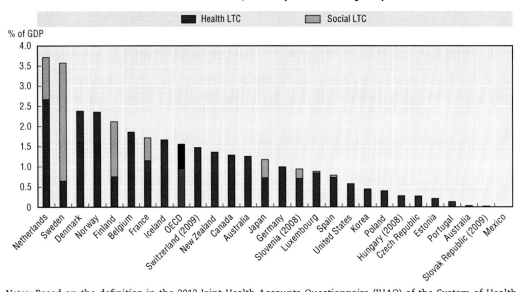

Notes: Based on the definition in the 2012 Joint Health Accounts Questionnaire (JHAQ) of the System of Health Accounts (SHA), long-term care expenditure comprises long-term (health) care and social services of long-term care. Health component of LTC spending relates to health and nursing care for patients who need assistance on a continuing basis due to chronic impairments and a reduced degree of independence and activities of daily living (ADL). The following items are included in LTC (Health): i) palliative care; ii) long-term nursing care; iii) personal care services (assistance with ADL restrictions); iv) services in support of informal (family) care. Social component of LTC includes i) home help (help with IADL); ii) residential (care) services; iii) other social services provided in a LTC context.
Data for Australia, Austria, Belgium Canada, Czech Republic Denmark, Estonia, Germany, Hungry, Iceland, Mexico, New Zealand, Norway, Portugal, Slovenia (from the Ministry of Labour and Social Affairs), Slovak Republic, Switzerland and the United States refer to both long-term (health) care and social services of long-term care. Data for Australia excludes all expenditures for residential aged care facilities in welfare (social) services. Data for Finland might be underestimated because long-term care within health centres hospitals is included in in-patient long-term care nursing care expenditure. Data for Poland might be underestimated due to a lack of data on medical component of all services delivered within centres/homes/hostels under social care. Data for Slovak Republic excludes in-patient long-term care expenditures. Data for Slovenia excludes services provided at home and paid by beneficiaries exclusively. Data for Spain only includes the long-term care provided by hospitals. Expenditure related to personal care services (help with ADL) is reported under social care services of long-term care in data for Sweden.
Source: OECD Health Data 2012.

High-quality LTC services should protect vulnerable persons and caregivers from potential abuses. Being dependent on others to perform basic activities of daily living can easily make individuals more vulnerable to abuse, which can take many forms, ranging from physical or mental abuse to financial exploitation. Those who fall victim to abuse might not be aware of their own vulnerability and less able to protect themselves against such events.

Figure 1.5. **Growth in public expenditure on LTC (health),
2000-10 (or nearest year)**

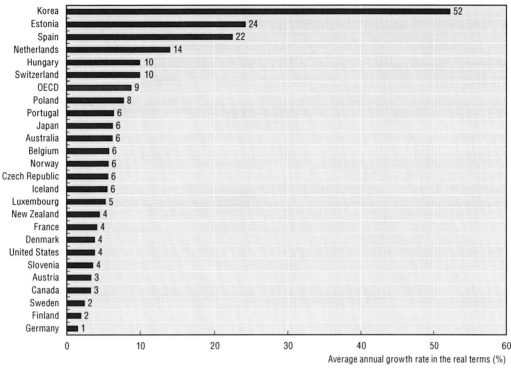

Average annual growth rate in the real terms (%)

Note: Data for Estonia refer to 2001-10; data for Poland refer to 2002-10; data for Japan and Australia refer to 2000-09; data for Belgium refer to 2003-10; data for Luxembourg refer to 2000-08; data for New Zealand refer to 2004-10; data for Slovenia refer to 2004-10.
See footnotes for Figure 1.4.

Source: OECD Health Data 2012.

This report uses an outcome-based framework for assessing long-term care quality

There is wide diversity across countries relative to services for people with reduced physical or cognitive functioning, and around what is meant by "quality" in long-term care. For example, services vary from short-term care, to longer-term care spanning many months or years, to recovering from surgery (post-acute care) to end-of-life care (palliative care). Measuring quality in each of these services raises its own set of methodological challenges. Whilst in most countries the vast majority of LTC recipients are over 65, beneficiaries of long-term care are not limited to the elderly and include those younger than 65 years old with disability or conditions requiring care for a long period of time. Some measures of quality – as well as policies to improve quality – may well be used across care services, but others would need to be tailored to different groups.

Relative to the health sector, LTC services have emerged as a formal system only relatively recently. Policies and regulations have therefore not yet been fully developed, especially for emerging services such as home care for palliative services. Guidelines for professionals are also in their infancy. Developing evidence-based practices poses many challenges given the often complex nature of the conditions affecting people receiving care, their diverse needs, the difficulties of navigating across care settings, and the involvement of multiple different professionals. Practices are less standardised, and different forms of care provision coexist.

Good quality care aims to maintain or improve outcomes of frail elderly, chronically ill, or physically disabled people, whether they receive care in nursing homes, assisted living facilities, community-based or home care settings. Unlike health care, the main focus is not on improving overall health status, but rather assisting a dependent person with maintaining control over health status, and, where possible reduce dependency and disability.

After reviewing national quality frameworks used in a selection of OECD countries, the rest of this chapter briefly describes two existing analytical frameworks used for describing quality in LTC that can be used to address long-term care quality. This approach presents *safe, timely, effective, efficient and user-centred* care as the main elements of quality. Box 1.2 at the end of the chapter contains all key definitions used in this report.

National long-term care quality frameworks focus on care effectiveness, safety and user centredness

Several OECD countries have produced policy or operational documents to monitor and improve LTC quality. These documents specify dimensions regarded as important to deliver quality in LTC, as well as specific outcomes to be monitored. A review of six frameworks used in Australia, Ontario, Canada, England, Finland, the Netherlands, and the United States (Box 1.1), highlights the following:

- All the countries reviewed consider care effectiveness and user safety as a key quality dimension. Patient centredness and responsiveness are the second most often identified priority area, followed by care co-ordination and integration (Australia, Canada, the Netherlands, and the United States).

- Population health focus, and prevention and adoption of community-based approaches are also frequently referred to (Canada, England, Finland, and the United States). Maintaining sufficient focus on broad population health and prevention is seen as important to promote healthy ageing and reduce the need for LTC. Promoting a community-based approach is regarded as a means to respond to most people's preference for residing at home.

- Staffing and management are described as critical supporting inputs, rather than a quality domain in itself.

- Efficiency and better quality per spending are priority areas for quality in Canada and the United States. In other countries, discussions on efficiency are part of LTC expenditures or value for money issues and not specifically part of quality only (Australia, England).

- Providing a safe living environment to LTC users is identified as a key condition in assuring quality services, particularly in Finland and the Netherlands.

- Different aspects of quality of life (such as opportunities for social activities, preference for meals, respect for privacy, and cleanness of living space for residents in LTC facilities) have also been a focus in national frameworks (England and the Netherlands) while other countries regard this as the ultimate objective instead of a standalone quality domain (England and Finland).

Supporting the priorities in a selected number of countries, care effectiveness (as measured by clinical outcomes) and user safety (such as adverse events and medication errors) was ranked as the highest priority area in long-term care in a survey of OECD countries that scored various areas on a scale of 1 (low) to 5 (high). Patient-centredness, care co-ordination, and staffing were also regarded as important (Figure 1.6).

Box 1.1. **Frameworks to promote LTC quality in six OECD countries**

Australia. The Productivity Commission was requested by the Government of Australia to develop options for redesigning the country's aged care system. The Commission's report, published in June 2011, recommends developing a new quality assurance framework and quality indicators with greater focus on outcomes than on minimum standards. In its response, the government's aged care reform package provides a plan to develop and report in the *My Aged Care* website national aged-care quality indicators (QIs) and a rating system based on QIs for residential care from mid- 2014 and national aged-care QIs for home care services from mid-2016 (Government of Australia, 2012a; Government of Australia, 2012b).

Ontario, in **Canada's** largest province. Health Quality Ontario (HQO) monitors quality of health care, including LTC. According to the latest 2011 report, quality for health and LTC services are monitored through nine dimensions. Some indicators for LTC are still under development and data collection is currently limited to accessibility, effectiveness, safety, and resource appropriateness. Access is measured through length of time waiting for nursing-home placement and percentage of those who are placed in their first-choice LTC home. Effectiveness is monitored by a set of health outcome indicators such as the percentage of LTC recipients whose bladder function has recently declined, and the percentage of LTC recipients with worsening symptoms of depression. Safety is presented by the number of LTC recipients prescribed a drug that should be avoided, and the percentage of LTC recipients started on certain drugs (such as antipsychotics) without clear reason. Resource appropriateness is measured by the expenditure spent as a percentage of GDP, but the figure includes both health and LTC (Health Quality Ontario, 2011).

In **England**, the Department of Health is going through a transition from the previous national performance system to a new approach for adult social care (i.e. LTC) based on outcomes. The Department has proposed a new outcomes framework which sets quality as the determining factor in achieving the best possible outcomes for people. The proposal has identified effectiveness, positive experience, safety and efficiency (for value for money) as preconditions to ensure high quality services and best outcomes. The proposed Outcomes Framework focuses on four quality domains: *i)* enhancing quality of life for people with care and support needs, *ii)* delaying and reducing the need for care and support, *iii)* ensuring that people have a positive experience of care and support, and *iv)* safeguarding adults whose circumstances make them vulnerable and protecting from avoidable harm (Department of Health, 2010, Department of Health, 2011).

In **Finland**, the Ministry of Social Affairs and Health published, in 2008, a national quality framework for care of older people, which sets out a number of key dimensions. The first dimension is about promoting health and welfare, and related service structure aiming for prevention and early intervention and for comprehensive assessment. The second dimension is to ensure sufficient staffing and right management. The third one is about ensuring pleasant, safe and private living and care environment. The fundamental value under the Finnish Constitution guarantees the right to a good treatment, informed choices, dignity, security and involvement (Ministry of Social Affairs and Health, 2008).

In **the Netherlands**, the Steering Committee Responsible for Care set ten quality domains under the 2007 National Quality Framework. The ten domains are the following: *i)* care/life plan to assure LTC recipients' involvement in care and life planning, *ii)* communication and information to ensure that providers keep communication open and make efforts to listen to recipients' wishes, *iii)* physical well-being for recipients to receive adequate support and to feel satisfied with the care provided, *iv)* safety of care to prevent avoidable harms and restriction of freedom of movement, *v)* domestic and living conditions to respect recipients' privacy and their living atmosphere, *vi)* participation and autonomy to ensure sufficient opportunities to participate in various activities, *vii)* mental and

Box 1.1. **Frameworks to promote LTC quality in six OECD countries** (cont.)

autonomy to ensure sufficient opportunities to participate in various activities, vii) mental well-being to provide mental support (loneliness or depression) and pay attention to their choices and sense of purpose, viii) safety of living environment, ix) sufficient and competent personnel to ensure availability of qualified staff and sufficient care time, and x) care co-ordination across health and adult social care. Each domain includes a set of indicators reflecting the structure, process and outcomes of care (Steering Committee Responsible Care, 2007). In the Netherlands, in May 2012, a new version of the framework was launch after some criticisms received on its framework Quality Framework for Responsible Care (Normen Verantowoorde Zorg VVT).

The **US Department of the Health and Human Services** published a new national strategy, the National Strategy for Quality Improvement in Health Care (including LTC) in March 2011. It includes six priorities: i) safe care which aims to reduce the risk of injury from care and adverse medication events, ii) involvement of patients and their families (patient-centredness), iii) care co-ordination and communication to promote and encourage providers to better communicate among themselves for effective care and support, iv) effective prevention which targets those (including LTC recipients) with multiple chronic conditions to reduce their risk of complications, v) community-based approach by partnering with local health providers to promote healthy living, and vi) affordable care which aims to make sure the right care is delivered to the right person at the right time and at affordable price. Each priority will be measured against specific quantitative goals which are being developed (US Department of Health and Human Services, 2011).

Figure 1.6. **Care effectiveness and user safety judged the highest priority area in quality of LTC in OECD countries, 2012**

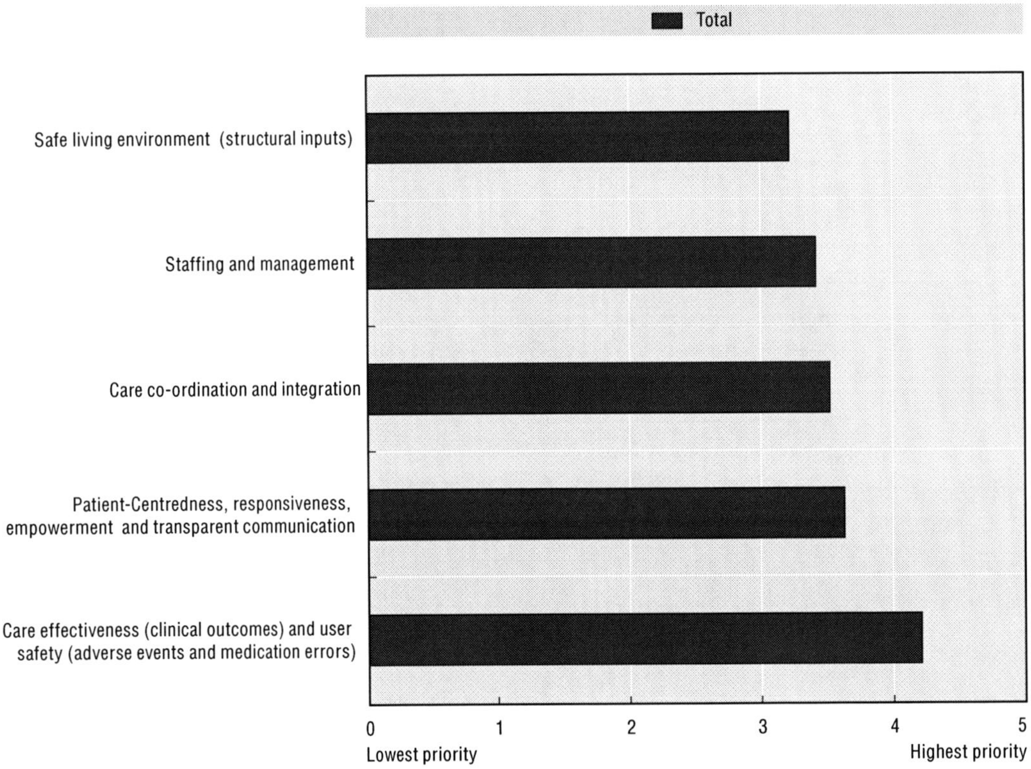

Note: Includes responses from 24 countries.

Source: OECD 2012 Questionnaire on Long-Term Care Quality.

A widely used framework links quality with structure, process and outcome of care

Historically, quality has been often described by Donabedian's framework linking quality with structure, process and outcome (Donabedian, 1966). These domains have since been frequently used over the last 50 years to measure quality in health care and have been extended to assessing the quality of LTC.

According to Donabedian's framework, structural measures refer to the organisational characteristics, material resources, or human resources associated with the provision of care. Process describes how the structure is put in place to provide services for and to the recipients of care. Outcome measures are the health outcomes and health status resulting from care (Castle and Ferguson, 2010; Committee on Redesigning Health Insurance, Performance Measures, Payment, and Performance Improvement Programmes, 2006; Sorenson and Mossialos, 2007).

Process and outcome indicators serve to provide different types of information. Process indicators assess whether certain services are provided or administered (Arling et al., 2009) while outcome indicators provide information about deviations from appropriate care which influence care outcome of residents and beneficiaries (Donabedian, 1966). Unlike input indicators, process and outcome indicators often require provider level information as well as the patient level data. Typically, patient level individual data is derived from clinical assessments of patients at specific intervals during their care. Process quality indicators are easy to interpret and translate into practice for improvement (Castle and Ferguson, 2010). A lack of certain procedures and neglect and abuse can be categorised as part of the process indicators. The prevalence of nursing home residents who are restrained in an example of a process indicator, while the proportion of home care beneficiaries who improve in their ability to transfer from bed to chair is an outcome of care (E-Qalin Model, 2010). Statistically speaking, many process indicators are also easy to enumerate and do not require adjustment (Castle and Ferguson, 2010). However, the applicability of process measures may be restricted unless there is clear evidence of inappropriate care and a lack of safety procedure such as physical restraints and medication errors (Arling et al., 2009) Empirical evidence showing linkage between process measures and causes of inappropriate care is yet to be evaluated (Kelley and Hurst, 2006; Sorenson and Mossialos, 2007).

Outcome indicators represent changes in health status and conditions (physical and cognitive functions) attributable to care provided or not provided and can give directions for desirable results of care provided to residents and beneficiaries (Mor, 2006). Quality measures are an aggregation of assessment data, reflecting how well the providers achieve certain clinically relevant goals such as preventing pressure ulcers or promoting functional improvement.

The Donabedian's concept proposes that each component has a direct influence on the next, starting from structure to process and from process to outcomes. Using the concept, the 2005 OECD report on long-term care summarised the variety of quality regulations and quality improvement measures taken in OECD member countries (OECD, 2005). Quality and safety of buildings and staff ratios were categorised under quality of structure, while providing well-balanced diet to residents in LTC institutions are under quality of process. Prevalence of pressure sores and malnutrition were categorised under outcomes. The Donabedian's concept has been widely used to conceptualise the boundaries and dimensions of LTC quality in research projects such as the European INTERLINKS, PROGRESS, ANCIEN projects (Dandi et al., 2012; Dandi and Georgia, 2012; European Centre for Social Welfare Policy and Research et al., 2010; Nies et al., 2010) and in the development of national quality monitoring frameworks and quality indicators including in Japan, Korea, the Netherlands, the United States, and many other countries (Health Insurance Review & Assessment Service, 2011; Japan Ministry of Health, Labour and Welfare, 2011; Steering Committee Responsible Care, 2007; Wunderlich and Kohler, 2001). In MEDLINE from 2005 to 2010, about 60% of articles applied his concept in conducting nursing home studies (Castle and Ferguson, 2010).

The OECD Health Care Quality Indicator (HCQI) project started in 2003 provides an alternative to the Donabedian framework, and aims at developing a set of quality indicators to assess performance of health care system across OECD countries (Kelley and Hurst, 2006). Building on countries' experiences with the assessment of health care performance and quality of care, the HCQI project identified three most commonly mentioned quality dimensions in OECD member countries, namely, effectiveness, safety and responsiveness. It then applied Donabedian's concept to identify a set of indicators to measure each of these quality priorities, focusing on both process and outcome measures.

The OECD long-term care quality framework focuses on outcomes most relevant to care

The framework used for this report borrows from the six national and sub-national frameworks on LTC quality and also from the two analytical frameworks presented above, pointing to key elements and explaining presumed relationships for the assessment of quality (Miles and Huberman, 1994; Hurtado et al., 2001).

Three quality dimensions seem to capture well what quality means in LTC settings. These dimensions relate both to technical quality (safety and care effectiveness) as well as the experience that LTC users will have and the way care is harmonised across settings:

- Effectiveness and care safety.
- Patient-centredness and responsiveness.
- Care co-ordination.

In addition, this report devotes special attention to three structural inputs, which appear to be instrumental for good care:

- Staffing and management.
- Care environment.
- Information and communication technology (ICT) and non-ITC assistive technologies.

Figure 1.7 illustrates this conceptual framework within a general LTC model. The health and well-being of older people (which could be summarised as quality of life) are the ultimate objective of LTC services and systems. The performance of LTC services which include notions of quality, access, and cost are shown in the central part of the framework. Waiting time to get the first LTC contact and placement in nursing homes is included under access. Efficiency and cost are defined as how to maximise benefits in a resource-constrained environment. Apart from LTC, other factors influencing health and well-being of older people such as socio-economic and behavioural factors are also covered in Figure 1.7. Key definitions are presented in Box 1.2.

Figure 1.7. **Conceptual framework for OECD long-term care quality**

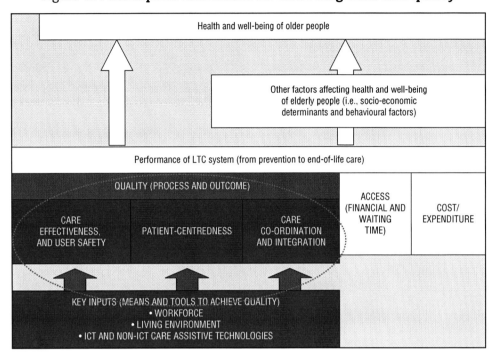

Box 1.2. **Key concepts and definitions of long-term care
and quality in long-term care**

Long-term care is a range of services required by persons with a reduced degree of functional capacity, physical or cognitive, and who are consequently dependent for an extended period of time on help with basic activities of daily living (ADL). This "personal care" component is frequently provided in combination with help with basic medical services such as "nursing care" (wound dressing, pain management, medication, health monitoring), as well as prevention, rehabilitation or palliative care.

a) **Dimensions of quality**

Care effectiveness (Clinical effectiveness) describes the degree to which the provision of care delivers the best possible health and social care, to achieve the best functional outcomes and prevent conditions from worsening more rapidly than otherwise expected. This domain looks at LTC users' outcomes resulting from a range of policies including the effectiveness of care-needs assessment and treatment, and the provision of continuum of care and rehabilitation.

User safety refers to the safeguarding aspect of care provision to "avoid, prevent and ameliorate adverse outcomes or injuries" (Kelley and Hurst, 2006). This quality domain focuses on the process of care delivery and LTC users' outcomes and is closely linked with policies delivering effective care and skilled LTC workforce and management.

Patient-centredness, responsiveness, and empowerment refers to providing users with opportunities to be actively involved in their care, and to ensure that their expectations are met and their care experience pleasant. It is the degree to which a system actually functions by placing the patient/user at the centre of its delivery of care. Empowerment of LTC users can take the form of providing choices with respect to the type of services and the selection of provider (Lundsgaard, 2005).

Box 1.2. **Key concepts and definitions of long-term care
and quality in long-term care** *(cont.)*

Care co-ordination and integration is the degree to which health and social care are interconnected and transitions harmonised (US Department of Health and Human Services, March 2011). LTC systems operate in close link with health care. LTC users often suffer from multiple morbidities due to chronic conditions and disabilities, necessitating a continuum of care and follow-ups at different levels of care provision. Many LTC users move from health care to LTC back and forth, but support for transfer and information sharing throughout the process can be inefficient, sporadic, and inadequate, thereby affecting the overall quality of care provided.

b) Key inputs affecting quality

Workforce. Staff is central to the provision of care for LTC users in both institutional and home care settings because of their frontline role. For a dependent person it can take the form of receiving support for intimate/private acts on a regular basis by someone outside their network, while for the caregivers it can take the form of having to deal with difficult and unseen behaviours linked to specific physical or cognitive conditions (Nies et al., 2010; Ministry of Social Affairs and Health, 2008).

Living environment refers to the physical safety of the facilities, home and care environment relative to accidents, harm, fire and other hazards, as well as the extent to which the living environment protects individual privacy and promotes users' quality of life. A safe environment helps prevent incidents leading to a dependent person's conditions to degenerate more rapidly than otherwise expected. For nursing homes and residential care facilities, the physical environment of the facility can contribute to the physical safety and functional mobility of residents. This also applies to the extent to which a dependent person's home is adapted to their needs. A pleasant and safe living environment also means creating a sense of physical, mental and social safety (Steering Committee Responsible Care, 2007) which leads to improved quality of life.

ICT and non-ICT care assistive technologies have attracted more attention in LTC as tools to drive improvement in the delivery of care (including care co-ordination) and enhance quality of life of LTC recipients. Monitoring technologies such as alarm systems enable LTC recipients to be more at ease at living independently at home. These also help family members and caregivers monitor at distance, for example by providing them instructions on medication intakes and daily tasks (OECD, 2011b). ICT enables LTC recipients and families to communicate with professional caregivers and health care providers.

Conclusions

At the same time as the number of people in need of care is growing, LTC users are demanding greater flexibility, more choice, more autonomy, and a higher quality of services. This occurs at a time when higher spending on long-term care and public stories of inadequate standards put pressures on government to increase transparency over the quality of care delivered to frail and disabled elderly.

Based on a review of national frameworks for LTC quality in six OECD countries, as well as a review of the analytical frameworks used in the academic literature, this project identified three key domains that appear to be both central and that are generally accepted as being critical factors underpinning LTC quality. These include: effectiveness and care safety, patient-centredness and responsiveness and care co-ordination. The project also identifies three structural factors key to LTC quality: 1) staffing and management; 2) care environment; and 3) assistive devices.

The rest of this report will analyse policy initiatives and indicators on LTC quality across OECD countries.

References

Administration on Aging (2011), *2010 National Ombudsman Reporting System Data Tables*, Department of Health and Human Services, Washington, DC.

Arling, G. et al. (2009), "Medicaid Nursing Home Pay for Performance: Where Do We Stand?", *The Gerontologist*, Vol. 49, No. 5, pp. 587-595.

Australian Institute of Health and Welfare (2002), *Aged Care Assessment: Program Data Dictionary*, Australian Institute of Health and Welfare, Canberra.

Castle, N.G. and J.C. Ferguson (2010), "What Is Nursing Home Quality and How Is It Measured?, *The Gerontologist*, Vol. 50, No. 4, pp. 426-442.

Colombo, F. et al. (2011), *Help Wanted: Proving and Paying for Long-Term Care*, OECD Health Policy Studies, OECD Publishing, Paris, *http://dx.doi.org/10.1787/9789264097759-en*.

Committee on Redesigning Health Insurance, Performance Measures, Payment, and Performance Improvement Programs (2006). *Performance Measurement: Accelerating Improvement,* National Academy of Sciences, Washington, DC.

Dandi, R. and C. Georgia (2012), "Quality Assurance Indicators of Long-Term Care in European Countries", *ENEPRI Research Report* No. 110, April.

Dandi, R. et al. (2012), "Long-Term Care Quality Assurance Policies in the European Union", *ENEPRI Research Report* No. 111, March.

Donabedian, A. (1966), "Evaluating the Quality of Medical Care", *The Milbank Memorial Fund Quarterly*, Vol. 44, No. 3, Suppl., pp. 166-206.

Department of Health (2010), *Transparency in Outcomes: A Framework for Adult Social Care – A Consultation on Proposals*, Department of Health, London.

Department of Health (2011), *Transparency in Outcomes: A Framework for Quality in Adult Social Care – A Response to the Consultation and Next Steps*, Department of Health, London.

Department of Health (2012), *Transparency in Outcomes: A Framework for Quality in Adult Social Care – The 2012/2013 Adult Social Care Outcomes Framework*, 30 March, Department of Health, London.

E-Qalin Model (2010), *www.e-qalin.net/index.php?id=17&L=1*.

European Centre for Social Welfare Policy and Research (2010), "Measuring Progress: Indicators for Care Homes", European Centre for Social Welfare Policy and Research, Vienna.

Fiske, A. et al. (2009), "Depression in Older Adults", *Annual Review of Clinical Psychology*, Vol. 5, pp. 363-389.

Gouvernement du Québec (2012), "Bilan statistique du suivi des recommandations des visites d'appréciation de la qualité", *http://publications.msss.gouv.qc.ca/acrobat/f/documentation/2011/11-830-04.pdf*.

Government of Australia (2012a), "Australian Government Response Productivity Commission's Caring for Older Australians Report", Department of Health and Ageing, Government of Australia, Canberra.

Government of Australia (2012b), "Living Longer. Living Better. Aged Care Reform Package (Technical Document)", Department of Health and Ageing, Government of Australia, Canberra.

Health Insurance Review and Assessment Service (2011), "Comprehensive Quality Report of National Health Insurance 2010", Health Insurance Review and Assessment Service, Seoul.

Health Quality Ontario (2011), *Quality Monitor: 2011 Report on Ontario's Health System*, Health Quality Ontario, Ontario, Canada.

Hirdes, J.P. et al. (2011), "Beyond the 'Iron Lungs of Gerontology': Using evidence to shape the future of nursing homes in Canada", *Canadian Journal on Aging/La Revue canadienne du vieillissement*, Vol. 30, No. 3, pp. 371-390, September.

Hurtado, M.P. et al. (eds.) (2001), *Envisioning the National Health Care Quality Report*, Committee on the National Quality Report on Health Care Delivery, Institute of Medicine, Washington, DC.

Japan Ministry of Health, Labour and Welfare (2011), *www.mhlw.go.jp/stf/shingi/2r9852000001qyj1-att/2r9852000001qz5h.pdf,* accessed 15 October, 2012.

Kelley, E. and J. Hurst (2006), "Health Care Quality Indicators Project: Conceptual Framework Paper", *OECD Health Working Papers*, No. 23, OECD Publishin, Paris.

Lafortune, G. and G. Balestat (2007), "Trends in Severe Disability Among Elderly People: Assessing the Evidence in 12 OECD Countries and the Future Implications", *OECD Health Working Papers*, No. 26, OECD Publishing, Paris, *http://dx.doi.org/10.1787/217072070078.*

Lundsgaard, J. (2005), "Consumer Direction and Choice in Long-Term Care for Older Persons, Including Payments for Informal Care: How Can It Help Improve Care Outcomes, Employment and Fiscal Sustainability?", *OECD Health Working Papers*, No. 20, OECD Publishing, Paris, *http://dx.doi.org/10.1787/616882407515.*

Miles, M.B. and A.M. Huberman (1994), "Focusing and Bounding the Collection of Data", *Qualitative Data Analysis: An Expanded Sourcebook,* 2nd ed., Sage Publications, Newbury Park, United States, pp. 18-22.

Ministry of Social Affairs and Health (2008), *National Framework for High-Quality Services for Older People,* No. 5, Ministry of Social Affairs and Health, Helsinki.

Mor, V. (2006), "Defining and Measuring Quality Outcomes in Long-term Care", *Journal of the American Medical Directors Association,* Vol. 7, No. 8, October, pp. 532-540.

Nies, H. et al. (2010), "Quality Management and Quality Assurance in Long-Term Care – European Overview Paper", Vilans/European Centre for Social Welfare Policy and Research (INTERLINKS REPORT #2 – *http://interlinks.euro.centre.org/project/reports*), Utrecht and Vienna.

OECD (2005), *Long-Term Care for Older People,* OECD Publishing, Paris, *http://dx.doi.org/10.1787/9789264015852-en.*

OECD (2011a), *Health at a Glance 2011: OECD Indicators,* OECD Publishing, Paris, *http://dx.doi.org/10.1787/health_glance-2011-en.*

OECD (2011b), *The Future of Families to 2030,* OECD Publishing, Paris, *http://dx.doi.org/10.1787/9789264168367-en.*

OECD (2012), *OECD Health Data 2012,* OECD Publishing, Paris, *http://dx.doi.org/10.1787/health-data-en.*

Productivity Commission (2011), *Caring for Older Australians,* Report No. 53, Final Inquiry Report, Canberra.

Sorenson, C. and E. Mossialos (2007), *Measuring Quality and Standards of Long-term care for Older People,* European Commission, Brussels.

Steering Committee Responsible Care (2007), *Quality Framework Responsible Care – Nursing, Care and Home Care.*

United States Department of Health and Human Services (2011), *National Strategy for Quality Improvement in Health Care,* US Department of Health and Human Services, Washington, DC.

WHO/Europe – World Health Organization Regional Office for Europe (2011), *European Report on Preventing Elder Maltreatment,* Copenhagen.

Williams, K. et al. (2003), "Improving Nursing Home Communication: An Intervention to Reduce Elderspeak", *The Gerontologist,* Vol. 43, No. 2, pp. 242-247.

Wunderlich, G.S. and P.O. Kohler (eds.) (2001), *Improving the Quality of Long-Term Care,* Committee on Improving Quality in Long-Term Care, Division of Health Care Services, Institute of Medicine, Washington, DC.

PART I

Chapter 2

Measuring quality in long-term care

by

Yuki Murakami

and
Francesca Colombo,
OECD Health Division

Quality is a difficult concept to define and operationalise for measurement purposes. A majority of countries do not systematically collect information on quality and many have not reached a national consensus regarding which indicators ought to be collected and reported regularly. The measurement of quality is held back by definitional and methodological challenges and the lack of a mandate to collect these data. This chapter discusses these challenges by documenting the approaches to measure long-term care quality in a selection of OECD countries, evaluates the advantages and limitations of the indicators used, and provides recommendations for the development of indicators to monitor LTC quality across OECD and EU countries.

Quality measurement in LTC needs further development

As stories about poor-quality long-term care are regularly reported in the media, there has been impetus and pressure on governments to develop better evidence-based approaches to LTC quality improvement. National reports, audits, individual studies and patient satisfaction surveys point to poor quality and instances of "sub-standard" care in nursing homes, assisted living or home-care services (Hurtardo et al., 2001; Wiener et al., 2007a; Capitman, 2005). To take one example, in 2010, 34% of nursing homes in the United States were reported as having inadequate quality of care and 23% of them as causing harm to residents (Wiener, 2012). This pressure has been accelerated by trends in long-term care markets – such as government reliance on decentralised authorities or care users themselves for purchasing care – which have increased the need for reliable data to assess the quality of services or the performance of providers government are contracting with (Malley and Fernández, 2010).

However, quality measurement in LTC lags behind developments in the health care sector. While nearly four-fifths of countries have indicators of inputs, such as staff ratios, the number of single rooms in nursing homes or the number of skilled LTC workers, only a handful of OECD and EU countries collect or systematically report LTC quality measures – for example some Canadian provinces (e.g., Ontario), Finland, Iceland, Korea, Germany, the Netherlands, Norway, Portugal and the United States. Still fewer collect measures of experiences of LTC users (Sorenson and Mossialos, 2007; Castle and Ferguson, 2010). Information on diagnosis, functional status, and medical complexity is generally not available.

There are clearly measurement and data collection challenges. Quality is not an easy concept to define and operationalise for measurement purposes. Unlike efforts to enhance quality of acute care, which mainly focus on achieving specific health outcomes and eliminating medical errors, measuring LTC quality is made complex because of the degenerative nature of long-term care and the multiple care settings involved in care provision. The combination of these factors makes it especially challenging to specify expected outcomes or set benchmarks for outcome improvement. Also challenging is to set measures that go beyond clinical aspects and focus on the overarching quality of life of recipients of care. Last, the fragmentation of responsibilities for care between central and local government and across health and social care authorities add to the complexity of data collection and measurement.

This chapter discusses some of these challenges, starting by documenting the approaches to measure LTC quality in a selection of OECD countries, identifying indicators used, the source of information, and the type of data collected. A small set of data on six quality indicators collected across six countries is presented. The chapter discusses some of the advantages and limitations of the indicators, and the methodological difficulties related to the use of quality indicators. Recommendations for the development of indicators to monitor quality in LTC across OECD countries are included in the chapter's conclusion, and some of the challenges and complexity in realising such a process are then discussed.

Measuring clinical as well as social outcomes of care is crucial, despite the challenges

Measuring safety, effectiveness and responsiveness of care is beneficial in several ways. It allows regulators to identify which facilities and issues to focus upon in their quality improvement efforts. Such benchmarking exercises can also help encourage competition among providers. For purchasers of care, such as local authorities and municipalities, information on LTC quality helps inform recourse allocation decisions. For providers, quality measures help internal quality improvement, while information on quality care offers consumers a basis for selecting care providers and offers workers information to select their employer. Measurement of LTC quality can help establish baselines and benchmark performance over time or across geographical areas, allowing intra and cross-national comparison of performance of the services delivered.

In practice, however, measuring LTC quality is challenging and complex, both in its conceptualisation and the identification of indicators that can be expressed numerically. There are important questions to be asked, for example about the right scope of measurement. While a number of countries collect information on inputs such as staff ratios and service utilisation, changes in health status, physical and cognitive functions attributable to care are the outcomes that are ultimately of most relevance. Another important conceptual consideration regards whose outcomes should be considered when measuring LTC quality – should measurement focus on LTC users alone, or on the family carers and LTC workers. For example, there is a growing interest in quantifying the outcomes of care of each provider.

Some countries have initially focused on the development of measurements of clinical aspects of care (such has some Canadian provinces, Iceland, Germany, Korea, the Netherlands, the United States), while others have devoted much attention to social outcomes, the experience of LTC users, and their quality of life (England, the Netherlands and Sweden). This focus is somewhat influenced by whether the long-term care is conceptualised as social care or as nursing care. Over time, however, quality frameworks used to assess LTC for example in Australia, Canada (Ontario), England, Finland, the Netherlands, and the United States, have identified both clinical-quality outcomes (care effectiveness and safety) as well as user-experience outcomes (user centredness and care co-ordination) as being the main dimensions of LTC quality.

Defining a start point and an end point (or outcome) for LTC is not always clear-cut, making it challenging to quantify changes and set benchmarks. The start of a LTC "pathway" is not necessarily the initial onset of illness, rather the use of LTC services. The priority for LTC users is the good management of their conditions and relief in everyday life. Practices are less standardised, and different forms of care provision coexist, further complicating the development of quality measures.

Despite the challenges, there have been notable examples of countries that collect and report aggregate measures of LTC quality (Box 2.1). Various international projects are also underway to validate quality indicators.

> ## Box 2.1. **Examples of quality indicators identified in national and cross-national projects**
>
> **Victoria, Australia.** The Aged Care Branch of the DHS in Victoria, Australia, carried out a project from 2003 to 2004 to identify a set of quality indicators to assist in monitoring and improving the quality of care provided to residents in the state's residential aged care services (RACS). Their final recommendation was to use six quality indicators including, incidence of stage 1-4 pressure ulcers, incidence of new fractures as a proportion of falls, incidence of daily physical restraints, incidence of residents using nine or more different medications, incidence of weight change (i.e. a significant increase or decrease from the norm), and prevalence of symptoms of depression. Recommendations suggested to investigate additional four indicators including incidence of behavioural symptoms, resident experiences of care, health related QOL of residents, and staff experience of care. In 2007, the Victorian government published a resource manual for quality indicators in RACS which included all but the prevalence of symptoms of depression. The quality indicators were implemented from July 2006 and RACS started to report the required data for each indicator to DHS (Victorian Government Department of Human Services, 2007; Aged Care Branch of the Department of Human Services, 2004).
>
> **Germany.** In 2011, Germany reported the results of a project to develop and implement outcome quality indicators in residential long-term care facilities. In the project, outcome measurements were based on empirical evidence, suitable to be used in internal quality management, verifiable during inspections, comparable across LTC facilities, and applicable in today's practice (Berringer, 2012). The German project recommended a set of indicators covering not only functional (e.g. steadiness of mobility, self-care ability and ability to organise everyday life) and safety outcomes (e.g. pressure sores acquired during stay in facility, malnutrition, incidence of falls) but also lodging and household assistance, activities and communication, outcomes related to particular needs, and co-operation with resident's relatives (Berringer, 2012).
>
> **Iceland.** Iceland has 20 quality indicators that provide a valuable insight into quality of care in nursing homes and are shown to be statistically stable over at least three months, suggesting a high degree of reliability (Karon et al., 1999). These indicators are based on research findings that identified ten clinical quality indicators that were more sensitive in categorising facilities as good, average or poor. The sensitive quality indicators are: falls; depression; depression without treatment; use of 9+ different medications; urinary tract infection; weight loss; dehydration; bedfast residents; decline in late-loss ADLs; stage 1-4 pressure ulcers.
>
> **Portugal.** GestCare CCI monitors assessments of recipients across transitory care and long-term care. Referrals, admissions, transitions, waiting times and patients waiting to be admitted, as well as outcomes of care are collected. For providers who are part of Hospital Discharge Teams (EGA) and Primary Care Referral Teams (CS) are required to submit medical, nurse and social evaluation, evaluation of physical autonomy, pressure ulcers, pain evaluation. Providers in Integrated Home Care ECCI and inpatient facilities are responsible for the same information as EGA and CS, but at admission, during care and at discharge. In addition, they also need to submit data on falls, diabetes, and pressure ulcers risk and elaborate individual intervention plans. Indicators are comparable across geographical areas and overtime and include care related indicators (i.e. pressure ulcers, falls) but also mortality rate, access and user surveys.
>
> **United States.** The Centers for Medicare and Medicaid Services has recently launched version 3.0 of the Minimum Data Set (MDS). Prior to the launch, a national project was initiated to improve the clinical relevance and accuracy of MDS assessments, increase the voice of residents in assessments, improve user satisfaction, and increase the efficiency of reports.

Box 2.1. **Examples of quality indicators identified in national and cross-national projects** (cont.)

The MDS collects information on nursing residents based on the RAI assessment. Among the indicators measured are the percentage of residents whose ability to perform certain activities of daily living had deteriorated. There are also indicators to measure those receiving post-acute care such as the percentage of post-acute residents with delirium, with delirium adjusted by the facility admission profile, whose walking ability had improved or been maintained since admission, and with moderate pain or excruciating pain at any frequency (Mukamel et al., 2008). Another function of MDS is to produce a set of quality indicators and a set of quality measures. The revision process also made changes to the set of quality indicators and measures. For example, new fractures, falls, behaviour symptoms affecting others, depression, urinary tract infection, lost weight, tube feeding, lost control of their bowels or bladder, pressure ulcers are among the list of indicators without a major change while the following list of indicators was dropped: use of nine or more different medications, prevalence of fecal impaction, prevalence of dehydration, prevalence of hypnotic use, and prevalence of little or no activity (Salida and Buchanan, 2008).

The OASIS-C dataset specifically developed to capture information of home care service also set out a list of quality measures by three dimensions: process, outcomes and avoidable events. Such quality measures include, timely initiation of care, depression assessment conducted, pain intervention in care plan, improvement in bathing, improvement in toileting hygiene, stabilisation in light meal preparation, improvement in dyspnea, emergent care for injury caused by fall, and development of urinary tract infection (CMS, 2011a; CMS 2011b; CMS 2011c).

A set of result-oriented quality indicators in care homes (i.e. nursing homes) was published in *Measuring Progress: Indicators for Care Home* in 2010. This handbook is one of the products of the EU co-funded-project "Quality management by result-oriented indicators: Towards benchmarking in residential care for older people", co-ordinated by the European Centre for Social Welfare policy and Research (Austria) with working partners across Europe. The project looked at the issue of measurement from the different perspectives of residents, staff, management, families and other stakeholders. Based on experiences in selected European Union Member States, 94 quality indicators related to the quality of care (24 indicators such as dehydration, weight loss, falls), quality of life (46 indicators, such as staff feel supported and residents with a defined key worker), economic performance (4 indicators, staff cost per care days, degree of capacity utilisation), leadership (17 indicators, such as complaints addressed, satisfaction with care quality, HRM records) and social contexts (three indicators, such as average length of employment per staff) were selected (European Centre for Social Welfare Policy and Research et al., 2010).

The ANCIEN project. An EU-funded project focusing on the future of long-term care for the elderly in Europe, collected 390 quality indicators from 11 European counties and categorised them by "organisation type" (institutional and home nursing and home-based care), quality dimensions (effectiveness, safety, patient responsiveness, co-ordination) and system dimensions (inputs, process and outcomes). The collected indicators are used either at a national level or are recommended to be used at a local level by a national authority. Across these 11 countries, more indicators are available to assess quality of institutional care and there is a large difference in the availability of quality indicators in different countries, with a low of 5 in Hungary to a high of 119 in France. Most of the indicators concern effectiveness of care while there is a fewer availability of indicators on safety and co-ordination. In terms of system dimensions, there is a large difference in the available number of process indicators (247 indicators) comparing to the number of inputs (76 indicators) and outcomes (68 indicators) across 11 countries (Dandi and Casanova, 2012).

Clinical indicators help to identify adverse events and problems in the provision of care

Indicators on clinical aspects of care help providers and administrations identify quality problems and point to adverse events in the provision of care (OECD, 2005; Joint Commission, 2012). For example, pressure ulcers, falls, incontinence, and acute infections may all point to adverse clinical events and unmet needs (Naylor et al., 2009). A high prevalence of pressure ulcers, malnutrition and dehydration may imply that care workers do not devote sufficient time to care recipients or are not adequately qualified, motivated or trained. This can also reflect poor management or insufficient resources (Productivity Commission, 2011). Indicators commonly used in health care, such as avoidable hospital admission for chronic conditions, can also point to the effectiveness in the management by primary care and LTC systems.

There is convergence around a small selection of care effectiveness and safety indicators

A review of country experiences (Box 2.2) revealed six quality indicators related to care effectiveness and user safety most commonly used in institutional settings and available nationally (Box 2.3):

- Prevalence of pressure ulcers (i.e. bedsores).
- Incidence of falls and fall-related fractures.[1]
- Incidence of use of physical restraint.
- Incidence of over medication and medication errors.
- Prevalence of unplanned weight loss.
- Incidence of depression.

Box 2.2. Examples of indicators on clinical aspects on care effectiveness and user safety

Canada: Incidence of pressure ulcers, percentage of pressure ulcers worsened, incidence of depression, percentage of residents whose behavioural symptoms worsened/improved, percentage of residents with symptoms of delirium, percentage of residents whose ADL functioning worsened/improved/remained, percentage of residents whose bowel/bladder continence worsened/improved, prevalence of tube feeding, percentage of residents whose cognitive ability worsened, percentage of residents whose ability to communicate worsened, percentage of residents with pain worsened, percentage of residents on antipsychotics without a diagnosis of psychosis, percentage of residents with one or more infections, percentage of residents who developed a respiratory condition.

Germany: Provision of medication in accordance with doctor's instruction, appropriate handling of medication, systematic assessment of pain, close co-operation with doctor's in case of patients with chronic pain, residents with chronic pain receive prescribed medication, appropriate handling of tracheal cannula, time and place documented when chronic wound/ulcer was first diagnosed, measures taken to battle chronic wounds or ulcers are state of the art, assessment of individual risk of falling, assessment of individual risk of decubitus/ulcer, implementation of falling prophylaxis, development of weight of patient in last six months, implementation of measures in case independent food intake is limited, appropriate nutritional condition of patients, documentation of individual resources and risks for patient with incontinence or catheter, consideration of biography and daily routine of dementia patient in care planning, implementation of appropriate measures of

---

Box 2.2. **Examples of indicators on clinical aspects
on care effectiveness and user safety** (*cont.*)

body hygiene, assessment of legal and professional control of restricting measures, implementation of necessary provisions for residents with incontinence or a catheter, state of nutrition (as being influenced by the nursing home) (both items also apply to the supply of liquids), assessment of individual resources and risks.

Korea: Prevalence of pressure ulcers, prevention and management of bedsores, mini-mental state examination (MMSE) test rate, proportion of patients with declined ability to perform daily activities, percentage of clients with urinary tract infection, HbA1c test rate for diabetic patients, prevalence of use of physical restraints, residents with indwelling catheters.

Netherlands: Prevalence of pressure ulcers, prevalence of unplanned weight loss, incidence of depression, prevalence of behaviour symptoms affecting others, percentage of residents with UTI, percentage of residents given the seasonal influenza vaccine, incidence of falls, prevalence of use of physical restraints, the organisational unit can prove that they have a demonstrable policy for the prevention of restricting measures, the percentage of clients that has used anti-psychotic, anti-anxiety medication, the percentage of clients that has been involved in a medicine-related incidents over the past 30 days, residents with indwelling catheters.

Portugal: Prevalence of pressure ulcers, prevalence of unplanned weight loss, outcomes in physical autonomy by typology of care, incidence of falls, percentage of residents with one or more infections.

United States: Prevalence of pressure ulcers (i.e. bedsores), prevalence of unplanned weight loss, incidence of depression, prevalence of behaviour symptoms affecting others, percentage of residents whose need for help with activities of daily living has increased, prevalence of tube feeding, percentage of residents who were assessed and appropriately given the seasonal influenza vaccine and pneumococcal vaccine, incidence of falls, residents with indwelling catheters.

Box 2.3. **Six quality indicators: Definitions, risk factors and relevance**

Pressure ulcers, also known as bedsores, are clinical conditions of soreness on the skin. Frail elderly people whose mobility is limited are at risk of getting pressure ulcers because pressure ulcers are caused by unrelieved pressures to soft tissues of the skin. The level of severity can be categorised into four stages.

While this definition is commonly acknowledged, some countries do not include those with stage 1 pressure ulcers in data collection. As a preventive measure, assessing the risk of residents and recipients, providing special mattresses and/or padding, avoiding incontinence, keeping skin dry, providing good nutrition, and above all, regularly turning if mobility is limited help to reduce the risk of pressure ulcers and avoiding conditions to become severe and fatal (CIHI, 2011; National Pressure Ulcer Advisory Panel, 2011).

Falls are leading causes of hospitalisation or death among elderly people, especially among women. Falls can be accounted for muscle weakness and walking problems of older people in nursing home residents and home-care recipients (CDC, 2012). Environmental hazards such as conditions of facilities, vision problems and side effects from medications are known risk factors (CIHI, 2011). Fall incidents most commonly result in hip and wrist fractures, hip and shoulder dislocations, head injuries and bruises.

Box 2.3. **Six quality indicators: Definitions, risk factors and relevance** (cont.)

The use of physical restraints is a method used to limit or restrict the movement of residents and recipients. There are different types of restraints including physical and mechanical restraints (hand mitts, restrictive chairs such as Gerichairs, vests that tie nursing home residents to their chairs or beds, wrist and ankle restraints, and bedrails.), chemical restraints (medications given to residents to lessen pacing, restlessness, and unco-operative behaviour), and environmental restraints. Research shows that restraints can increase falls, as well as increase the risk of pressure ulcers and asphyxiation, worsen an injury if a fall occurs while in restraint, and worsen depression and a sense of helplessness (Health Quality Ontario, 2011).

Medication errors and over prescribed medication refer to cases such as inappropriate and wrong medication causing or potentially causing harms to residents and recipients of care. Such examples include prescribing, monitoring, administration or dispensing. Medication errors and over use of medication are known to be common across health care and long-term care, however, more so among residents of nursing homes. LTC users with multi-morbidity conditions can take many medications a day, however, other factors that lead physicians to prescribe medications or may cause medication errors are: inappropriate resident behaviours, such as aggressiveness, a lack of information sharing about a complete list of prescriptions available to physicians and pharmacists for the review of safety, especially for home care users who see multiple doctors (e.g. specialists) and fill prescriptions at different pharmacies (Health Quality Ontario, 2011).

Involuntary weight loss seen among elderly people can be a cause for acute and chronic illnesses and normal (hyperthyroidism, diabetes mellitus, or mal-absorption) and reduced appetites (cancer, chronic infections, cardiovascular, pulmonary, or renal disease) (Huffman, 2002). Depression is also known to trigger unintentional weight loss and it is usually higher among those living in nursing home than receiving care at home. Bereavement is another significant factor and men are shown to be more influenced than women. Importantly, elderly people with dementia are at high risk of unintentional weight loss. Drugs and medications also play a role in reduced appetites (Rehman, 2005). Increasing age, disability, coexisting medical conditions, history of hospital admission, low education level, presence of cognitive impairment, smoking, and low baseline body weight are also associated with unintentional weight loss among elderly people (Rehman, 2005). Although there is no clear consensus, the most well-accepted definition of clinically important weight loss is 5% over a period of 6-12 months (Rehman, 2005).

Depressions, also known as mood disorders, are the most common mental illness among elderly people. However, symptoms tend to be under reported because it is often under detected or considered natural reaction to physical conditions. Depressions are more prevalent among those living in nursing homes than those receiving care at home. Residents express social isolation especially with initial move to Long-term care facilities. A decline in general health makes people feel depressed. Depression in later life frequently coexists with other medical illnesses and disabilities. Major causes of depression are known to be related to health problems (illness and disability, chronic pain, cognitive decline, etc.), loneliness and isolation, reduce sense of purpose, fears, and recent bereavement. Deaths of friends and family which become more common with age can lead to depression (Health Quality Ontario, 2011). Although it is not feasible to see zero prevalence of depression, there are known to be effective measures available including providing meaningful activities, social networks, visitors, medications or pet therapy (CIHI, 2011).

> **Box 2.3. Six quality indicators: Definitions, risk factors and relevance** (*cont.*)
>
> These six indicators chosen satisfy soundness criteria such as: 1) the indicators focus on an important performance aspect, are scientifically sound, and potentially feasible; 2) the indicator focuses on quality and not utilisation; 3) the indicator reflect technical quality; 4) the indicator can be used for quality assessment at the health care system level, not just at the provider level; 5) the indicator can be constructed from administrative data or registries using uniform or standardised coding systems; and 6) the indicator is widely available and could be standardised for cross-country comparison.

Collection of six quality indicators in selected countries

This section illustrates some key indicators on care effectiveness and safety available in a small sample of countries. This data shows some of the challenges in collecting data on LTC quality across countries:

- Nation-wide data on the six indicators remain limited, mainly because efforts to collect such indicators are not always part of a national data collection. Only five countries (Ontario, Canada; Finland; Iceland; Norway and Portugal) submitted actual data to the OECD. Data on the use of physical restraints is the most often collected indicator. Data on pressure ulcers, falls and fall-related fractures are commonly available, while depression was the least available (Table 2.1).

- Poor availability of indicators such as medication use, weight loss and depression can be explained by a lack of consensus regarding their relevance to both care effectiveness and measurement difficulties. Differences in definitions limits cross-country comparability.

- Measuring LTC quality largely focuses on institutional care, and far less attention is paid to care at home and in the community. Only Finland reported data on all six quality indicators for both nursing homes and home care services. Semi-residential care tends to be less targeted.

Table 2.1. **Data availability**

	Pressure ulcers	Falls and fall-related fractures	Use of physical restraints	Over medications or medication errors	Unvoluntary weight loss	Depression	Care setting
Ontario, Canada	Yes	Yes	Yes	No	No	Yes	Nursing homes
Finland	Yes	Yes	Yes	Yes	Yes	Yes	Nursing homes and home care
Iceland	No	Yes	Yes	Yes	Yes	Yes	Nursing homes
Germany							In-patients and out-patients
Korea	Yes	No	No	No	No	No	Long-term care hospitals
Netherlands	Yes	Yes	Yes	No	Yes	Yes	Nursing homes and home care
Norway	No	No	Yes	No	No	No	Nursing homes
Portugal	Yes	Yes	Yes	Yes	Yes	No	Nursing homes and home care (pressure ulcers and falls only)
United States	Yes	Yes	Yes	No	Yes	Yes	Nursing homes and home care

Source: OECD 2012 Questionnaire on Long-Term Care Quality.

Pressure ulcers or bedsore

Pressure ulcers are known to affect a large number of LTC recipients in nursing homes. The data submitted to OECD present large variations in the prevalence of pressure ulcers by setting and by severity (Figure 2.1). For all countries and settings, prevalence is the lowest for those with stage 4 pressure ulcers. For those countries with time-series data, the prevalence of pressure ulcers among nursing home residents decreased gradually, while the prevalence among home care recipients went up, suggesting there might be a need to monitor mobility for this category of LTC recipients.

Falls

Falls are one of the most relevant causes of hospitalisation among elderly people. In the United Kingdom, a report indicated that one old person dies due to a fall every five hours (Department of Health, 2001). About 30% of the population over 65 years and between 32% and 42% of the population over 75 years are estimated to experience a fall each year (Royal College of Physicians, 2011). A study from the United States reported that 34% of nursing home residents had experienced at least one fall in the last 180 days and 9% in the last 30 days (Jones et al., 2009). Although one quarter of falls can be due to weak muscles and walking problems, another quarter can be due to environmental hazards, facilities' conditions, vision problems and the side-effects of medications, which could be addressed or prevented (CDC, 2012; CIHI, 2011). The pilot data collection showed that the incidence of falls is higher in home settings relative to nursing homes (Finland, Portugal), although fall-related fractures were higher in nursing homes (4.2%) compared to home settings (2.7%) in 2011. Differences in definitions limit cross-country comparisons; for example, Ontario, Canada and Iceland define the number of falls in the last 30 days recorded on their target assessment, while Finland uses 180 days for nursing home and 90 days for home care (Figure 2.2).

Figure 2.1. **Prevalence of bedsores and pressure ulcers**
Percentage of LTC recipients
Portugal

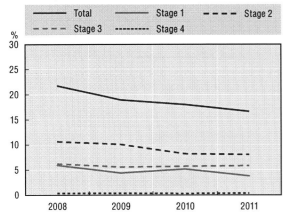

Note: The numbers include those with pressure ulcers on admission.
Source: Ministry of Health, GestCare CCI.

Source: Ministry of Health, GestCare CCI.

Finland

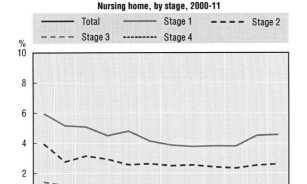

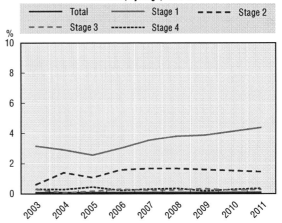

Note: Institutions participate in the RAI MDS quality network voluntarily. Coverage is approximately 40% of LTC residents, with 100% coverage in certain communities. Coverage has increased annually.
Source: THL RAI MDS 2.0.

Note: Home care providers (municipalities) participate in the RAI HC MDS quality network voluntarily. The number of participating municipalities increases annually. Because many large cities were the first to participate, the covarage of all home care clients is approx. 30% in 2011, even if the number of non-participating minicipalities is large.
Source: THL RAI MDS 2.0.

Ontario, Canada, pressure ulcers, Stage 2-4, LTC residents, 2010 and 2011

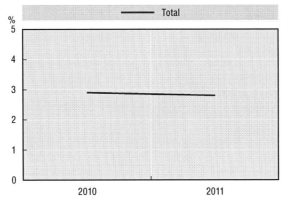

Note: The data covers approx. 300 LTC homes out of 600+.
Source: Canadian Institute for Health Information, Ministry of Health and Long-Term Care.

Figure 2.2. **Incidence of falls and fall-related fractures**
Percentage of LTC recipients

Portugal

Inpatient units and ECCI (home care), 2008-11

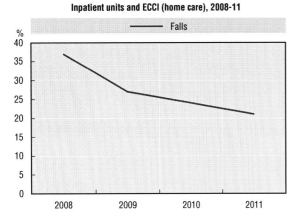

Source: Ministry of Health, GestCare CCI.

Home care recipients, 2010 and 2011

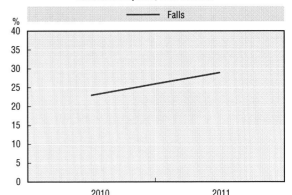

Note: Home Care data is available since 2010.
Source: Ministry of Health, GestCare CCI.

Finland

Nursing home, 2000-11

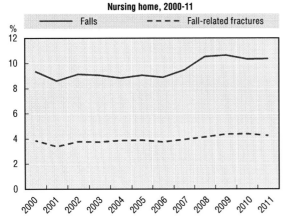

Note: Institutions participate in the RAI MDS quality network voluntarily. Coverage is approximately 40% of LTC residents, with 100% coverage in certain communities. Coverage has increased annually.
Source: THL RAI MDS 2.0.

Home care, 2003-11

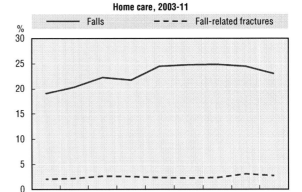

Note: Home care providers (municipalities) participate in the RAI HC MDS quality network voluntarily. The number of participating municipalities increases annually. Because many large cities were the first to participate, the covarage of all home care clients is approx. 30% in 2011, even if the number of non-participating minicipalities is large.
Source: THL RAI MDS 2.0.

Nursing home residents, 2010 and 2011

Canada, Ontario

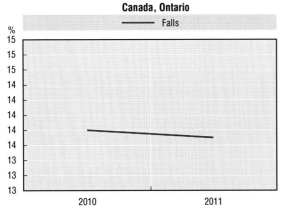

Note: The data covers approx. 300 LTC homes out of 600+.
Source: Canadian Institute for Health Information, Ministry of Health and Long-Term Care.

Iceland

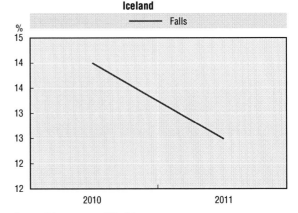

Source: Directorate of Health.

Use of physical restraints

The justification for the use of physical restraints is a subject of some divergence. Restraints might prevent falls and protect residents who may harm themselves or put other residents in danger, especially for LTC recipients with higher levels of disability. A Canadian study using a Resident Assessment Instrument (RAI) data found that restraint use was higher among those with late-loss ADLs,[2] while restraint use rates were lower, typically below five per cent, in the case of elderly with early to mid-loss ADLs (Hirdes et al., 2011). However, there is a general consensus that physical restraints should not be used as a fall prevention strategy as they do not lower the risk of fall-related injuries and can, conversely, increase the risk of pressure ulcers, muscle atrophy, agitation and depression (Health Quality Ontario, 2011). The use of physical restraints varies significantly across countries (Figure 2.3) – for example from 0.3% in Norway to 16% in Finland. For home care, incidence is low. These variations can be explained in part by data issues, but also by different policy approaches around the use of physical restraints. There is no sign of a consistent decline in the incidence of physical restraint use.

Use of nine or more medications

Medication errors can harm older people, for example, if inappropriately or wrongly prescribed. In a study in the United Kingdom, two-thirds of LTC users in institutions were exposed to one or more medication errors with the average of two errors per recipient (Barber et al., 2009). The most common types of prescribing error, accounting for 87% of the total, were due to "incomplete information", "unnecessary drug" (24%), "dose/strength error" (14%) and "omission" (12%). Measuring overuse or overprescribing of medication is tricky because the link between an excess number of medications and quality is not straightforward. Older people may take more than nine medications a day due to multiple chronic conditions and disabilities, rather than because of prescription errors or overprescribing. Variation in data from Iceland, Finland and Portugal reported can be explained by the different definitions used (e.g., Finland counts the number of medications taken in the previous seven days and Iceland defines the number of use of nine or more medications per resident reported while Portugal does not specify criteria in their definition), different prescription practices, and different compliance with practice guidelines (Figure 2.4). This suggests that such an indicator is unsuitable for comparative analysis as it stands.

Involuntary weight loss

Elderly patients with unintentional weight loss are at higher risk of infection, depression and death. Causes of weight loss could be a medical condition (e.g., cancer, cardiac disorder, or gastrointestinal diseases) or depression. Definitions of involuntary weight loss are not consistent across countries. Iceland measures the number of residents who experienced an unplanned weight loss of 3 kg of total body weight in the previous three months. In Finland, involuntary weight loss refers to a 5% body weight loss over 30 days or more than 10% of body weight loss over 180 days. Portugal did not specify weight loss rate in its definition. Finnish data showed an increase in involuntary weight loss over time. A UK study found that at least one in two people admitted to hospital from a care home setting are at risk of malnutrition, although the prevalence of malnutrition declined slightly from 40% to 37% between 2008 and 2010 (BAPEN, 2011; Figure 2.5).

Figure 2.3. **Use of physical restraints**
Percentage of LTC recipients

Portugal
Inpatient units, 2008-11

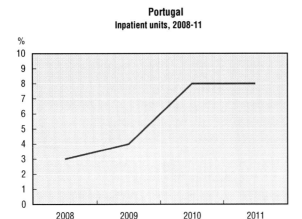

Source: Ministry of Health, GestCare CCI.

Iceland
Nursing home, 2010 and 2011

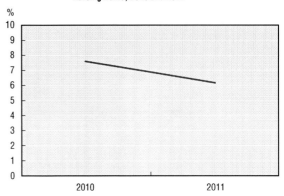

Source: Directorate of Health.

Finland

Nursing homes, 2000-11

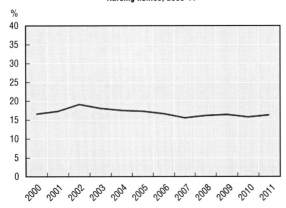

Note: Institutions participate in the RAI MDS quality network voluntarily. Coverage is approx. 40% of LTC residents, with 100% coverage in certain communities. Coverage has increased annually.
Source: THL RAI MDS 2.0.

Home care, 2003-11

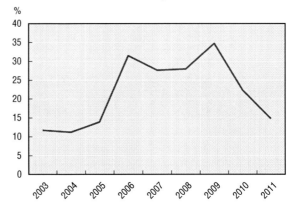

Note: Home care providers (municipalities) participate in the RAI HC MDS quality network voluntarily. The number of participating municipalities increases annually. Because many large cities were the first to participate, the coverage of all home care clients is approx. 30% in 2011, even if the number of non-participating municipalities is large.
Source: THL RAI MDS 2.0.

Canada, Ontario
Nursing home, 2010 and 2011

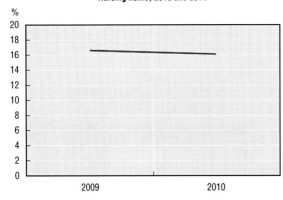

Note: The data covers approx. 300 LTC homes out of more than 600.
Source: Canadian Institute for Health Information, Ministry of Health and Long-Term Care.

Norway
Nursing home, 2009 and 2010

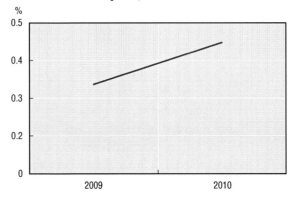

Source: IPLOS (national register of LTC), Norwegian Directorate of Health.

Figure 2.4. **Prevalence of use of nine or more medications**
Percentage of LTC recipients

Portugal
Inpatient units and ECCI (home care), 2008-11

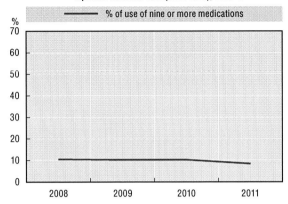

Note: The registry of medication is made in an open field in GestCare CCI. The evaluation cannot be done by a simple query to the data set. This evaluation can only be done by individual registry analysis. For this determination it was used a sample of patients in inpatient units –25%.

Source: Ministry of Health, GestCare CCI.

Iceland
Nursing home, 2010-11

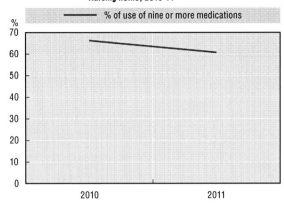

Source: Directorate of Health.

Finland

Nursing homes, 2000-11

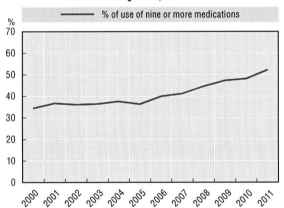

Note: Institutions participate in the RAI MDS quality network voluntarily. Coverage is approx. 40% of LTC residents, with 100% coverage.

Source: THL RAI HC MDS 2.0.

Home care, 2003-11

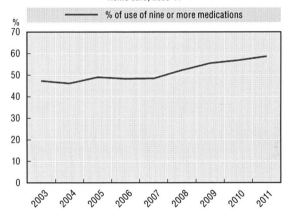

Note: Home care providers (municipalities) participate in the RAI HC MDS quality network voluntarily. The number of participating municipalities increases annually. Because many large cities were the first to participate, the coverage of all home care clients is approx. 30% in 2011, even if the number of non-participating municipalities is large.

Source: THL RAI HC MDS 2.0.

Figure 2.5. **Prevalence of unvoluntary weight loss**
Percentage of LTC recipients

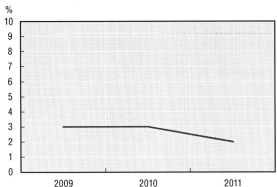

Portugal
Inpatient units and ECCI (home care), 2009-11

Source: Ministry of Health, GestCare CCI.

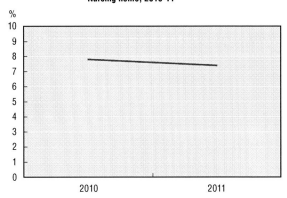

Iceland
Nursing home, 2010-11

Source: Directorate of Health.

Finland

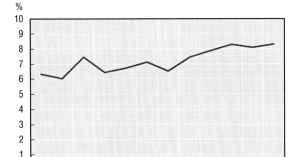

Nursing home, 2000-11

Note: Institutions participate in the RAI MDS quality network voluntarily. Coverage is approx. 40% of LTC residents, with 100% coverage in certain communities. Coverage has increased annually. *Source:* THL RAI MDS 2.0.

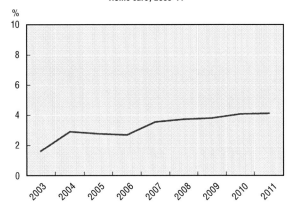

Home care, 2003-11

Note: Home care providers (municipalities) participate in the RAI HC MDS quality network voluntarily. The number of participating municipalities increases annually. Because many large cities were the first to participate, the coverage of all home care clients is approx. 30% in 2011, even if the number of non-participating municipalities is large. *Source:* THL RAI MDS 2.0.

Depression

Depression is very common and a growing condition in the older population. According to a UK report, at least 30% of older people in acute hospitals and 40% of older people in care homes meet the clinical criteria for a diagnosis of depression. Up to 25% of people aged 65 and over living in the community have symptoms of depression severe enough to warrant intervention, 2% of older people living in the community meet the criteria for major depression, and 11% have minor depression (Lee, 2007). Incidence of depression can be defined differently depending on the instrument employed. One of the most widely used instruments is the Yesavage Geriatric Depression Scale (GDS) and its shorter versions, including Geriatric Depression Scale shorter versions called GDS-30 items, GDP-15 items and GDS-5 items (ABUEL, 2008). The data submitted by Finland and Iceland showed a downward trend and a higher prevalence of depression among nursing home residents (Figure 2.6).

Figure 2.6. **Prevalence of depression**

Percentage of LTC recipients

Finland

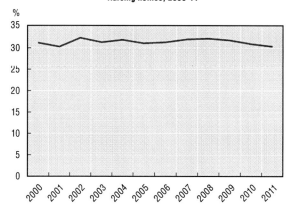

Nursing homes, 2000-11

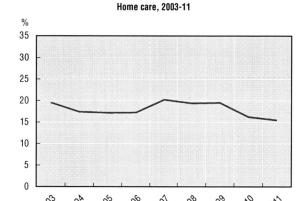

Home care, 2003-11

Note: Institutions participate in the RAI MDS quality network voluntarily. Coverage is approx. 40% of LTC residents, with 100% coverage in certain communities. Coverage has increased annually.

Source: THL RAI MDS 2.0.

Note: Home care providers (municipalities) participate in the RAI HC MDS quality network voluntarily. The number of participating municipalities increases annually. Because many large cities were the first to participate, the coverage of all home care clients is approx. 30% in 2011, even if the number of non-participating municipalities is large.

Source: THL RAI HC MDS 2.0.

Iceland

Nursing home, 2010-11

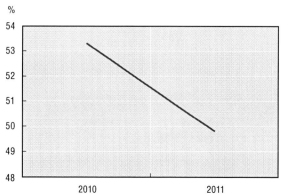

Source: Directorate of Health.

Measuring patient-centredness in long-term care is an important outcome dimension

As concern is growing that LTC quality measures should go beyond physical and cognitive functions and take into consideration the preservation of autonomy and well-being of LTC users, indicators addressing patient-centredness and quality of life, including user experience and waiting times to care, are increasingly considered as important (Kane et al., 2003; Mor, 2006). Expectations from care users and family members is that care services will help them maintain physical and cognitive functions, a good quality of life, ability to remain independent, to take part in decisions over everyday matters, and maintain social activities.

Measuring quality of life and user experiences

Quality of life seeks to measure "intangible" factors such as consumer choice, autonomy, dignity, individuality, comfort, well-being and security, relationships and meaningful social activity (Wiener, 2007b). Specific items identified include domestic and living conditions, privacy, control over daily life and autonomy, food and nutrition, involvement and information, personal cleanliness and comfort, experience of safety, and social participation (Social Care Institute for Excellence, 2010; Steering Committee Responsible Care, 2007). Efforts to express users' experiences and to incorporate aspects of quality of life, satisfaction and psychosocial well-being into a national reporting system have started to emerge in a selection of EU and OECD countries. Among the countries that regularly collect such indicators are England, Korea, Germany, Portugal and the Netherlands, as described in Box 2.4.

Box 2.4. List of indicators expressing patient-centredness, responsiveness, and empowerment collected by a selected number of countries

England (ASCOT): How happy are you with the way staff help you? Thinking about the good and bad things that make up your quality of life, how would you rate the quality of your life as a whole? Do care and support services help you to have a better quality of life? Which of the following statements best describes how much control you have over your daily life? Which of the following statements best describes how much control you have over your daily life? Do care and support services help you in keeping clean and presentable in appearance? Do care and support services help you to get food and drink? Do care and support services help you in feeling safe? Do care and support services help you in having social contact with people? In the past year, have you generally found it easy or difficult to find information and advice about support, services or benefits?

Germany: Active communication with doctor, patients can choose own clothes, care staff is friendly and polite.

Korea: Patient rights and/or dignity, documentation related to benefit and compensation, information service availability, bath and toilet assist services, beneficiary management, client satisfaction assessment.

Netherlands: The extent to which clients or representatives experience a good care plan, a good evaluation of that plan, good participation, good consultation, good treatment, good communication, good meals, good physical care, and good information. The extent to which clients or representatives experience adequate independence/autonomy, the extent to which representatives experience adequate respect for clients' rights in relation to restriction of freedom of movement, the extent to which clients or representatives experience adequate possibilities to spend the day and to participate in society and to experience mental support.

Portugal: Promotion of physical anatomy, patients' rights and/or dignity.

One main example is the Adult Social Care Outcomes Toolkit (ASCOT) developed in England. ASCOT is a tool designed to capture information about social care outcomes, which is expressed as a scale of an individual's LTC related quality of life (SCRQoL) and has been developed for application across different care settings and users. This is a similar approach to the EQ-5D, a standardised instrument for measuring health-related quality of life that is widely accepted in health care (AHRQ, 2012). ASCOT assesses LTC outcomes such as cleanliness and comfort, good nutrition, safety, control over daily life, social interaction, occupation, accommodation and dignity. The questions used in ASCOT are based on multiple choices (i.e. four response options) reflecting four different outcome states (Malley et al., 2012).

For example, a question on food could ask to describe a respondent's situation, followed by four choices ranging from "I get all the food and drink I like when I want" to "I don't always get adequate or timely food and drink, and I think there is a risk to my health" (NHS, 2012), which is then translated into a rating. Data are usually collected through surveys involving interviews with users or their legal representatives. In England, a National Adult Social Care Survey has used ASCOT to survey all LTC users at national level. Some other OECD countries, such as Denmark, Austria, Finland, and the Netherlands, are starting to use ASCOT (HSCIC, 2012). This may provide an opportunity for comparative analysis on social aspects of care, although often data and analysis on quality of life are not available at the national level.

The Health and Social Care Information Centre in England recently released a second annual report detailing the findings of the Personal Social Services Adult Social Care Survey for the period from 2011 to 2012. A stratified random sampling was used and 40% of the total sample recipients of care services replied to the questionnaire (n = 164.570).[3] The survey responses were used to populate six of the measures in the Adult Social Care Outcomes Framework (ASCOF), first launched by the Department of Health in March 2011 (Department of Health, 2012), including social care related quality of life, dignity, satisfaction, information, safety, and health, results suggest that quality of life was very good for 27% of the respondents, while only 10% of the respondents say quality of life is bad. More than 75% of the respondents have adequate control over their daily life. For feelings of safety, 64% of respondents feel as safe as they want and only 2% answered to not to feel at all safe (Figure 2.7).

SCRQoL scores are generated by combining the answers from eight questions (including control, personal care, food, accommodation, personal safety, social life, occupation, dignity) with a score of zero indicating high level needs (i.e. low quality of life) and a maximum possible score is 24 being the highest quality of life. For 2011-12, the average score for the SCRQOL was 18.7 similar to the score in 2010-11. There tends to be correspondence between being in good health and having a god quality of life: 65% of respondents in good health rated their quality of life as good, very good or could not be better. To the contrary, only 10% of respondents in poor health say their quality of life is very good (NHS Information Centre, 2012).

Denmark, Spain, the Netherlands, England, and the United States survey patients and user-experiences, although availability and comparability of data are limited and these surveys tend to be on an ad-hoc basis. For example:

● In the Netherlands, all LTC facilities are required to carry out surveys of users' experience using the so-called CQ-Index® Long-Term Care (Steering Committee Responsible Care, 2007). This national tool, used to measure and compare consumer experience, was developed based on the national quality framework for "responsible care" which specifies indicators for ten quality domains[4] (Triemstra et al., 2010). Each domain has an associated set of indicators developed on the basis of the structure-process-outcome concept (see Annex 2. A1). The indicators provide a picture of what users find important and what their experience with care is (van der Veen and Mak, 2010). Some studies analysing the effects on quality improvement suggest that providers are motivated to improve the care they provide but need further support in the use of information for improving quality of care (Zuidgeest et al., 2012).

● In the United States, the minimum data set (MDS, 2.0 version) has two indicators on quality of life – physical restraints (which could be regarded as a clinical measures) and prevalence of little or no activity (Zimmerman, 2003); experience of pain has been recently added (Saliba and Buchanan, 2008). The selection and definition of "quality of life" and "user experience" influenced by the way data are collected, in that indicators

Figure 2.7. **Responses to four different questions on quality of life of LTC users in ASCOT, England, 2011-12**

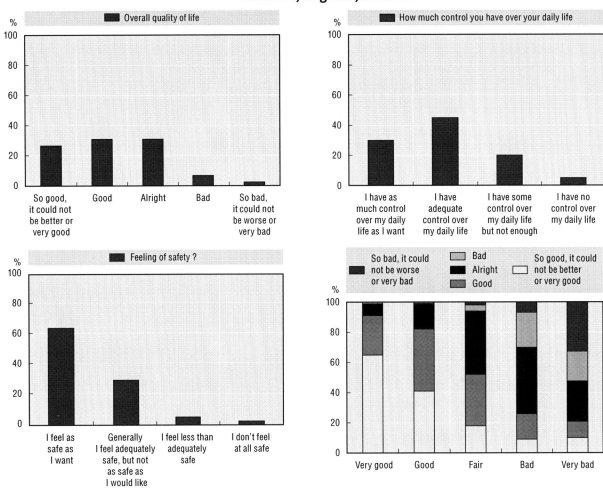

Source: NHS Information Centre, 2012.

are centred around clinical indicators collected through standardised instruments. Consumer surveys are mandatory for home health agencies, although they might only be for a short-duration of time or for post-acute care (Wiener, 2012).

The development of measure on quality of life faces similar challenges to the development of care quality indicators – such as validity, reliability, coherence, comparability, sampling and non-response biases, and relevance (The NHS Information Centre, 2012). For example, self-reporting is not always possible among LTC users and responses are always necessarily limited to those service users who have the physical and mental capacity to respond, and normally for those for whom responses are facilitated by carers. Responses also express a subjective view not easy to standardise. The distinction between subjective view and objective assessment is sometimes hard to draw and there is no consensus around specific indicators to use.

Measuring care responsiveness

One important dimension of patient-centred care is care responsiveness. While various policies seek to make care services more attuned with individual wants and needs (for example, by increasing the scope for choice of service provider and patterns of care), measures of responsiveness are hardly collected on a regular basis across OECD and EU countries, with the notable exception of the Netherlands and England (Box 2.4).

One alternative measure is waiting times for admission to a nursing home or receipt of other care services. Waiting times are regarded as an indicator of poor access and a major challenge for delivering high-quality care services. Waiting may occur when older people needing LTC are discharged from acute care to a more appropriate care setting such as community care and residential care for which there is a waiting. This may lead to patients occupying acute care beds when no longer in need of acute care services. Waiting times can also occur when older people in their own homes wait for a placement in a nursing home.

According to a 2012 survey, 13 out of 14 EU and OECD countries reported problems or growing concerns about waiting times for LTC services. For example, Iceland's 2010 National Health Plan identified waiting times for nursing homes as the third of eight priority areas. About half of these countries collect data on waiting times to access long-term care facilities (Table 2.2) (OECD, 2012b). Information regarding waiting time is collected in England as part of data collection on delayed transfers of care for non-acute and acute care patients. A delayed transfer is defined as a patient awaiting transfer from a hospital bed although she or he is ready for transfer based on a clinical or multi-disciplinary team decision (Knowledge and Intelligence, 2010; Figure 2.8).

Figure 2.8. **Delayed transfer of care by number of patients and days in England**

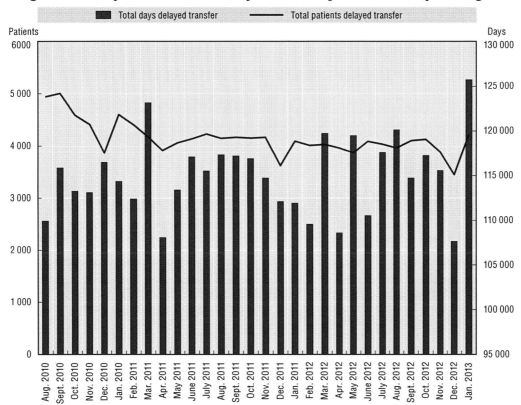

Source: Delayed Transfer of Care, NHS Organisation, England (2013).

A main reason for waiting times can be inadequate capacity in nursing homes or home-care services and supports. In Japan, the average length of stay for long-term care in hospitals is 179.5 days which is about ten times higher the average length of stay for acute care in hospital (18.5 days); this is mainly due to a lack of nursing home beds and home care service capacity (MHLW, 2011a; MHLW, 2011b). In Ontario, Canada, waiting times to access long-term care has been a challenge. The median wait for placement into a nursing

Table 2.2. **Countries with LTC waiting times and data collection on waiting**

	Waiting times for LTC are an issue	National data collection on waiting times for LTC
Australia	Yes	
Canada	Yes	
Czech Republic	Yes	
England	Yes	
Finland	Yes	
Germany		Yes
Iceland	Yes	
Ireland	Yes	Yes
Netherlands	Yes	Yes
Norway	Yes	
Poland	Yes	Yes
Portugal	Yes	Yes
Slovenia	Yes	Yes
Turkey	Yes	

Source: OECD 2011 Waiting Times Policy and Data Availability Questionnaire.

home was 113 days in 2012, compared to 103 days in 2011. Over a longer period, the average waiting time for admission into a nursing home has grown from 30 days to almost four months over the last decade (Health Quality Ontario, 2011; Health Quality Ontario, 2012). A report produced by the Canadian Institute for Health Information shows that only half of older people waiting in acute care were discharged to a residential care facility, while 18% of them discharged to home with support. Of those older people discharged, those with dementia needed to wait a longer period in order to receive specialised services (CIHI, 2012). The majority (86.5%) of acute care clients aged 65 and older were discharged to their own home or to a residential care facility. Of the persons discharged with no waiting days, the majority were discharged to home settings without support (CIHI, 2012).

There is hardly any measurement of care co-ordination in long-term care

Despite the significant challenges in LTC care co-ordination across settings, it is hard to operationalise measures of care co-ordination. Some countries (Canada, the Czech Republic, France, Ireland, Singapore, Sweden, England and Scotland) carry out surveys that attempt to measure patient experience with care co-ordination and integrated care.

LTC users are frail and increasingly multiple chronic conditions. They are therefore at high risk of hospitalisation for health conditions. Poor care integration is a main cause of unsatisfactory quality and can lead to preventable hospital (re)admissions. Hospital admissions data have the potential to permit the development of indicators of care co-ordination. They represent a rich source of information, which refers to routine administrative records rather than direct contact with respondents (OECD, 2012c). Possible indicators of care co-ordination based on these sources of data include:

● Preventable admissions by old people for chronic conditions (Asthma, COPD, and uncontrollable diabetes). These indicators are collected across OECD countries by age group and the data is available by 65 years old and over and 80 years old and over (Figure 2.9).

● The rate of admissions of older people from home, community care and LTC settings to an emergency department could be seen as one indicator of (poor) care co-ordination, although there are hardly cross-country statistics concerning re-admissions of old frail people or detailed statistics of admissions from home and other LTC settings.

Figure 2.9. **Asthma, COPD and uncontrolled diabetes hospital admission rates, population aged 80 years old and over, 2009 (or nearest year)**

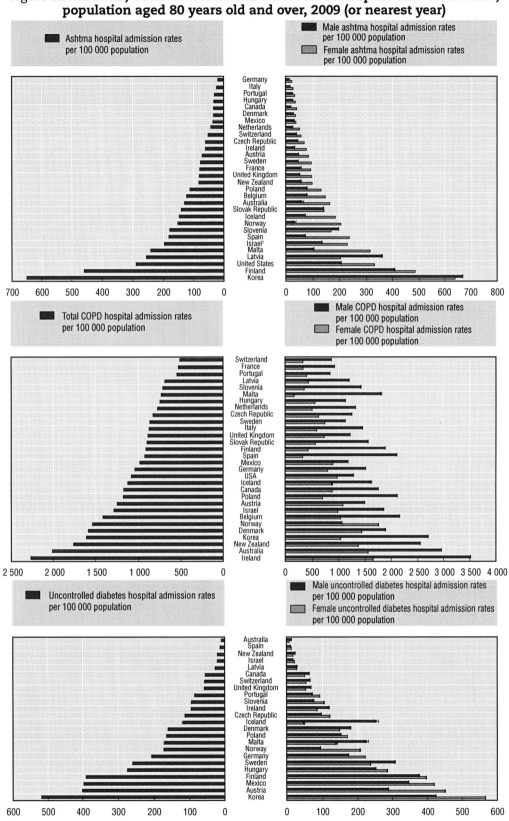

1. Information on data for Israel: http://dx/doi.org/10.1787/888932315602.

Source: OECD Health Data 2011.

Structural indicators provide a proxy of quality where outcome measures are unavailable

Structural inputs are preconditions and instrumental to making high-quality services available (IOM, 1986; Kelley and Hurst, 2006). Indicators such as the characteristics of LTC facilities, the qualification level and training of staff, the safety and appropriateness of the care environment, and information and communication technology (ICT) and other assistive technologies can be indirectly linked to good quality, although they are only indirect measures of outcomes (Sorenson and Mossialos, 2007). For example, resident turnover influences the quality of care provided to old people (Spilsbury et al., 2004). Japan and Korea, among others, regard structural inputs, in particular the living environment and staffing, as key items worthy of measurement and reporting.

Box 2.5 presents a list of indicators related to structural inputs (staffing, care environment and ICT) used in Germany, Korea, the Netherlands and Portugal. These indicators continue to be collected at inspection or through administrative data. For example, in the United States, inspection of care environment and staffing are part of the system to grade the level of providers' quality.

Box 2.5. List of indicators on structural inputs commonly collected in countries

Staffing

Korea: Staff ratios, number of beds per doctor, mix of staff qualification, average length of employment per staff, turnover rate of nursing personnel, information management: privacy protection.

Netherlands: The extent to which clients or representatives experience staff to be adequately reliable, the extent to which clients or representatives experience adequate professionalism (and safety) in administering care, the organisational unit can prove that staff members working with transfer lifts have been instructed to do this, the organisational unit can show that for the function residence combine with nursing and/or treatment there is a nurse available seven times 24 hours, and that the nurse can be on location within ten minutes, the extent to which clients or representatives experience sufficient availability of staff and continuity, the organisation unit can show that over the reported past year competencies of staff that carry out reserved or risky treatment have been tested and found to be up to standards, the organisational unit can show that for the function residence combined with nursing and/or treatment a doctor can be reached and called in seven times 24 hours and that the doctor will react within ten minutes and be on location within 30 minutes?

Living environment

Germany: Appropriate community rooms, community space outside of institution is safe.

Korea: Sanitation and infection control, emergency or disaster situation, availability of pharmacy (including pharmacist), rate of safety grip installed, rate of wards with toilet, percentage of multi-patient wards, rate of thresholds or bumps removed, rate of non-slip floors installed.

Portugal: Number of beds in facilities.

Netherlands: The extent to which clients or representatives experience a safe living environment.

Technology (ICT and non-ICT device)

Korea: Availability of alarm system equipped at LTC recipients' home or nursing homes, living environment.

Only a few OECD countries have well-established information systems for care quality

Sources of data for LTC quality vary widely, reflecting the way countries organise data collection and depending on the sources of the data. Some countries have well advanced systematic quality collection – for example several Canadian provinces, Finland, Iceland, Portugal, Korea, the Netherlands, Germany and the United States. Of these, Canada, Iceland, Portugal, Finland and the United States use information from *standardised assessment systems*, such as the Resident Assessment Instrument – RAI, to measure needs of LTC users in institutions and generate indicators of care quality. As these countries use similar definitions and similar data categorisation to calculate the indicators, there is a potential for cross-country comparisons. Since 2007, Portugal's National Network of Integrated Continuous Care (RNCCI) manages information collected through an integrated evaluation tool, collecting data on need (Katz evaluation, ADL, age), psychosocial well-being (emotional complaints) and social indicators (social status and habits). In Japan, where clinical information generated from the needs assessment database could be used to develop quality indicators (JPHA, 2009; JPHA, 2011).

Another important source of information are *administrative databases* generated from acute care and long-term care discharge data, claim data, inspection reports, or mandatory reporting of a minimum set of data from providers. Korea, for example, derives quality indicators for patients receiving care in LTC hospitals on the basis of claims and administrative data collected by the Health Insurance Review Agency. In the United States, Medicare claims data enable tracking the use of medicine among nursing-home residents (and to some extend home-care recipients). The Department of Health and Human Services uses these data to identify inappropriate and over-use of atypical antipsychotic drugs for the treatment of schizophrenia and/or bipolar disorder in nursing homes (Department of Health and Human Services, 2011). GestCare CCI in Portugal collects administrative data as well as quality indicators for patients receiving care in the continuous post-acute and long-term care network. This enables the monitoring of (intermediate) outcomes over the course of care. The Canadian Institute for Health Information links three administrative database including the Home Care Reporting System (HCRS), Continuing Care Reporting System (CCRS) built on RAI data, and Discharge Abstract Database (DAD) to analyse the waiting times and quality indicators of newly admitted long-stay home care and residential care recipients who had been discharged from an acute care facility (CIHI, 2012).

Audits and inspections can contain useful information on structural inputs, staffing, as well as care effectiveness and safety. For example, in England, compliance with essential standards is published in a quarterly report by the Care Quality Commission, which is responsible for regulating and inspecting health and social care services in England (CQC, 2012). A recent publication from England used the results of the national audits to examine the prevention, incidences, and treatment of hip fractures in people aged 65 and over in hospitals, care homes and primary care (Royal College of Physicians, 2011).

A few OECD countries have registries for LTC users that would enable them to derive quality measures: In the United Kingdom, the National Hip Fracture Database, a web-based registry launched in 2007, builds on the work of established hip fracture audits across the United Kingdom. There are plans to cover in detail the care of patients with hip fracture and related outcomes. Norway national registry of statistics for nursing and care services in the municipalities (IPLOS) includes indicators on the use of restraints of nursing home residents and is used to inform decisions regarding the planning of services. Sweden has a set of well-developed registries in a number of clinical areas or specific conditions, for example:

- The Senior Alert Registry, started in 2009, gathers individual data on falls (incidence), pressure sores and malnutrition. This registry helps identifying elderly at risk that could be targeted through preventive interventions. By 2012, 274 municipalities (out of 290) reported data to the registry.

- The Palliative Registry, started in 2007, collects information on structural inputs (such as beds and access to staff, care plan) associated with end-of-care, as well as information about fatalities. In 2011, some 53% of all deaths were recorded in the registry.

- The Swedish Dementia Registry (SveDem), started in 2007, collects information on age, gender, heredity, BMI, Mini-Mental State Examination scores, diagnoses, dementia development, medical treatment, community support, and time from referral to diagnosis. The Swedish Registry on Behaviour and Psychiatric Symptoms in Dementia, launched in 2010, aims to collect individual data on care and treatment of demented persons with behaviour and psychiatric symptoms. Dementia registries are being built also in England, Northern Ireland and Scotland. In England, GPs are required to keep a register of patients with a diagnosis of dementia.

A recent *Dementia in Australia* report draws on a wide range of administrative and clinical databases, periodic national surveys, research and targeted longitudinal studies, and ad hoc surveys to provide a comprehensive national overview. Among others, the report considers various data sources and implications for assessing the quality of services and the quality of life of people with dementia (Australian Institute of Health and Welfare, 2012).

Ad-hoc surveys at facility or individuals constitute another source of information. These surveys collect information on patient characteristics, socioeconomic status, diagnostics, co-morbidity or multimorbidity, care/treatment history, and the number of beds and staff in facilities. In some cases, questionnaires include topics related to quality for specific conditions, mostly dementia, end of life care and elder abuse. For example, the Health Quality Council of Alberta, Canada, conducted in 2007/08 and in 2010/11 a survey – addressed to residents and their family – on LTC residents' experience and satisfaction with the quality of care provided (Health Quality Council of Alberta, 2011).

The data coverage and the availability of time-series data differ significantly from country to country and are mostly limited. For example, Finland has expanded data coverage through a voluntary process representing about 40% of LTC residents and 30% of home-care clients, while Iceland, Norway and Portugal collect quality data at the national level through compulsory data submissions. Compliance to data submission improved in Iceland after tri-annual needs assessment of each resident became pre-condition for reimbursement of services to nursing homes. The data collection started as early as in 1996 in Iceland and aggregated findings were made available to all nursing homes although the longitudinal data was not submitted. The availability of time-series is relatively long in Finland – since 2000 for nursing home and 2003 for home care services – while other countries have started more recently, for example Portugal started data collection with the establishment of the RNCCI in 2007 (integrated home care began in 2009) for inpatients units and 2010 for home-care services. Annex 2.A1 reports definitions used by countries for these indicators.

A few countries have recently announced plans to collect LTC quality data. Australia, for example, plans to develop quality indicators and a rating system to be reported in the *My Aged Care* website by mid2012 for residential care and mid-2016 for home care services (Government of Australia, 2012). England has two projects aimed at developing the foundation for data collection. *Transparency and Quality Compact* (managed by the Department of Health) involved voluntary reporting by social care providers on key quality metrics. *Present on Admission Flags* is a project for hospitals to help monitor pressure ulcer care management, continence care, falls, injuries, infections and possibly neglect.

Technical, implementation and wider measurement difficulties remain

Despite the valuable efforts described above, measurement of LTC quality still faces significant methodological and implementation difficulties.

At the first level, without regulatory requirements to collect and report on LTC quality, it is unlikely that widespread measurement and reporting develops. Providers may resist the introduction of quality indicators for fears of scrutiny over their performance, and need to recognise that the use of indicators will facilitate their daily jobs or improve their capacity to deliver good care. Finland has collected quality indicators on a voluntary basis for more than a decade and still the coverage does not reach all providers. A useful way to overcome resistance is by creating a culture of transparency. There seems to be good examples for example from the Netherlands and the United States.

Significant barriers to improving care quality measurement include the split responsibilities between health and social care, fragmentation of service points, and differences in coverage of data. These pose significant challenges to data comparability and collection on a national level. Data might be collected at primary care level (e.g. the dementia registry in the United Kingdom) and at acute health (e.g. secondary reasons for (re)-admissions to hospitals) but might not be linked to LTC data. Countries with decentralised governance have large regional variations in eligibility rules, benefits, and quality enforcement policies, resulting in non-comparable systems, structures or measures. This could reduce ability to gather comparable data and evaluate service quality. When data access rights lie with local authorities, opportunities for sharing of data at the national level are limited (e.g., Spain).

Concerns have also grown around data protection and privacy issues. For example, there are concerns about misuse of personal information from assessment of care needs (OECD, 2012a). Approaches to minimise these risks have included specific patient protection legislation, requiring informed consent for the use of personal data, de-identifying data, or centralising access and supervising rights to access data. For example, the Health Information Act of Alberta (Canada) requires a privacy impact assessment and the Office of the Information and Privacy Commissioner has to approve requests for use of personal data. Belgium also has enacted a Privacy Act enacted in 1992 to protect the use of data.

Data management requires significant financing and technical capacity. Data development takes a long time and requires routine data collection, substantial resources and appropriate technical equipment and computerised systems (Progress, 2010). Staff must be trained to collect, manage, monitoring and maintain the dataset. The experience of the United States shows that primary factors for setting up a successful data infrastructure for LTC quality are computerisation and the use of standardised, mandatory, patient assessment systems. When the US Centers for Medicare and Medicaid Services (CMS) began using OASIS for monitoring home care quality in 2002, all eligible home health agencies had to undergo training to collect, analyse, and use information on quality of care (AHRQ, 2003; Capitman et al., 2005). Today, all US nursing homes and home health agencies serving Medicare beneficiaries have computer-based standardised needs assessment tools and protocols (Mor, 2006).

Other barriers to the development of statistically reliable and valid quality indicators exist when different providers serve different LTC beneficiaries and make different assessments (Capitman et al., 2005; Mor, 2010). For example, to make valid comparisons across provider serving population with different care needs, it is necessary to adjust data for casemix. It is important to differentiate a person with terminal prognoses who deteriorate faster from post-acute care patients who have a much faster potential for improvement (Mor, 2006). When users receive multiple services or combinations of health and social services, it is difficult to tease out what aspect of care acts has determined what outcome.

Last, while setting benchmarks and targets can be important for stimulating quality improvements, there are still no established LTC standards that could inform where a minimum might be established (Mor, 2006). There are questions also about the most appropriate way to set benchmarks: national or local; different or identical benchmarks for different types of providers; fixed or adjusted over time; based upon the empirical observations across providers or upon some external standard or guideline.

Conclusions

There is a growing impetus to improve measurement on LTC quality. Information on LTC quality benefits providers, purchasers, consumers and regulators in several important ways:

● It helps providers manage care services and workers.

● It helps care workers choosing high-performing facilities where they may wish to work.

● It offers consumers information for choosing across different care providers.

● It helps purchasers make informed resource-allocation decision.

● It helps policy maker to set benchmarks for providers.

● It enables cross-national comparisons of performance, although, to get to this, at least some of the others are necessary.

While LTC quality measurement still lags behind developments in health care, there are important exceptions. Many countries including Finland, the United States, Iceland, Canada and Portugal use quality indicators by applying needs assessment data to carry out regular data collection. Some countries use indicators that are rather self-reported (through surveys) and clinical evaluation (multi-item scales). However, a review of a single set of quality indicators collected within OECD counties showed that very few are able to report data on six commonly used and accepted clinical quality indicators. While the data show significant variations across countries and over time, they can offer a useful indication regarding trends, especially in their longitudinal dimension.

There is a growing interest of applying the evaluation of social outcomes through studying satisfaction and experience, incorporating user perspectives, and investigating social aspects or user experiences, such as in the Netherlands and England. While indicators on care co-ordination are difficult to operationalise, international data collection by the OECD of avoidable admissions for chronic conditions such as COPD, uncontrollable diabetes and asthma among older people offers useful indicators.

Collection of LTC quality data within countries is not yet a regular endeavour. There are implementation costs, among them the large investment costs of developing data systems (such as the Minimum Data Set). Many countries do not systematically collect information of quality or have not reached a national consensus regarding whether and which indicators ought to be collected and reported regularly. Definitional challenges (e.g., whether the right focus of measurement should be inputs and processes or outcomes; whether the focus should be clinical aspects or responsiveness and quality of life), methodological challenges (e.g., the fact that outcomes for frail care recipients deteriorate over time regardless of how good is the care received), and lack of requirements to collect data delay measuring efforts. Among the countries where quality is not yet part of regular data collection efforts, Australia, England, Japan and Spain have quality indicator development plans in the pipeline.

Although much work remains to be done to harmonise definitions, there is a potential for harmonising data collection on LTC quality at the international level. The few available data offer a useful indication of trends in individual countries.

Notes

1. In Canada, falls, restraints, depression are measured in prevalence.

2. Within ADL, people first become dependent in activities related to dressing and personal hygiene (early loss ADLs), followed by transfer, locomotion and toilet use (middle-loss ADLs) and eating and being mobile in bed (late-loss ADLs) (Doupe et al., 2011).

3. One limitation of the survey is that it does not include people who pay entirely for their own care estimated about 45% of the residents in registered care home places in England. Furthermore, about 170 000 older people paying for their care at home are also not included in the survey. In 2011-12, 1.5 million adults received social care services in the country fully or partially funded by their Local Authority.

4. Care/life plan, communication and information, physical well-being, safety of care, domestic and living conditions, participation and autonomy, mental well-being, safety of living environment, sufficient and competent personnel, and coherence in care.

References

ABUEL (2008), *Matrix of Instruments for Measuring Health and Well-being of People between 60 and 84 Years*, ABUEL. *www.abuel.org/docs/pub03_matrix_of_instruments.pdf*.

Adult Social Care Outcomes Toolkit (2012), *www.pssru.ac.uk/ascot/index.php*, accessed on 19 October 2012.

Aged Care Branch of the Department of Human Services (Victoria) (2004), *Public Sector Residential Aged Care: Quality of Care Performance Indicator Project Report*, Victoria, Australia.

AHRQ – Agency of Healthcare Research and Quality (2003), *National Healthcare Quality Report*, Rockville, United States, December.

AHRQ (2012), "U.S. Valuation of the EuroQol EQ-5D™ Health Statistics", Rockville, United States, January, *www.ahrq.gov/rice/EQ5Dproj.htm*, access on 21 March 2012.

AIHW – Australian Institute of Health and Welfare (2012), *Dementia in Australia*, Cat. No. AGE 70, Canberra.

American Health Quality Association (2012), "Improving Quality of Care at Home: QIOs Training Home Health Agencies Nationwide", Fact Sheet: Home Health Quality Initiative, American Health Quality Association, *www.ahqa.org/pub/media/159_766_4134.CFM*, accessed on 1 October 2012.

BAPEN – British Association for Parenteral and Enteral Association (2011), "Nutrition Screening Survey in the UK and Republic of Ireland in 2010: Hospitals, Care Homes and Mental Health Units", Nutrition Screening Week Survey and Audit, Main Data Collection, BAPEN, 12-14 January 2010.

Barber, N.D. et al. (2009), "Care Homes' Use of Medicines Study: Prevalence, Causes and Potential Harm of Medication Errors in Care Homes for Older People", Quality & Safety in Health Care, Vol.18, pp. 341-346.

Capitman, J. et al. (2005), "Long-Term Care Quality: Historical Overview and Current Initiatives", Report for the National Commission for Quality Long-term Care, Washington, DC.

Castle, N.G. and J.C. Ferguson (2010), "What Is Nursing Home Quality and How Is It Measured?", The Gerontologist, Vol. 50, No. 4, pp. 426-442.

CDC – Centers for Disease Control and Prevention (2012), "Falls in Nursing Homes", Division of Unintentional Injury Prevention, National Center for Injury Prevention and Control, Centers for Disease Control and Prevention, www.cdc.gov/HomeandRecreationalSafety/Falls/nursing.html, accessed 27 August 2012.

CIHI – Canadian Institute for Health Information (2011), Health Care in Canada, 2011: A Focus on Seniors and Aging, CIHI, Ontario.

CIHI (2012), "Seniors and Alternate Level of Care: Building on Our Knowledge, Executive Summary", Analysis in Brief, CIHI, Ontario.

CIHI (2013), When a Nursing Home is Home: How Do Canadian Nursing Homes Measure Up on Quality?, Ontario.

CMS – Centers for Medicare & Medicaid Services (2011a), "Home Health Potentially Avoidable Event Measures", revised August, pp. 1-3.

CMS (2011b), "Home health Outcome Measures", June, pp. 1-7.

CMS (2011c), "Home Health Process Measures", June, pp. 1-11.

CMS (2012), "OASIS Dataset", www.cms.gov/Medicare/Quality-Initiatives-Patient-Assessment-Instruments/OASIS/DataSet.html, accessed on 4 October 2012.

CQC – Care Quality Commission (2012), "Market Report", Care Quality Commission, Vol. 1, London, June, www.cqc.org.uk/sites/default/files/media/documents/20120626_cqc_market_report_issue_1_for_website_final_0.pdf.

Dandi, R. and G. Casanova (2012), "Quality Assurance Indicators of Long-term Care in European Countries", ENEPRI Research Report No. 110.

Degenholtz, H.B. et al. (2006), "Predicting Nursing Facility Residents' Quality of Life Using External Indicators", Health Services Research, Vol. 41, No. 2.

Department of Health (2001), National Service Framework for Older People, Department of Health, London.

Department of Health (2012), Transparency in Outcomes: A Framework for Quality in Adult Social Care – The 2012/13 Adult Social Care Outcomes Framework, Department of Health, London, 30 March.

Department of Health and Human Services (2011), Medicare Atypical Antipsychotic Drug Claims for Elderly Nursing Home Residents, Office of Inspector General, Department of Health and Human Services, Washington DC, May.

Drösler, S. et al. (2009), "Health Care Quality Indicators Project: Patient Safety Indicators Report 2009", OECD Health Working Papers, No. 47, OECD Publishing, Paris.

European Centre for Social Welfare Policy and Research (2010), Measuring Progress: Indicators for Care Homes, European Centre for Social Welfare Policy and Research, Vienna.

Forder, J. et al. (2012), "Evaluation of the Personal Health Budget Pilot Programme", Discussion Paper No. 2840-2, Department of Health, 30 November 2012, www.personalhealthbudgets.dh.gov.uk/_library/Resources/Personalhealthbudgets/2012/PHBE_personal_health_budgets_final_report_Nov_2012.pdf.

Government of Australia (2012), "Living Longer. Living Better. Aged Care Reform Package (Technical Document)", Department of Health and Ageing, Government of Australia, Canberra.

Health Insurance Review and Assessment Service (2011), Comprehensive Quality Report of National Health Insurance 2010, Health Insurance Review and Assessment Service, Seoul.

Health Quality Council of Alberta (2011), "Long-term Care Family Experiences Survey", Health Quality of Alberta, Alberta, November.

Health Quality Ontario (2011), *Quality Monitor: 2011 Report on Ontario's Health System*, Health Quality Ontario, Ontario.

Health Quality Ontario (2012), *Quality Monitor, 2012 Report on Ontario's Health System*, Health Quality Ontario.

Hirdes, J.P. et al. (2011), "Beyond the 'Iron Lungs of Gerontology': Using Evidence to Shape the Future of Nursing Homes in Canada", *Canadian Journal on Aging/La Revue canadienne du vieillissement*, Vol. 30, No. 3, pp. 371-390, September.

HSCIC – Health and Social Care Information Centre, Social Care Team (2012), *Personal Social Services Adult Social Care Survey Guidance Document – 2012-13*, Health and Social Care Information Centre.

Huffman, G.B. (2002), "Evaluating and Treating Unintentional Weight Loss in the Elderly", *American Family Physician*, Vol. 65, No. 4, pp. 640-651, 15 February.

Hurtado, M.P. et al. (eds.) (2001), "Envisioning the National Health Care Quality Report", Committee on the National Quality Report on Health Care Delivery, Institute of Medicine, Washington, DC.

IMO – Institute of Medicine (1986), "Improving the Quality of Care in Nursing Homes", Committee on Nursing Home Regulation, Institute of Medicine, Washington, DC.

Joint Commission (2012), *National Patient Safety Goals Slide Presentation*, 7 February, *www.jointcommission.org/2012_npsgs_slides/*.

Jones, A.L. et al. (2009), *The National Nursing Home Survey: 2004 Overview*, National Center for Health Statistics, *Vital Health Stat Series*, Vol. 13, No. 167.

JPHA – Japan Public Health Association (2011), *www.kantei.go.jp/jp/singi/kinkyukoyou/suisinteam/TF/kaigo_dai4/sankou3.pdf*, Tokyo, accessed on 30 August 2012.

JPHA (2009), *www.jpha.or.jp/sub/pdf/menu04_5_05_all.pdf*, Tokyo, accessed on 30 August 2012.

Kane, R.A. et al. (2003), "Quality of Life Measures for Nursing Home Residents", *Journals of Gerontology*, Series A, Biological Sciences and Medical Sciences, Vol. 58, No. 3, pp. 240-248.

Kelley, E. and J. Hurst (2006), "Health Care Quality Indicators Project: Conceptual Framework Paper", *OECD Health Working Papers*, No. 23, OECD Publishing, Paris.

Knowledge and Intelligence (2010), "Monthly Delayed Transfer of Care SitReps, Definitions and Guidance", version 1.06, Unify 2, Department of Health, London.

Lee, M. (2007), "Improving Services and Support for Older People with Mental Health Problems: Second Report from the UK Inquiry into Mental Health and Well-Being in Later Life. Age Concern", Age Concern England, London.

Leichsenring, K. (2010), "Achieving Quality Long-term Care in Residential Facilities", Peer review in Social Protection and Social Inclusion 2010, European Commission Employment, Social Affairs and Inclusion.

Lyder, C.H. and E.A. Ayello (2008), "Pressure Ulcers: A Patient Safety Issue", Chapter 12 in R.G. Hughes (ed.), *Patient Safety and Quality: An Evidence-Based Handbook for Nurses*, Agency for Healthcare Research and Quality, Rockville, United States.

Malley, J. and J.L. Fernández (2010), "Measuring Quality in Social Care Services: Theory and Practice", *Annals of Public and Cooperative Economics*, Vol. 81, No. 4, pp. 559-582.

Malley, J.N. et al. (2012), "An Assessment of the Construct Validity of the ASCOT Measure of Social Care-related Quality of Life with Older People", *Health and Quality of life Outcomes*, Vol. 10, No. 21.

Mattke, S. et al. (2006), "Health Care Quality Indicators Project: Initial Indicators Report", *OECD Health Working Papers*, No. 22, OECD Publishing, Paris, *http://dx.doi.org/10.1787/481685177056*.

McGeary, M.G.H. (1990), "Medicare Conditions of Participation and Accreditation for Hospitals", in K.N. Lohr (ed.), *Medicare: A Strategy for Quality Assurance, Volume II: Sources and Methods*, Committee to Design a Strategy for Quality Review and Assurance in Medicare, Institute of Medicine, Washington, DC.

MDS – Medizinischer Dienst des Spitzenverbandes Bund der Krankenkassen e.V. (2012), *3. Bericht des MDS nach § 114a Abs. 6 SGB XI, Qualität in der ambulanten und stationären Pflege*, MDS, Essen.

MHLW – Ministry of Health, Labour and Welafare (2011a), "Heisei 22 Nen Ban Kosei Rodo Hakusho" (The Annual Health, Labour and Welfare Report 2009-2010), Part 3 References, Nikkei Printing, Tokyo, *www.mhlw.go.jp/english/wp/wp-hw4/02.html*.

MHLW (2011b), "Data of Medical Institutions", MHLW, Tokyo, *www.mhlw.go.jp/stf/shingi/2r9852000001qd1o-att/2r9852000001qdig.pdf*.

Mor, V. (2006), "Defining and Measuring Quality Outcomes in Long-term Care", *Journal of the American Medical Directors Association*, Vol. 7, No. 8, pp. 532-540, October.

Mor, V. (2010), "Improving the Quality of Long-term Care", *CESifo DICE Report* No. 2/2010.

Mukamel, D.B. et al. (2008), "Publication of Quality Report Cards and Trends in Reported Quality Measures in Nursing Homes", *Health Service Research*, Vol. 43, No. 4, August.

National Health Services (2012), "User Survey Guidance 2010-2011, Adult Social Care Survey", *www.ic.nhs.uk/services/social-care/social-care-collections/user-surveys/user-survey-guidance-2010-11#cmsanchorquestion*, accessed on 25 October 2012.

National Pressure Ulcer Advisory Panel (2007), *NPUAP Pressure Ulcer Stages/Categories*, Washington, DC.

Naylor, M.D. et al. (2009), "Transitions of Elders Between Long-term Care and Hospitals", *Policy, Politics and Nursing Practices*, Vol. 10, No. 3, pp. 187-194.

NHS Information Centre (2012), "Personal Social Services Adult Social Care Survey, England – 2011-12 – Provisional Release", Social Care Team, NHS Information Centre.

OECD (2005), *Long-Term Care for Older People*, OECD Publishing, Paris, *http://dx.doi/org/10.1787/9789264015852-en*.

OECD (2012a), "Privacy Protection Challenges in Developing Health Information Infrastructure for Health, Health Care Quality and Health System Performance Monitoring and Research", DELSA/HEA, 18, OECD, Paris.

OECD (2012b), *Waiting Times Policies in the Health Sector: What Works?*, Fast-Track Paper, DELSA/HEA, 19, OECD, Paris.

OECD (2012c), "Health Care Quality Indicators, Data Collection 2012-2013: Patient Experiences", DELSA/HEA/HCQ, No. 9, OECD, Paris.

Park-Lee, E. and C. Caffrey (2009), "Pressure Ulcers Among Nursing Home Residents: United States, 2004", *NCHS Data Brief*, No. 14, National Center for Health Statitsics, Centers for Disease Control and Prevention, US Department of Health and Human Services.

Productivity Commission (2011), "Caring for Older Australians", Report No. 53, Final Inquiry Report, Commonwealth of Australia, Canberra.

Raleigh, V.S. and C. Foot (2010), *Getting the Measure of Quality: Opportunities and Challenges*, Kings Fund, London.

Rehman, H.U. (2005), "Involuntary Weight Loss in the Elderly", *Clinical Geriatrics*, Vol. 13, No. 7.

RNCCI – Rede Nacional de Cuidados Continuados Integrados (2012), "Relatório de monitorização do desenvolvimento e da atividade da Rede Nacional de Cuidados Continuados Integrados (RNCCI) 2011", February, Lisbon.

Royal College of Physician (2011), *Falling Standards, Broken Promises: Report of the National Audit of Falls and Bone Health in Older People 2010*, Royal College of Physician, London.

Saliba, D. and J. Buchanan (2008), "Development & Validation of a Revised Nursing Home Assessment Tool: MDS 3.0 Appendices", Quality Measurement and Health Assessment Group, Office of Clinical Standards and Quality, Centers for Medicare & Medicaid Services, Baltimore, United States.

Social Care Institute for Excellence (2010), "Finding Excellence in Adult Social Care Services: An Overview of Selected Approaches to Excellence in Social Care", Excellence Definition Materials, Social Care Institute for Excellence.

Sorenson, C. and E. Mossialos (2007), "Measuring Quality and Standards of Long-term Care for Older People", Research Note, European Commission, Brussels.

Spilsbury, K. et al. (2011), "The Relationship Between Nurse Staffing and Quality of Care in Nursing Homes: A Systematic Review", *International Journal of Nursing Studies*, Vol. 48, No. 6, pp. 732-750.

Steering Committee Responsible Care (2007), *Quality Framework Responsible Care – Nursing, Care and Home Care*.

Triemstra, M. et al. (2010), "Measuring Client Experiences in Long-Term Care in the Netherlands: A Pilot Study with the Consumer Quality Index Long-Term Care", *BMC Health Services Research*, Vol. 10, No. 95.

UMCCI – Office of Mission Units for Continuous Care (2012), "Relatório de monitorização do desenvolvimento e da atividade da Rede Nacional de Cuidados Continuados Integrados (RNCCI), 2011" (Monitoring report of the development and activity of continuous care), Cuidados Continuados, February 2012, Lisbon.

Van der Veen, R. and S. Mak (2010), "Developing and Ensuring Quality in Long-term Care: Netherlands National Report", Utrecht (INTERLINKS National Report), available at *http://interlinks.euro.centre.org/ countries/netherlands*.

Victorian Government Department of Human Services (2007), "Resource Manual for Quality indicators in Public Sector Residential Aged Care Services, 2007-2008 version 1", Rural and Regional Health and Aged Care Services Division, Victorian Government Department of Human Services, Melbourne, Victoria, Australia.

White Paper (2012), "Developing an Effective Quality Assurance Program: Turning Minimum Requirements into a Comprehensive Strategy".

Wiener, J.M. et al. (2007a), *Quality Assurance for Long-Term Care: The Experiences of England, Australia, Germany and Japan*, AARP, Washington, DC.

Wiener, J.M. et al. (2007b), *Strategies for Improving the Quality of Long-Term Care*, Final Report for National Commission for Quality Long-Term Care, RTI International, Washington, DC.

Wiener, J.M. (2012), "Quality Assurance for Long-Term Care: The Case of the United States", Long-Term Care Quality Expert Meeting, unpublished document, OECD, Paris.

Zimmerman, D.R. (2003), "Improving Nursing Home Quality of Care through Outcomes Data: The MDS Quality Indicators", *International Journal of Geriatric Psychiatry*, Vol. 18, pp. 250-257.

Zuidgeest, M. et al. (2012), "Using Client Experiences for Quality Improvement in Long-term Care Organizations", *International Journal for Quality in Health Care*, pp. 1-6, 6 April.

ANNEX 2.A1

Summary of quality indicators in selected OECD countries

Category	Examples of indicators in nursing homes	Countries using the indicator
Care effectiveness		
Pressure ulcers	Prevalence of pressure ulcers (i.e. bedsores)	United States (for long and short-stay), Korea, Canada, Portugal, Netherlands (at home)
	Incidence of pressure ulcers (i.e. bedsores)	Canada, Portugal
	Percentage of pressure ulcers worsened	Canada
	Assessment of individual risk of decubitus/ulcer	Germany
	Prevention and management of bedsores	Korea (LTCF)
Nutrition/Weight	Prevalence of unplanned weight loss	United States (for long stay), Canada, Portugal, Netherlands
Depression/ behaviour/Delirium	Incidence of depression	United States (for long stay), Netherlands
	Prevalence of symptoms of depression without antidepressant therapy	United States (for long-stay)
	Prevalence of behaviour symptoms affecting others	United States (for long-stay), Netherlands
	Percentage of residents whose behavioural symptoms worsened/improved	Canada
	Percentage of residents with symptoms of delirium	Canada
	Mini-mental state examination (MMSE) test rate for patients aged 65 years or older when hospitalised	Korea
	Percentage of residents whose mood from symptoms of depression worsened	Canada
ADL	Percentage of residents whose need for help with activities of daily living has increased	United States (for long stay)
	Percentage of residents whose (late-loss/mid-loss/late-loss) ADL functioning worsened/improved/ remained independent	Canada
	Proportion of patients with declined ability to perform daily activities	Korea
	Outcomes (dependency maintained/reduced) in physical autonomy by typology of care	Portugal
Continence-related	Percentage of long-stay residents/clients with a urinary tract infection	United States (for long stay), Korea, Netherlands
	Prevalence of occasional or frequent bladder or bowel incontinence without a toileting plan (United States)	United States (for long stay)
	Percentage of residents whose bowel/bladder continence worsened/improved	Canada
Chronic condition	HbA1c test rate for diabetic patients	Korea
Tube feeding	Prevalence of tube feeding	United States (for long stay), Canada (CCRS)
Vaccination	Percentage of residents who were assessed and appropriately given the seasonal influenza vaccine	United States (for long stay), Netherlands
	Percentage of residents assessed and appropriately given the pneumococcal vaccine	United States (for long stay)
Cognitive function	Percentage of residents whose cognitive ability worsened/improved	Canada
Communication	Percentage of residents whose ability to communicate worsened/improved	Canada
Mobility	Percentage of residents whose ability to locomotion worsened/improved	Canada

Category	Examples of indicators in nursing homes	Countries using the indicator
Pain	Percentage of residents with pain/whose pain worsened	Canada
	Systematic assessment of pain	Germany
Falls	Incidence of falls and fall-related fractures	United States (for long stay), Portugal, Netherlands
	Assessment of individual risk of falling	Germany
Restraints	Prevalence of use of physical restraints	United States (for long stay), Canada (CCRS), Netherlands, Korea (LTCF)
	The organisational unit can prove that they have a demonstrable policy for the prevention of restricting measures concerning freedom of movement	Netherlands
Medications	a) The percentage of clients that has used anti-psychotic, anti-anxiety medication or hypnotica one or more days over the past week b) The percentage of clients that has used anti-depressants one or more days over the past week	Netherlands
	Percentage of residents on antipsychotics without a diagnosis of psychosis	Canada
	The percentage of clients that has been involved in a medicine-related incidents over the past 30 days	Netherlands
	Appropriate handling of medication	Germany
	Provision of medication in accordance with doctor's instruction	Germany
	Administration of medication	Korea (LTCF)
Continence	Residents with indwelling catheters (for a certain period of time)	United States (for long stay), Korea, Canada (CCRS), Netherlands
Infection	Percentage of residents with one or more infections	Canada, Portugal
	Percentage of residents who developed a respiratory condition or have not gotten better	Canada
Re-admission	Re-admission rate	
Patient centredness		
Experience	The extent to which clients or representatives experience a good care plan and a good evaluation of that plan	Netherlands
	The extent to which clients or representatives experience good participation and good consultation	Netherlands
	The extent to which clients or representatives experience good treatment	Netherlands
	The extent to which clients or representatives experience good communication and they can easily reach staff by phone	Netherlands
	The extent to which clients or representatives experience good physical care	Netherlands
	The extent to which clients or representatives experience good meals	Netherlands
	The extent to which clients or representatives experience good information.	Netherlands
Anatomy	Promotion of physical anatomy	Portugal
	The extent to which clients or representatives experience adequate independence/autonomy	Netherlands
Rights	Patient rights and/or dignity	Portugal, Korea (LTCF)
	The extent to which representatives experience adequate respect for clients' rights in relation to restriction of freedom of movement	Netherlands
Duties	Documentation related to benefit and compensation	Korea(LTCF)
	Information service availability	Korea (LTCF)
Support	The extent to which clients or representatives experience adequate possibilities to spend the day and to participate in society.	Netherlands
	The extent to which clients or representatives experience adequate mental Support	Netherlands
	Bath and toilet assist services	Korea (LTCF)
	Beneficiary management	Korea (LTCF)
Communication	Active communication with doctor	Germany
Satisfaction	Patients can choose own clothes	Germany
	Care staff is friendly and polite	Germany
	Client satisfaction assessment	Korea (LTCF)
Care co-ordination		
	Availability of electronic medical records, tracking tools and support team used to monitor co-ordination across providers and settings	
	Availability of comprehensive needs assessment and care planning	Korea (LTCF)
	Availability of multidisciplinary team	

Category	Examples of indicators in nursing homes	Countries using the indicator
	Discharges with attained objectives of individual care plan by typology of care	Portugal
	Close co-operation with doctor's in case of patients with chronic pain	Germany
	Compliance with care plan and care record	Korea (LTCF)
	Transfer	Korea (LTCF)
	Case management meeting	Korea (LTCF)
Staffing		
	Staff ratios, number of beds per doctor, nurse and nursing personnel	Korea
	Mix of staff qualification	Korea
	On-call doctor availability in nights/ holidays	Korea
	Average length of employment per staff, staff turnover	Korea
	The extent to which clients or representatives experience adequate professionalism (and safety) in administering care	Netherlands
	Multidisciplinary teams	Portugal
	Turnover rate of nursing personnel	Korea
	The extent to which clients or representatives experience staff to be adequately reliable	Netherlands
	The organisational unit can prove that staff members working with transfer lifts have been instructed to do this.	Netherlands
	The extent to which clients or representatives experience sufficient availability of staff (and continuity)	Netherlands
	The organisational unit can show that for the function Residence combined with Nursing and/or Treatment a doctor can be reached and called in seven times 24 hours and that the doctor will react within 10 minutes and be on location within 30 minutes?	Netherlands
	The organisational unit can show that over the reported past year competencies of staff that carry out reserved or risky treatment have been tested (practical test) and found to be up to standard	Netherlands
	The extent to which clients or representatives experience adequate coherence in care	Netherlands
	The organisational unit can show that for the function residence combine with nursing and/or treatment there is a nurse available seven times 24 hours and that the nurse can be on location within 10 minutes	Netherlands
	Human resource operation	Korea (LTCF)
	Welfare of employees	Korea (LTCF)
	Employee education	Korea (LTCF)
	Information management: privacy protection	Korea (LTCF)
Living environment		
	Size of rooms	Korea
	Average space per ward bed	Korea
	Availability of adequate bathroom	Korea
	Percentage of multi-patient wards	Korea
	Quality and safety of buildings or home	Korea
	Rate of patient amenities furnished	Korea
	Rate of wards with toilet	Korea
	No. of beds	Portugal
	Rate of thresholds or bumps removed	Korea
	Rate of non-slip floors installed	Korea
	Rate of safety grip installed	Korea
	No. of beds per physical therapist	Korea
	Availability of radiation cabin (including radiologist) and clinical laboratory and technologist	Korea
	Availability of pharmacy (including pharmacist)	Korea
	The extent to which clients or representatives experience adequate living comfort	Netherlands
	The extent to which clients or representatives experience a good atmosphere	Netherlands
	The extent to which clients or representatives experience adequate privacy (and living accommodation)	Netherlands
	Appropriate community rooms	Germany
	Community space outside of institution is safe	Germany

Category	Examples of indicators in nursing homes	Countries using the indicator
	The extent to which clients or representatives experience a safe living Environment	Netherlands
	Sanitation and infection control	Korea (LTCF)
	Emergency or disaster situation	Korea (LTCF)
Technology		
	Availability of alarm system equipped at LTC recipients' home or nursing homes	Korea
	No. of EKG monitor per 100 beds	Korea
	No. of oxygen supply equipment per 100 beds	Korea

Notes: Many countries collect many indicators, but this summary table only includes those that are defined as quality indicators in their definition.

This summary table is not minimum data set collected in countries, but represents indicators that are considered for assessment of quality in care provision.

Data for the United States: Development & Validation of a Revised Nursing Home Assessment Tool MDS 3.0 – Appendices, prepared by Saliba and Buchanan (2008), Rand Corporation, April.

Korea: Information refers to long-term care hospitals under health care insurance. Comprehensive Quality Report of National Health Insurance 2010 (2011) Health Insurance Review & Assessment Service.

Canada: Continuing care reporting system.

Portugal: Rede National de Cuidados Continuados Integrados (RNCCI, 2012).

Netherlands: Steering Committee Responsible Care (2007).

Germany: MDS (2012).

ANNEX 2.A2

Definitions and data avalability by function and type for quality indicators collected in four OECD countries

Table 2.A2.1. **Definition of pressure ulcers**

	Definition	Availability by physical and cognitive function (ADL, IADL, ICF)
Ontario, Canada	Numerator: Residents who had a pressure ulcer at stages 2 to 4 on their target assessment and the stage of pressure ulcer is greater on their target compared with their prior assessment Denominator: Residents with valid assessments excluding those who had a stage 4 ulcer on their prior assessment	Data is risk-adjusted with Case Mix Index (CMI) but not available broken down
Finland (NH)	Numerator: (LTC) Residents with stage 1-4 pressure ulcers in latest assessment Denominator: All long-term residents	Yes
Finland (HC)	Numerator: Regular Home Care clients with stage 1-4 pressure ulcer in the most recent assessment Denominator: All regular Home Care clients	Yes
Portugal (NH)	Numerator: Number of patients with pressure ulcers Denominator: Patients treated in inpatients units (in the National Network of Integrated Continuous Care) and home care	Yes
Portugal (HC)	Numerator: Number of patients with pressure ulcers Denominator: Patients treated in home care	Yes

Note: ADL: Activities of daily living, IADL: Instrumental activities of daily living, International Classification of Functioning, Disability and Health.

Source: OECD 2012 Questionnaire on Long-Term Care Quality.

Table 2.A2.2. **Definition of incidence of falls and fall-related fractures and data availability by function**

Column 1	Definition: Incidence of falls and fall-related fractures	Availability by physical and cognitive function (ADL, IADL, ICF)
Ontario, Canada	Falls Numerator: Residents who had a fall in the last 30 days recorded on their target assessment Denominator: Residents with valid assessments	Data is risk-adjusted with Case Mix Index (CMI) but not available broken down
Finland (NH)	Falls Numerator: Residents who experienced one or more falls in the preceding 180 days (90 days in facilities using RAI-HC) Denominator: All long-term residents Fall-related fractures Numerator: Residents who experienced one or more falls AND a new fracture in the preceding 180 days (90 days in facilities using RAI-HC) Denominator: All long-term residents	Yes
Finland (HC)	Falls Numerator: Clients who experienced one or more falls in the preceding 90 days Denominator: All regular home care clients Fall-related fractures Numerator: Clients who experienced one or more falls AND one or more fractures in the preceding 90 days Denominator: All regular home care clients	Yes
Portugal (NH)	Falls Numerator: Patients with Falls Denominator: Patients treated in inpatients units and home care	Yes
Portugal (HC)	Falls Numerator: Patients with Falls Denominator: Patients treated in home care	Yes

Note: ADL: Activities of daily living, IADL: Instrumental activities of daily living, International Classification of Functioning, Disability and Health.

Source: OECD 2012 Questionnaire on Long-Term Care Quality.

Table 2.A2.3. **Definition of use of physical restraints and data availability by function and type**

	Definition	By physical and cognitive function (ADL, IADL, ICF)	By type of restrains
Ontario, Canada	Numerator: Residents who were physically restrained daily on their target assessment Denominator: Residents with valid assessments, excluding comatose residents and those who are quadriplegic	Data is risk-adjusted with Case Mix Index (CMI) but not available broken down	Data is available for percentage of residents who were physically restrained
Finland (NH)	Numerator: Residents, whose care involved a physical restraints, not including bed rails Denominator: All long-term care residents	Yes	Yes
Finland (HC)	Numerator: Clients whose care involved a physical restraints Denominator: All regular home care clients	Yes	No
Norway	Numerator: Number of LTC receivers with decision of physical restraint as of 31 December Denominator: All receivers of LTC as of 31 December	Yes	Yes
Portugal	Numerator: Patients with restraints Denominator: Patients treated in inpatient units	Yes	No

Note: ADL: Activities of daily living, IADL: Instrumental activities of daily living, International Classification of Functioning, Disability and Health.

Source: OECD 2012 Questionnaire on Long-Term Care.

Table 2.A2.4. **Definition of over prescribed medication and medication errors and availability by function**

Column 1	Definition: Use of nine or more medications, Medication Errors	By physical and cognitive function (e.g. ADL, IADL, ICF, etc.)
Finland (NH)	Use of nine or more medications Numerator: Residents who received nine or more medications (different preparations) during the previous seven days Denominator: All long-term care residents	Yes
Finland (CH)	Use of nine or more medications Numerator: Clients who received nine or more medications (different preparations) during the previous seven days Denominator: All regular home care clients	Yes
Portugal	Use of nine or more medications Numerator: Patients with nine or more medications Denominator: Patients treated in inpatient units	No

Note: ADL: Activities of daily living, IADL: Instrumental activities of daily living, International Classification of Functioning, Disability and Health.

Source: OECD 2012 Questionnaire on Long-Term Care Quality.

Table 2.A2.5. **Definition of involuntary weight loss and availability by function**

	Prevalence of unplanned weight loss: Numerator	By physical and cognitive function (e.g. ADL, IADL, ICF, etc.)
Finland (NH)	Numerator: Residents, who experienced weight loss of more than 5% of body weight over 30 days OR more than 10% of body weight over 180 days Denominator: All long-term care residents	Yes
Finland (CH)	Numerator: Clients, who experienced an unplanned weight loss of more than 5% of body weight over 30 days OR more than 10% of body weight over 180 days Denominator: All regular home care clients	Yes
Portugal	Numerator: Patients with unplanned weight loss Denominator: Patients treated in inpatients units and home care	No

Note: ADL: Activities of daily living, IADL: Instrumental activities of daily living, International Classification of Functioning, Disability and Health.

Source: OECD 2012 Questionnaire on Long-Term Care Quality.

Table 2.A2.6. **Definition of depression and availability by function**

Column 1	Numerator	By physical and cognitive function (e.g. ADL, IADL, ICF, etc.)
Finland (NH)	Numerator: Residents with a Depression Rating Scale score of 3 or more Denominator: All long-term care residents	Yes
Finland (HC)	Numerator: Clients with a Depression Rating Scale score of 3 or more Denominator: All regular home care clients	Yes

Note: ADL: Activities of daily living, IADL: Instrumental activities of daily living, International Classification of Functioning, Disability and Health.

Source: OECD 2012 Questionnaire on Long-Term Care Quality.

PART I

Chapter 3

Using interRAI assessment systems to measure and maintain quality of long-term care[1]

by

Iain Carpenter,
Royal College of Physicians, London

and

John P. Hirdes,
University of Waterloo, Ontario

Rapidly ageing populations and increasing prevalence of chronic diseases present major challenges for policy makers. Populations as well as individuals have different prevalence of conditions related to ageing and chronic disease. This is compounded by cultural and institutional differences in care service provision, eligibility criteria and funding models. Comparing differences at population and individual level helps policy makers address the complexities of maintaining quality in long-term care. This chapter describes how evolution in development of needs assessment instruments has led to a way of producing high-quality data for policy makers. It describes in detail the interRAI system of standardised needs assessment instruments for routine care that generate aggregatable data. Data driven algorithms generate outcome scales, care planning support protocols, quality indicators, and a resource-use casemix system. The chapter then illustrates, with data from nine OECD countries and regions, how needs assessment data recorded at the point of care using the interRAI system can inform policy. It ends with a discussion of factors for consideration when implementing sophisticated needs assessment tools.

The quality challenge in long-term care

Providing for the health and social care needs of the growing numbers of older people and people with chronic diseases in the face of rising costs, limited budgets and increasing dependency ratios is a major challenge for industrialised countries. In emerging economies, the rate of population ageing is accelerating, increasing the pressures on policy makers attempting to respond to the needs of rapidly growing numbers of older people. For example, it is estimated that the proportion of people aged 65+ in China will double from 7% to 14% of the population in 26 years (Kinsella and He, 2009). In France this change took place over 115 years. For countries that are already "old" demographically, as well as for those that are ageing rapidly, concerns about the costs and quality of care for older people are inextricably linked. Good quality integrated services across the continuum of care can slow the rate of health-related declines, reduce health care expenditures related to avoidable conditions and improve quality of life.

This challenge is immense as the nature of ageing-related conditions and factors relating to provision of care and support are multiple and varied. They include variation in prevalence of conditions commonly related to ageing, different configurations of service provision and different funding models. The result is a tangle of interdependent factors that connect in different patterns from care provider to care provider, region to region and nation to nation.

Only by using reliable data with understandable and comparable constructs can one begin to make progress in determining cost effective services that maintain quality of care. A logical starting point would be aggregating reliable valid data on those individuals receiving care, thus allowing for analysis of the benefits of different models of care for people with comparable care requirements.

The interRAI system for assessment of care needs (*www.interRAI.org*) generates data that can be aggregated from routine clinical practice to provide evidence that is highly relevant to key questions facing decision makers in long-term care. For example, policy makers and service providers must understand the needs and resource requirements of persons across the continuum of care. The inherent complexity of the populations served in nursing home and community settings means that this evidence must be multidimensional and provide a comprehensive view of the person – one that cannot be obtained from administrative records alone.

The information can be used for planning purposes to determine the nature and intensity of the health and social services that are needed. Longitudinal information is essential at the person-level to evaluate the effectiveness of care plans and at the organisational level to evaluate the quality of care. Comparative regional and cross-national data provide insights about practice patterns and policy decisions that may not be self-evident if comparisons are made only between like-minded organisations within a limited geographic region.

This chapter describes the background to the formation of the interRAI collaboration, the development, design, distribution, and potential contribution of the interRAI approach to assessment for care and systematic embedding of a quality driven assessment system in care delivery. It also presents data from use of the interRAI system in nine OECD and non-OECD countries and regions, demonstrating the potential for international benchmarking of performance in long-term care.

Poor care quality led to a call for more systematic assessments of care needs in the United States

In the United States, major scandals in long-term care of older people prompted Congress to ask the US National Academy of Sciences and its Institute of Medicine (IOM) to examine nursing home quality and report on how to improve nursing home regulation. The IOM's expert committee issued its report in 1986 after a 2.5 year study and a series of hearings (Institute of Medicine, 1986; Hawes, 1990). One of the central recommendations was the development of a uniform, comprehensive resident assessment system.

The IOM Committee argued that a uniform, comprehensive assessment of each resident was essential to improving the quality of care in the nation's nursing homes. Comprehensive assessment of physical, cognitive and social functional status was (and still is) seen as the cornerstone of high quality care of older people, identifying issues requiring individualised care planning so that the best outcome of care can be achieved. The IOM recognised that resident-level data from routine assessment of care needs would be the most likely to provide reliable data on quality and outcomes of care. In fact it is not possible to monitor or improve quality of care without being able to measure and compare progress over time or performance between organisations, regions or nations.

Many clinical and care services adopt structured approaches to assessment, and the tradition of standardised assessment is strong in many clinical domains. Many disciplines such as neuropsychology, physical, occupational, speech and respiratory therapy have specific assessment tools for structured recording of care need, severity and care outcomes. In care of older people, there is now a long tradition of assessment and there are many publications listing historical best practice (Kane and Kane, 1981; Rubenstein et al., 1995).

As a result of the IOM report, development of the nursing home Minimum Data Set – Resident Assessment Instrument (MDS-RAI) was embedded in a set of reforms enacted by the United States Congress in the Omnibus Budget Reconciliation Act of 1987 (OBRA '87).

The original RAI project development consortium was commissioned by the Health Quality Bureau of the US Health Care Finance Administration. The process began by reviewing more than 80 existing assessment instruments incorporating inputs from the designers of those assessments and the long tradition of behavioural and performance assessments and symptom reviews, including that of developmentally disabled individuals. The importance of the review of these kinds of assessments was that they enabled the measures developed within the MDS-RAI, the assessment devices, records of symptoms present and other pieces of information about the resident, to substantially increase the breadth, depth and strength of the assessment system (Morris et al., 1990).

Development was completed in 1990 and the first version of the MDS-RAI was implemented in all US nursing homes in 1990-92.

The evolution of assessment instruments and the interRAI collaboration has provided an answer

Standardised assessment instruments enable the structured recording of information about an individual in such a way that the data generated can be used to create performance scales. These scales measure, for example, physical abilities (activities of daily living, or ADLs) cognitive impairment and quality of life. The information recorded can be observed performance against assessment items or self-reported responses to questionnaires. The data can be aggregated to show change in performance of individuals and populations over time and in response to treatment and service developments.

The evolution of assessment instruments can be divided into three generations. First generation instruments, of which there are very large numbers, are standalone scales designed to measure a single construct for a single purpose [e.g., Barthel Index for Activities of Daily Living; (Mahoney and Barthel, 1965), Mini Mental State Examination – MMSE (Folstein et al., 1975), Geriatric Depression Scale – GDS (Yesavage et al., 1982), "MUST" for nutrition (Stratton et al., 2004)]. The strength of the single domain assessments lies in their discrete measurement rules and (for the best) extensive testing of psychometric properties (i.e., reliability and validity) and use in clinical trials. However, these limited domain assessment instruments cannot be used together to produce efficient and reliable integrated multi-dimensional assessment tools. Attempts to use clusters of these instruments typically result in cumbersome assessment approaches employing overlapping assessment items and conflicting assessment methods. The use of clusters of stand-alone instruments also lacks proven utility and acceptability across different care settings.

Second-generation instruments are multidimensional instruments that address many clinical domains with applicability in many settings. Individual items are constructed to record focused information about the individual, and it is the assembly of these items into specific sections that form the backbone of a comprehensive assessment schedule. Examples include CAPE (Pattie et al., 1979), FACE (*www.face.eu.com*) and EASYCARE (*www.easycare.org.uk*). The other principal feature is that they are designed to support care planning, rather than just to record function in particular domains. The combination of assessment items covers specific medical, functional and social issues that need to be addressed in order to provide optimal care to the individual as a whole person. Some include the ability to trigger action through care planning protocols for conditions identified in the assessment.

A secondary but very significant by-product of good multi-dimensional assessment instruments is that the data can be aggregated to produce measures of outcome, casemix, quality of care and eligibility criteria for access to services (Hirdes et al., 1999). Databases consisting of aggregated data from quality second-generation instruments provide a basis for comparisons between regions and nations as well as changes over time.

Adoption and use of these assessment scales and assessment systems are largely dependent on the local choice of practitioners, though the more sophisticated second generation scales may be adopted by provider organisations or local and regional jurisdictions. Two systematic reviews describe and compare the characteristics of the most widely available instruments including the first versions of the interRAI assessment instruments. Box 3.1 provides an overview of the history and evolution of the interRAI collaboration (Lincoln Centre for Ageing and Community Care Research, 2004; and *www.nzgg.org.nz/resources/57/Assess_Processes_GL.pdf*).

Box 3.1. **The interRAI collaboration and the interRAI integrated suite**

InterRAI is a not-for-profit collaboration, now composed of around 70 clinicians, researchers and health administrators from over 30 countries. It was founded in 1992 with the vision statement "the assembly of accurate clinical information in a common format within and across services sectors and countries enhances both the well-being of frail persons and the efficient and equitable distribution of resources" (Fries et al., 2003).

During the first two years, the founding members from Europe, Nordic countries and the United States focussed on the use of the MDS-RAI and the application of the RUGs casemix system in long-term residential care (Resource Utilization Groups – RUG-III – see below). Introduction of the MDS-RAI into nursing home (NH) care was associated with measurable improvements in the standard of care, particularly when quality indicators derived from the instrument were introduced (Mor et al., 1997; Mor et al., 2005). Work soon began on a community care version of the MDS-RAI, and in 1994 the initial version of the Resident Assessment Instrument for Home Care (RAI-HC) was introduced as a model for comprehensive assessment in a community setting (Morris et al., 1997). By 1997, interRAI researchers had completed a revision of the MDS-RAI (v 2.0) and the initial focus of interRAI on care of older persons had broadened, applying the assessment technology to other vulnerable populations. To date assessment instruments have been developed for: acute care (Carpenter et al., 2001), post-acute care, community health, home (community) care, long-term care facilities, assisted living, initial contacts, deaf blind persons, emergency psychiatric screening, hospital and community mental health Hirdes et al., 2002a), palliative care (Steel et al., 2003), physical and intellectual disability (Martin et al., 2007), child and youth intellectual disability, and quality of life (www.interrai.org/index.php?id=3).

InterRAI's work continued to evolve toward development of a fully integrated assessment system (known as the interRAI Suite), the first third-generation assessment system. A new set of subjective quality of life instruments is about to be released as companions to the assessor-rated interRAI instruments, the combination of which will comprise the first fourth generation assessment system for use in the continuum of care.

The number of items and their distribution in the interRAI home care and long-term care facilities assessment instruments

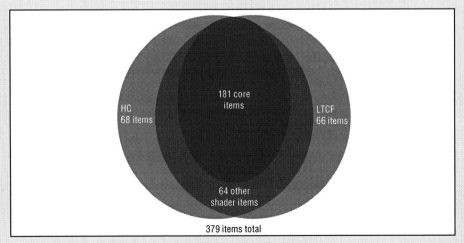

Source: Illustration of interRAI home care and long-term care facilities assessment instruments.

Box 3.1. The interRAI collaboration and the interRAI integrated suite *(cont.)*

The first versions of interRAI instruments all had a comparable look and feel, since they were developed sequentially from 1993 through 2001. However, specific items did not always measure identical phenomena in identical ways across settings and care groups. While not a problem within any given care setting or for general comparisons of populations across settings, these inconsistencies limited the extent to which interRAI assessment information could flow seamlessly across all boundaries. An integrated system enables transfer of common information across transitions across care settings, both orienting the recipient caregiver and reducing the need for completing paper work. In 2001, interRAI therefore established a systematic process to create a third-generation assessment system – a fully integrated suite of instruments – the interRAI Suite. It is composed of a unified set of items that are used to populate the full range of assessment instruments.

A principal benefit of the interRAI Suite is that it delivers consistent recording of information across care settings, allowing comparison of immediate or long term change in status and across settings. Clinicians in one care setting can understand the language and information from health and social care professionals in another, and the data are directly transferrable. The assessment items are standard, the core items used in all settings, with other items used in many, several, or even only a single setting (see figure above). Thus, design of software systems to support multi-sector assessment and care planning is facilitated by having consistent items across multiple different assessment instruments. This also greatly facilitates the development of assessments in new care settings or for new care groups. Training of assessors is also simplified as, for example, a nurse trained in the use of an instrument in one sector can quickly learn to use a companion instrument in another.

Third-generation instruments extend the concept of second-generation tools to multiple care settings. They provide assessment processes that can be used across different populations and care settings. Moreover, they comprise an integrated suite of instruments designed to support continuity of assessment practices across the continuum of care. They create person-focussed, longitudinal records that can be viewed, understood and used irrespective of care setting. The use of the same protocols to support care planning in sectors between which people may move (e.g. acute, community and residential care) allow for a collaborative approach to service provision that spans the continuum of care. The focus is on recording the information about the individual, their changing strengths, abilities and preferences rather than the information required only by a particular care setting where that person happens to be at any given time. Currently the interRAI suite of assessment instruments is the only example of this type (see Box 3.1). This integrated system enables transfer of common information across care settings, thereby facilitating continuity of care across transitions. A number of regional and national jurisdictions are now introducing the interRAI instruments in response to growing pressures on care delivery services (*http://interrai.org/index.php?id=7*).

Combining observations and subjective ratings by the person describing his/ her experience in a care setting will become the next generation of interRAI solutions. These instruments will combine the physical, cognitive and social functional measures in assessor-rated instruments with self-reported quality of life surveys completed by the person.

Structure and use of the interRAI assessment instruments

InterRAI instruments include manuals to support training on standardised assessment items. They also include Clinical Assessment Protocols (CAPs) and numerous clinical summary scales and algorithms that help to "interpret" the clinical findings and describe the severity of impairment or risk of problems in a variety of domain areas. The manuals give an extensive description of the assessment process. They also describe the intent of assessing that domain and the process for conducting a high quality assessment of the domain. In addition, they outline coding rules for each item and provide case examples to illustrate key principles associated with appropriate assessment and coding. They are designed to be used by care professionals for the assessment of the care needs of individuals and to support and inform best practice care planning. Once the assessment is completed, scales summarising major domains (e.g., depression, cognition, and physical function) are calculated. These scales are automatically constructed from the aggregation of information that has been recorded for the sole purpose of determining the care that a person will require.

Assessments are mostly commonly completed by registered nurses, but are also undertaken by therapists and care managers from social work who have been trained in their use. The process of assessment includes a conversational dialogue between the care professional and person whose care needs are being assessed, covering all relevant domains. A number of items are specifically addressed to the person being assessed, such as aspects of mood, self-reported perception of health and preferences for activities, etc. However, to complete other items, assessors also review all available relevant records and talk with formal and informal care givers and relatives who are associated with the person whose assessment is being completed. Typically assessments will take around 40 minutes to one hour to complete where assessors are familiar with the assessment instruments. Those people with complex care needs will require more time, up to two hours. In nursing home populations in particular, this time is likely to be distributed across more than one day as carers and assessors get to know residents and their family and carers.

The assessment records what is achieved by the person, not his or her hypothetical "potential". Where there is uncertainty (e.g., conflicting information from different sources), the assessor records information based on his/her best judgement. Where there is evidence of cognitive or communication impairment, there will be increased reliance on information provided by care-givers and staff, driven by clear protocols laid out in the instrument training manuals. The process has been shown to be reliable and valid in systematic evaluation of the instruments with data from a wide range of settings and nations (Morris et al., 1990; Morris et al., 1997a, Morris et al., 1997b; Poss et al., 2008).

The assessment instruments themselves have a *uniform structure* that gives them their inherent strength. The suite of instruments are constructed around a set of data items that are assembled and configured differently for given care populations and care settings. There is a set of core items addressing key aspects of domains common to all settings and populations that appears in all the instruments. Each complete interRAI instrument consists of the core set and additional data items relevant for assessments in the care setting and care group. The figure in Box 3.1 shows the number of data items in the interRAI Home (community) Care (HC) and interRAI Long-term care Facilities (LTCF) assessment instruments. Each complete assessment instrument also includes a training manual, calculated scales (including screeners and severity measures), a set of algorithms that trigger "Clinical Assessment Protocols" (CAPs), quality indicators and casemix measures relevant to resource use.

The assessment items

The assessment items are organised into sections dealing with issues such as cognitive patterns, communication and hearing patterns, physical functioning, health conditions and preventive health measures. Typically, an assessment instrument will have around 20 sections within which there are a number of items to characterise each issue in various ways (e.g., frequency, severity, presence/absence). Every item and response code has concise and precise definitions including time frames. Most, but not all items refer to the past three days and define specific exclusions (e.g., excluding the washing of the back as part of assessing ability to bathe), as well as giving examples (e.g., vision is measured "with glasses or with other visual appliance used"). These characteristics ensure high inter and intra – observer reliability. Table 3.1 shows the sections and number of core and additional items in the interRAI Long-term care Facilities (LTCF) assessment instrument

Table 3.1. **Sections and number of core and additional items in the interRAI long-term care facility (LTCF) assessment instrument**

Section	Core items	Additional items	Section	Core items	Additional items
Identification information	24	11	Admission and initial history	11	8
Cognition	9	1	Communication and vision	4	3
Mood and behaviour	20	1	Psychosocial well-being	3	16
Physical functioning	15	4	Continence	2	
Disease diagnoses	25	0	Health conditions	33	2
Oral and nutritional status	11	3	Skin condition	7	0
Activity pursuits	0	18	Medication	11	0
Treatment and procedures	2	46	Responsibility and directives[1]	0	10
Discharge potential	0	4	Discharge	2	3
Assessment information	2	0			

1. Legal matters.
Source: InterRAI long-term care facility assessment instrument.

Complex issues are addressed by recording information about each component. For example, in the assessment of symptoms of pain, the interRAI assessment items address frequency, intensity, consistency and pain control. The pressure ulcer item records precise descriptive information about the most severe ulcer present – persistent skin redness, partial loss of skin layers, deep craters in the skin, breaks in skin exposing muscle or bone, and the presence of necrotic eschar.

The scales

Once an interRAI assessment has been completed, algorithms generate scales to provide severity measures (e.g., the extent of dependency in activities of daily living – ADL) or diagnostic screeners (e.g., whether a person has dementia). Scales are constructed from information recorded for care purposes alone. For example, the well validated Cognitive Performance Scale (CPS) is constructed from four items, short term memory, ability to make self understood, ability to feed oneself and whether or not comatose (Morris et al., 2004). The scales are computed by the assessment software.[2] Thus, automatic presentation of the CPS score, for example, informs the care professional of the degree of cognitive impairment, overcoming the well-reported phenomenon of cognitive impairment being under-recognised (McDonald et al., 2003). Numerous scales are currently available (*www. interrai.org/index.php?id=106*) encompassing cognition, communication, mood (depression), instrumental and personal ADL, pain and health stability, social engagement, etc. (Morris et al., 1999; Carpenter et al., 1999; Burrows et al., 2000; Fries et al., 2001; Hirdes et al., 2003; Mor et al., 1995).

The Clinical Assessment Protocols

InterRAI's Clinical Assessment Protocols (CAPs) are clinical algorithms that identify the need for care plans to address factors that may lead to adverse outcomes that are amenable to clinical intervention (Table 3.2 shows the list of CAPs of the interRAI Home Care (HC) instrument). They are an integral feature of each individual assessment instrument in the Suite and have a standard structure. CAPs were each written by multinational groups of academics and clinicians (both interRAI members and others) selected for their expertise in each CAP domain. The development method included review of the relevant scientific literature and expert opinion, and analysis of existing extensive interRAI data sets to identify sub-populations with adverse (or in some cases positive) outcomes across multiple assessment periods.

Table 3.2. **List of CAPs for the interRAI home care assessment instrument**

Clinical issues	Functional performance
Falls	Physical activities promotion
Pain	Instrumental activities of daily living
Pressure ulcer	Activities of daily living
Cardiorespiratory conditions	Home environment optimisation
Undernutrition	Institutional risk
Dehydration	Physical restraints
Feeding tube	**Cognition/Mental health**
Prevention	Cognitive loss
Appropriate medications	Delirium
Tobacco and alcohol use	Communication
Urinary incontinence	Mood
Bowel conditions	Behaviour
	Abusive relationship
	Social life
	Activities
	Informal support
	Social relationship

Source: InterRAI home care assessment instrument.

The text of a CAP begins with a description of the problem/issue and provides information on epidemiology of the CAP target condition. This is followed by a statement of the overall goals of care and the items from the assessment that "trigger" the CAP, together with information about the estimated proportion of a care population who will trigger it. Box 3.2 shows an extract of a CAP from the interRAI HC. The final section provides care planning guidelines for the target condition and a list of references to publications that can be used as additional resources. The CAPs may be used in their own right as a form of clinical guideline, or they may be used in conjunction with existing guidelines in any given jurisdiction. The interRAI assessment system, manuals and CAPs are themselves used as resources in general training of care professionals.

Box 3.2. **Extract from the trigger for the CAP addressing potential for improving abilities in activities of daily living**

Activities of daily living CAP trigger

The goal of this CAP is to improve performance or prevent avoidable functional decline in persons who already have some ADL deficits. The CAP applies to persons living in independent community housing, persons receiving services from home care programmes, persons in assisted living housing, and persons residing in nursing homes (long-stay care residents). The following rules specify the two types of persons triggered for specialised follow-up. A key difference between the two triggered groups is whether the person has a fluctuating functional status or condition at the initial assessment, often indicative of a person who has had a recent acute event.

Triggered to facilitate improvement

● Included in this group are persons who have all the following characteristics.

● Receive at least some help in ADLs (but are not totally dependent in all ADLs).

● Have at least some minimal cognitive assets (as indicated by having a Cognitive Performance Scale [CPS] score of less than six).

● Are not at imminent risk of dying.

● And, have two or more of the following indicators that suggest the person has experienced a recent acute event or has a fluctuating functional status, such as:

  – Experiencing an acute episode or a flare-up of a chronic condition.
  – Delirium.
  – Changing cognitive status (either improving or worsening).
  – Fluctuating care needs (with service supports either increasing or decreasing).

The quality indicators

The person-level data from interRAI instruments can be aggregated to inform decision making at the population level by managers, policy makers, planners, and evaluators (Mor et al., 2003a). Indicators of processes and outcomes of care are available for most established instruments in the interRAI suite, and they are a key application developed with any new instrument. In the nursing home sector, the initial set of quality indicators (QIs) created by Zimmerman and colleagues described a variety of quality problems that could be measured using the MDS-RAI, ranging from the prevalence of pressure ulcers to prevalence of untreated symptoms of depression (Zimmerman et al., 1995). These initial QIs included stratification criteria to provide basic differentiations of risk levels for adverse outcomes, and they had inclusion/exclusion criteria to identify the populations to which the indicator applied.

An extensive evaluation of QIs developed in the 1990s combined with new research on risk adjustment methodologies resulted in the release of updated quality indicators with more emphasis on longitudinal outcomes in nursing homes and post-acute care (Berg et al., 2002; Mor et al., 2003a; Mor et al., 2003b). Rather than considering only the prevalence of indicators at a given point in time, these indicators emphasized changes in clinical status in areas that could potentially respond to intervention. A further refinement was additional enhancements to risk adjustment through direct standardisation of populations (Jones et al., 2010; Table 3.3). The newest QIs involved three levels of adjustment: a) use of inclusion and exclusion criteria to limit the application of the indicator to subgroups for whom the indicator would represent a true potential quality problem (e.g., persons at the end of life are excluded from many QIs because their changes in health are less likely to be a function of quality); b) individual level adjustment for related factors likely to lead to a higher or lower baseline rate of the indicator for reasons likely to be unrelated to quality (e.g., ADL problems related to locomotion are used as adjusters for falls); and c) computation of QI rates within strata of variables with strong associations with the indicator and then standardisation of facility populations using a fixed distribution of those strata as a reference (e.g., facility distribution of Case Mix Index values from the RUG-III classification system for comparing facilities with similar levels of dependency).

Table 3.3. **Examples of interRAI risk adjusted quality indicators for nursing homes**

Improvements in:	Presence of:
Mid-loss ADL (mobility, transfer)	Stage 2-4 pressure ulcers
Behaviour	**Occurrence of:**
Worsening of:	Falls
Mid-loss ADL	**Use of:**
Behaviour	Physical restraints
Bladder continence	Antipsychotics without related diagnosis
Mood	Catheter
Pain	Feeding tube

Source: InterRAI nursing home assessment instrument.

By 2004, interRAI had released a comparable set of QIs for home care settings (Hirdes et al., 2004; Table 3.4). Similar work is underway to extend QI development to acute care (Brand et al., 2011) and mental health settings (Hirdes et al., 2001).

Public reporting on nursing home QIs was first made available in the United States through the Nursing Home Compare website (www.medicare.gov/NursingHomeCompare); but the indicators reported include relatively basic risk adjustment strategies. In Canada, the Canadian Institute for Health Information (www.cihi.ca) and Health Quality Ontario (www.hqontario.ca) have collaborated to develop a web-based public reporting system that provides fully risk adjusted QI information to the public on all nursing homes in the province of Ontario.

Table 3.4. **Examples of home care quality indicators (QIs)**

Prevalence QIs	
Inadequate meals	Delirium
Weight loss	Negative mood
Dehydration	Disruptive/intense daily pain
No medication review by MD	Inadequate pain control
Neglect or abuse	Any injuries
ADL/rehab potential and no therapies	No flu vaccination
Falls	Social isolation with distress
Difficulty in locomotion and no assistive device	
Failure to improve/incidence QIs	
Bladder incontinence	Impaired locomotion in home
Skin ulcers	Cognitive function
ADL impairment	Difficulty in communication

Source: InterRAI home care assessment instrument.

The next stage in the evolution of performance measurement based on the interRAI assessment instruments is cross-national comparisons of quality. As these instruments begin to be adopted on a large scale internationally, the opportunity to perform "natural experiments" using population level data to compare health system performance will become possible. QIs from the interRAI Home Care instrument have been used to compare the performance of home care services in a pilot study in 11 European nations (Bos et al., 2007).

Casemix systems to describe resource use

Resource Utilisation Groups (RUGs) is a classification system that uses a subset of MDS-RAI assessment items to determine the relative cost of caring for a nursing home resident. RUGs is frequently used in payment systems to reimburse costs (Fries et al., 1994). The system of seven clinical categories was devised as a hierarchy ranked by cost. Residents can qualify for more than one group, but are placed in the most resource intensive one. A resident failing to fulfil the criteria for the rehabilitation groups would be checked against criteria for extensive treatments; those failing to meet the criteria would be checked against special care and so on. The reduced physical function group contains those residents who fail to meet the criteria for any of the other (Table 3.5). ADL (activities of daily living) scores, presence of depression and nursing rehabilitation needs are then assessed to allow subdividing of each of these clinical groups, to identify a final RUG group.

RUGs has proven to be an extremely robust system (Carpenter et al., 1997) and it is used in several nations as a basis of a payment system for funding long-term care, including the United States, Canada, Iceland and Finland. The aggregated data provide a powerful capacity to compare caseload complexity and service responses between facilities, regions and nations. The RUG system has also been shown to be effective in measuring casemix for persons receiving home care (Bjorkgren et al., 2000) and those with intellectual disability in institutional settings (Martin et al., 2011) Another casemix system has been developed for inpatient psychiatry (Hirdes et al., 2002b), and others are in development for sectors ranging from acute care to developmental services (Martin et al., 2011).

Table 3.5. **Criteria for allocation to main RUG-III categories**

Rehabilitation ↓	**Very high intensity multidisciplinary rehabilitation:** 450 minutes or more of rehabilitation therapy per week; and at least five days per week of one type of therapy; and at least two of the three therapies provided.
	High intensity rehabilitation: 300 minutes or more of rehabilitation therapy per week; and at least five days per week of one type of therapy.
	Medium intensity: 150 minutes or more of rehabilitation therapy per week; and at least five days per week of rehabilitation therapy.
	Low Intensity: 45 minutes or more of rehabilitation therapy per week; and at least three days per week of rehabilitation therapy; and at least two types of rehabilitation nursing, each provided five days per week.
	Note: Rehabilitation therapy is any combination of physical, occupational or speech therapy. Rehabilitation nursing includes: Amputation care, active/passive range of motion, splint/brace assistance; training in locomotion/ mobility; dressing/grooming; eating/swallowing; transfer.
Extensive services ↓	**If the resident fails to fulfil these criteria, the next category is considered**
	ADL index score of at least seven and meet the following criteria: Parenteral feeding, suctioning, tracheotomy, ventilator/respirator.
Special care ↓	**If the resident fails to fulfil these criteria, the next category is considered**
	ADL index score of at least seven and meet at least one of the following criteria: Burns; coma; fever with vomiting, weight loss, pneumonia or dehydration; Multiple Sclerosis; pressure ulcers of stage 3 or 4; quadriplegia; septicaemia; IV medications; radiation treatment; tube feeding.
Clinically complex ↓	**If the resident fails to fulfil these criteria, the next category is considered**
	Meet at least one of the following criteria: Aphasia, aspiration, cerebral palsy, dehydration, hemiplegia, internal bleeding, pneumonia, stasis ulcer, terminal illness, urinary tract infection, chemotherapy, dialysis, four or more physician visits per month, respiratory therapy, transfusions, wound care other than ulcer care including active foot care dressing.
Impaired cognition ↓	**If the resident fails to fulfil these criteria, the next category is considered**
	ADL score of 4-10 and cognitive impairment in all three of the following: Decision making, orientation (recall), short-term memory.
Behavioural problems ↓	**If the resident fails to fulfil these criteria, the next category is considered**
	ADL scores of 4-10 and residents who display daily problems with the following: Inappropriate behaviour, physical abuse, verbal abuse, wandering, hallucinations.
Physical functions	**If the resident fails to fulfil these criteria, the final category is considered**
	Residents who do not meet any of the above criteria.

Source: InterRAI.

Cross-national comparisons of recipients of long-term care services

This section illustrates the potential of person level operational data to address matters of importance for evaluating and monitoring quality and efficiency of long-term care services. It uses data from a range of international research projects on interRAI assessment systems and data from nine of the many countries in which the interRAI system is in use. The data presented are selected to show how different components of the interRAI system described above could be used to show systematic differences between nations. The data are illustrative data from a range of implementations and are not presented as being representative of whole region or nation from which the data are derived.

Before analysing the data from the nine countries, this section reviews the results of two major EU-funded research projects that have used data collected from the interRAI system. This is illustrative of the potential for using data generated from assessment instruments to appraise the quality of care received by care users and to identify priority areas for intervention.

Results from two major European projects using interRAI instruments

These projects tested the reliability of the interRAI system in community care and nursing home care. The objective of the ADHOC study (Carpenter et al., 2004) of recipients of community care services in 11 countries was to link the characteristics of community care recipients, the services they receive, and the outcomes they experience. In each country a cohort of 250 people receiving community care services were assessed using the interRAI HC assessment at baseline, six months and 12 months. Use of formal care services and amount of informal care were also recorded for the same period. The SHELTER study (Onder et al., 2012) assessed the reliability of the interRAI LTCF instrument in nursing home care when translated into the languages of eight participating EU countries and tested the implementation of the instrument on a large scale. 450 nursing home residents were assessed at baseline, six months and 12 months using the interRAI LTCF. Mortality, admissions to hospital and discharge from nursing home care were also recorded. In both studies data on configuration, staffing and models of management of the community and the nursing homes services was also recorded.

Figure 3.1 uses data from ADHOC and SHELTER to show how the community and nursing home care services of the nations that participated in both studies provide for people with very different degrees of cognitive and physical impairment. The axes in the graph show the degree of physical impairment using the interRAI ADL hierarchy scale and degree of cognitive impairment using the interRAI cognitive performance score (CPS). Both scales have a range zero (no impairment) to six (very severe impairment). The rectangular data points are the median values for recipients of community care (ADHOC) and the diamond shaped points, the median values for residents of nursing homes (SHELTER).

Figure 3.1. **Relationship between mean Cognitive Performance Scale score and mean ADL hierarchy scale score by country in the SHELTER (black) and ADHOC (grey) samples**

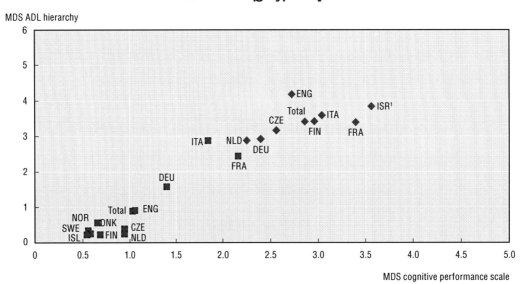

1. Information on data for Israel: *http://dx/doi.org/10.1787/888932315602.*
Source: ADHOC and SHELTER studies.

The community and nursing home populations are distributed in two distinct clusters, with the community populations in lower left of the chart having much lower levels of impairment than the nursing home residents in the upper right. While there are clear differences between the countries in each cluster, the populations in Italy (IT) and France (FR) are markedly different. The community care recipients in these two nations (the two rectangular data points at the lower left extremity of the cluster of diamond shaped data points on the upper right) have the same degree of impairment as the nursing home population in the Netherlands (NL). Providing for such extremely dependent older people in their own homes must be due to different patterns of service provision and/or support of extended families. In either case, there are clearly lessons to be learned, as there will be significant differences between the eligibility criteria for access to services, and the financial and social costs of community and nursing home care.

The potential for insight into a wide range of clinical and social indicators requires only some processing of data from operational practices. For example, Figures 3.2 and 3.3 present further data from the nursing homes that participated in the SHELTER study.

Figure 3.2. **Pain and pain medication in residents with pain in nursing homes in eight EU countries**

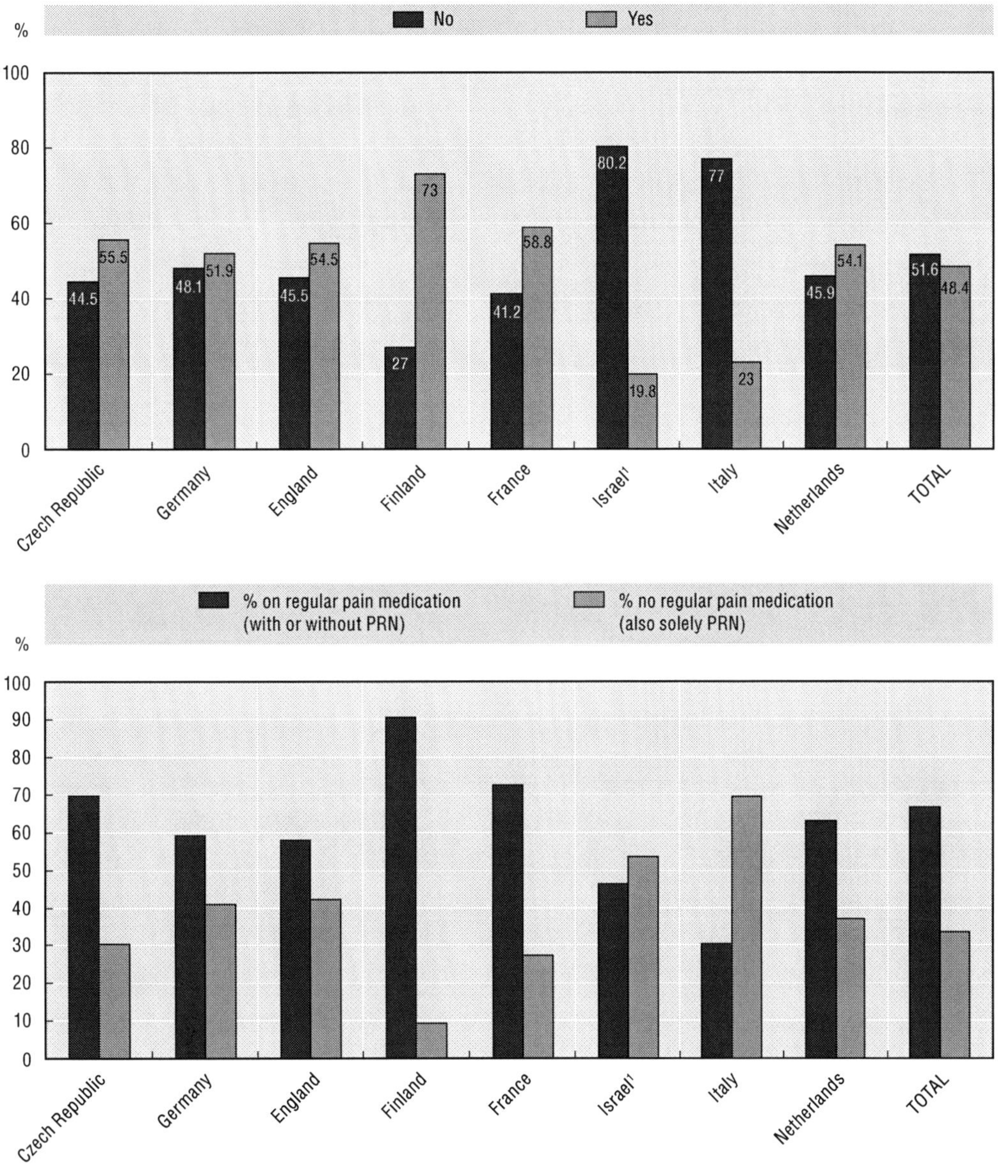

1. Information on data for Israel: http://dx/doi.org/10.1787/888932315602.
Source: SHELTER study.

Figure 3.2 shows the prevalence of pain and use of pain relieving medication. The upper graph shows the percentage of residents who complain of daily pain (lighter columns). The lower graph shows the percentage with pain who are not receiving regular pain relieving medication (pale section of each column). There are wide differences between countries, with 73% of nursing home residents in the Finnish sample (FI) reporting daily pain (light column upper graph), although only a small proportion are not receiving regular medication (pale column section in lower graph). In Italy (IT), just 23% of the residents of the participating homes reported daily pain (pale column in upper graph), but only 30% of these received regular pain relieving medication (dark column section in lower graph).

Figure 3.3 shows how the degree of social activity relates to physical disability and severity of dementia in the participating nursing homes. The upper graph shows how the degree of engagement in social activities reduces as physical disability increases for the resident in the homes from the United Kingdom and France. For the United Kingdom, the level of activity is higher than in the French homes across nearly all levels of disability, and falls more slowly with increasing disability than the SHELTER average. The lower graph

Figure 3.3. **Relationship between engagement in social activity physical and cognitive impairment in residents in nursing homes in eight EU countries**

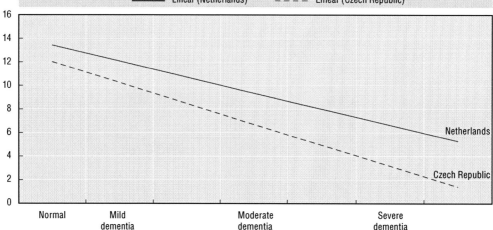

Source: SHELTER study.

shows reduction in social activity with increasing severity of dementia. However the slope of the line is less marked for the Netherlands, showing that the severity of dementia in the residents of the participating homes has a smaller impact on their participation in social activities than for those in the Czech Republic homes. Exploring the factors and management practices underlying these differences can increase knowledge and improve quality of care.

Data from nine OECD and non-OECD countries and regions

Data are shown from nine of the OECD and non-OECD countries and regions in which the interRAI assessment system is in use. The data are from interRAI fellows in the countries and regions that have contributed to this report: Ontario Province (Canada), Michigan State (United States), Iceland, Finland, Hong Kong (China), New Zealand, the United Kingdom, Belgium and Italy. In all of these countries except the United Kingdom, the data are derived from operational use of the interRAI assessment instruments for long-term care facilities (LTCF) and home (community) care (HC). The UK data are from the two EU-funded research projects conducted in South East England, ADHOC and SHELTER.

While countries like the United States and Canada have large data holdings for interRAI data, other nations such as Finland, New Zealand, and Belgium are well underway in their progress toward similar population level data, derived from the operational use of the interRAI assessment system. This report does not include direct comparisons of fully risk adjusted QIs, but it does provide some basic examples of stratified comparisons of potential quality issues in nursing home and home care settings.

Box 3.3. Summary of use of the interRAI assessment system in nine OECD and non-OECD countries

There are national collections of InterRAI data in six of the countries, with one other country considering establishing a national collection. Quality indicators using InterRAI data are reported in Canada, the United States, and Iceland. This practice will begin in New Zealand in 2012. In other countries, the data are used internally, and for reimbursement.

Canada is able to cite use of InterRAI data as a basis for changing policy (e.g., changing service caps for homecare, prioritising access to services, and inclusion of casemix in funding formulas). The United States and Iceland have used InterRAI data to assess eligibility for care and for quality monitoring. Finland uses interRAI data in national reports on health and social care projects. Belgium also plans to use the data to support quality and reimbursement from 2013.

There are examples of the impact of changes in policy. The United States has examples of where use of interRAI data has led to substantial changes in cost structures for nursing home and home care. In the state of Michigan, the use of InterRAI data led to a reduction in duplicative care that resulted in a saving of USD 1 billion. In Canada, there has been a substantial reduction in the use of restraint in nursing homes following a quality initiative that built on InterRAI data.

InterRAI data are also used for regulatory purposes in Canada (e.g., in public reporting and nursing home inspection), and in the United States and Iceland.

Four countries provide the public with access to summary data or quality indicators. In the United States, summary data are available through a public website.

Iceland, Finland and New Zealand present data from the national data repositories. Michigan (entire state), Ontario (entire province), Italy (Umbria Region) and Hong Kong (China) present data from their entire region, with the exception that the HK nursing home data are from ten participating nursing homes. Belgium data come from pilot implementations prior to national deployment of the interRAI system; UK data are from the EU projects SHELTER (NH) and ADHOC (HC) only. The most recent deployments of Italy, Belgium and UK NH are data from implementations of the interRAI suite; the remainder are from implementations of the interRAI NH and HC versions 2.0.

The report represents the beginning of the opportunity to benchmark care internationally. The following sections reference tables listed in the annex.

Comparing demographics

Annex Table 3.A1.1 ("demographics worksheet") shows age, gender, marital status and prevalence of common clinical diagnoses in nursing home (NH) and home care (HC) populations. Both home care and nursing home settings serve a predominantly older, female population. All nations show the NH residents being marginally older than those cared for in the community, with the exception of Italy, where the age distribution is the same across both settings. Figure 3.1 showed how the levels of impairment in the community dwelling older people were remarkably similar to the NH residents in the other countries in the SHELTER study. There is likely something quite different about the way that NH and HC services are provided in Italy.

Women are more likely to not be married in both settings, and males in home care settings are generally more likely to be married than those in nursing homes. The lowest proportions of married people were in Finland (NH and HC) and the NH residents in Italy. This points to the importance of informal supports as a resource for maintaining older persons in the community, especially in Italy where the community dwelling older people are so dependent (see above in relation to Figure 3.1).

There are also clear differences in the diagnoses of persons in community and institutional settings. For example, the prevalence of Alzheimer's disease and related dementia is notably higher in nursing homes than in home care. The lowest NH prevalences are seen in Michigan, where there is a major initiative to provide increased care in the community, in Hong Kong (China) and in the United Kingdom. In the case of the United Kingdom, it could be simply that it is under-diagnosed in NH populations in spite of the high prevalence of cognitive impairment in the United Kingdom (McDonald et al., 2003). There are cross-national differences in the rates of diabetes (highest in Michigan of both populations and lowest in Belgium). However there are only modest differences in the rates of diabetes between the NH and HC settings within the same country. This demonstrates that some conditions are important risk factors for institutionalisation, whereas others may be managed effectively in either care settings. It also points to the importance of rising prevalence rates of dementia in many developed nations. Current approaches to community based care may not be sufficiently well equipped to deal with the rapidly growing population of people with cognitive impairment in later life.

Comparing casemix and quality indicators

Annex Table 3.A1.2 shows prevalence of triggered Client Assessment Protocols (CAP) that give an indication of the clinical syndromes requiring care planning in both NH and HC settings. Table 3.A1.3 (Scales) shows the mean scores of some of the principal outcome scales that demonstrate the prevalence of functional impairment (cognitive performance and activities of daily living – ADL) and clinical syndromes (pain and depression).

Physical disability is an important area of need in both care settings cross-nationally. The ADL Hierarchy Scale (Morris et al., 1999) shows higher proportions of older people in the severe impairment groups in NH settings with more than 75% in the higher two groups (ADL Hierarchy scores 3-4 and 5-6) across all countries (Table 3.A1.3). The fact that a high proportion of NH residents trigger[3] the "ADL Prevent Decline" CAP (Table 3.A1.2) also implies that these residents are more physically impaired and less likely to benefit from physical rehabilitation in dressing, transferring between bed and chair, eating and mobility in bed (ADL Facilitate improvement CAP) than is the case in the HC populations. A striking difference is the high proportion of nursing home resident in Michigan that trigger "ADL Facilitate improvement". This is most likely as a result of policy in the United States which provides Medicare funding for rehabilitation in nursing homes, which likely enables earlier discharge from hospital with rehabilitation and discharge home from NHs. The fact that the "Delirium" CAP is also triggered in a greater proportion of Michigan NH residents (33.9% cf. <15% in all other countries except Italy – 24.8%) also suggests more acutely ill residents discharged from hospital to NH or possibly poor recognition of the critical clinical syndrome.

In addition, there are cross-national differences of note with the United Kingdom reporting about two-thirds of its nursing home residents to have the most severe levels of impairment compared with about one third in Hong Kong (China) and Canada. Similar patterns are evident with respect to cognitive impairment. These are likely to reflect differences in eligibility criteria for admission to NH between countries.

Use of physical restraints

Restraint use is an important issue with respect to quality in nursing homes. Table 3.A1.4 shows the percentage of residents triggering the "restraints" CAP in those who are relatively physically disabled and those with little physical disability. In most countries the CAP is triggered for more of the physically disabled (unable to perform early/mid loss ADLs – 13% to 25%) than the less disabled (able to perform early/mid loss ADLs – 1% to 3%). Rates of restraint use in the United Kingdom (0.6% and 0%) and the United States (0.3% and 1.1%) are substantially lower than in Canada (16% and 1.6%) and Hong Kong, China (20.7% and 3.5%). These differences are evident even though there has been a substantial *reduction* in restraint use in Canada in the last decade (see Figure 3.6). The differences between countries can only be explained by differences in policy and culture.

Depression

Depression (Annex Table 3.A1.3) is an important problem affecting the quality of life of older persons in community and institutional settings. However, a reasonably consistent pattern of more depression in nursing home settings is evident in most countries, except Hong Kong (China). For that country, the question of the adequacy and quality of home care services is important, particularly given the relatively lighter care needs of Hong Kong (China) home care clients. This finding is important given the recognised phenomenon of under-detection of depression (Huang et al., 2011) and many may take for granted that sadness/depression in nursing home residents is normal. In other countries, policy makers must consider whether there are alternative strategies that may be used in nursing home settings to respond to or prevent the onset of depressive symptoms.

Pain

Pain (Annex Table 3.A1.2) is a pervasive problem affecting older persons around the world. The rates and severity of pain appear to be higher in home care settings; however, that may be associated with cross-sector variations in the severity of cognitive impairment (making pain more difficult to detect). In fact, in each country, the *minority* of home care clients report no pain. Therefore, effective pain management should be an important dimension of any country's strategy to improve the quality of life of older persons in the community.

Resource use

Casemix classification systems can provide summary information about the overall resource needs of health care service recipients. The RUGs system identifies those residents with higher and more complex care needs that make greatest demand on the skills and time of nursing care staff. By linking the RUGs system to payment systems, jurisdictions are able to direct funding to those with greatest need. Integral within the RUGs system is a linkage to good practice. Thus, the fact that it can take more time to support the good practice of enabling residents to, for example, dress themselves rather than care staff actually dressing the resident is recognised as "nursing rehabilitation" within RUGs, and is reflected in the casemix measure. Indicators of poor care are also embedded in the system, so that "gaming" the system to increase payments is difficult and not without consequences. In addition, statistical methods have been developed by interRAI researchers to identify dubious coding practices.

The Resource Utilisation Groups algorithms for nursing homes (RUG-III) and for home care (RUGIII/HC) have been extensively validated in cross-national studies of staff time use in those settings. The RUG algorithms differ somewhat between the two settings. Annex Table 3.A1.4 shows the distribution between the RUG system clinical groups of the nursing home (NH) and home care (HC) populations. These clinical groups are listed in the order of highest resource use (Rehabilitation) through to the lowest resource use group (Physical Function Reduced).

In all comparisons and all settings, the largest group of persons served are in the Physical Function Reduced RUG level, which includes persons with physical disabilities but few other medical complexities. The next most common groups are the impaired cognition and clinically complex groups. There are notable cross-national differences in the rehabilitation levels,[4] suggesting international variations in access to therapies, probably reflected in the funding available to provide care. There are also differences between home care and nursing homes with home care having larger proportions of persons in the clinically complex level but nursing homes having more in the somewhat more resource intensive special care level.

Despite the various differences that may be found with respect to specific RUG levels, perhaps the more interesting finding is the general *similarity* of RUG distributions in nursing homes and home care settings. This implies that in most places the two sectors are serving a relatively comparable population with respect to clinical factors associated with resource use. It also suggests that other, *non-clinical* factors (e.g., social support) may be important differentiating factors determining who is in facility versus community settings.

Comparing sub-populations

Annex Table 3.A1.5 shows health and social care indicators within sub-populations in nursing home and community care across the nations. In this example, the data have been subdivided into four groups by degree of physical and cognitive impairment. The sub-groups are those with good physical function and good cognitive function, poor physical function but good cognitive function, poor physical function but good cognitive function and both poor physical function and poor cognitive function. The creation of the sub-groups is identical for both nursing home and community (home) care.

The prevalence of bladder incontinence as one would expect is higher in the "poor cognition" groups than "good cognition" groups. It is also higher in the "poor physical function" groups than the "good physical function" groups, with highest prevalence of all in those with both poor physical function and poor cognition. In addition there is a general pattern of bladder incontinence being higher in nursing home than home care populations in all sub-groups, with the exception of those with good physical function and poor cognition, where the pattern is reversed in all the country data, with the exception of the United Kingdom and Hong Kong (China). What is striking is that in Michigan, prevalence in home care is higher than any other country and greater than in nursing homes in all sub-groups. This could be of interest as it may reflect quality of care provision differences, or an impact of a policy decision that has an ill-understood or unexpected impact.

Use of physical restraints is highly related to culture and policy. Examining the data in Annex Table 3.A1.5, there is virtually no restraint use in any nation or in those people with good physical function and either good or poor cognition. However where there is poor physical function there are significant differences between nations. For those with poor physical function, but who still have good cognition, Finland (9.2%), Belgium (9.5%) and Hong Kong, China (19.2%) have the highest rates of use. In the most impaired group, the differences between nations are the greatest. In the United Kingdom (1%) and Michigan (2.7%), there is virtually no restraint use in those with poor physical and cognitive function. The rates in the other nations is much higher in this sub-group – Ontario (23.1%), Finland (18.7%), Belgium (19.9%), Italy 23.1%) and Hong Kong, China (54.2%). These differences can only represent differences in policy.

A further example of differences that stimulate thought, are in relation to the prevalence of feeling lonely. The highest rates of loneliness are seen in all the home care sub-groups in the United Kingdom and Belgium and Finland. In Belgium, a significant proportion of nursing home residents also feel lonely.

Falls

Falls are an important threat to the autonomy and well-being of older adults. As shown in Table 3.A1.5 in the annex, falls are more common in community settings (except in Italy) where exposure to risk and physical mobility is greater. Not all falls result in injury, and a balance must be struck between maintaining mobility and independence and the risk of falling. Much can be done to reduce the risks associated with falling (OECD, 2007).[5] Routinely available comparable data highlights variations in incidence that permits exploration of different policies and practices associated with reduced risk of injury.

Longitudinal information and relation to policy

When longitudinal data are available from the routine use of interRAI assessments, it is possible to monitor quality of care and to evaluate the impact of policy decisions on the quality of care.

New Zealand introduced the interRAI home care assessment system in 2005. Straightforward aggregation of the assessment data and running of the quality indicator (QI) algorithms enables monitoring of the prevalence of quality indicators over time. Figures 3.4 and 3.5 present a selection of QI data from the national repository of data covering all home care assessments undertaken in New Zealand. Disaggregation by care provider or municipal district would enable benchmarking and comparison of performance.

Figure 3.4. **Selected quality indicators from home (community) care in New Zealand, 2005-12 (indicator list 1)**

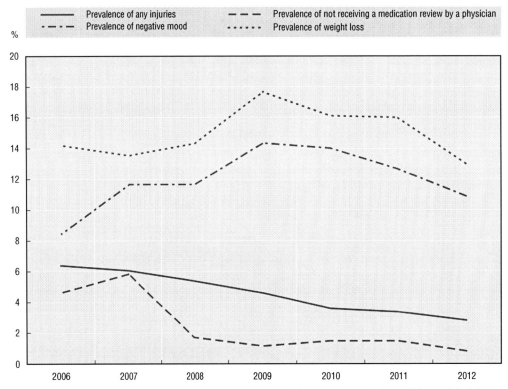

Source: National New Zealand interRAI Software Service (on behalf of New Zealand District Health Boards). Elaborated based on data from InterRAI.org.

Figure 3.5. **Selected quality indicators from home (community) care in New Zealand, 2005-12 (indicator list 2)**

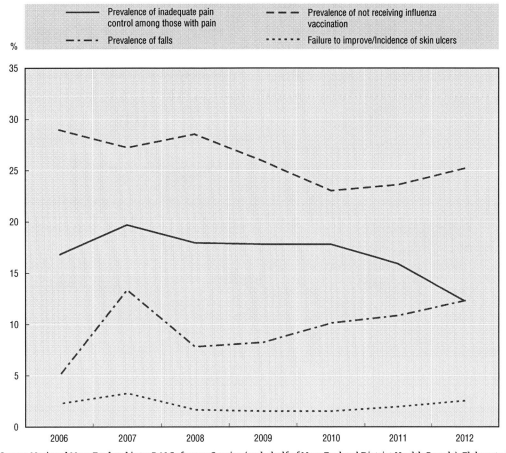

Source: National New Zealand interRAI Software Service (on behalf of New Zealand District Health Boards). Elaborated based on data from InterRAI.org.

In Canada, the use of restraints in nursing homes emerged as an important quality issue in the late 1990s, when international comparisons suggested that the rate of restraint use in that country was high by international standards (Feng et al., 2009). In a recent study funded by the Public Health Agency of Canada, longitudinal trends in restraint use were examined among Canadian provinces/territories that have implemented the interRAI nursing home instrument. Figure 3.6 provides clear evidence of substantial reductions in restraint use in four regions that reported their data to the Canadian Institute for Health Information. Two provinces had no major changes in restraint use, but their levels were already at the level to which other regions improved over time. Only one province (Saskatchewan) had a high rate of restraint use that remained effectively unchanged over a five year time period.

Figure 3.6. **Restraint use among nursing home residents without neurological conditions, by province, Canada, 1996-2010**

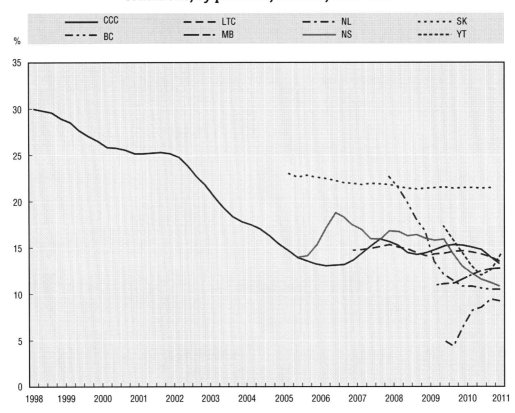

Note: BC: British Columbia; CCC: Ontario Complex Continuing Care Hospitals; LTC: Ontario nursing homes; MB: Manitoba; NL: Newfoundland and Labrador; NS: Nova Scotia; SK: Saskatchewan; YT: Yukon Territory.
Source: Canadian data set available from InterRAI.org.

The United States introduced policies to reduce admissions to nursing homes and limit admission to those with greatest need, through the Medicaid Waiver programme. Figure 3.7 shows the impact of these policies with a progressive reduction of the proportion of nursing home residents classified as "low care". These residents will typically have no complex clinical conditions and be relatively independent in their activities of daily living. The data in the figure are derived from completely reliable aggregations of MDSRAI assessments undertaken for care purposes and submitted to the national repository (*www.ltcFocus.org*).

Figure 3.7. **Percentage of long stay residents needing only limited care are in US nursing homes**

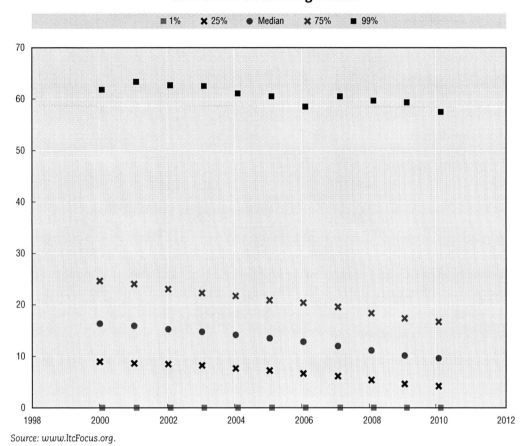

Source: www.ltcFocus.org.

Implementation issues and opportunities

The need to move toward evidence-informed decision making is a relatively uncontroversial proposition. The question is what conditions are required in order to implement solutions like the interRAI instruments on a large scale basis, as has been achieved in a number of countries including Canada, United States, New Zealand, Finland, Iceland, and currently underway in Belgium.

Political will, leadership and effective partnerships are essential. Decision makers often need information to address:

● policy challenges that lie ahead;

● clinical information for the entire jurisdiction;

● the needs of vulnerable populations across the continuum of care.

These can only be met by a common cross-sectoral information standard, without which all comparisons are subject to doubt and the evidence needed to inform decisions will be equivocal. This point is illustrated in the NHS Information Strategy for England which specifically addresses the importance of standards and comparable information in all aspects of health care (Department of Health, 2012).

However, to select and implement a single standard is a substantial political challenge because even if most agree with the decision, it is highly unlikely that all stakeholders will support any single choice. The issues encompass consensus, technical issues, education and providing feedback to the care providers.

The nature of the challenge

Availability of integrated multi-setting person level data provides a wide array of opportunities for clinicians, administrators and researchers. This proposition is not unique to long-term care. It has been the focus of a major health informatics programme in the United Kingdom, led by the Health Informatics Unit at the Royal College of Physicians (*www.rcplondon.ac.uk/policy/improving-healthcare/health-informatics*) and is a major component of the EU eHealth interoperability roadmap (Calliope, 2011) for example. However achieving the goal of implementing a standardised integrated approach to assessment, such as the interRAI system, across whole jurisdictions presents challenges that are not insignificant. In 2003 the Millbank Memorial Fund published a series of case studies that illustrated the challenges of implementing the interRAI system in the United States, Canada, Iceland, Israel, Italy, Japan, Spain and the United Kingdom (Milbank Memorial Fund, 2003). Some of these countries have made significant progress (United States, Israel, Canada) but others remain embroiled in dialogue over models for assessment, funding and information management (e.g. United Kingdom). The report listed seven key issues that are still relevant today:

● It is difficult to introduce compatible, consistent assessment instruments across different systems and domains, each of which has a culture, history, and current approach to gathering and using information.

● The interRAI assessment system can be seen by persons in various professions as unnecessarily burdensome, less precise than existing instruments, too medically oriented, and an encroachment on the responsibilities of particular professions.

● The [interRAI assessment system] can be the basis for reimbursement based on nursing home residents' levels of acuity and thus disrupt the status quo in reimbursement.

● The introduction, maintenance, and full exploitation of a data system can only develop over time and with a significant expenditure of resources.

● Staff turnover impedes the consistent, continuing use of the instrument.

● The use of the [interRAI assessment system] is affected by such contingent factors as perceived crises that claim public attention.

● The [interRAI assessment system] can assist but not determine the judgment of policy makers.

The increasing pressures associated with ageing populations and constrained resources, together with the rapid development of information technology is leading to the development of models for successfully addressing the challenge.

Introducing new integrated assessment instruments across different systems and domains

The establishment of systems across regions, nations and care settings is likely to require significant political and administrative investment by governments. Specific services are often separately administered by different agencies under the jurisdiction of different levels of government – national, state, and regional. Even within one level of government, administrative "silos" can develop which attend to each service type (e.g., hospitals and community care). To further complicate matters, the health and social service systems are frequently organised in their own administrative silos with belief and delivery models which may be perceived as being very different. Many elements of service systems may be provided by private agencies with varying levels of independence from government administration. Finally, the distribution of personal information across care settings, notably when the care is provided by different agencies, requires careful attention to privacy issues. Protocols are required to ensure that individuals are comfortable with the sharing of information among their caregivers.

The introduction of a single integrated clinical information system to such a complex mosaic of services thus seems formidable. However a number of nations and services have shown that full implementation is feasible.

Table 3.6. **Example of an interRAI assessment instrument section and assessment items**

SECTION C.   COGNITION

1. COGNITIVE SKILLS FOR DAILY DECISION-MAKING

Making decisions regarding tasks of daily life – e.g., when to get up or have meals, which clothes to wear or activities to do

0. **Independent** – Decisions consistent, reasonable, and safe
1. **Modified independence** – Some difficulty in new situations only
2. **Minimally impaired** – In specific recurring situations, decisions become poor or unsafe; cues/supervision necessary at those times
3. **Moderately impaired** – Decisions consistently poor or unsafe; cues/supervision required at all times
4. **Severely impaired** – Never or rarely makes decisions
5. **No discernible consciousness, coma [Skip to Section G]**

2. MEMORY/RECALL ABILITY

Code for recall of what was learned or known

0. Yes, memory OK   1. Memory problem

a. **Short-term memory OK** – Seems/appears to recall after 5 minutes
b. **Long-term memory OK** – Seems/appears to recall distant past
c. **Procedural memory OK**– Can perform all or almost all steps in a multitask sequence without cues
d. **Situational memory OK** – Both: recognises caregivers' names/faces frequently encountered AND knows location of places regularly visited (bedroom, dining room, activity room, therapy room)

3. PERIODIC DISORDERED THINKING OR AWARENESS

[Note: Accurate assessment requires conversations with staff, family or others who have direct knowledge of the person's behaviour over this time]

0. Behaviour not present
1. Behaviour present, consistent with usual functioning
2. Behaviour present, appears different from usual functioning (e.g., new onset or worsening; different from a few weeks ago)

a. **Easily distracted** – e.g., episodes of difficulty paying attention; gets sidetracked
b. **Episodes of disorganised speech** – e.g., speech is nonsensical, irrelevant, or rambling from subject to subject; loses train of thought
c. **Mental function varies over the course of the day** – e.g., sometimes better, sometimes worse

4. ACUTE CHANGE IN MENTAL STATUS FROM A PERSON'S USUAL FUNCTIONING – e.g., *restlessness, lethargy, difficult to arouse, altered environmental perception*

0. No   1. Yes

5. CHANGE IN DECISION MAKINGCOMPARED TO 90 DAYS AGO (OR SINCE LAST ASSESSMENT)

0. Improved   2. Declined
1. No change   8. Uncertain

Note: Copies of interRAI instruments and manuals may be purchased by contacting interRAI at *http://catalogue.interrai.org/*. Instruments are copyright; however interRAI provides royalty-free use licenses to governments and caregivers.
Source: InterRAI.

An incremental approach to introduction is likely to be more successful than a blanket introduction across all care providers. Administrations operating two or more related services may introducing one of the instruments followed by a second and third (e.g., acute and post-acute care; community and institutional mental health). Services with relationships to the organisations that implement instruments may then see opportunities to improve sharing of interoperable data by implementing other instruments from the suite. Ultimately, the choice not to share instrumentation may place an organisation at considerable disadvantage (e.g., inability to avail themselves of the opportunity to benchmark their performance). This effect is likely to be particularly pronounced in adjacent health or social service sectors providing care to overlapping populations.

In New Zealand, the interRAI Home Care assessment system and interRAI Contact Assessment are used across all of community care. Introducing the LTCF assessment is being linked to the development of an information model for the interRAI system that will support interoperability of the data across computer systems of the full range of care providers. The New Zealand model of implementation was cited as an example of innovation in the NHS England Information Strategy 2012 (Department of Health, 2012). Other countries that have, or plan, advanced implementations of multiple instruments of the interRAI suite include Canada (Hirdes, 2006), Finland and Belgium.

Consensus

Reluctance to share instrumentation is also evident between health and social care disciplines, particularly in multi-disciplinary settings. Each professional group uses its own instrument set to evaluate aspects such as cognition, ADL and mood. There is often a division of labour in which each profession attends to aspects of the problem – medical staff to cognition, occupational therapists to functional activities, and nurses to pressure ulcer prevention. The introduction of a "shared" clinical dataset can be perceived to compromise the quality of instrumentation and threaten professional autonomy.

Conversely, the use of a shared dataset presents the opportunity to improving productivity through reduction in duplication of data recording, particularly if this information is linked to a wider system that brings previous data to the current setting, and offers an opportunity to efficiently pass on information to subsequent care settings.

The Canadian experience points to two important decision making dynamics. First, a consensus building process is often needed to reach a critical mass of opinion leaders of differing types (clinicians, administrators, researchers, policy makers) who will support the selection of a given information standard. Second, mandated use will ensure *full* implementation across all settings, including organisations that may be indifferent to or unsupportive of the recommendation. It is telling that the only province to recommend, but not mandate, use of the interRAI instruments (Nova Scotia) was not able to expand use beyond five opinion-leader homes.

Technical issues

InterRAI instruments are intimately dependent on computerisation, since an integral feature is a series of complex algorithms that generate scales, CAPs and numerous other administrative by-products. High quality, computer-based information systems are required to collect, compile and report on interRAI data to decision makers at all levels from the bedside to the minister's office. Paper based solutions are untenable, as are poorly designed

IT systems. Considerations that will affect data quality range from the human-computer interface at the clinical level to information standards for national databases. In addition, tools for on-going monitoring and correction of data quality issues (e.g., auditing systems, data submission standards, statistical controls). Information governance (including privacy, access to and secondary uses of interRAI information) need to be built into the implementation model from the start. Consent models for sharing and transmission of person identifiable data across care settings and between care professionals are increasingly available.

Thus, a major challenge to implementation is access to computers and the need for a reasonable degree of computer literacy among front line staff. Many service settings are not yet ready for this level of sophistication, and see investment in computerisation as a significant cost barrier. However, as the benefits of such systems grow and with the development of lower cost web based solutions, the development of the formal interRAI information model and the increasing availability of cheaper computer hardware, the case for investment in these capabilities become increasingly powerful.

Education and training

Education is another core requirement for successful implementation. This includes training on the technical task of completing assessments correctly, but it also includes: education to support transitions to a culture of evidence, role modelling on collaborative exchange and use of data to inform decision making, and training on the use of interRAI's decision support algorithms address clinical, service delivery and policy related questions. The educational strategy must be multidimensional (e.g., in-person education, e-learning solutions, workshops, conferences), dynamic (to change with evolving learning needs), and ongoing (e.g., to deal with staff turnover, emergence of new evidence or applications).

Feedback to care providers

Feedback is a critical requirement at all levels of implementation. The required cycle times for feedback vary depending on the information user and the application of the information. For example, clinicians should receive virtually instantaneous feedback on the results of the person's assessment in order to initiate care planning and interventions in a timely manner. Managers require information on a somewhat longer time period to support internal administrative decisions and for governance purposes (e.g., reports to boards of directors). Governments may find a quarterly to annual information cycle adequate to inform population level decisions and public accountability. Despite the different time frames for feedback, each of these levels of consumers must see a "payback" of evidence arising from the investments made to gather these data.

Data quality

Continually monitoring, evaluating and protecting data quality is important. The maintenance of data quality is a continuous responsibility for all stakeholders and it can be addressed through a variety of educational and technical strategies. The fact that assessment data is generated at the interface between the patient/resident/care recipient, for the purpose of day to day care planning and delivery is itself a powerful driver for data quality.

Conclusions

Ageing and its associated chronic diseases and disability will be one of the major global challenges of this century. Almost all middle and high income nations are experiencing growth in the size of the older population, and the rate of population ageing is accelerating as birth rates and mortality rates decline. The availability of high quality evidence to inform policy development will be an essential resource to governments at all levels. It is not possible to monitor or improve quality of care without being able to measure and compare progress over time or performance between organisations, regions or nations. Assessment instruments such as the interRAI family of assessment instruments provide a unique, scientifically sound evidence base that can provide insights into the service needs, quality of care, and impact of policy choices on vulnerable persons across the continuum of care.

This chapter has described the history, scope and use of the interRAI assessment system. It also presented data illustrating how standardised person level data, recorded for the purpose of care planning and provision of care, can be aggregated to compare quality of care and efficiency of care services. Data from cross-national studies illustrate how only person level data (as opposed to service level data) can provide comparisons of the characteristics of nursing home and community care service populations and how these same data provide information on quality indicators of health and social care. Comparisons have illustrated differences that suggest improved outcomes can be achieved by examining policies and practices across organisations, regions and nations.

Standardisation of assessment in routine care practice is the most efficient means of delivering both high quality care and performance data. Standardising assessment and implementing sophisticated technologies such as the interRAI system on a large scale has the potential for huge transformational change. It is a significant undertaking that requires political commitment and presents a significant challenge. This chapter has described the nature of the challenge, highlighting the importance of overcoming interdisciplinary defensiveness and reluctance to change practice, commitment to generating reliable evidence to inform policy and investing in training, education and feedback to the care professionals and managers whose practice is required to change. There are also essential technology requirements. Investing in appropriate IT infrastructure seems an expensive investment. However it is probable that in the face of demographic change and financial pressure, it is only developing technology that is likely to deliver year on year improved efficiencies in service organisation and delivery.

Currently it would appear that the interRAI technology is unique in the depth and breadth of assessment and the well developed products in the form of quality, outcome and resource use indicators. All constructed entirely on the basis of supporting care professionals in assessing care needs and developing plans and delivering care. However great the challenge, governments must address the transformational change of introducing technology of this nature. OECD countries and regions' data used in this chapter demonstrate that this is feasible.

HL7 is the standard for the safe transmission of computerised clinical messages and the coded clinical information they contain. Health Level Seven International (HL7 – *www.hl7.org*) is the global authority that maintains and develops the HL7 standards. SNOMED CT is the international coding standard for clinical terminology that enables recording, transmission and retrieval of clinical information in a coded digital format. The International Health Terminology Standards Development Organisation (IHTSDO –

www.ihtsdo.org) is an international organisation with nation stake holders, created to support and develop – SNOMED CT. For functional assessment of care needs and the reliable use of valid comparable person level data, the interRAI assessment technology is the uniquely powerful system that delivers a full range of reliable aggregatable data from the day to day care of vulnerable populations. A move from an informal collaboration to a more formal international organisation such as IHTSDO will help manage the care challenges of population ageing.

Box 3.4. Suggestions for countries considering the use of standardised assessment systems

1. Foster a culture of evidence-informed decision making and a shared commitment to high data quality: the introduction of standardised assessment instruments with the sophisticated associated constructs (such as outcome scales, quality indicators and casemix systems) can provide a foundation of evidence to inform decision making; however, the use of evidence in this way itself requires a cultural shift at all levels of health and social service delivery. The protection of the quality of evidence must become a fundamental concern for all stakeholders investing in the implementation of these systems.

2. Engage a broad range of stakeholders as "consumers" of information from standardised assessment generated from routine practice: the key value of the interRAI assessments lies not in the collection of data, but rather the application of those data to create evidence that different stakeholders can use immediately to inform their decisions. Operational person level data should become a major source of evidence for decision makers at "the bedside" through to their counterparts in government. The information will also be of interest to patients, residents and other service users as they review their own care and compare quality of care across care providers. The engagement of these stakeholders supports improved data quality and cost-effectiveness for the implementation investment.

3. Integrate the assessment systems into normal clinical and social care practice: interRAI assessments should replace redundant systems and those with weak psychometric evidence as the required standard assessment approach for service recipients.

4. Invest in good quality IT systems to support data collection, reporting and information exchange: poorly designed computer systems can have profound negative consequences for any implementation effort. In addition to basic considerations related to the human-computer interface for a given solution, it is important that the system is able to process data into meaningful information to support the care professional in day to day work as well as providing performance data. In the case of the interRAI system this means all the major interRAI applications (e.g., care planning, outcome measures, quality indicators, casemix) across sectors and over time for individuals.

5. Employ the suite of instruments across adjacent sectors: although it may not be feasible to implement *every* instrument in a short period of time, health and social service providers serving overlapping populations (e.g., home care and nursing homes) should adopt instruments with interoperable data.

Box 3.4. **Suggestions for countries considering the use of standardised assessment systems** (cont.)

6. Ensure that information feedback loops are responsive to stakeholders' needs: clinicians should get virtually instantaneous results from having completed an assessment, but these results should be shared among all colleagues in the "circle of care" in a timely manner. Similarly, aggregated data should be available to support decisions related to governance, regulation and policy development as those decisions are being formulated.

7. Promote transparency in the use of data: evidence should be available to all decision makers including consumers, clinicians, managers, administrators and policy makers. Transparency supports "buy-in" to the introduction of these systems, enhances data quality, identifies best practices and industry leaders, helps to establish appropriate quality targets, and fosters and diffuses innovations through collaborative quality improvement initiatives.

8. Use casemix applications based on person level data to support appropriate allocation of limited resources to those most in need: in any economic circumstance, but particularly when resources are constrained by economic pressures, needs based solutions to funding through proven casemix methodologies provide an equitable approach to resource allocation.

Notes

1. The authors of the chapter wish to acknowledge the following interRAI fellows for their contribution: Vincent Mor, Brant Fries, President of interRAI; Pálmi Jónsson; Harriet Finne-Soverei; Anja Declercq; Roberto Bernabei; Iris Chi; Nigel Miller; and contributions from Graziano Onder; Andrew Downes; Anna Bjorg Aradottir; Ingibjorg Hjaltadottir; and Johanna De Almeida Mello.

2. InterRAI instruments are intimately dependent on computerisation, since an integral feature is the suite of complex algorithms that generate scales, assessment protocols, resource use casemix products etc. Some software packages developed to deliver the interRAI system include full care planning, rostering and staffing tools and links to knowledge databases, features that are not interRAI products.

3. Trigger – have assessed care needs that trigger a CAP which draws the attention of the care provider to a matter that should be considered in the care plan and provides guidance on the specific issues that should be addressed

4. Some of the differences between United States and other nursing home sites regarding the RUGs distribution may be a function of the US sampling strategy, which would favour new admissions that tend to receive more post-acute care services.

5. The goals of care are specified in the interRAI Falls CAP: Identify and change underlying risk factors for falls; Promote activity in a safe manner and in a safe environment. Recognise common pathways among falls, incontinence, and functional decline. Fall prevention is not an isolated goal but part of a larger objective of promoting physical activity and improved quality of life.

References

Berg, K., V. Mor, J. Morris, K.M. Murphy, T. Moore and Y. Harris (2002), "Identification and Evaluation of Existing Nursing Homes Quality Indicators", *Health Care Financing Review*, Vol. 23, pp. 19-36.

Bjorkgren, M.A., B.E. Fries, A. Arbor and L.R. Shugarman (2000), "A RUG-III Casemix System for Home Care", *Canadian Journal on Aging 2000*, Vol. 19 (Suppl. 2), pp. 106-125.

Bos, J.T., D.H. Frijters, C. Wagner, G.I. Carpenter et al. (2007), "Variations in quality of Home Care between sites across Europe, as measured by Home Care Quality Indicators", *Aging Clinical and Experimental Research*, Vol. 19, No. 4, pp. 323-329, August.

Brand, C.A., M. Martin-Khan, O. Wright et al. (2011), "Development of Quality Indicators for Monitoring Outcomes of Frail Elderly Hospitalised in Acute Care Health Settings: Study Protocol", *BMC Health Services Research*, Vol. 11:281, 20 October.

Burrows, A.B., J.N. Morris, S.E. Simon, J.P. Hirdes and C. Phillips (2000), "Development of a Minimum Data Set-based Depression Rating Scale for Use in Nursing Homes", *Age and Ageing*, Vol. 29, No. 2, pp. 165-172.

Calliope (CALL for InterOPErability) Network (2011), "European eHealth Interoperability Roadmap – Final European Progress Report", Belgium, retrieved at *www.epractice.eu/en/library/5318244*.

Carpenter, G.I., N. Ikegami, G. Ljunngren, E. Carrillo and B.E. Fries (1997), "RUG-III and Resource Allocation: Comparing the Relationship of Direct Care Rime with Patient Characteristics in Five Countries", *Age and Ageing*, Vol. 26-S2, pp. 61-65.

Carpenter, G.I., G.F. Teare, K. Steel, K. Berg, K. Murphy, J. Bjornson, P.V Jonsson and J.P. Hirdes (2001), "A New Assessment for Elders Admitted to Acute Care: Reliability of the MDS-AC", *Aging Clinical and Experimental Research*, Vol. 13, pp. 316-330.

Carpenter, G.I., S. Gill et al. (1999), "A Comparison of MDS/RAI Activity of Daily Living, Cognitive Performance and Depression Scales with Widely Used Scales", *Age and Ageing*, Vol. 28(S2), p. 29.

Carpenter, G.I., G. Gambassi, E. Topinkova et al. (2004), "Community Care in Europe: The Aged in Home Care Project (AdHOC)", *Aging Clinical and Experimental Research*, Vol. 16, pp. 259-269.

Department of Health (2012), "The Power of Information. Putting All of Us in Control of the Health and Care Information We Need", London, retrieved at *www.dh.gov.uk/prod_consum_dh/groups/dh_digitalassets/@dh/@en/documents/digitalasset/dh_134205.pdf*.

Feng, Z., J. Hirdes, T. Smith, H. Finne Soveri et al. (2009), "Use of Physical Restraints and Antipsychotic Medications in Nursing Homes: A Cross-national Study", *International Journal of Geriatric Psychiatry*, Vol. 24, pp. 1110-1118.

Folstein, M.F., S.E. Folstein and P.R. McHugh (1975), "Mini-mental State. A Practical Method for Grading the Cognitive State of Patients for the Clinician", *Journal of Psychiatric Research*, Vol. 12, No. 3, pp. 189-198.

Fries, B.E., S.E. Simon, J.N. Morris, C. Flodstrom and F.L. Bookstein (2001), "Pain in U.S. Nursing Homes: Validating a Pain Scale for the Minimum Data Set", *The Gerontologist*, Vol. 41, No. 2, pp. 173-179.

Fries, B.E., D.P. Schneider, W.J. Foley, M. Gavazzi, R. Burke and E. Cornelius (1994), "Refining a Case-mix Measure for Nursing Homes: Resource Utilisation Groups (RUG-III)", *Medical Care*, Vol. 32, pp. 668-685.

Fries, B.E., C.J. Fahey, C. Hawes, B.C. Vladeck, J. Morris, C. Phillips, H. Fredeking, J. Hirdes, D.G. Sinclair, J.T. King et al. (2003), "Implementing the Resident Assessment Instrument: Case Studies of Policymaking for Long-term Care in Eight Countries", Milbank Memorial Fund, p. 129.

Hawes, C. (1990), "The Institute of Medicine Study: Improving Quality of Care in Nursing Homes", in P. Katz, R.L. Kane and M. Mezey (eds.), *Advances in Long-term Care*, Springer, New York.

Hirdes, J.P., B.E. Fries, J.N. Morris, K. Steel, V. Mor, D. Frijters, S. LaBine, C. Schalm, M.J. Stones, G. Teare et al. (1999), "Integrated Health Information Systems Based on the RAI/MDS Series of Instruments", *Health Manage Forum*, Vol. 12, No. 4, pp. 30-40.

Hirdes, J.P. et al. (2002a), "A System for Classification of Inpatient Psychiatry (SCIPP): A New Case Mix Methodology for Mental Health", Joint Policy and Planning Committee, Toronto.

Hirdes, J.P., T.F. Smith, T. Rabinowitz, K. Yamauchi, E. Perez, N.C. Telegdi, P. Prendergast, J.N. Morris, N. Ikegami, C.D. Phillips et al. (2002b), "The Resident Assessment Instrument-Mental Health (RAI-MH): Inter-rater Reliability and Convergent Validity", *Journal of Behavioral Health Services & Research*, Vol. 29, pp. 419-432.

Hirdes, J.P., G. Ljunggren, J.N. Morris, D.H. Frijters, H. Finne Soveri, L. Gray, M. Björkgren and R. Gilgen (2008), "Reliability of the InterRAI Suite of Assessment Instruments: A 12-country Study of an Integrated Health Information System", retrieved at *www.biomedcentral.com/1472-6963/8/277*.

Hirdes, J.P., D.H. Frijters and G.F. Teare (2003), "The MDS-CHESS Scale: A New Measure to Predict Mortality in Institutionalized Older People", *Journal of American Geriatrics Society*, Vol. 51, No. 1, pp. 96-100.

Hirdes, J.P., B.E. Fries, J.N. Morris, N. Ikegami et al. (2004), "Home Care Quality Indicators (HCQIs) Based on the MDS-HC", *The Gerontologist*, Vol. 44, No. 5, pp. 665-679, October.

Hirdes, J.P., M. Marhaba, T.F. Smith et al. (2001), "Development of the Resident Assessment Instrument – Mental Health (RAI-MH) Resident Assessment Instrument-Mental Health Group", *Hospital Quarterly*, Vol. 4, No. 2, pp. 44-51, Winter.

Hirdes, J.P. (2006), "Addressing the Health Needs of Frail Elderly People: Ontario's Experience with an Integrated Health Information System", *Age and Ageing*, Vol. 35, No. 4, pp. 329-331, July.

Huang, Y. and G.I. Carpenter (2011), "Identifying Elderly Depression Using the Depression Rating Scale as Part of Comprehensive Standardised Care Assessment in Nursing Homes", *Aging and Mental Health*, Vol. 15, No. 8, pp. 1045-1051.

Institute of Medicine (1986), "Improving the Quality of Care in Nursing Homes", National Academy of Sciences Press, Washington, DC.

Jones, R.N., J.P. Hirdes, J.W. Poss, M. Kelly, K. Berg, B.E. Fries and J.N. Morris (2010), "BMC Adjustment of Nursing Home Quality Indicators", *Health Services Research*, Vol. 15, 10:96, April.

Kane, R.A. and R.L. Kane (1981), Assessing *the Elderly: A Practical Guide to Measurement*, Lexington, United States.

Kinsella, K. and W. He (2009), *An Aging World: 2008*, US Department of Commerce, Washington.

Lincoln Centre for Ageing and Community Care Research (2004), "The Review and Identification of an Existing, Validated, Comprehensive Assessment Tool", retrieved at *www.health.vic.gov.au/subacute/assess.pdf*.

Mahoney, F. and D. Barthel (1965), "Functional Evaluation: The Barthel Index", *Maryland Medical Journal*, Vol. 14, pp. 61-65.

Martin, L., B.E. Fries, J.P. Hirdes and M. James (2011), "Using the RUG-III Classification System for Understanding the Resource Intensity of Persons with Intellectual Disability Residing in Nursing Homes", *Journal of Intellectual Disabilities*, Vol. 15, No. 2, pp. 131-141, June.

Martin, L., J.P. Hirdes, B.E. Fries and T.F. Smith (2007), "Development and Psychometric Properties of an Assessment for Persons with Intellectual Disability – The interRAI ID", *Journal of Policy and Practice in Intellectual Disabilities*, Vol. 4, pp. 23-29.

McDonald, A.J.D. and G.I. Carpenter (2003), "The Recognition of Dementia in 'Non-EMI' Nursing Home Residents in South East England", *International Journal of Psychology*, Vol. 18, pp. 105-108.

Milbank Memorial Fund (2003), "Implementing the Resident Assessment Instrument:Case Studies of Policymaking for Long-Term Care in Eight Countries", retrieved at *www.milbank.org/uploads/documents/interRAI/ResidentAssessment_Mech2.pdf*.

Mor, V., K. Branco, J. Fleishman, C. Hawes, C. Phillips, I. Morris and B. Fries (1995), "The Structure of Social Engagement Among Nursing Home Residents", *Journals of Gerontology Series B-Psychological Sciences & Social Sciences*, Vol. 50, pp. P1-P8.

Mor, V., O. Intrator, B.E. Fries, C. Phillips, J. Teno, J. Hiris, C. Hawes and J. Morris (1997), "Changes in Hospitalization Associated with Introducing the Resident Assessment Instrument", *Journal of the American Geriatrics Society*, Vol. 45, No. 8, pp. 1002-1010.

Mor, V., J. Angelelli, D. Gifford, J. Morris and T. Moore (2003), "Benchmarking and Quality in Residential and Nursing Homes: Lessons from the US", *International Journal of Geriatric Psychiatry*, Vol. 18, No. 3, pp. 258-266, March.

Mor, V., J. Angelelli, R. Jones, J. Roy, T. Moore and J. Morris (2003a), "Inter-rater reliability of nursing home quality indicators in the U.S.", BMC Health Services Research, Vol. 4, No. 3(1), p. 20, November.

Mor, V., K. Berg, J. Angelelli, D. Gifford, J. Morris and T. Moore (2003b), "The Quality of Quality Measurement in U.S. Nursing Homes", *The Gerontologist*, Vol. 43, Spec. No. 2, pp. 37-46.

Mor, V. (2005), "Improving the Quality of Long-term Care with Better Information", *Milbank Quarterly*, Vol. 83, No. 3, pp. 333-364.

Morris, J., C. Hawes, B.E. Fries, C. Phillips, V. Mor and S. Katz (1990), "Designing the National Resident Assessment System for Nursing Homes", *The Gerontologist*, Vol. 30, No. 3, pp. 293-307.

Morris, J.N., B.E. Fries, K. Steel, N. Ikegami, R. Bernabei, G.I. Carpenter et al. (1997), "Comprehensive Clinical Assessment in Community Setting – Applicability of the MDS-HC", *Journal of the American Geriatrics Society*, Vol. 45, pp. 1017-1024.

Morris, J.N., S. Nonemaker, K. Murphy, C. Hawes, B.E. Fries, V. Mor and C. Phillips (1997), "A Commitment to Change: Revision of HCFA's RAI", *Journal of the American Geriatrics Society*, Vol. 45, No. 8, pp. 1011-1016, August.

Morris, J.N., B.E. Fries, D.R. Mehr, C. Hawes, C.D. Phillips, V. Mor and L.A. Lipsitz (1994), "MDS Cognitive Performance Scale", *Journal of Gerontology*, Vol. 49, pp. 174-182.

Morris, J.N., B.E. Fries and S.A. Morris (1999), "Scaling ADLs within the MDS", *Journals of Gerontology Series A: Biological Sciences and Medical Sciences*, Vol. 54, No. 11, pp. 546-553.

OECD (2007), *Reviews of Risk Management Policies: Sweden – The Safety of Older People*, OECD Publishing, Paris, *http://dx.doi.rg/ 10.1787/9789264027077-en*.

Onder, G., I. Carpenter, H. Finne-Soveri, J. Gindin, D. Frijters, J.C. Henrard, T. Nikolaus, E. Topinkova et al. (2012), "Assessment of Nursing Home Residents in Europe: The Services and Health for Elderly in Long-term Care (SHELTER) Study", *BMC Health Services Research*, Vol. 12, No. 5, *www.biomedcentral.com/1472-6963/12/5*.

Pattie, A.H. and C.J. Gilleard (1979), "Manual of the Clifton Assessment Procedures for the Elderly (CAPE)", Hodder and Stoughton Educational, Sevenoaks, United Kingdom.

Poss, J.W., N.M. Jutan, J.P. Hirdes, B.E. Fries, J.N. Morris, G.F. Teare and K. Reidel (2008), "A Review of Evidence on the Reliability and Validity of Minimum Data Set Data", *Health Management Forum*, Vol. 21, No. 1, pp. 33-39, Spring.

Rubenstein, E., L.Z. Wieland and D. Bernabei (1995), *Geriatric Assessment Technology – The State of the Art*, Editris Kurtis, Milan.

Steel, K., G. Ljunggren, E. Topinkova, J.N. Morris, C. Vitale, J. Parzuchowski, S. Nonemaker, D.H. Frijters, T. Rabinowitz, K.M. Murphy et al. (2003), "The RAI-PC: An Assessment Instrument for Palliative Care in All Settings", *American Journal of Hospice & Palliative Care*, Vol. 20, pp. 211-219.

Stratton, R.J., A. Hackston, D. Longmore, R. Dixon, S. Price, M. Stroud, C. King and M. Elia (2004), "Malnutrition in Hospital Outpatients and Inpatients: Prevalence, Concurrent Validity and Ease of Use of the 'Malnutrition Universal Screening Tool' ('MUST') for Adults", *British Journal of Nutrition*, Vol. 92, No. 05, pp. 799-808.

Yesavage, J.A., T.L. Brink, T.L. Rose et al. (1982), "Development and Validation of a Geriatric Depression Screening Scale: A Preliminary Report", *Journal of Psychiatric Research 198283*, Vol. 17, No. 1, pp. 37-49.

Zimmerman, D.R., S.L. Karon, G. Arling, B.R. Clark, T. Collins, R. Ross and F. Sainfort (1995), "Development and Testing of Nursing Home Quality Indicators", *Health Care Financing Review*, Vol. 16, No. 4, pp. 107-127, Summer.

ANNEX 3.A1

*Reference tables from nine OECD
and non-OECD countries and regions using interRAI*

Table 3.A1.1. Demographics/Demographic data and prevalence of common diseases in nursing home (NH) and home (community) care (HC) populations

Characteristic	Ontario, Canada		Michigan, United States		Iceland		Finland		United Kingdom		Belgium		Italy		Hong Kong, China		New Zealand	
	NH (N=90 115)	HC (N=w152 558)	NH (N=83 893)	HC (N=14 621)	NH (N=2 307)	HC (N=)	NH (N=5 699)	HC (N=13 041)	NH (N=481)	HC (N=250)	NH (N=765)	HC (N=4 070)	NH (N=3 661)	HC (N=2 417)	NH (N=3 016)	HC (N=103 001)	NH (N=)	HC (N=11 163)
	%	%	%	%	%	%	%	%	%	%	%	%	%	%	%	%	%	%
Female	69.9	65.3	67.0	69.5	66.1	–	73.4	71.8	72.1	74.4	75.9	68.4	69.4	63.5	65.3	–	–	60.3
Age group																		
< 65	6.2	17.5	13.6	25.9	2.6	–	4.1	9.5	4.2	0	4.3	5.6	4.7	8.2	3.7	–	–	4.7
65-74	9.4	14.9	16.2	21.4	7.8	–	11.6	13.3	10.6	18.3	10.4	16	11.2	11.1	19.2	–	–	18.4
75-84	32.1	34.2	32.7	31.1	31.3	–	34.8	39	33.7	41.9	38.6	48.5	37.1	37.4	38.8	–	–	43.6
85+	52.3	33.5	37.5	24.0	58.3	–	49.5	38.2	51.6	39.8	46.7	29.9	47.1	43.4	38.4	–	–	32.4
Married																		
Male	42.9	58.3	44.1	34.5	37.8	–	–	50.7	37.3	41.9	42.5	59.8	32.1	65	56.2	–	–	–
Female	16.0	28.5	20.0	17.2	17.8	–	–	49.3	11.2	15.3	12.6	27.3	11.7	25.7	15.1	–	–	–
Both sexes	24.1	38.8	27.9	22.4	19.5	–	15.7	17.6	18.5	22.1	19.7	37.6	17.8	40.1	29.4	–	–	37
Diagnosis																		
Alzheimers disease or other dementia	56.3	19.3	38.1	25.1	62.1	–	64.7	29.9	30.9	12.1	46.4	15.6*	53.3	33.5	25.1	21.4	–	21
Heart failure	12.4	11.4	27.0	30.6	16	–	13	19.5	6.4	20.4	28.2	9.9	13.3	25	9.6	18.1	–	17
Emphysema or other chronic obstructive pulmonary disease (COPD)	14.4	16.9	23.0	23.6	10.2	–	4.2	11.2	6	13.5	9.7	4.2	19.9	17	5.5	11.2	–	19

Table 3.A1.1. Demographics/Demographic data and prevalence of common diseases in nursing home (NH) and home (community) care (HC) populations (cont.)

Characteristic	Ontario, Canada NH (N=90115) %	Ontario, Canada HC (N=w152558) %	Michigan, United States NH (N=83893) %	Michigan, United States HC (N=14621) %	Iceland NH (N=2307) %	Iceland HC (N=) %	Finland NH (N=5699) %	Finland HC (N=13041) %	United Kingdom NH (N=481) %	United Kingdom HC (N=250) %	Belgium NH (N=765) %	Belgium HC (N=4070) %	Italy NH (N=3661) %	Italy HC (N=2417) %	Hong Kong, China NH (N=3016) %	Hong Kong, China HC (N=103001) %	New Zealand NH (N=) %	New Zealand HC (N=11163) %
Diabetes	25.0	26.3	33.9	37.4	14.1	–	18	26	14.8	14.2	18	10.3	21.7	19	24.1	25.9	–	19
Cancer	8.9	15.0	8.7	9.9	8.5	–	7.1	6.9	12.7	6.6	7.4	4.7	10.2	15.1	5.4	6.7	–	11.1
Stroke	21.2	17.0	15.9	22.5	22.7	–	10.5	8.2	26.4	25.3	19.8	12.3	20.7	15.8	29.1	32.0	–	18

Note: For the Belgian nursing home (NH) data, about 20% of cases have missing values for diagnosis. For those cells, rates are computed based on non-missing cases only. This table offers a demonstration of potential for cross-national comparisons using data from the interRAI assessment system in nine OECD and non-OECD countries.

Source: New Zealand: National New Zealand interRAI Software Service (on behalf of New Zealand District Health Boards); Belgium: BelRAI-data, Federal Public Service Health, Food chain safety and Environment; Iceland: The Icelandic data is on all skilled NH's in Iceland from a national data base on NH care, as per MDS 2.0. The supervisor of the data base is the Director General for Health in Iceland and the data base is maintained by Stiki ehf, data warehouse company; Italy: Italy are obtained from the Umbria region; Michigan, United States: Nursing home: from Michigan MDS 2.0 – the federally mandated assessment instrument for nursing homes – for 10/1/09 – 9/30/10); Home care: Michigan Home- and Community-Based Waiver interRAI HC data – the State-run community-based home care program (MI CHOICE) for persons in need of care at the nursing home level (Calendar year 2010); Hong Kong, China: RAI-HK HC data, SWD Elderly Services, HK SAR Government.

Table 3.A1.2. **CAPs (Client Assessment Protocols)/Prevalence of clinical syndromes as indicated by the prevalence of triggered CAPs in nursing home (NH) and home (community) care (HC) populations**

Clinical assessment protocol	Ontario, Canada		Michigan, United States		Iceland		Finland		United Kingdom		Belgium		Italy		Hong Kong, China		New Zealand	
	NH (N=90 115)	HC (N=152 558)	NH (N=83 893)	HC (N=14 621)	NH (N=)	HC (N=)	NH (N=5 699)	HC (N=13 041)	NH (N=481)	HC (N=250)	NH (N=765)	HC (N=4 070)	NH (N=3 661)	HC (N=2 417)	NH (N=3 016)	HC (N=103 001)	NH (N=)	HC (N=)
	%	%	%	%	%	%	%	%	%	%	%	%	%	%	%	%	%	%
ADL CAP																		
Facilitate improvement	30.6	13.2	69.1	23.3	–	–	36.0	15.8	18.3	15.6	29.4	25.9	27	30.1	4.0	7.3	–	–
Prevent decline	44.2	22.7	24.1	28.8	–	–	39.0	11.6	52.6	0	34.3	9.8	45	28.6	42.1	38.9	–	–
Communication CAP																		
Facilitate improvement	11.1	6.8	17.4	5.6	–	–	9.1	12.4	10.6	3.4	8.1	8.6	6.7	10.7	8.1	7.7	–	–
Prevent decline	23.0	11.6	6.1	17.9	–	–	31.1	13.9	23.1	16.9	27.3	13.1	25.8	19.7	10.6	0.4	–	–
Delirium CAP	10.1	1.9	33.9	4.1	–	–	7.4	5.1	14.8	9	15.6	15.8	24.8	26.6	3.8	3.4	–	–

Table 3.A1.2. CAPs (Client Assessment Protocols)/Prevalence of clinical syndromes as indicated by the prevalence of triggered CAPs in nursing home (NH) and home (community) care (HC) populations (cont.)

Clinical assessment protocol	Ontario, Canada NH (N=90 115) %	Ontario, Canada HC (N=152 558) %	Michigan, United States NH (N=83 893) %	Michigan, United States HC (N=14 621) %	Iceland NH (N=) %	Iceland HC (N=) %	Finland NH (N=5 699) %	Finland HC (N=13 041) %	United Kingdom NH (N=481) %	United Kingdom HC (N=250) %	Belgium NH (N=765) %	Belgium HC (N=4 070) %	Italy NH (N=3 661) %	Italy HC (N=2 417) %	Hong Kong, China NH (N=3 016) %	Hong Kong, China HC (N=103 001) %	New Zealand NH (N=) %	New Zealand HC (N=) %
Restraints CAP																		
Unable to perform early/mid-loss ADLs	16.0	n.a.	0.3	n.a.	–	–	22.3	n.a.	0.6	n.a.	13.5	n.a.	16.1	n.a.	20.7	n.a.	–	–
Able to perform early/mid-loss ADLs	1.6	n.a.	1.1	n.a.	–	–	2.4	n.a.	0	n.a.	1.8	n.a.	1.6	n.a.	3.5	n.a.	–	–
Cardiorespiratory CAP	11.6	40.5	15.1	53.5	–	–	27.0	47.0	18.1	38.2	37.5	38.4	39	53.5	8.3	33.5	–	–

Notes: The ADL CAP (Activities of Daily Living Client Assessment Protocol): triggered where there is potential to improve performance or prevent avoidable functional decline in persons who already have some ADL deficits. Examples of the characteristics of those who are in the "Facilitate improvement" group are shown in Box 3.2 of the report. The aim of care for these resident is a) to manage the new onset acute problem and work to return the person to his or her pre-acute functional level and b) watch to ensure the person does not enter a cycle of spiraling ADL decline. Persons who are in the "Prevent decline" group have the attributes listed in Box 3.2, but only one of the ten clinical items is present. The principal approach to care for these residents is a) Institute a plan of care to help the person preserve current ADL self-sufficiency levels and b) to watch for the onset of acute health problems or new medications that could drive ADL decline (for example, delirium, change in cognition, pneumonia, new hospitalisation) and treat or respond in the earliest phase. The onset of such acute problems will be the principal force that drives functional decline in the months ahead

Communication CAP: Triggered where there is potential to work to improve communication ability or prevent avoidable communication decline.

Delirium CAP: Triggered when a person has active symptoms of delirium.

Restraints CAP: Identifies persons who are physically restrained. Those in the "Unable to perform early/Mid-loss ADLs" group (e.g. personal hygiene, dressing, and walking) are more likely to have a history of falls and behavioural problems than the subgroup not triggered. About 70% of these persons have severe cognitive loss and a like number are unable to walk or use a wheelchair. About 40% will be unable to sit upright on their own, over one-quarter will have severe problems in seeing or understanding others, and about 15% will be tube fed. With effective restraint reduction programmes, few, if any, such persons will require restraints. Those in the "Able to perform early/mid loss ADLs" group tend to be restrained because of concerns about falling, wandering, and behavioural problems (for example, resisting care, physical abuse, or socially inappropriate behaviour). About one in five restrained persons will fall into this group. Organisations with effective restraint reduction programmes have been able to eliminate restraints in caring for such persons.

Cardiorespiratory CAP: Alerts the health care professional to the need to assess and manage the person for possible cardiovascular or respiratory problems.

This table offers a demonstration of potential for cross-national comparisons using data from the interRAI assessment system in nine OECD and non-OECD countries.

Source: New Zealand: National New Zealand interRAI Software Service (on behalf of New Zealand District Health Boards); Belgium: BelRAI-data, Federal Public Service Health, Food chain safety and Environment; Iceland: The Icelandic data is on all skilled NH's in Iceland from a national data base on NH care, as per MDS 2.0. The supervisor of the data base is the Director General for Health in Iceland and the data base is maintained by Stiki ehf, data warehouse company; Italy: Italy are obtained from the Umbria region; Michigan, United States: Nursing home: from Michigan MDS 2.0 – the federally mandated assessment instrument for nursing homes – for 10/1/09 – 9/30/10); Home care: Michigan Home- and Community-Based Waiver interRAI HC data – the State-run community-based home care program (MI CHOICE) for persons in need of care at the nursing home level (Calendar year 2010); Hong Kong, China: RAI-HK HC data, SWD Elderly Services, HK SAR Government.

Table 3.A1.3. Scales/Physical impairment, cognitive impairment, severity of depressive symptoms and severity of pain in nursing home (NH) and home (community) care (HC) populations

Scale name	Ontario, Canada		Michigan, United States		Iceland		Finland		United Kingdom		Belgium		Italy		Hong Kong, China		New Zealand	
	NH (N=90 115)	HC (N=152 558)	NH (N=83 893)	HC (N=14 621)	NH (N=2 307)	HC (N=)	NH (N=5 699)	HC (N=13 041)	NH (N=481)	HC (N=250)	NH (N=765)	HC (N=4 070)	NH (N=3 661)	HC (N=2 417)	NH (N=3 016)	HC (N=103 001)	NH (N=)	HC (N=11 163)
	%	%	%	%	%	%	%	%	%	%	%	%	%	%	%	%	%	%
Cognitive performance scale																		
0	15.2	44.4	34.6	33.2	4.9	–	4.9	35.0	21.4	52.6	17.7	41.5	7.6	24.2	36.0	10.3	–	38.3
1-2	26.4	44.2	26.3	40.3	17.6	–	16.8	37.6	28.5	26.3	21.6	27.3	30.4	27.3	26.9	83.0	–	31.6
3-4	33.4	7.3	30.2	15.9	30.1	–	35.5	21.8	20.8	9.3	33.6	20.9	21.5	14.0	18.4	5.0	–	25.1
5-6	25.0	4.2	8.8	7.5	47.4	–	42.8	5.7	29.5	8.0	27.1	10.3	40.5	34.5	18.6	1.7	–	5.0
ADL hierarchy																		
0	7.9	62.6	2.3	41.3	–	–	2.8	72.2	6.9	67.8	7.9	23.4	5.6	10.6	42.5	53.7	–	65.3
1-2	17.1	24.0	19.0	26.6	–	–	15.2	17.7	ore	11.1	12.8	24.4	16.1	8.4	12.0	38.0	–	22.3
3-4	38.2	10.0	57.1	20.3	–	–	28.7	8.4	20.8	16.6	46.8	41.1	31.6	27.6	12.1	7.6	–	9.3
5-6	36.8	3.4	21.6	9.6	–	–	53.4	1.8	64.7	4.5	32.5	11.1	46.6	53.5	33.4	0.8	–	3.1
Depression rating scale																		
0	34.1	60.5	61.3	60.6	33.4	–	35.0	62.9	39.3	>2	31.1	46.1	37.9	49.9	83.2	64.8	–	60.5
1-2	33.0	23.1	29.8	24.0	42.1	–	34.1	20.9	28.3	26.3	30.3	24.6	28.1	20.3	13.6	27.6	–	23.4
3+	32.9	16.4	8.8	15.4	24.5	–	30.9	16.3	32.2	g	38.6	29.3	34.0	29.8	3.3	7.6	–	16.1

Table 3.A1.3. Scales/Physical impairment, cognitive impairment, severity of depressive symptoms and severity of pain in nursing home (NH) and home (community) care (HC) populations (cont.)

Scale name	Ontario, Canada		Michigan, United States		Iceland		Finland		United Kingdom		Belgium		Italy		Hong Kong, China		New Zealand	
	NH	HC	NH	HC	NH	HC	NH	HC	NH	HC	NH	HC	NH	HC	NH	HC	NH	HC
	(N=90 115)	(N=152 558)	(N=83 893)	(N=14 621)	(N=2 307)	(N=)	(N=5 699)	(N=13 041)	(N=481)	(N=250)	(N=765)	(N=4 070)	(N=3 661)	(N=2 417)	(N=3 016)	(N=103 001)	(N=)	(N=11 163)
	%	%	%	%	%	%	%	%	%	%	%	%	%	%	%	%	%	%
Pain scale																		
0	57.5	32.4	39.8	28.4	24.5	–	51.0	38.7	63.2	29.4	ges	50.0	77.9	63.5	72.4	48.8	–	40.4
1-2	39.6	53.8	56.1	51.0	63.9	–	45.6	53.9	34.1	51.6	37.0	40.6	20.2	31.0	21.5	46.6	–	45.9
3	3.0	13.8	4.0	13.5	11.6	–	3.3	7.5	2.7	19.0	4.3	9.3	1.9	5.5	6.1	4.6	–	13.7

Cognitive Performance Scale: Combines information on memory impairment, level of consciousness, and executive function, with scores ranging from 0 (intact) to 6 (very severe impairment). Scores of 3 or greater indicate likely presence of dementia (www.interrai.org/assets/files/Scales/Cognitive%20Performance%20Scale.pdf).

ADL (activities of daily living) hierarchy groups activities of daily living according to the stage of the disablement process in which they occur. Early loss ADLs (for example, dressing) are assigned lower scores than late loss ADLs (for example, eating). The ADL Hierarchy ranges from 0 (no impairment) to 6 (total dependence). (www.interrai.org/assets/files/Scales/ADL%20Hierarchy.pdf).

Depression rating scale: Used as a clinical screen for depression. Scores of 3 or greater indicate likely presence of major or minor depressive disorders (www.interrai.org/assets/files/Scales/Depression%20Rating%20Scale.pdf).

Pain scale: Uses two items to create a score from 0 to 3. It has been shown to be highly predictive of pain as measured by the Visual Analogue Scale (www.interrai.org/assets/files/Scales/Pain%20Scale.pdf).

This table offers a demonstration of potential for cross-national comparisons using data from the interRAI assessment system in nine OECD and non-OECD countries.

Source: New Zealand: National New Zealand interRAI Software Service (on behalf of New Zealand District Health Boards); Belgium: BelRAI-data, Federal Public Service Health, Food chain safety and Environment; Iceland: The Icelandic data is on all skilled NH's in Iceland from a national data base on NH care, as per MDS 2.0. The supervisor of the data base is the Director General for Health in Iceland and the data base is maintained by Stiki ehf, data warehouse company; Italy: Italy are obtained from the Umbria region; Michigan, United States: Nursing home: from Michigan MDS 2.0 – the federally mandated assessment instrument for nursing homes – for 10/1/09 – 9/30/10); Home care: Michigan Home- and Community-Based Waiver interRAI HC data – the State-run community-based home care program (MI CHOICE) for persons in need of care at the nursing home level (Calendar year 2010); Hong Kong, China: RAI-HK HC data, SWD Elderly Services, HK SAR Government.

Table 3.A1.4. Casemix/Distribution of populations in nursing home (NH) and home (community) care (HC) populations by the clinical groups of the Resource Utilisation Groups (RUGs) resource use casemix system

RUG-III hierarchical groups[1]	Ontario, Canada NH (N=90115) %	Ontario, Canada HC (N=152558) %	Michigan, United States NH (N=83893) %	Michigan, United States HC (N=14621) %	Iceland NH (N=2307) %	Iceland HC (N=) %	Finland NH (N=5699) %	Finland HC (N=13041) %	United Kingdom NH (N=481) %	United Kingdom HC (N=250) %	Belgium NH (N=765) %	Belgium HC (N=) %	Italy NH (N=3661) %	Italy HC (N=2417) %	Hong Kong, China NH (N=3016) %	Hong Kong, China HC (N=103001) %	New Zealand NH (N=) %	New Zealand HC (N=11163) %
Rehabilitation	15.0	3.7	65.0	9.6	19.2	–	2.6	1.8	1.6	1.0	43.5	–	0.0	1.1	17.0	4.7	–	6.7
Extensive services	1.6	0.7	4.0	2.2	3.2	–	1.1	0.3	0.0	0.7	1.0	–	10.8	11.4	0.1	0.0	–	0.4
Special care	9.0	1.6	3.5	5.3	9.8	–	8.0	4.4	10.3	1.0	5.5	–	21.1	8.9	1.8	0.7	–	1.0
Clinically complex	16.5	22.0	9.4	44.5	19.5	–	16.9	1.4	20.7	31.1	11.5	–	20.1	32.5	21.7	40.1	–	18.8
Impaired cognition	10.8	7.3	4.4	8.3	13.5	–	16.3	20.4	6.6	4.8	13.5	–	9.6	2.8	8.5	1.1	–	19.4
Behaviour problems	2.8	1.2	0.1	0.9	1.6	–	2.8	6.3	2.7	1.7	2.0	–	2.0	0.4	0.4	6.7	–	0.7
Physical function reduced	44.3	63.5	13.6	28.9	33.1	–	52.2	55.4	57.8	59.5	23.0	–	36.3	42.9	50.5	46.6	–	53.2

1. Group: Outline of the clinical criteria for each group.
Rehabilitation group: Those receiving rehabilitation services
Extensive services: Physically dependent and requiring high intensity services parenteral feeding, suctioning, tracheostomy, ventilator/respirator.
Special care: Physically dependent and with clinical conditions associated with high nursing care input.
Clinically complex: Presence of clinical conditions that are associated with medical conditions.
Impaired cognition: Intermediate physical impairment and significant cognitive impairment.
Behaviour problems: Intermediate physical impairment and disruptive behavioural symptoms.
Physical function reduced: Those who do not match any of the above criteria.
For full explanation of the RUGs Casemix system see:
Fries, B.E., D.P. Schneider, W.J. Foley, M. Gavazzi, R. Burke and E. Cornelius (1994), "Refining a Case-mix Measure for Nursing Homes: Resource Utilisation Groups RUG-III", *Medical Care*, Vol. 32, pp. 668-685.
Carpenter, G.I., A. Main and G. Turner (1995), "Case Mix for the Elderly In-patient. Resource Utilisation Groups (RUGs) Validation Project", *Age and Ageing*, Vol. 24, pp. 513.
Carpenter, G.I., N. Ikegami, G. Ljunngren, E. Carrillo and B.E. Fries (1997), "RUG-III and Resource Allocation: Comparing the Relationship of Direct Care Time with Patient Characteristics in Five Countries", *Age and Ageing*, Vol. 26-S2, pp. 61-65.
Bjorkgren, M.A., B.E. Fries, A. Arbor and L.R. Shugarman (2000), "A RUG-III Casemix System for Home Care", *Canadian Journal on Aging*, Vol. 19, Suppl. No. 2, pp. 106-125.
This table offers a demonstration of potential for cross-national comparisons using data from the interRAI assessment system in nine OECD and non-OECD countries.

Source: New Zealand: National New Zealand interRAI Software Service (on behalf of New Zealand District Health Boards); Belgium: BelRAI-data, Federal Public Service Health, Food chain safety and Environment; Iceland: The Icelandic data is on all skilled NH's in Iceland from a national data base on NH care, as per MDS 2.0. The supervisor of the data base is the Director General for Health in Iceland and the data base is maintained by Stiki ehf, data warehouse company; Italy: Italy are obtained from the Umbria region; Michigan, United States: Nursing home: from Michigan MDS 2.0 – the federally mandated assessment instrument for nursing homes – for 10/1/09 – 9/30/10); Home care: Michigan Home- and Community-Based Waiver interRAI HC data – the State-run community-based home care program (MI CHOICE) for persons in need of care at the nursing home level (Calendar year 2010); Hong Kong, China: RAI-HK HC data, SWD Elderly Services, HK SAR Government.

Table 3.A1.5. **Casemix/Prevalence of clinical and social indicators by physical and cognitively impaired sub-groups in nursing home (NH) and home (community) care (HC) populations**

Sub-groups[1]	Characteristic	Ontario, Canada NH (N=90115)	Ontario, Canada HC (N=152558)	Michigan, United States NH (N=83893)	Michigan, United States HC (N=14621)	Finland NH (N=5699)	Finland HC (N=13041)	United Kingdom NH (N=481)	United Kingdom HC (N=250)	Belgium NH (N=765)	Belgium HC (N=4070)	Italy NH (N=3661)	Italy HC (N=2417)	Hong Kong, China NH (N=3016)	Hong Kong, China HC (N=103001)	New Zealand NH (N=)	New Zealand HC (N=11163)
		%	%	%	%	%	%	%	%	%	%	%	%	%	%	%	%
Good physical condition/Good cognition (ADLH 0-1/CPS 0-1)	% (N) in this sub-population	8.3 (6,210)	50.2 (76,636)	3.6 (2,985)	32.2 (4714)	3.5 (202)	49.2 (6416)	7.3 (35)	58.1 (168)	8.9 (68)	24.0 (975)	5.8 (213)	11.3 (272)	36.3 (1096)	38.7 (39881)	–	46.9 (5222)
	Uncontrolled pain	20.7	17.5	34.3	11.5		19.5	0	19	10.8	11.8	1.9	5.1	12.2	9.6	–	16.5
	Falls (any in past 90 days)	16.5	26.6	11.6	21	5.5	21.3	14.3	31	11.3	30.3	9.4	8.4	9.3	29.1	–	27.7
	Any use of trunk restraint/chair prevents rising	0	n.a.	0	n.a.	0	n.a.	0	n.a.	0.1	n.a.	2.8	n.a.	0.2	n.a.	–	n.a.
	Bladder incontinence daily or more freq.	9.4	10.2	1.7	28.6	13.9	12.9	17.1	15.5	25.9	21.38	7	9.5	1.1	1	–	17.6
	Pressure ulcers (any > grade 1)	1.1	1.7	2.7	2	1.5	2	0	2.4	4.7	2.2	0.5	4	0.3	0.4	–	0.9
	No flu shot in past year	n.a.	27.1	n.a.	22.1	n.a.	34.1	25.7	19	7.8	23.6	17.8	16.4	–	44.2	–	23.6
	Lonely	n.a.	13.7	n.a.	18.7	n.a.	24.2	8.6	36.3	26.5	37.1	15	15	–	28.8	–	19.4
	Depression (DRS > 2)	15.7	12.4	5.3	9.3	21.3	11.9	17.1	20.2	20.2	24.9	26.8	19.3	2.1	8.1	–	n/a
Poor physical condition/Good cognition (ADLH 2+/CPS 0-1)	% (N) in this sub-population	17.9 (13,418)	10.9 (16,608)	40.7 (34,177)	21.7 (3171)	10.1 (574)	5.6% (726)	27.7 (133)	14.5 (42)	21.2 (162)	34.8 (1417)	19.6 (717)	28.8 (696)	14.0 (421)	9.2 (9460)	–	8.2 (916)
	Uncontrolled pain	25.5	21.5	39	13	25.3	27.1	4.5	33.3	14.5	9.6	3.5	8.8	18.5	10.7	–	17
	Falls (any in past 90 days)	21.4	35.2	11.9	24.4	8	26.9	5.3	23.8	32.1	36.6	29.1	16.8	11.9	37.1	–	33.2
	Any use of trunk restraint/chair prevents rising	5	n.a.	0.2	n.a.	9.2	n.a.	0	n.a.	8.2	n.a.	5.3	n.a.	19.2	n.a.	–	n.a.
	Bladder incontinence daily or more freq.	52	22	15.1	43.7	62.7	37.3	64.7	11.9	41.18	30.52	41	31.2	39.9	0.9	–	32.4
	Pressure ulcers (any > grade 1)	6.8	5.2	11.1	9	4.7	5.9	6	7.1	7.1	2.9	9.5	16.7	2.9	6.1	–	4
	No flu shot in past year	n.a.	31.7	n.a.	30.6	n.a.	36.8	29.3	33.3	10.3	17.8	12.4	14.2	–	45.6	–	32.2
	Lonely	n.a.	11.1	n.a.	17.8	n.a.	19.2	21.8	28.6	35.1	29.6	11.2	10.8	–	27.5	–	15
	Depression (DRS > 2)	28.3	18.3	5.8	12.7	29.6	19	30.8	23.8	27.5	22.8	32.6	30	3.6	7.3	–	n/a

Table 3.A1.5. Casemix/Prevalence of clinical and social indicators by physical and cognitively impaired sub-groups in nursing home (NH) and home (community) care (HC) populations (cont.)

Sub-groups[1]	Characteristic	Ontario, Canada NH (N=90 115)	Ontario, Canada HC (N=152 558)	Michigan, United States NH (N=83 893)	Michigan, United States HC (N=14 621)	Finland NH (N=5 699)	Finland HC (N=13 041)	United Kingdom NH (N=481)	United Kingdom HC (N=250)	Belgium NH (N=765)	Belgium HC (N=4 070)	Italy NH (N=3 661)	Italy HC (N=2 417)	Hong Kong, China NH (N=3 016)	Hong Kong, China HC (N=103 001)	New Zealand NH (N=)	New Zealand HC (N=11 163)
		%	%	%	%	%	%	%	%	%	%	%	%	%	%	%	%
Good physical condition/Poor cognition (ADLH 0-1/CPS 2+)	% (N) in this sub-population	5.7 (4,295)	23.0 (35,061)	2.9 (2,442)	19.4 (2840)	5.7 (322)	35.2 (4586)	2.1 (10)	12.8 (37)	5.1 (39)	11.1 (453)	3.5 (127)	2.3 (55)	10.9 (329)	30.4 (31313)	–	30.4 (3385)
	Uncontrolled pain	13.5	11.9	8.4	9.6	11.8	15.1	0	24.3	2.2	5.7	0.8	1.8	8.5	5.5	–	9
	Falls (any in past 90 days)	19.5	33.4	20.7	26.3	6.8	25.8	20	27	23.8	34.7	12.6	14.5	13.1	31	–	28.9
	Any use of trunk restraint/ chair prevents rising	0.1	n.a.	0	n.a.	0	n.a.	0	n.a.	0	n.a.	1.6	n.a.	3.7	n.a.	–	n.a.
	Bladder incontinence daily or more freq.	11.1	15.3	4.9	38	12.7	16.7	30	5.4	23.9	26.1	13.4	27.3	5.5	2	–	19.9
	Pressure ulcers (any > grade 1)	0.8	0.7	0.9	1.3	1.2	1.3	0	0	0	2.5	0.8	5.5	0	0.4	–	0.8
	No flu shot in past year	n.a.	24.3	n.a.	24.2	n.a.	34.1	20	27	8.1	25.9	12.6	27.3	–	38.9	–	29.9
	Lonely	n.a.	16.4	n.a.	22	n.a.	32	10	35.1	25	32.2	10.2	27.3	–	24.9	–	19.9
	Depression (DRS > 2)	27.8	19.8	12	20.4	32	19.1	0	29.7	39.1	42.4	29.9	38.2	4.6	8.6	–	n/a
Poor physical condition/Poor cognition (ADLH 2+/CPS 2+)	% (N) in this sub-population	68.0 (50,926)	15.9 (24,253)	52.8 (44,289)	26.7 (3896)	80.7 (4,601)	10.1 (1,313)	62.8 (302)	14.5 (42)	64.8 (496)	30.1 (1,225)	71.1 (2,604)	57.6 (1,392)	38.8 (1170)	21.7 (22,347)	–	14.7 (1640)
	Uncontrolled pain	15.7	12	14.1	7.5	19	19.9	2.6	14.3	10.7	8.2	1.7	5	7.4	5.2	–	12
	Falls (any in past 90 days)	28.4	39.7	21.1	28.9	6.6	34.4	6.3	45.2	28.7	41.8	19.9	14.5	9.3	30.8	–	37.7
	Any use of trunk restraint/ chair prevents rising	23.1	n.a.	2.7	n.a.	18.7	n.a.	1	n.a.	19.9	n.a.	23.1	n.a.	54.2	n.a.	–	n.a.
	Bladder incontinence (daily or more freq.)	77.2	46.5	50.9	66.5	85.6	55.5	85	57.1	66.2	47.4	67.8	60.5	76.3	41.8	–	55.7
	Pressure ulcers (any > grade 1)	6.4	3.2	10.5	7.9	4	3.7	8.9	21.4	8.1	1.2	20.5	27.1	4.3	8.5	–	3.7

Table 3.A1.5. Casemix/Prevalence of clinical and social indicators by physical and cognitively impaired sub-groups in nursing home (NH) and home (community) care (HC) populations (cont.)

Sub-groups[1]		Ontario, Canada		Michigan, United States		Finland		United Kingdom		Belgium		Italy		Hong Kong, China		New Zealand	
	Characteristic	NH	HC	NH	HC	NH	HC	NH	HC	NH	HC	NH	HC	NH	HC	NH	HC
		(N=90115)	(N=152558)	(N=83893)	(N=14621)	(N=5699)	(N=13041)	(N=481)	(N=250)	(N=765)	(N=4070)	(N=3661)	(N=2417)	(N=3016)	(N=103001)	(N=)	(N=11163)
		%	%	%	%	%	%	%	%	%	%	%	%	%	%	%	%
	No flu shot in past year	n.a.	27	n.a.	26.4	–	29.2	20.9	26.2	7.6	21.2	12.6	11.8	–	50.1	–	33.3
	Lonely	n.a.	9.4	n.a.	15.3	–	27	15	14.3	29.8	28.6	9.3	10.1	–	17.3	–	11.2
	Depression (DRS >2)	34.5	22	11.3	21.2	31.4	25.9	35	26.2	44	36.7	35.1	31.5	3.9	5.2	–	n/a

1. Sub-groups are created by dividing the population into physical function groups – good (interRAI Cognitive Performance Score 0-1) or poor (interRAI Cognitive Performance Score ≥ 2), and combining them to give four distinct sub-groups. The ADL hierarchy groups activities of daily living according to the stage of the disablement process in which they occur. The ADL hierarchy ranges from 0 (no impairment) to 6 (total dependence) (www.interrai.org/asets/files/scales/ADLhierarchy.pdf).

Cognitive performance scale: Combines information on memory impairment, level of consciousness, and executive function, with scores ranging from 0 (intact) ɔ6 (very severe impairment). Scores of 3 or greater indicate likely presence of dementia (www.interrai.org/assets/files/Scales/Cognitive Performance Scale.pdf).

This table offers a demonstration of potential for cross-national comparisons using data from the interRAI assessment system in nine OECD and non-OECD countries.

Source: New Zealand: National New Zealand interRAI Software Service (on behalf of New Zealand District Health Boards); Belgium: BelRAI-data, Federal Public Service Health, Food chain safety and Environment; Iceland: The Icelandic data is on all skilled NH's in Iceland from a national data base on NH care, as per MDS 2.0. The supervisor of the data base is the Director General for Health in Iceland and the data base is maintained by Stiki ehf, data warehouse company; Italy: Italy are obtained from the Umbria region; Michigan, United States: Nursing home: from Michigan MDS 2.0 – the federally mandated assessment instrument for nursing homes – for 10/1/09 – 9/30/10); Home care: Michigan Home- and Community-Based Waiver interRAI HC data – the State-run community-based home care program (MI CHOICE) for persons in need of care at the nursing home level (Calendar year 2010); Hong Kong, China: RAI-HK HC data, SWD Elderly Services, HK SAR Government.

PART II

Policies to drive quality
in long-term care

PART II

Chapter 4

Regulation to improve quality in long-term care

by

Yuki Murakami

and
Francesca Colombo,
OECD Health Division

The complexity of care services means that identifying the most appropriate policy approaches to drive long-term care quality can be challenging. This chapter and the next two review the approaches and policies used by OECD and EU countries to promote care quality. Three approaches are identified: 1) imposing external regulatory controls to safeguard and control quality; 2) developing standards to standardise care practice and monitor indicators to ensure that care outcomes match desired levels; and 3) stimulating quality improvement through the use of market-based incentives directed at providers and users, including the use of performance-based financial incentives and competition among care providers. This chapter focuses on external regulatory controls such as the development of minimum standards, licensing or accreditation of facilities and training requirements for workers. Standardisation policies and the use of incentives to drive quality will be analysed in the next two chapters.

There has been an evolution in policy approaches to encourage quality in long-term care

Evidence of elderly abuses, misuse of care, opaqueness of living conditions in nursing and home-care settings, have all called into question the ability of self-regulation by care providers to lead to optimal care services. Left to self-regulation, there can be a tendency for care providers to provide low-quality services to ill-informed care recipients. However, the complexity of care services, which include a mix of health and social care, involvement of family carers, and users' moving across settings, challenges the identification of the most appropriate policy approaches to drive quality in LTC.

This chapter and the two following chapters review the range of policies and instruments that OECD countries have set up to drive quality in LTC. These can be broadly classified into three groups, reflecting, to some extent, the way different policy approaches to LTC quality are evolving. A first step to overcome poor incentives or the failure of providers to self-regulate is to impose certain external regulatory controls in order to safeguard and control quality. These are typically focused on controlling inputs (labour, infrastructure) by setting minimum acceptable standards, and then enforcing compliance. A second approach is to develop standards seeking to standardise care practice in desirable ways, and then monitor quality indicators to ensure that care outcomes match the desired objectives. A third approach is to stimulate quality improvement through the use of market-based incentives directed at providers and at users, including the use of financial incentives and the encouragement of competition among care providers based on performance measures. Table 4.1 provides a summary.

This chapter focuses specifically on the first cluster. It starts by describing the legislative framework for protecting old people and safeguarding care. Essentially, regulatory oversight involves setting external controls over nursing homes and, in some cases, home care and assisted living facilities. Such oversight begins with the regulation of physical and human resources employed in the care process. This can be accompanied by standards prescribing structural and procedural requirements. The assumption is that because providers are accredited and licensed to practise, they will meet the terms of the requirements, even if regulation does not interfere with care providers' decisions or choices regarding care practices, processes and approaches. Compliance can be audited and the public can be informed about the fact that providers meet set standards. Results or details of the assessment and inspection processes and not necessarily diffused publicly.

Table 4.1. **Quality policies: Inputs, monitoring and standardisation, system improvement**

Policy/Instrument
Regulation and control over inputs
Care quality and elderly protection legislation
Minimum quality standards
Accreditation and certification of providers and organisations
Facilities auditing
Qualification and certification of workforce
Monitoring and standardisation of processes
Needs assessment, care planning
Practice guidelines
Policies for monitoring user outcomes,
Policies for monitoring user satisfactions (e.g., consumer surveys, etc.)
Policies for public reporting of outcomes and performance
System improvement through incentives
Pay for performance
User direction and choice
User protection policies and instruments (such as ombudsmen)
Public reporting and grading
Integration and co-ordination polices
Use of ICT

Source: Authors for the OECD.

Legislation sets the framework underpinning oversight of care quality

In all OECD countries and EU countries, the central government has an overarching responsibility for ensuring the effectiveness and safety of care for elderly and disabled people, principles that are typically embedded into legislation. Legislation aims to ensure that older people have the right to access quality care, receive the appropriate care, and exercise choice and control over care arrangements. It also defines the role of providers in ensuring the quality of services and duties such as reporting, as well as the minimum standards expected from providers (Table 4.2). In some countries, such as Australia, Iceland, and Sweden, legislation sets specific rights for self-determination, fair funding, quality care from skilled workers, protection against abuse, and the legal duty to report any witnessed abuse of elderly or dependant persons. With a growing prevalence of dementia and Alzheimer's, some EU and OECD countries have enacted specific dementia acts, which include principles of safeguard of safety and effectiveness of care.

Most OECD countries regulate LTC system inputs, although the way they do differs widely across countries, especially concerning LTC workers qualifications and skills level. While ultimately, the main goal of regulation is to guarantee accountability for resources invested in care processes, generally speaking government seeks to achieve three main objectives:

● guide providers and facilities on how to improve quality and safety of services;

● inform service users and their families as to what they can reasonably expect from a service; and

● inform regulators on various aspects of care provision, helping to identify gaps.

While the central government is the principle regulator of LTC quality, many countries assign the responsibility for implementing quality control and monitoring compliance to a range of decentralised bodies, sub-national governments, or arm's length organisations. Almost a third of OECD countries have decentralised the governance of LTC to state, regional or local level authorities, which are responsible for providing and supervising the quality of providers (Colombo et al., 2011).

Several OECD and EU countries have charged national or regional oversight bodies with the task of monitoring the level of LTC quality and compliance with regulations. In Germany, for example, responsibilities for quality assurance have been traditionally assigned to provider bodies, such as the medical advisory service of the Federal Association of Health Insurance Funds and its operative units on the regional level. These are responsible for training medical doctors and specialist nurses who assess the needs of applicants for LTC benefits, as well as carrying out quality inspections (Leichsenring, 2010). In the Netherlands, each LTC institution reports on an annual basis to the Healthcare Inspectorate (IGZ), which has an advisory and monitoring role. In Portugal, five regional co-ordinating teams monitor compliance according to minimum standards for providers participating in the continuous care programme and produce annual audits. All providers are required to report quality indicators (UMCCI, 2011). In the United States, federal law gives each state the responsibility for monitoring the quality of care in its nursing homes and other LTC settings (Capitman et al., 2005). This can result in cross-state differences in the enforcement of quality monitoring and improvement.

Table 4.2. Legislation concerning LTC quality, responsible bodies

	Legislation addressing LTC quality	Responsibility for regulating LTC quality	Responsibility for monitoring compliance and controls	A national framework addressing LTC and quality
Australia	1997 Age care Act, 1997 Quality of Care Principles, 1997 User Rights Principles	Central government	States	Yes (based on Living Longer Living Better)
Austria	15a B-VG Agreement between the federal state and the provinces (1993), Health Reform Act of 2005, Health Quality Act	Federal Ministry of Labour, Social Affairs and Consumer Protection, the Federal, Ministry of Health		
Belgium	Arrêté royal fixant les normes pour l'agrément spécial comme maison de repos et de soins, comme centre de soins de jour ou comme centre pour lésions cérébrales acquises	Federal and regional government	Regional	
Canada	Protection for Persons in Care Act (Ontario, 2010), Long-Term Care Homes Act (Ontario, 2007), Ontario Regulation 79/10 (2010), Act Respecting Health Services and Social Services (Québec), Nursing Homes Act (New Brunswick), Co-ordinated Home Care Act (Nova Scotia)	Provinces and territories, Health Quality Councils at provinces		No, but yes by region
Croatia	Act of Social Welfare (Narodne novine, No. 33/2012) and Strategic plan of the Ministry of Social Policy and Youth		Social welfare centres and independent body for administrative supervision and inspection, petitions, complaints and co-ordination of the social welfare system	Strategic plan of the Ministry of Social Policy and Youth
Czech Republic	2007 Act on Social Services (Social Services Act No. 108/2006)	Ministry of Health, Ministry of Labour and Social Affairs		
Denmark	Act on Social Services	Municipalities		National framework of mechanisms to monitor quality in the elderly care has been developed
Estonia	Labour Contract Act, Social Welfare Act, Health Insurance Act	Government	Estonian Health Insurance Fund (EHIF).	
Finland	The Act on the Status and Rights of Patients and The Act on the Status and Rights of Social Welfare Clients, Health Care Act (No. 1326/2010), and The Act on Services for the Aged (presented to the Parliament in Oct 2012)	Central government for accreditation and supervision, municipalities for implementation and funding	Municipalities, National Supervisory Authority	National Framework for High-Quality Services for Older People
France	APA (20/07/2001) par la loi n° 2001-647, PCH (11/02/2005)	Ministry of Social Affairs, Ministry of Labour	National Agency for Assessing LTC Organisations (ANESM)	
Greece	Name unknown	Ministry of Health and Social Welfare		
Germany	Act on Residential Homes (Heimgesetz) and the Act on Long-Term Care Insurance (SCB XI) (2008 and 2012)	Lander and municipalities	Medical advisory services of the Federal Association of Health Insurance Funds	The 2008 and 2012 acts strengthen quality assurance mechanisms such as the co-ordination of services and auditing mechanisms acts
Hungary	Act III of 1993 on social administration and social allowances (Social Act)	Ministry of State responsible for Social, Family and Youth Affairs		

Table 4.2. **Legislation concerning LTC quality, responsible bodies** (cont.)

	Legislation addressing LTC quality	Responsibility for regulating LTC quality	Responsibility for monitoring compliance and controls	A national framework addressing LTC and quality
Iceland	Local Authorities' Social Services Act, No. 40/1991, the Act on the Affairs of the Elderly, No. 125/1999, Health Service Act	Directorate of Health, Ministry of Welfare (after the merger of the ministries of Health and of Social Affairs and Social Security on 1 Jan. 2011), the Medical Director of Health	Directorate of Health	National Health Plan
Ireland	Health Act (Care and Welfare Regulations) (2007), Health Act (Nursing Homes Support Scheme) (2007)	National government with the Health Service Executive (HSE)		National Clinical Programme for Older People (e.g. reduction of falls and access, integration of acute and community care)
Israel		Municipalities		
Italy	National Insurance Act		Regional agencies for quality assurance	National framework legislation
Japan	Long-Term Care Insurance Act	Ministry of Health, Labour and Welfare	Prefectures and municipalities	Quality standard framework for nursing homes, Public reporting system
Korea	Long-Term Care Insurance for the Elderly, National Health Insurance Act (for long-term care, hospitals), Elderly Welfare Act, Act on Health and Family Standard Ac, Act to Increase and Secure Convenience of the Disabled, Aged and Pregnant	Ministry of Health and Welfare	National Health Insurance Corporation (for Long-term care facilities) Health Insurance Review and Assessment service (for Long-term care hospitals)	Guidelines for the Protection of Human Rights and Safety Management in Welfare Facilities for the Elderly
Latvia	Law on Social Services and Social Assistance (came into force on 1 January, 2003).			
Lithuania	1. Law on Social Services dated February 20, 2006, No X-493. 2. Social Care Standards approved by the Minister of Social Security and Labour in 2007. (Order of the Minister of Social Security and Labour dated April 20, 2007, No A1-46.)	1. For social care quality are responsible social care institutions. 2. Data collection on in-patient health care quality will start form 2013 on the national level. Indicators such as incidence of pressure ulcers in LCT and user satisfaction are included to the list.	1. Department of Supervision of Social Services under the Ministry of Social Security and Labour	1. Law on Social Services, Social Care Standards, Licencing Rules of Social Care Establishments. 2. Lithuanian health system's development framework for 2011-20.
Malta		Superintendence of Public Health	Department for Health Care Standards, Department of the Elderly and Community Care	
Netherlands		Healthcare Authority depending on the Ministry of Health, Welfare and Sport		Quality Framework for Responsible Care
New Zealand	Health and Disability Services (Safety) Act 2001			

A GOOD LIFE IN OLD AGE? MONITORING AND IMPROVING QUALITY IN LONG-TERM CARE © OECD/EUROPEAN COMMISSION 2013

Table 4.2. Legislation concerning LTC quality, responsible bodies (cont.)

	Legislation addressing LTC quality	Responsibility for regulating LTC quality	Responsibility for monitoring compliance and controls	A national framework addressing LTC and quality
Norway	Municipal Health and Care Services Act, Patient's and User's Rights Act	Local authorities		
Poland	Law on health care units (1991 and amended), Law on health care benefits financed from public sources (2004, amended 2009), Law on the nursing and midwifery professions (1996), Law on social assistance (1990, significantly changed in 2004),	Central government and Territorial governments		
Portugal	The Directive related to Quality policy and strategy	Ministry of Health and the Ministry of Labour and Social Solidarity		
Turkey		Ministry of Health, Ministry of Family and Social Policies and their related agencies		
Slovak Republic	Act on Social services	Ministry of Labour, Social Affairs and family		
Slovenia		Ministry of Labour, Family and Social Affairs and Ministry of Health		
Spain	Law 39/2006, Common Criteria on Accreditation	Autonomous Region and the Central Administration, for Ceuta and Melilla		
Sweden	Social Services Act (1982, 2009), Health and Medical Services Act and the Social Services Act (2010)	Municipalities	National Board of Health and Welfare	National Strategy of eHealth
Switzerland	National Health Insurance Law; additionally laws on the level of cantons	Federal Department of Home Affairs; cantons	Health insurance providers and cantons	Yes (see first column)
United Kingdom	Health and Social Care Act (2008)	Department of Health	Care Quality Commission	
United States	Omnibus Budget Reconciliation Act (1987)	States	States	

Source: OECD compilation based on country replies to the OECD 2009-2010 Questionnaire on Long-Term Care Workforce and Financing and OECD 2012 Questionnaire on Long-Term Care Quality.

Regulation of long-term care institutions through accreditation and standard settings

Accreditation recognises that a facility meets certain criteria

Regulatory oversight involves setting external controls over nursing homes and, in some cases, home care and assisted living facilities. Nearly all OECD countries require LTC institutions to be officially licensed (United States), registered (e.g. England), or certified. Generally, this procedure tends to be based on minimum requirements to minimise the risk that nursing homes operate in unsafe or underperforming conditions (Box 4.1). The set of requirements and procedures tends to be similar across countries, even if the term used varies, ranging from licence, to registration, and certification.

Box 4.1. Different forms of official recognition for the operation of LTC services in a selection of OECD countries

Registration and licensure. This is often a requirement for market entry. In England, the Care Quality Commission registers nursing homes, assisted living and home care services if they meet government standards. If they are not registered, they will not be able to provide services. This procedure usually follows a uniform and standardised form across the country but a set of requirements might vary depending on different care settings. In Iceland, any individual or entity wishing to operate nursing homes has to meet a set of certain criteria requested by the Medical Director of Health. A decision for licensure is made based on the submitted documents and the same procedure will be repeated for the renewal of such licensure.

Certification and accreditation. Accreditation bodies are often not-for-profit, but can be private. They are independent bodies that carry out an external peer review process to assess and improve services based on standards of "excellence". They, therefore, examine organisations and providers regularly and consistently, and promote greater uniformity of practice within organisations, allowing benchmarking comparisons across organisations (Wagner et al., 2012). Countries may define certification and accreditation differently. In the United States, there is a distinction between accreditation, a voluntary process with the Joint Commission, and certification, a condition for receiving federal funding. Other countries use certification synonymous with the license and registration of operations and services.

In addition to such official recognition, it is not uncommon for regulators to require additional quality conditions to be met by institutions, in some cases as a condition for public funding. This chapter uses the terms "accreditation" and "certification" to refer to these sets of requirements that are above minimum obligations for practising. Accreditation involves an evaluation process that assesses quality of care and services provided in LTC intuitions, and sometimes assisted living facilities, and gives recognition that providers are competent, comply with the regulations and meet certain quality standards in their services. The purpose of accreditation is to encourage quality and safety through a mix of compliance and quality elements, which can extend to continuous quality improvement. National accreditation bodies are often independent authorities, and can be private (e.g., Australia), although most often they are public bodies. More than two-thirds of the 27 OECD and EU countries reviewed have systems in place to accredit LTC institutions (Table 4.3).

Table 4.3. Accreditation, registration and certification of LTC providers

	Accreditation, registration or certification	Providers being accredited/ certified	Accreditation organisation	Standards	Is accreditation/ registration/ certification mandatory or precondition for reimbursement/ contract?	Voluntary accreditation body	Inspection
Australia	Accreditation	Institutions, assisted living, home	Aged Care Standards and Accreditation Agency Ltd (for residential aged care homes), state or territory governments or the Department of Health and Ageing (for community care)	Effective management, appropriate access and service delivery, service user rights and responsibilities, management systems, staffing and organisational development, health and personal care, resident lifestyle, physical environment and safe systems	Yes for residential aged care homes		
Austria	Registration				Yes	Third party audits are then provided in the context of the still voluntary Austrian "National Quality Certificate" for care homes.	
Belgium	Accreditation	Institutions	National and regional		Yes, but not precondition		
Canada	Accreditation	Varies by province, but, in general, institutions, assisted living and home	Varies by province and Canadian Council on Health Service Accreditation		Yes/No	Accreditation Canada	
Denmark	Accreditation	Institutions and home care providers	National body	The local council is required to set up and publish quality standards and price requirements that must be observed by all suppliers of personal and practical assistance.	No		
Finland	Accreditation	Institutions, assisted living, home care services	National Supervisory Authority Valvira	Personnel, facilities, management systems, self-regulatory procedure	Mandatory		Regional supervisory authorities, municipalities
France	Accreditation	Residential care and home care providers	ANESM	Privacy, confidentiality, co-ordination of work, organisation of a high-quality reception, tailoring operations, clarity and quality in the offer of the service, operation methods, monitoring and evaluating operations, selection and qualification of staff and workers,	Yes		
Germany	Accreditation	Institutions and home-based care	Insurance funds	Qualified personnel, adequate wages for employees, quality management system introduced, use of expert standards.	Yes		

Table 4.3. Accreditation, registration and certification of LTC providers (cont.)

	Accreditation, registration or certification	Providers being accredited/ certified	Accreditation organisation	Standards	Is accreditation/ registration/ certification mandatory or precondition for reimbursement/ contract?	Voluntary accreditation body	Inspection
Iceland	Certification	Nursing homes	Medical Director of Health	Type of health service, personnel, equipment and premises	Yes		As needed? Directorate of Health
Ireland	Registration	Nursing homes	Health Information and Quality Authority	Rights, protection, health and social care needs, quality of life, staffing, the care environment, governance and management, and dementia-specific residential care units for older people	Yes		
Italy	Accreditation	Residential and semi-residential institutions	States	Structural, technological and organisational requirements	Yes (but not enforced)		
Japan	Certification and Registration	All the service providers who get LTC fee covered by LTC Insurance	Prefecture, Municipality	Human Resources, Complaints and protection, Management and administration, quality of care	Yes		Yes
Korea	Accreditation for Long-term care hospitals	Long-term care hospitals	Korean Institute for Healthcare Accreditation	Now on process	Not yet		
Japan	Certification	Residential care, assisted living, and home care providers	Ministry of Health, Labour and Welfare	Human Resources, Complaints and protection, Management and administration, quality of care	Yes		
Lithuania	Licensure	(From 2015) All establishments of social care (From 2013) voluntary licensure	1. Department of Supervision of Social Services under the Ministry of Social Security and Labour. 2. State Health Care Accreditation Agency under the Ministry of Health.	1. Social Care Standards (Order of the Minister of Social Security and Labour, 2007). 2. Regulation on Supporting treatment and nursing services approved by the Minister of Health in 2012. Regulation on Nursing services in out-patient health care institutions and at home is approved by the Minister of Health in 2007. Regulation on Palliative care services for adults and children approved by the Minister of Health in 2007.	Yes, from 2015 to obtain the license is necessary. From 2013, establishments of social care could licence voluntary.	Yes, institutions can implement self – assessment, according to Social Care Standards.	1. Minimum once per five years The Department of Supervision of Social Services under the Ministry of Social Security assesses and inspects social care standards in institutions. 2. State Health Care Accreditation Agency performs planned and unplanned inspections in health care providing institutions.
Malta	Licensure	Homes for older people	Licensing Authority (Superintendent of Public Health)		Valid licence is a precondition for contracts		Annually by Health Care Standards Directorate within the Superintendence of Public Health

Table 4.3. **Accreditation, registration and certification of LTC providers** (cont.)

	Accreditation, registration or certification	Providers being accredited/ certified	Accreditation organisation	Standards	Is accreditation/ registration/ certification mandatory or precondition for reimbursement/ contract?	Voluntary accreditation body	Inspection
Netherlands	Accreditation	Institutions and home-based care	Dutch Institute for Accreditation in Hospitals; Harmonisation of quality review in health care and welfare	Client's perceptions, outcomes for informal care, service utilisation, care workers' qualifications and satisfactions, and clinical outcomes	Yes but not precondition		
Norway							
Portugal							
Spain	Accreditation	All the service providers (including private entities)	Territorial Council	Material resources and equipment, human resources	Yes		
Sweden	In the process of initiation	LTC institutions					
Switzerland	Certification (only in some cantons, but no uniform model)	Nursing homes	Private organisations	Varying standards for each certification model	Only in some cantons mandatory	Private organisations	
United Kingdom	Registration	Registration for residential care, assisted living, and home care providers	Care Quality Commission	Involvement and information, Personalised care, treatment and support, Safeguarding and safety, Suitability of staffing, Quality and management, Suitability of management,	Yes		
United States	Accreditation	Institutions, assisted living, home	Joint Commission		No	Joint Commission	
	Certification		States, but federal governed sets the requirements	Resident rights, admission, transfer and discharge, quality of life, services, environment, nutrition and administration	No but precondition		
	Accreditation, registration or certification	Providers being accredited/certified	Accreditation organisation	Standards	Is accreditation/ registration/ certification mandatory or precondition for reimbursement/ contract?	Voluntary accreditation body	Inspection

Source: OECD compilation based on country replies to the OECD 2009-2010 Questionnaire on Long-Term Care Workforce and Financing and OECD 2012 Questionnaire on Long-Term Care Quality.

The accreditation process usually involves self-assessment by care providers, a review of performance against certain standards set by the accreditation body, and the monitoring of ongoing performance against such standards. Generally speaking, the process involves both an internal and external review. During the internal review, providers and facilities draw up documentation describing aspects of the services under question or work through the list of accreditation criteria. The external review is usually carried out by a government authority or an independent body that evaluates providers and facilities against a set of quality criteria. An assessor or a team of assessors carry out a desk review, make an on-site visit and conduct a comprehensive assessment that, in some countries, involves interviewing LTC residents, staff, and family members.

Safety requirements and workforce standards are a common feature of accreditation standards. In Australia, accreditation criteria cover the management systems; the physical and human resources employed in the care process; the safety of the physical environment; and the lifestyle or quality of life of LTC recipients (see Box 4.2). In the United States, accreditation requirements set by the non-governmental Joint Commission accreditation (which is a

---

Box 4.2. Accreditation standards in Australia

In **Australia**, the Australian Aged Care Quality Agency (replacing the Aged Care Standards and Accreditation Agency) manages accreditation. According to Aged Care Act of 1997, all services, with the exception of the 11 multipurpose services, are required to be accredited (The Aged Care Branch of the Department of Human Services, Victoria, 2004). Accreditation is the arrangement established by the Australian Government to verify that nursing homes provide quality care and services for residents. Without accreditation a provider is not eligible to receive a residential care subsidy from the government. In order to receive Australian Government subsidies, providers of residential, community and flexible LTC services are required to seek approved provider status.

Residential care. The Aged Care Standards and Accreditation Agency Ltd. is an independent accreditation body under the Aged Care Act 1997 and the Accreditation Grant Principles 2011. The Agency is responsible for managing the accreditation process and for the ongoing monitoring for residential care services. The Agency assesses performance of residential aged-care homes against a set of legislated standards into four main areas, which consists of a total of 44 expected outcomes. There is a greater focus on outcomes of care and support in their standards. Residential aged care homes must comply with all 44 expected outcomes. The majority of services are usually awarded three years' accreditation, but a shorter period may be given, if a service is assessed as not performing well and if there is a history of non-compliance with the accreditation standards. The legislation does not specify a maximum period of accreditation. There are four accreditation standards:

1. Management systems, staffing and organisational development. This Standard concerns the management style of a care home and how it should respond to the needs of residents and their family members. Expected outcomes are that care homes should have complaint mechanisms, written visions and values, appropriately skilled and qualified staff and information systems.

2. Health and personal care. This standard refers to appropriate clinical care and specialised nursing care to meet the needs to residents, lead to safe and appropriate medication, conduce pain management and behavioural management, and others.

Box 4.2. **Accreditation standards in Australia** (cont.)

3. Resident lifestyle. This standard promotes residents' dignity and rights with expected outcomes of care to provide independence, choice, privacy and dignity, and leisure activities.

4. Physical environment and safe systems. This focuses on the physical safety of a facility to lead to a safe and comfortable environment for quality of life and welfare of residents. It regulates occupational health and safety, fire hazard, infection control and cleaning and laundry services.

Home care services. The Quality of Care Principles 1997 establishes the community care standards. Performance against these standards is monitored through the Community Care Quality Reporting Programme. The Australian government further monitors the delivery of quality care through the Charter of Rights and Responsibilities of Community Care, established under the User Rights Principles 1997. In order to integrate and standardise accreditation for community care services, (up until recently, the quality of services varied across jurisdictions), a set of common community care standards have been implemented by most jurisdictions from 2011. According to this regulation, there are 18 indicators and associated expected outcomes covering three broad standards:

1. effective management;

2. appropriate access and service delivery; and

3. service user rights and responsibilities.

Source: Aged Care Standards and Accreditation Agency Ltd. (2007); Department of Health and Ageing (2010; 2011).

---

voluntary process that many nursing homes undergo) encompass standards and safety goals (see Chapter 8). In Canada, standards for LTC facilities under Accreditation Canada focus on safe and appropriate LTC services, the workforce, the maintenance of clinical information systems and quality of life. Decisions are usually made such that organisations and providers receive "accredited", "accredited with commendation", "accredited with exemplary standing" or "not accredited" (Accreditation Canada, 2012). In France, the ANESM, a national public agency, created in response to the law on equality of rights and opportunities, set criteria for professional best practice, staff certification, and accreditation for residential care and home care providers (Naiditch and Com-Ruelle, 2011). In the Netherlands, the Centre Client Experience Care (the owner of the CQ Index) produces standards derived from the CQ Index and accredits organisations (that use CQ Index) (Steering Committee Responsible Care, 2007).

In many cases, accreditation is a precondition to access public funding, for registration in the public LTC programme or for entering into contractual arrangement with public purchasers (e.g., England, Spain, Ireland, France, Australia, Germany and Portugal; for certification in the United States). In all these countries, a large number of publicly funded LTC institutions and home care providers are accredited or certified. To the contrary, countries without such requirements face difficulties in enforcing accreditation among providers.

Once they are registered, providers are subject to inspection, assessment or review of their status. Failure to meet any of the responsibilities set out in the regulations can lead to the imposition of sanctions and the revoking of approved provider status. For example, in the United States, only nursing home facilities granted a certification of compliance by the Centers for Medicare and Medicaid are permitted to participate in Medicaid as a nursing facility or in Medicare as a skilled nursing facility (CMS, 2010). The frequency of re-accreditation and inspection varies and may not be the same as the duration of accreditation.

Inspections are more generally conducted annually or every two years, although in some cases inspections may take place only once every five years, or according to specific needs. In France, institutional care and home care providers are required to go through a re-certification process every five years (Naiditch and Com-Ruelle, 2011). In Japan, accreditation has to be renewed every six years while inspections can occur more regularly.

Even if standards and accreditation are imposed at national level, inspections and supervision can take place at sub-national level. Nursing homes in the United States must comply with national certification standards if they are to be reimbursed by Medicare or Medicaid. Because they are licensed by state governments, however, they must comply with standards set and monitored at the state level. Some countries have regional accreditation processes that may cumulate with national systems. For example, in Quebec (Canada), every institution must have a permit delivered by the minister of health and social services in the province, while a few also receive national accreditation by the Canadian Council on Health Service Accreditation. France sets rules at the national level, but enforcement takes place within each local council, and the latter can apply its own inspection methodology and criteria (Naiditch and Com-Ruelle, 2011). Variation in inspection standards across sub-national jurisdictions may be a concern in some countries.

Standards to ensure safety and effective care have extended to quality of life and dementia management

Minimum standards, often overseen by a national quality agency – and referred to as quality standards, expert standards or, simply, standards – have been used to ensure quality in LTC institutions or residential homes, although they are not compulsorily enforced by all countries. Such standards are often key elements of evaluation criteria for accreditation or authorisation to practise. They are designed to ensure minimum safety and effective care through a number of criteria around inputs (e.g., the living environment, the care workforce and financial solvency), the care process (e.g., user involvement, quality management systems, medication management) and expected outputs (e.g., rights, quality of life). They can be found in many OECD and EU countries (e.g., Austria, Australia, England, Germany, Ireland, Japan, the Netherlands, Portugal Slovenia, Spain, and the United States).

The depth of information covered in standards varies. However, there are common requirements across OECD countries. The ratio of LTC workers (nurses and/or personal carers) to LTC recipients and the number of qualified skilled workers are often included as a proxy for physical safety and functional mobility of residents. Arrangements concerning living environments are set in order to prevent accidents. Other aspects covered are administrative matters and governance of care provision. More recently, elements have included aspects beyond physical safety and functional mobility, such as quality of life of recipients, basic human rights as well as human dignity (the Netherlands, England, and the United States) and individualised care planning processes and reporting systems for adverse incidents and complaints (Ireland, United States). Some countries – e.g., England, Australia, Japan and the United States – set minimum standards or national license for managers. The English Care Standards Act requires any person who manages a nurse agency to be registered (Department of Health, 2003). In Portugal, providers are obliged by contract to have multi-disciplinary teams and local co-ordination teams.

Some examples from selected countries include:

- England's Care Standard Act and the National Minimum Standards establish basic expectations for providers of social and health care services around safety, staffing and personalised care (see Box 4.3).

- In Germany, provider authorisation to practice is based on structural standards (e.g., personnel and finances), the use of expert quality standards and a requirement to participate in a quality management system (see Box 4.6). Legislation offers a road map of the criteria to be included, while specific standards are often developed based on empirical evidence and best practice, and the involvement of service providers, LTC recipients, health care professionals, advocacy groups, and the central or regional government.

- In Ireland, the Health Information and Quality Authority produces standards for residential care services (including nursing homes), covering rights of older people, quality of life, staffing, the care environment, and the care management process.

- National quality standards for nursing homes in Australia include the following: i) rights and dignity: rights for information, consultation and participation, consent, privacy and dignity, civil, political and religious rights, complaints; ii) care effectiveness: based on assessment, care plan, prevention or health promotion, medication arrangement, end of life care; iii) quality of life: autonomy and independence, expectation, social contacts and behaviours, privacy; iv) staffing: recruitment, staffing levels and qualifications, training and supervision; v) care environment and safety: physical environment, hygiene, safety, fire hazards; vi) governance and management: operational management, quality assurance and continuous improvement, financial procedures, registration, information management system.

- In the United States, standards set by the federal government for certification span from staffing requirements to transfer or discharge. Over 150 regulatory standards including safe storage, preparation of food, and protection against elder abuse are inspected (Nursing Home Compare, 2012).

Standards specifically related to dementia care are receiving wider attention. In addition to the National Quality Standards for all residential care settings, Ireland has set criteria for dementia care that apply to those caring for people with dementia and to residential care settings exclusively hosting people with dementia. In England, quality standards set out by NICE state that people with dementia should receive care from staff appropriately trained in dementia care, while people with suspected dementia are referred to a memory assessment. People with dementia develop high levels of dependency and morbidity, as well as behavioural and psychological symptoms. Some of the challenges that LTC workers face caring for people with dementia can include aggressive behaviour, restlessness and wandering, eating problems, incontinence, delusions and hallucinations, and mobility difficulties that can lead to falls and fractures (NICE, 2012).

Some countries require organisations to use quality management systems

Among others, Germany, Spain, Slovenia, Austria and France require the use of quality management systems as part of the minimum standards (see also Chapter 7). These are internal quality assurance mechanisms to measure quality at an organisational level. Well-known quality management systems include EFQM, ISO 9000, Qualicert, E-Qalin (Box 4.4), AFNOR, Total Quality Management, and the Balanced Score Card, but which specific system should be used may not be mandated. For example, municipalities and care organisations in Finland are free to choose their quality assurance mechanism and Total Quality Management and Balanced Score Care are the most popular.

Box 4.3. **Minimum standards in England**

In England, National Minimum Standards are set to ensure that care provision meets the needs of people using LTC services. The Care Quality Commission (CQC) inspects and reviews activities of all registered care homes and home-care services to make sure they meet national minimum standards (CQC, 2011; CQC, 2012a). The CQC registers care homes and home-care service providers if they meet these standards. The CQC aims to strengthen the quality monitoring through frequent inspections and unannounced visits and by making information accessible to public (e.g. online reporting and publications such as quarterly and annual reports) (CQC, 2012b). However, compliance with the standards is not, strictly speaking, enforceable. In order to standardise processes and judgement for compliance, the CQC's produced a judgement framework to reduce variations in practices and procedures (CQC, 2012c; CQC, 2012d; CQC, 2012e; CQC, 2012f).

Minimum national standards set acceptable levels of care in six key areas including i) involvement and information (respecting, involving people use services, consent, fees), ii) personalised care, treatment and support (care and welfare of users, nutrition, co-operating with other providers), iii) safeguarding people and environment (prevention of abuse, cleanliness and infection control, management of medicine, safety and sustainability of premises and equipment), iv) staffing (sustainability, recruiting, supporting workers), v) quality and management (complaints, notifications of death and incidents and records), and vi) sustainability of management (registration of managers) (CQC, 2010).

Standards also concern managers. Registered managers have to undergo a criminal records check to proof that they are not banned from working with vulnerable adults. "Skills for Care" has introduced a core set of standards for registered managers (Skills for Care, 2012; CQC, 2012g).

Under the 2012 Health and Social Care Act, the National Institute for Health and Clinical Experience (NICE) has been give new responsibilities to develop quality standards and other guidance for social care in England, from April 2013. Currently, pilot programmes on care of people with dementia, and the health and well-being of looked-after children, are being undertaken (NICE, 2012).

Quality systems seek to engage organisations in ongoing monitoring with the aim of enhancing care processes and improving care outcomes. Larger organisations may adopt such mechanisms to comply with external requests for transparency and as a competition tool (Nies et al., 2010). However, these systems can require expensive paper work, and a long time spent writing reviews, carrying out surveys, training staff, recording outcomes and describing processes, which can lead to higher costs for service providers and reduced time spent with care recipients (Nies and Leichsenring, 2012; Capitman et al., 2005).

Accreditation and standards for home and community care are less common

Although standards for residential care settings are a relatively common practice in most countries, there is less regulation of home care and community-based care services. Minimum standards for domiciliary care are usually established separately from those for institutional care.

For example, in the Netherlands, care outside of institutions is less strictly regulated than institutional care, although the National Quality Organisation (NZA) monitors competition in the home-based nursing care sector (Mot, 2010; Anne-Wietske, 2009). In the United States, home-care agencies are required to be certified, or accredited with the Joint-Commission, in order to receive public funds by Medicare or Medicaid, but the regulatory responsibility over home care providers, and assisted living facilities, rests with the states (Chapter 8).

> ### Box 4.4. **Quality management systems in selected countries: The case of E-Qalin**
>
> In some European countries, LTC quality indicators have been introduced through the quality management system E-Qalin, which applies a bottom-up approach to establish standards and methodologies for quality management in social care (Dandi and Casanova, 2012). The system focuses on organisational development, learning and training. Staff, stakeholders and care recipients are involved. By involving all these stakeholders in self-assessment and continuous quality improvement, E-Qalin strives to strengthen the staff responsibility and their ability to co-operate across professional and hierarchical boundaries. The E-Qalin quality management system also attempts to involve residents of care homes and their relatives in quality assessment and measures for improvement, for example in specific assessment workshops or through classical satisfaction surveys.
>
> The system includes training for process managers and a self-assessment process in the organisation, during which 66 "structures and processes" criteria and 25 "results" are assessed. "Results" are considered from five different perspectives: residents, staff, leadership, social context (social accountability) and "earning organisation" (future orientation). The self-assessment process is implemented by two process managers, a steering group (with representatives of all major stakeholders (including the residents' council and/or other advocates of residents and families/friends), and specific assessment groups (Nies et al., 2010; Rupel et al., 2012).
>
> E-Qalin is increasing coverage. About 150 care homes in Austria, Germany, Italy, Luxembourg and Slovenia have introduced the model. Evaluation results have shown significant improvements in quality thinking in participating pilot organisations. Some regions in Austria have also introduced quality management systems for care homes based on E-Qalin, and in collaboration with partner countries such as Germany, Italy, Luxembourg and Slovenia (Frings et al., 2010; Leichsenring, 2010).

In Spain, any centre providing care during the day (or night), including private entities are required to be accredited in order to be able to provide care (Sistema para la Autonomía y Atención a la Dependencia, SAAD). In order to be accredited, entities must fulfil certain minimum standards (Ministry of Education, Social Policy and Sports, 2008). In France, accreditation is mandatory for agencies providing services at home and specifically for commercial agencies to access the market. Accreditation gives entitlement to specific benefits and a lower rate of social security charges. In Australia, minimum standards for home care services – including home and community care, dementia care at home and respite for carers – are monitored through the Community Care Quality Reporting Programme (Department of Health and Ageing, 2011). Standards cover effective management (e.g., risk management, regulatory compliance and continuous improvement), access (e.g., assessment, care plan, referral) and user rights (e.g., privacy, information and complaints).

Criteria for care provided at home often differ markedly from those set for institutional care. They broadly seek to regulate the extent to which a dependent person's home is adapted to their needs (e.g., the need for the installation of safety rails), and the main areas covered are safety and staffing ratios. The frequency of inspections and evaluations varies (every two years in Korea; every five years in France, Naiditch and Com-Ruelle, 2011). Australia requires that all community care providers undergo a quality review every three years.

Qualification and certification of care workers

Human resources in the LTC sector provide hands-on care, supervision and emotional support to older people with chronic illness and disabilities as well as their entourage. Formal LTC workers can be distinguished into two main categories of care providers: (registered) nurses and personal care workers. Although job content and responsibilities might be similar, the titles of personal care workers vary: ancillary workers (Australia), care assistants (Austria), social and health care assistants (Denmark), elderly carer (Germany), home helper (Japan) and auxiliary nurse (Sweden). The challenges related to LTC workforce – low pay, low qualifications, high stress and high turnover – are well documented (Colombo et al., 2011). High turnover and lack of targeted qualifications can pose challenges to the quality of services (Castle, 2008); reducing turnover, improving staff training, and empowering workers can have a positive impact on improving care quality.

The minimum approach to regulate the quality of care workers seen in most countries is to set the educational and training requirements of personal care workers (Colombo et al., 2011). These requirements set the minimum hours of theoretical and practical training, content and final certification process. Educational requirements, certification, and, ultimately, qualification of personal care workers vary significantly across countries and sometimes across sub-national jurisdictions within a country – ranging from the United States' 75 hours to Japan's three years of experience to obtain a similar job description (Table 4.4). They are not strictly regulated in all countries. In Iceland, where there is no formal certification programme for nurse assistants working in nursing homes, informal in-house education is provided to staff. Some countries have different levels of training. For example, Korea has a two-step approach requiring all applicants to complete a first training of 240 hours, before entering a second degree of training of 120 hours. A step-wise approach has also been introduced in Japan in 2012, with a view to encourage career development among LTC workers and simplify the process of LTC workers certification.

Educational requirements have been strengthened in some counties, although mostly for institutional settings. Sweden has started a four-year education programme targeting LTC staff with no formal qualifications. The initiative also aims to provide more specialised training to meet the demand of complex health and social care needs of LTC users. Municipalities successfully raising the competence level of workers are granted a financial reward at the end of the training period. In Spain, the Agreement on Common Criteria for Accreditation (2008) requires every LTC worker to obtain an appropriate professional qualification by 2015 (either a university degree, vocational degree, or suitable professional certificate). This qualification is required for facility directors, personal and home care workers. In the United States, all nurse aides who work in nursing homes receiving federal funding are required to complete a state-approved training programme and be certified as nursing aides. Japan has a qualification system for LTC workers that include requirements related to training and recertification. Since the 2011 LTC reform, the role of certified LTC workers has been expanded and they are now allowed to perform certain simple medical procedures (e.g., aspiration of sputum). According to a 2010 national survey, nursing homes welcome the use of quality indicators on staffing (such as on career development and skill improvement) and safety (accident prevention management systems).

Table 4.4. LTC workforce requirements by country

	National training available for LTC workers/minimum requirements in curriculum	Job title or category	Training content and duration
Australia	Yes/National curriculum	Ancillary worker	430 hours, five weeks in practical and theoretical training
	Yes/National curriculum	Residential aged care worker	Personal care Worker Certificate III in Aged Care: 555 hours/8 to 16 weeks. Practical and theoretical
	No/National curriculum	Specialisation for care worker	Home and Community Care CHC40208: 730-740 hours/ up to 18 weeks. Includes work placement Additional training, voluntary
Austria	Yes	Home assistants (Heimhilfe)	200 hours theoretical course, 120 hours of practical training in ambulatory working stations and 80 hours in stationary departments
	Yes	Care assistants (Pflegehilfe)	Minimum 17 years of age, mental and physical fitness. One year/1 600 hours of theoretical and practical instruction
Belgium			
Canada	No/Regional curriculum	Ontario: Personal Support worker (PSW)	PSW training programme: Two academic years (eight months), 384 hours of in class theory. 386 hours of practical experience. In-service training with employers
	No/Regional curriculum	Personal attendants	Similar to PSW programme but shorter in duration
	Yes/National curriculum	Worker of basic social care	Basic education + 150 hours expert course Duty of 24 hours of additional education annually
Czech Republic	Yes	Health assistant	(Eight years elementary school +) four years high school
		Nurse (assistant)	(Eight years elementary school +) three years high school
Denmark	Yes/National curriculum	Social and health care helper	One year seven months: 20 week basic course, 24 weeks school study, 31 weeks practical training
	Yes/National curriculum	Social and health care assistant	One year, eight months, 32 weeks school study, 48 weeks practical training periods
Estonia		Social care worker	Training of two years, of which 25% practice
Finland	National Curriculum	Long-term care worker	Vocational education, three years, 120 credits in total, with at least 29 credits of on-the-job training.
France	No/National Curriculum	Home aid (aide à domicile) Household Assistant (aide ménagère) Family and Life Assistant (auxiliaire familiale et de vie)	Qualification for Social Carer (Diplôme d'État d'auxiliaire de vie sociale): 504 hours of technical and methodo ogical training, 560 hours of practical training. Voluntary, Employer based
Greece			
Germany	No/Local (Lander) curriculum	Elderly carer	In accordance to Geriatric Nursing Act (2004), three years training programme, 200 hours theoretical training and 2 500 hours professional practice teaching.
	National curriculum	Additional institutional care workers (Betreuungskräfte)	Five day orientation internship, three modules of at least 160 hours total, plus two weeks internships

Table 4.4. LTC workforce requirements by country (cont.)

	National training available for LTC workers/minimum requirements in curriculum	Job title or category	Training content and duration
Hungary			
Iceland	Yes	Registered nurses	
	Yes	Licensed practical nurses	
Ireland	Yes/National curriculum	Care assistant for elderly	FETAC Level 5 Certificate in Healthcare Support: 36 weeks. 16 weeks training with Training and Employment Authority (FAS), 15 weeks integrated training (FAS and host employer), and five weeks on-the-job training with a host employer.
Japan	No (Regional)/National curriculum	Home care worker/LTC worker (entry level)	Total of 130 hours: of theoretical and practical instruction
	No (Regional)/National curriculum	Practical care worker	Total of 500 hours: 360 hours of theoretical instruction and 140 hours of practical training (total 450 hours since FY 2013)
	Yes/National curriculum	(Nationally) Certified care worker	– Completion of two-year programme at training facility (1 650 hours), or – Training programme in high school (1 190 hours) and State Examination for Certified Care Workers, or – Three years of experience in personal care-related occupation and State Examination for Certified Care Workers
	Yes/National curriculum	(Nationally) Certified social worker	To be eligible for State Examination for Certified Social Workers: completion of a combination of theoretical and practical training for two to four years or college/university education in care-related subject
Korea	Yes	2nd degree	120 hours dedicated training
		1st degree	240 hours dedicated training
Lithuania	Yes	Nurse Nurse assistant (helper) Social worker	In 2012, the Minister of Social Security and Labour approved the Programme of Competence trainings for the employees of social services establishments (The Order of the Minister of Social Security and Labour 2012, No. A1-303). Two years 160 h of specialisation after training as a nurse Three years (in College) Four years (in University) 160 h of specialisation after training as a nurse Requirement of education for social workers, from 1 of July 2011, stipulated in the Law on Social Services, only persons who have the acquired higher (university or non-university) education in social work or equivalent education shall be entitled to the position of a social worker.
Malta	No		Training for formal carers are provided through the government's established Malta College of Arts, Science and Technology (MCAST), the Employment and Training Corporation (ETC) and the Department of Elderly.

Table 4.4. **LTC workforce requirements by country** (cont.)

	National training available for LTC workers/minimum requirements in curriculum	Job title or category	Training content and duration
Netherlands	Yes	Care work assistant	Vocational Training Level 1: One year of training, no prior requirement. Mainly practice based
	Yes/National curriculum	Care work/social care work helper	Vocational Training Level 2: At least age 16, two years full-time assistant vocational education. Theory based
	Yes/National curriculum	Individual carer	Vocational Training Level 3: Requires preparatory intermediate vocational education (VMBO) or equivalent prior education (incl. diploma level 2); three years
Norway	Yes	Skilled Care worker (Health and Social Care Programme)	Completion of lower secondary education. 2-3 years, 50% theory, 50 GBP practice
Slovak Republic			High school for nurses. 220 hours, emphasis on practical experiences.
Spain	Yes	Carers, home carers, personal assistants and directors of institutions.	All formal workers must obtain minimum professional qualifications
Sweden	Yes/National curriculum	Auxiliary nurse	Three years – upper secondary level education
	No		Depending on programme: a few days to a month – private association training
Switzerland	National curriculum	Registered nurse	3 years
United Kingdom	Yes/National curriculum	Care and support workers	Level 3: Two years – eight units, four compulsory and four optional. Units of study vary according to educational institution.
United States	Yes/National curriculum	Home health aide	Two weeks training
	/National curriculum	Personal care assistant	No federal training requirements, fewer than a fifth have a certification requirement for PCAs and 19 states have uniform training requirements for PCAs across programmes, only 35% of states have a training hours requirement for PCAs in one or more programmes, and, of these, 68% require 40 hours or less (Paraprofessional Healthcare Institute, 2012).
	No (regional) /National curriculum	Certified nursing aide	75 hours of classroom and practical training (some states require 120 hours). Competency evaluation within four months of work.

Source: OECD compilation based on country replies to the OECD 2009-2010 Questionnaire on Long-Term Care Workforce and Financing and OECD 2012 Questionnaire on Long-Term Care Quality.

A number of training programmes are targeting improved knowledge in dementia care, a highly skilled work that is emotionally and physically demanding and requires continuous training. The 2010 US Affordable Care Act requires specific training in caring for LTC residents with dementia and in preventing abuse. In Ireland, health and social care staff in close contact with dementia patients can take specialist training programmes to improve their knowledge in dementia care. These programmes were also rolled out as part of the National Dementia Education Project throughout the Health Service Executive Centres for Nurse Education (Cahill et al., 2012).

A threat to quality might come from home settings, where qualification requirements are often less stringent. For example, the United States requires only two weeks training for workers with a high-school diploma, while 75 hours of classroom and practical training is necessary for certified nursing aides working in a federally certified nursing home. Austria requires 1 600 hours of theoretical and practical instruction for care assistants, but only 400 hours in total for home assistants (Colombo et al., 2011). In addition, qualifications are often not required or enforced during recruitment. According to data from the Netherlands, Australia, and the United States, between 17% and 60% of care workers lack the relevant qualifications, especially in home settings. Less than half of home-care workers have a relevant qualification in Germany (Colombo et al., 2011). In the United Kingdom, social care workers have a fairly low qualification level. While across OECD countries, most LTC workers operate in institutional settings (see Figure 4.3), people and government preferences for arranging care at home mean that maintaining quality standards in home settings will become a necessity.

Pre-employment checks are often used to ensure that care workers have no criminal history, have the required training, and satisfy other market entry criteria. A danger however is that significantly more resources are allocated to the pre-employment phase of ensuring a qualified LTC workforce than the post-employment phase. For example, in the United States the focus of facilities is on pre-screening applicants before employment, and there are structures and regulations in place that support this effort. However, once a worker is hired, there is less guidance regarding how best to train, continuously educate and monitor existing employees to drive quality. In the event of employees' complaints or allegations of abuse, the effectiveness of US state systems often breaks down due to a lack of co-ordination between multiple state entities involved in the investigation and reporting process.

This is an issue common to other countries. Many OECD countries do not have a process in place to monitor whether an active employee commits a fault that would have prohibited them from working during their background check prior to employment. Improving LTC quality is more about post-employment workforce policies to ensure a qualified workforce than pre-employment checks. However, most postemployment continuing education is on a voluntary basis, apart from in a few cases (Iceland requires continuing for nurses working in nursing homes and in the in United States nurse aides must complete 12 hours of continuing education annually).

Figure 4.1. **More than half of care workers operate in institutional settings in most countries**

Care workers per 1 000 population aged 65 years old and over (head counts)

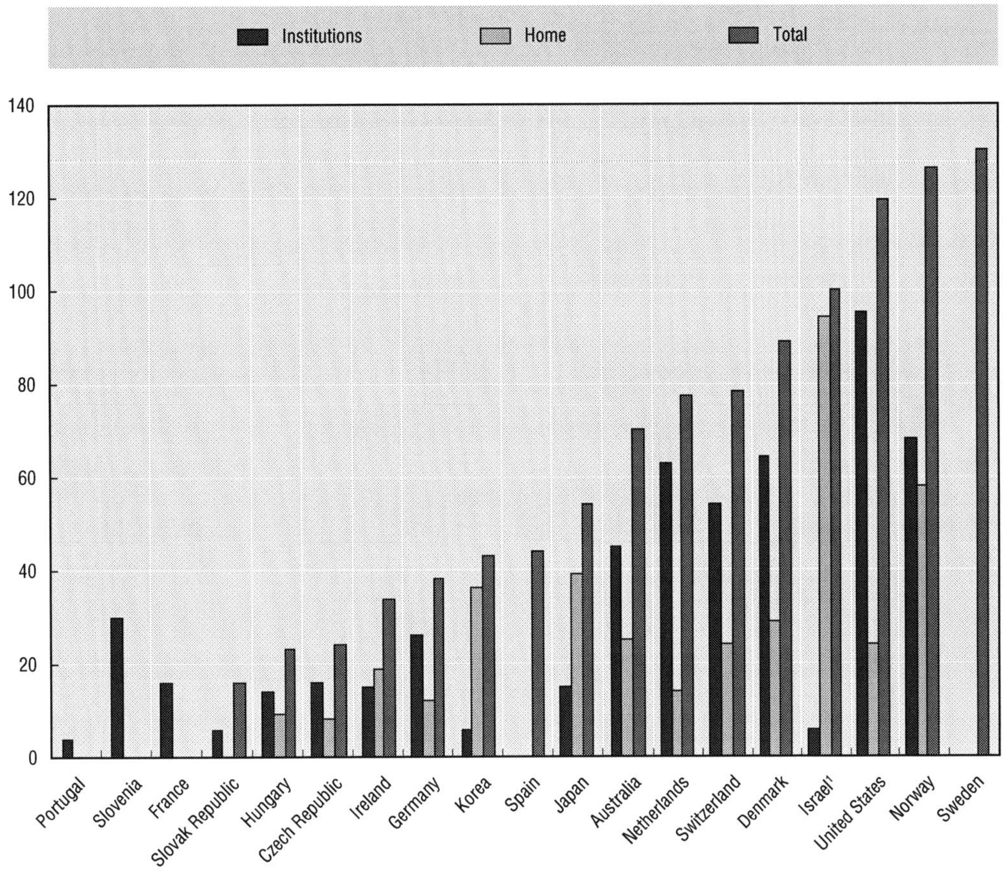

1. Information on data for Israel: http://dx/doi.org/10.1787/888932315602.
Source: OECD Health Data 2012.

Inspections and auditing of compliance

Surveys and inspections are the main mechanisms for monitoring compliance with set standards and validate accreditation or certification. By checking adherence to desired quality levels, inspections encourage quality and counter elderly abuse. Their role is to test whether they are in compliance with set standards and regulation. Although inspections can be part of the accreditation process, they can cover a wider set of topics than the minimum standards. The role of auditors can involve the review of medical records and interviewing care recipients and their families (e.g., United States) or more traditional visits evaluating infrastructure, living environments and respect of human rights (e.g., Korea). Self-reported inspections are rare (Japan is a case).

Box 4.5 describes inspection procedures in a selection of countries. Similar to accreditation, the government sets rules and regulations, while independent agencies or regional governments often have responsibilities for supervising procedures and protocols. In Germany, for example, although audits by the medical advisory boards of sickness funds are co-ordinated at federal level, each of the German Länder is responsible for nursing homes surveillance and monitoring compliance (Box 4.5). In Australia, the Aged Care Standards Accreditation Agency performs visits to facilities and assesses their performance

---

Box 4.5. **Inspection procedures in Ireland, France, Sweden and Luxembourg**

The Irish Health Information and Quality Authority has developed specific national standards for the operation of nursing homes and residential centres for old people, in consultation with users and providers. Inspections are made against these standards and other regulation set by the Department of Health and Children. Inspectors from the Social Services of the Inspectorate of the Health Information and Quality Authority report to the Chief Inspector of Social Services. The inspector meets with the applicant and carries out an interview to assess fitness of the provider. A full inspection of the premises is also undertaken including reviewing documentation, observing practices and speaking with staff and residents. Ireland uses two different audits on the use of physical restraints in residential care. The Healthcare Audit Team carries out a national audit and the nursing director in each residential facility conducts a local audit to identify if the processes used are in line with the 2010 Health Service Executive policy on the use of physical restraints. A further audit is carried out for every episode of planned or unplanned use of physical restraint (National Working Group on Restraint, 2011).

In France, the National Inspectorate for Social Affairs (IGAS) is responsible for quality control in residential facilities. Quality assurance is the responsibility of health insurance, the local authority (Département) and the residential care facilities. Co-ordinating doctors facilitate care planning and the regular assessment of care quality. Some facilities have acquired third-party certification using AFNOR or SGC-Qualicert, although these privately funded certifications do not replace the statutorily required inspections. These external assessments take place every five to seven years. Since 2002, the external assessment is to be conducted by an authorised body during the seven years upon the authorisation of services provision. In 2007, the National Agency for the Assessment of Nursing Home and Home Care Providers (ANESM) was tasked with adapting guidelines and recommendations to support providers in internal and external quality assessment processes.

In Sweden, the National Board of Health and Welfare is responsible for supervision, follow-up and evaluation of municipal and county council services. Sweden's 290 municipalities have a statutory duty to meet the social service and housing needs of older citizens. External quality assurance for nursing homes are carried out mostly by local authorities and only in cases of complaints or reporting of abuse through external follow-ups by the National Board of Health and Welfare (Leichsenring, 2010).

In Luxembourg, the Ministry of the Family and Integration stipulates minimum standards for structural and organisational quality for authorisation of residential care providers. The Ministry of Health and Social Security has set up a quality commission to regulate the provision of services under LTC Insurance. The commission establishes qualification standards and promotes expert standards and guidelines for good practices. The Ministry of the Family and Integration carries out follow-up visits to evaluate if providers meet the framework. Compliance with the contractual agreement is checked at least one a year. The Department of Evaluation and Orientation inspects facilities' compliance with the procedures of LTC insurance (Leichsenring, 2010).

against accreditation standards. In the Czech Republic, conversely, inspections on services managed by the regions are carried out by the Federal Ministry of Labour and Social Affairs (Leichsenring, 2010). In Ireland, inspections are carried out by the social services inspectorate of the Health Information and Quality Authority (Health Information and Quality Authority, 2012).

Despite cross-country variation, inspections are characterised by several common features, such as the use of paper-based inspections as well as on-site visits. Some countries require structured interviews with residents, family members and staff allowing direct observations of how care is delivered as well as targeted record reviews. Protocols guide inspectors throughout the process (Mor, 2010). For example, in Germany, assessors follow quality assurance guidelines (QPR) issued by the Central Federal Association of health insurance funds. Quality dimensions range from structural issues and satisfaction of recipients, to safeguarding resident rights, and accountability. The list of items covered in inspections varies across care settings and countries.

Inspections usually take place annually (e.g., Germany, Luxembourg, Portugal, Ontario, Canada), between one and two years (United States, Korea), over a longer time such as three years (Australia), five/seven years (France), or upon request following complaints (Finland, Sweden) (Leichsenring, 2010). In the United Kingdom, a 2009 national project named "Action on Elder Abuse", tasked safeguarding teams in local councils with responsibilities for raising alerts in case of abuse and monitoring the effectiveness of local authorities in preventing and responding to cases of abuse (Mandelstam, 2011; NHS Information Centre, 2012; NHS Information Centre, 2012b).

Inspections can be conducted by a single person (e.g., Spain), or, more often, by a team of inspectors. In the United States, a multidisciplinary team of professionals comprising, at least, one registered nurse survey skilled nursing facilities (CMS, 2010). In Germany, the audit team is usually comprised of nursing professionals but can also include physicians (Bavarian State Ministry of Labour and Social Welfare, Family Affairs, Women and Health and Federal Ministry of Health, 2010). Assessors normally complete training with an authorised accreditation body (e.g., in the United States, they need to pass a Surveyor Minimum Qualifications Test). Duration of training can be as short as twelve days like in Bavaria and ten days in Austria (NQZ), to a longer period. The frequency of inspection is not the same as the duration of accreditation. In Japan, accreditation has to be renewed every six years while inspections occur regularly.

Box 4.6. Germany quality assurance in LTC: Self-regulation, standards and inspections

Responsibility for quality assurance in Germany involves different components. First of all there is an element of *self-regulation*. Operators of care facilities have to ensure an appropriate level of quality in their services, facilities, staff and equipment and further improvement. Over time, this form of self-regulation has moved to forms of peer review and audit undertaken within the profession. For example, the Medical Advisory Boards of LTC insurance funds are responsible for external control, reporting and publishing audit results.

Provisional contracts' between the Federation of providers and regional branches of the LTC insurance give authorisation to the provider on the basis of a number of basic structural prerequisites, such as content of services, financial stipulations and personnel levels. Agreements concerning the funding of services also stipulate that authorised providers should use quality management systems although do not specify which system or method should be used (Leichsenring, 2010). These framework contracts spell out that care providers have to meet accreditation criteria including qualified personnel, adequate wages for employees, introduction of quality management system, and use of expert standards. There are minimum standards to exert control for, among others, personnel ratios introduced at the Länder level. Expert standards have to be continually updated and are expected to define what is generally recognised as the current state of the art in terms of medical and nursing care.

The associations of the LTC insurance funds tasks the medical advisory board of the health insurance funds (MDK) with *auditing* residential and non-residential long-term care

---

> ## Box 4.6. **Germany quality assurance in LTC: self-regulation, standards and inspections** (*cont.*)
>
> facilities licensed by means of the contract to provide benefits. MDK checks compliance with federal provisions. In addition, the supervisory authorities of the Land monitor compliance with the Land regulations governing residential accommodation and perform **inspections**. Inspections are carried out with or without prior notice, and are carried out by the Local Residential Homes Authorities (Heimaufsicht), a government agency. They include not only inspections of the rooms, living areas and documentation on relevant activities, but also personal visits among the residents to verify their care status. The inspections must be carried out each year, unless the Medical Advisory Boards have already audited the institutions. Close collaboration between the Residential Homes Authorities, the Medical Advisory Boards and local authorities is required to prevent homes from being inspected twice in one year (except where shortcoming have been identified).
>
> Annual audits include an assessment but also recommendations for improving quality. The assessment can be carried out as a regular event or may be necessitated for specific reasons or by a need for repeat assessment. If nursing home providers fail inspections, the Medical Advisory Board of sickness funds (Medizinische Dienste der Krankenversicherung, MDK) can cut payments or exclude care-homes providers entirely. The audit focuses on the physical state of the person in need of care and the effectiveness of the care and support measures. The assessment also includes an evaluation of the nursing process (process quality) as well as the framework conditions for providing care (structure quality). The underlying guidelines have to be regularly adapted to the latest innovations in medical and nursing care to reflect the most recent scientific findings related to appropriate patient care.
>
> The **quality audit** of a residential facility is based on 82 evaluation criteria that fall into the following five quality areas: 1) Nursing care and medical care (35 criteria); 2) Behaviour towards and interaction with residents who suffer from dementia (ten criteria); 3) Social care and daytime activities (ten criteria); 4) Accommodation, meals, home economics and hygiene (nine criteria); 5) Resident interviews (18 criteria). All criteria are evaluated both individually and grouped in one of the quality areas (area result). The overall result of the audit is compared to reference values. The marking of the audit results is modelled on the German school system, ranging from "excellent" (mark 1) to "poor" (mark 5). Quality audits of non-residential facilities are based on 49 assessment criteria that fall into four quality areas: 1) Nursing care services (17 criteria); 2) Medically prescribed nursing care services (ten criteria); 3) Service provision and organisation (ten criteria); 4) Client interviews (12 criteria). The overall result of the audit is determined on the basis of quality areas from 1 to 3 (i.e. without client survey). Otherwise, the procedure for non-residential care is identical to that for residential facilities.
>
> Parallel to these regulations, each of the Länder developed its own policies for surveillance of services and facilities – with their own regulations, structures and proceedings for monitoring compliance. In Bavaria, this is the role of the specialised bodies for quality development and monitoring of LTC facilities and facilities for disabled persons – the FQA. The FQA checks compliance with the quality requirements of the Bavarian Act on Long-Term Care and Quality of Life. The focus is on the services provided and the approaches taken to quality assurance.
>
> *Source:* Leichsenring, K. (2010), "Achieving Quality Long-term Care in Residential Facilities, Synthesis Report", Peer review in Social Protection and Social Inclusion 2010, European Centre for Social Welfare Policy and Research, 18-19 October, Murnau/Bavaria; Schulz, E. (2012), "Quality Assurance Policies and Indicators for Long-Term Care in the European Union Country Report: Germany", *ENEPRI Research Report* No. 104, Work Package 5, February.

Monitoring and enforcement

Compliance can be audited and the public can be informed about the fact that providers meet certain set standards. However, details of the assessment and inspection processes are typically kept confidential by regulators and not necessarily diffused publicly.

The results of inspections and audits furnish important information regarding gaps in care services. Common shortfalls reported through audits, surveys and inspections are safety and suitability of premises (e.g. infection control, fire hazard, safety), quality of care services and management (e.g. inadequate medication management and records), inadequate staff and training of the staff, including low understanding by care workers of safety and quality policies and procedures. Other shortfalls might relate to users' quality of life and the lack of regular re-assessment of recipients' needs and autonomy level (CQC, 2012d).

To ensure accountability for cases of poor quality and non-compliance with standards, inspectors or government bodies prepare a set of recommendations that providers or facilities can follow for improvement. There are several ways to inform and encourage providers to act on existing deficiencies, ranging from notification of non-compliance, to consultations and re-inspection, and sanctions such as fees, temporary banning from admitting new recipients and licence, termination of services and closure of facilities (Box 4.7). To give a few examples, in Australia, facilities found to be non-compliant are given a period to improve standards (Australian Government, 2011; European Peer Review, 2010). Follow-up visits are often scheduled to make sure that there is a visible improvement in the area of non-compliance in Ontario, Canada (Ontario Ministry of Health and Long-Term Care, 2012). Although the consequences on non-compliance are set in legislation, only a small proportion of providers fail to meet the standards or is sanctioned against non-compliance. For example, only 1% of the total social care services inspected were found to be seriously deviating from the minimum standards in England (CQC, 2012d). Closure of nursing homes is rarely imposed against many non-compliant providers.

A second indirect way to monitor compliance is by carrying out unannounced assessment visits. These are common for example in countries mandating accreditation (e.g., Australia, Germany) or are in plan (England). To help providers meet the standards and prepare for unannounced visits, some country agencies have developed self-assessment tools (e.g., the Australia Aged Care Standards and Accreditation Agency Australia; the "Fit-person Entry Programme" of Ireland). These self-assessment tools are designed for LTC recipients and their families and friends to understand what to expect from care services and give them sufficient information for informed judgment.

There is ongoing debate regarding the appropriateness and effectives of auditing and targeting strategy for facilities that perform poorly (Stevenson and Mor, 2009; Mor, 2010). While in the most blatant cases of shortcomings, termination of services or cuts in public payments is enforced, for other less serious cases, enforcement of standards on the basis of audits and inspections can be harder. In the United States, for example, there is evidence that enforcement of federal standards has been lenient and the stringency of the audit process varies across states.

Inspections can be costly for public or regulatory authorities, while adherence to norms and protocols can be expensive for providers. Providers complain about the time and expense involved in regulation leading to already scarce resources being directed away from actual provision of care (Wiener et al., 2007). According to a 2010 survey of care providers in Germany, only one in four nursing homes and one in three home care service providers were satisfied with the paper work, lack of focus on outcomes and arbitrariness of the audit carried out by the Medical Advisory Boards. This led to plans to change the audit process and the underlying guidelines (Schulz, 2012; Box 4.7).

Box 4.7. Sanctions against non-compliance: The case of the United States

In the United States, the Centers for Medicare and Medicaid Services (CMS) can take action against a nursing home according to the level of the problem. In case providers and organisations fail to meet standards, the law and regulations require "survey agencies" to perform:

- Consultation.
- Survey follow-up procedures (including plans of correction, initiation of formal enforcement).
- Sanctions (decertification and termination of the provider agreement, voluntary decertification, termination without decertification, automatic cancellation clause, suspension of payment) (Committee of Nursing Home Regulation, 1986).

The law permits CMS to take a variety of actions; for example, CMS may fine the nursing home, deny payment to the nursing home, assign a temporary manager, or install a state monitor. CMS considers the extent of harm caused by the failure to meet requirements when it takes an enforcement action. If the nursing home does not correct its problems, CMS terminates its agreement with the nursing home. As a result, the nursing home is no longer certified to provide care to Medicare and Medicaid beneficiaries. Any beneficiaries residing in the home at the time of the termination are transferred to certified facilities (Medicare, 2012).

Regulations to protect the elderly from abuses

Vulnerable old people are susceptible to maltreatment (Box 4.8). Many countries have specific legislation to safeguard the rights of LTC users (e.g., charters or bills of rights in Alberta and Ontario, Canada; Germany and Norway, US states and federal government) and elucidate role and responsibilities of individuals and organisations for addressing cases of abuses. Such legislation protects elderly from maltreatment and can target specific conditions, such as dementia. A multilateral convention based on the United Nations' Universal Declaration of Human Rights, the World Health Organization declared the global prevention of elder abuse in Toronto, and many countries policy documents stress that elder abuse is a violation of an older adult's fundamental rights to be safe and free of violence (WHO, 2007; AgePlatform Europe et al., 2010; EUROPEAN, 2012).

Legislation and regulations clearly state the right of older people and lay out means and procedures to protect against abuses, such as mandatory reporting of neglect or improper care (e.g., in Israel; Ireland; Ontario, Canada). These also set measures to encourage disclosure of cases or to set rules to guarantee standards of workers (e.g., mandatory criminal reference checks as in Canadian provinces, training requirements). The 2012 UK White Paper "Caring for Our Future: Reforming Care and support" clarifies legal responsibilities by requiring each local authority to establish a Safeguarding Adults Board (SAB) for strategic planning and co-ordination (including with the police, the National Health Service, and the local authorities). In Scotland, the Adult Protection and Support Act protects financial asset. In Japan, the 2005 Act on Prevention of Elderly Abuse and Support for Attendants of Elderly Persons sets, among others, measures to reduce the burden of guardians to reduce the likelihood of elderly abuses. The Netherlands, on the other hand, regulates the activities that providers can undertake, for example by identifying specific activities (e.g. catheterising and anaesthesia) that may be carried out only by qualified professionals.

Box 4.8. **Prevalence and forms of abuse**

Maltreatment could have significant impacts to the physical and mental conditions of older people. Older people are more frail than young people and are more likely to be subject to bruises, broken bones and head injuries, persistent physical pain and soreness, poor nutrition and dehydration, sleep disturbance. They can also experience fear and grief, isolation, depression, stress, and loss of self-confidence and self-esteem (WHO Europe, 2011).

Statistics on cases of elder abuse indicate the rising scale of problems. The Abuse and Health among Elderly in Europe (the ABUEL) studies urban populations in Germany, Greece, Italy, Lithuania, Portugal, Spain, and Sweden. Results across participating countries show different reasons for elder maltreatment in the region by different reason: 2.7% (equivalent to 4 million older people) have experienced physical abuse in the previous year; 0.7% (equivalent to 1 million older people) have experienced sexual abuse; 19.4% (equivalent to 29 million older people) have experienced mental abuse, and 3.8% (equivalent to 6 million) have experienced financial abuse. There are known risk factors that increase the susceptibility to maltreatment. Gender and age (women aged over 74 years old are more likely to experience abuses), high level of physical or intellectual disability, having dementia or Alzheimer's disease, or experiencing depression and challenging behaviour. Victims of elderly abuses tend to be financially dependent on the perpetrator, or be emotionally and physically dependent, but there are also cases of abuses in violent family settings or difficult living arrangement. Co-habitation, few social contacts and lack of social support tend to increase the probability of maltreatment. Surveys of family caregivers report widespread maltreatment also among caregivers (WHO/Europe, 2011). Typical perpetrators tend to be men in cases of physical abuse and women in the case of neglect.

Definitions of abuses

Physical abuse: Slapping, pushing, hitting, kicking, misuse of medication, inappropriate restraint (including physical and chemical restraint) or sanctions.

Sexual abuse: Rape, sexual assault, and/or sexual acts to which the older adult has not consented, or could not consent, or into which he or she was compelled to consent.

Psychological abuse: Emotional abuse, threats of harm or abandonment, deprivation of contact, humiliation, blaming, controlling, intimidation, coercion, harassment, verbal abuse, isolation or withdrawal from services or supportive networks.

Financial or material abuse: Theft, fraud or exploitation, pressure in connection with wills, property or inheritance, or financial transactions; or the misuse or misappropriation of property, possessions or benefits.

Neglect and acts of omission: Ignoring medical or physical care needs, failure to provide access to appropriate health, social care or educational services, the withholding of the necessities of life, such as medication, adequate nutrition and heating.

Discriminatory abuse: Ageism, racism, sexism that based on a person's disability, and other forms of harassment, slurs or similar treatment.

Source: Health Service Executive (2009).

In Ireland, aged care employers have a legal duty to refer people to the Health Information and Quality Authority in case of harms or risks to frail people, which can lead to care workers being banned from working with vulnerable people (Health Information and Quality Authority, 2012). The duty to report falls upon individuals including users, families and providers who witness incidences or have a concern regarding cases of elderly abuse. Such legal protection mechanisms usually allow and require consumers and those who are concerned about elderly abuse to report to a quality responsible body or individual. In Ireland, legislation restrict significantly the possibility for residential care and community hospital facilities to use physical restraints, requiring consensus or discussion with family members, legal representative, and within the nursing team.

Services and tools to protect older people from abuse and maltreatment can include adult protective services and complaint mechanisms. Protection mechanisms commonly seen across OECD countries range from personal directives to adult guardianship and trusteeship, as well as reporting mechanisms and ombudsmen's programmes acting as advocates of old people and seeking more generally to improve care. Findings and recommendations arising from Ombudsmen reports have been translated into specific action plans in some countries. These plans encompasses things such as: i) protective offices (e.g., British Columbia, Canada; Finland the United States; Israel); ii) improved communication services such as tool-free phone lines (British Columbia, Canada); iii) improved use of multidisciplinary teams, trained to prevent and intervene (e.g., Israel, the United States); and iv) involvement of consumer protection voluntary organisations.

In England, the Independent Safeguarding Authority* receives referrals concerning cases of abuses. In Finland, while there is separate legislation for both the rights of patients (in health care) and LTC recipients (in social services), both stipulate that hospitals, health care providers and social service providers must have a local patient/client ombudsman. Finland also has a parliamentary ombudsman service and a Chancellor of Justice service with good reputation in assessing and enforcing users' rights. In Iceland, complaints by users and providers may be made to the Medical Director of Health who is responsible for the interactions between providers and the public with respect to alleged negligence or errors in provision of health service.

In some countries, LTC providers and organisations (mainly nursing homes) are required to keep a record of incidences occurred in the premises and to submit to central data system. For example in Iceland, nursing homes are obliged to maintain a register of unforeseen incidents such as an accident, error, negligence, or any harmful event. Responsibilities for such recording lays upon health care practitioners who are involved, their professional superiors and other staff of the healthcare facility.

However, there can be disincentives for providers to record their own fault, which can lead to underreporting. Creating a culture of safety and transparency is a way to counter legitimate providers concerns that reporting adverse events would lead to penalties. Ensuring that procedures for investigations are fair and just for care workers and clearly important (Malley et al., in press). Other important issues to address include support and encouragement for frail older people to speak their concerns and have them be heard.

Conclusions

The development of minimum standards, licensure or accreditation of facilities, and training requirements for workers are, in a way, the starting point and bedrock of quality assurance in long-term care. Many OECD countries, including Australia, the United States, and many European countries, set standards for structural inputs and care process, and reward providers with licensing and public reimbursement for a share of the cost incurred. Some countries, most notable Japan, have emphasised educational and workforce standards as a quality assurance mechanism. Austria, Germany, Italy, Luxembourg and Slovenia have

---

* To merge with the Criminal Records Bureau to become the Disclosure and Barring Service.

developed quality management systems for organisations. Most have created external assessment bodies to oversee quality of care.

From the review of countries' experiences, the following key points have emerged:

● Providers in many European countries, Canada, Japan and the United States, particularly nursing homes, set quality goals for long–term care. However, leaving providers to self-regulate may not work well when results are sub-standard. Most OECD countries have set minimum requirements for LTC inputs and processes, as well as procedures for addressing low performance.

● All of 20 OECD and EU countries reviewed have legislation setting overarching principles of adequate and safe care. While standards are usually set at national level, most countries assign sub-national bodies or external organisations the task of monitoring and ensuring compliance to specific regulation.

● The main instruments to regulate LTC quality in institutional settings are licensure, standard settings and accreditation. In most OECD countries, such as Australia, Belgium, Canada, France, Germany, Ireland, Portugal, the Netherlands, and the United States, accreditation of facilities is either compulsory, a condition for reimbursement, or a common practice. Fewer OECD countries (e.g., Australia, Japan, Germany, Portugal, the United States, England, France) have accreditation for home care providers. Germany, Spain, Slovenia, Austria and France require the use of quality management systems at organisational level (such as ISO or E-Qalin) as part of minimum standards.

● Accreditation requirements and standards typically involve benchmarks for structure, workforce and safety. Staffing levels are included in quality standards or initiatives in nearly all countries, although some empirical studies do not find a significant relationship with improved quality of care (Castle, 2008; Castle and Ferguson, 2008). This suggests that processes of care, such as the way staff is employed in care activities, their roles and responsibilities, may have greater impact on quality.

● Quality dimensions built into accreditation and standards have evolved from inputs (e.g., ratio of skilled workers) to processes of care (e.g., management of medication, records keeping and management, infection controls), and, more recently, outcomes, quality of life, choice and human dignity, as demonstrated in the case of Germany, Australia, Ireland, England and the Netherlands.

● Qualification requirements for LTC workers mostly apply to institutional settings. There remains wide variance across countries regarding duration of training for LTC workers, varying from around 75 hours in the United States to 430 hours in Australia and 75 weeks of total training in Denmark to three years training for certified workers in Japan. Few countries require continuing education requirements. Most countries concentrate effort on pre-employment checks rather than post-employment improvement of standards.

● Despite regulation and standards, compliance and enforcement tools may not be strong enough. There is uncertainty regarding the most appropriate targeting and improvement strategies for facilities that perform poorly. For example, there are questions regarding the effectiveness of fines or warnings and threat of closure, or about how to minimise the administrative burden incurred and imposed on providers. Few OECD countries report on compliance and enforcement of regulation.

● Specific regulatory protection mechanisms to prevent elderly abuse have been embedded in "bills of rights" and legislation. These encourage disclosure of cases and range from ombudsman to adult guardianship systems and complaint mechanisms.

To what extent does regulation actually drive quality improvement? While regulation is necessary, too much of it can stifle innovation or discourage providers from going beyond minimum requirements. The answer to this question depends at least in part on the establishment and effectiveness of wider quality improvement mechanisms – from standardisation to incentives for quality and internal management systems – that complement regulatory frames, as explored in the next chapters of this book.

References

Accreditation Canada (2012), *www.accreditation.ca/about-us/message/*, accessed on 26 November 2012.

Aged Care Branch of the Department of Human Services, Victoria (2004), "Public Sector Residential Aged Care Quality of Care Performance Indicator Project Report", Victoria, Australia.

Aged Care Standards and Accreditation Agency Ltd. (2013), *Accreditation Standards*, Aged Care Standards and Accreditation Agency Ltd., Australia, *www.accreditation.org.au/site/uploads/30985_AgedCare_ ASENGLISHV1_3.pdf*, accessed on 21 March 2013.

Aged Care Standards and Accreditation Agency Ltd. (2009), *Results and Processes Guide*, Aged Care Standards and Accreditation Agency Ltd., Australia.

Age-Platform Europe et al. (2010), *European Charter of the Rights and Responsibilities of Older People in Need of Long-term Care and Assistance*, Brussels.

Anne-Wietske, E. (2009), "Self-Regulation through Quality Management Systems, How Nurses in Dutch Elderly Home Concretise the Goal of 'Responsible Care'", in M. Hertogh and P. Westerman (eds.), *Self-Regulation and the Future of the Regulatory State, International and Interdisciplinary Perspective*, Groningen.

Bavarian State Ministry of Labour and Social Welfare, Family Affairs, Women and Health and Federal Ministry of Health (2010), "Achieving Quality Long-term Care in Residential Facilities, Germany, Host Country Report", *Peer Review*, 18-19 October.

Cahill, S., E. O'Shea and M. Pierce (2012), "Creating Excellence in Dementia Care: A Research Review for Ireland's National Dementia Strategy", Ireland.

Capitman, J. et al. (2005), "Long-Term Care Quality: Historical Overview and Current Initiatives", Report for the National Commission for Quality Long-term Care, Washington, DC.

Casanova, G. (2012), "Quality Assurance Policies and Indicators for Long-Term Care in the European Union Country Report: Italy", *ENEPRI Research Report* No. 102, February.

Castle, N.G. (2008), "Nursing Home Caregiver Staffing Levels and Quality of Care: A Literature Review", *Journal of Applied Gerontology*, Vol. 27, pp. 375-405.

Castle, N.G. and J.C. Ferguson (2010), "What Is Nursing Home Quality and How Is It Measured?, *The Gerontologist*, Vol.5, No. 4, pp. 426-442.

CMS – Centers for Medicare and Medicaid Services (2010), "State Operations Manual: Chapter 7 – Survey and Enforcement Process for Skilled Nursing Facilities and Nursing Facilities, Rev. 63", *www.cms. gov/Regulations-and-Guidance/Guidance/Manuals/downloads/som107c07.pdf*.

Colombo, F. et al. (2011), *Help Wanted: Providing and Paying for Long-Term Care*, OECD Publishing, Paris, *http://dx.doi.org/10.1787/9789264097759-en*.

Committee on Nursing Home Regulation (1986), "Improving the Quality of Care in Nursing Homes", Institute of Health, National Academy Press, Washington, DC.

CQC – Care Quality Commission (2010), "Guidance about Compliance: Essential Standards of Quality and Safety, What Providers Should Do to Comply with the Section 20 Regulations of the Health and Social Care Act 2008", Care Quality Commission, London.

CQC (2011), "Registration under the Health and Social Care Act 2008, Quick Reference Guide to Regulated Activities by Service Type, Guidance for Providers", Care Quality Commission, *www.cqc.org.uk/sites/ default/files/media/documents/rp_poc2a_100521_20110831_v3_00_quick_reference_guide_-_to_regulated_ activities_by_service_type_for_publication.pdf*.

CQC (2012a), "Registration Under the Health and Social Care Act 2008, the Scope of Registration", July, London, *www.cqc.org.uk/sites/default/files/media/documents/20120621_100001_v4.0_scope_of_ registration_guidance_final_1.pdf*.

CQC (2012b), "Improving Our Work in 2011/2012", *www.cqc.org.uk/public/reports-surveys-and-reviews/ reports/cqc-annual-report-2011/12/improving-our-work-2011/12*, accessed on 26 October 2012.

CQC (2012c), "Annual Report and Accounts: 2011/2012" Care Quality Commission, London, *www.cqc.org. uk/sites/default/files/media/documents/cqc_annualreport_2012_tagged.pdf*.

CQC (2012d), "Market Report", Care Quality Commission, No. 1, June, London, *www.cqc.org.uk/sites/ default/files/media/documents/20120626_cqc_market_report_issue_1_for_website_final_0.pdf*.

CQC (2012e), "Judgment Framework, How We Judge Providers' Compliance with the Section 20 Regulations of the Health and Social Care Act", Care Quality Commission, London, April, *www. cqc.org.uk/sites/default/files/media/documents/20120321_final_judgement_framework_for_publication.pdf*.

CQC (2012f), "Preparing for CQC Inspection", Care Quality Commission, London, *www.cqc.org.uk/sites/ default/files/media/documents/cqc_preparing_for_inspection_-_cpa_version_-_final_0.pdf*.

CQC (2012g), "Criminal Record Bureau (CRB) Checks for Providers Registered Under the Health and Social Care Act 2008", Care Quality Commission, London, *www.cqc.org.uk/sites/default/files/media/ documents/20120822_100646_v_5_00_crb_checks_for_providers_registered_under_the_hsca_2008_-_ guidance_for_providers_and_cqc_staff.pdf*.

Da Roit, B. and B.L. Bihan (2010), "Similar and Yet So Different: Cash-for-Care in Six European Countries' Long-Term Care Policies", *Milbank Quarterly*, Vol. 88, No. 3, pp. 286-309.

Dandi, R. and G. Casanova (2012), "Quality Assurance Indicators of Long-term Care in European Countries", *ENEPRI Research Report* No. 110.

Department of Health (2003), *Nursing Agencies – National Minimum Standards: Nurses Agencies Regulations*, London.

Department of Health and Ageing (2011), "Quality Reporting: Community Care Common Standards and Quality Reporting Documentation", Department of Health and Ageing, Australian Government, *www.health.gov.au/internet/main/publishing.nsf/Content/ageing-commcare-qualrep-standards.htm*, accessed on 26 October, 2012.

Department of Health and Ageing (2010), *Community Care Common Standards Guide*, Department of Health and Ageing, Australian Government.

EUROPEAN (2012), "The European Reference Framework Online for the Prevention of Elder Abuse and Neglect", *www.preventelderabuse.eu/*, accessed on 20 October 2012.

Frings, S. et al. (2010), "Study in the Framework of PROGRESS Project, Best Quality (Benchmarking – European – Standards in Social Services – Transnationally)", TU Dortmund University, Olsberg, Germany.

Health Information and Quality Authority (2009), *National Quality Standards for Residential Care Settings for Older People in Ireland*, Health Information and Quality Authority, Ireland.

Health Information and Quality Authority (2012a), "Old People", available at *www.hiqa.ie/social-care/ older-people* accessed on 12 July 2012.

Health Information and Quality Authority (2012b), *www.hiqa.ie/getting-involved/how-we-involve-people/ inspections*, accessed on 26 November 2012.

Health Service Executive Elder Abuse Services (2009), "Open Your Eyes", HSE, Ireland.

Independent Safeguarding Authority (2012), "Our Role", available at *www.isa.homeoffice.gov.uk/Default. aspx?page=290*, accessed on 1 October 2012.

Joint Commission (2011a), "Facts About Joint Commission Accreditation and Certification", *www. jointcommission.org/assets/1/6/Accreditation_and_Certification_10_09.pdf*.

Leichsenring, K. (2010), "Achieving Quality Long-term Care in Residential Facilities, Synthesis Report", Peer review in Social Protection and Social Inclusion 2010, European Centre for Social Welfare Policy and Research, 18-19 October, Murnau/Bavaria.

Mandelstam, M. (2011), *Safeguarding Adults at Risk of Harm: A Legal Guide for Practitioners*, Social Care Institute for Excellence, London.

Malley, J. et al. (in press), "Regulating the quality and safety of long-term care in England", in V. Mor, T. Leone and A. Maresso (eds.), *Challenges in Regulating Long-term Care Quality: An International Comparison*, Cambridge University Press, Cambridge, in Press.

Medicare (2012), *www.medicare.gov/nursing/overview.asp*, accessed on 26 November 2012.

Ministry of Education, Social Policy and Sports (Ministerio de Educatión, Política Social y Deportes) (2008), 20450, 20451, y 452, 50722, BOE núm. 303 Miércoles 17 diciembre 2008.

Mor, V. (2010), "Improving the Quality of Long-term Care", CESifo DICE Report No. 2/2010.

Mot, E. (2010), *The Dutch System of Long-term Care*, CPB Document, No. 204, March 2010.

Naiditch, M. and L. Com-Ruelle (2011), *Quality Assurance and Quality Development in LTC: France*, Paris (INTERLINKS National Report), available at *http://interlinks.euro.centre.org/countries/france*.

National Working Group on Restraint (2011), "Policy on the Use of Physical Restraints in Designated Residential Care Units for Older People", Health Service Executive.

NHS Information Centre (2012a), "Abuse of Vulnerable Adults in England 2010-11: Experimental Statistics Final Report", Social Care Team, NHS Information Centre, 8 March.

National Institute for Health and Clinical Excellence (2012), "NICE Quality Standards in Social Care", *www.nice.org.uk/guidance/qualitystandards/socialcare/home.jsp*, accessed on 26 October 2012.

NHS Information Centre (2012b), "Information and Guidance for the Abuse of Vulnerable Adults Collection (AVA) 2011/2012", Adult Social Care Statistics, Health and Social Care Information Centre, April.

NICE (2012), "Dementia Quality standard", Issues on June 2010, last updated 7 June 2012, accessed on 16 July 2012. Available *http://www.nice.org.uk/aboutnice/qualitystandards/dementia/*.

Nies, H. and K. Leichsenring (2012), "Nine European Trends in Quality Management of Long-term Care for Older People", *Kwaliteit in zorg*, Vol. 3, pp. 24-271.

Nies, H. et al. (2010), "Quality Management and Quality Assurance in Long-Term Care – European Overview Paper", Vilans/European Centre for Social Welfare Policy and Research (INTERLINKS Report #2 – *http://interlinks.euro.centre.org/project/reports*), Utrecht and Vienna.

Nursing Home Compare (2012), *The Official U.S. Government Site for Medicare*, Washington DC, accessed on 12 September 2012, *www.medicare.gov/NursingHomeCompare/search.aspx?language=English&active Tab=2&subTab=0#HCAHPS1*.

Productivity Commission (2011), *Caring for Older Australians*, Report No. 53, Final Inquiry Report, Commonwealth of Australia, Canberra.

Rupel, V.P. et al. (2012), "Quality Assurance Policies and Indicators for Long-Term Care in the European Union Country Report: Slovenia", *ENEPRI Research Report* No. 103, Work Package 5, February.

Schulz, E. (2012), "Quality Assurance Policies and Indicators for Long-Term Care in the European Union Country Report: Germany", *ENEPRI Research Report* No. 104, Work Package 5, February.

Skills for Care (2012), "Manager Induction Standards – Refreshed 2012 web edition", Skills for Care, Leeds.

Steering Committee Responsible Care (2007), "Quality Framework Responsible Care", Steering Committee Responsible Care, Netherlands.

Stevenson, D.G. and V. Mor (2009), "Targeting Nursing Homes Under the Quality Improvement Organization Program's 9th Statement of Work", *Journal of the American Geriatrics Society*, Vol. 57, No. 9, pp. 1678-1684.

Unidade de Missão para os Cuidados Continuados Integrados (UMCCI – Unit of Mission for Integrated Continuous Care) (2011), "Manual do Prestador: Recomendações para a Melhoria Contínua" (Providers' manual: recommendations for better continuity), Rede Nacional De Cuidados Continuados Integrados, Unidade de Missão para os Cuidados Continuados Integrados, Lisbon, August.

Wagner, L.M., S.M. McDonald and N.G.Castle (2012), "Joint Commission Accreditation and Quality Measures in U.S. Nursing Homes", *Policy, Politics & Nursing Practice*, Vol. 13, No. 1, pp. 816.

WHO – World Health Organization (2007), *The Toronto Declaration on the Global Prevention of Elder Abuse*, Toronto.

WHO/Europe (World Health Organization Regional Office for Europe) (2011), *European Report on Preventing Elder Maltreatment*, Copenhagen.

Wiener, J.M. et al. (2007), *Quality Assurance for Long-Term Care: The Experiences of England, Australia, Germany and Japan*, February, AARP, Washington, DC.

PART II

Chapter 5

Standardisation and monitoring of care processes

by

Yuki Murakami

and
Francesca Colombo,
OECD Health Division

Setting standards that establish how to "do the right things" is one of the methods to make long-term care delivery safe and effective. Standardising needs assessment or care processes, and monitoring care processes or outcomes are effective tools to determine the needs of individuals, minimise variations in care for certain conditions and encourage providers to improve quality of care. This chapter reviews standardisation and monitoring approaches used by OECD and EU countries. It provides an overview of care needs assessment, looking specifically at the extent to which there is standardisation in the process of measuring and assessing care needs. It also reviews how information from needs assessment is used to formulate care plans, and the extent to which clinical guidelines and protocols are incorporated in care planning processes to drive good practices. The chapter concludes by reviewing care quality monitoring policies.

The importance of policies to standardise care processes

One of the methods for making LTC delivery safe and effective is the setting of standards for "doing the right things" based on best practices that reflect medical and nursing knowledge. The intention is to move from the setting of minimum requirements that institutional providers and workers need to follow to defining "ideal types" of care for different conditions. Standardisation of practice is a way to find more effective – and hopefully more efficient – solutions for driving care processes towards a desired level of care quality. This approach can overcome some of the drawbacks of regulation, for example the fact that strict regulation stifles innovative initiatives and management creativity. As standards for needs assessment and care practice are set, monitoring or external-oversight policies using these standards enable policy makers and providers to measure deviations from agreed benchmarks, before taking corrective measures.

Standardising needs assessment or care processes, and monitoring of care processes or outcomes can be effective tools to systematically determine the needs of individuals, minimise variations in care for certain conditions and encourage providers to improve quality of care. In many OECD countries, the introduction of these policies has been accompanied and facilitated by the use of assessment tools to record information about LTC users' needs. These improvements can be maximised when coupled with improved monitoring frameworks to oversee the care process and outcomes – such as monitoring of users' functional outcomes, auditing, indicators of quality and the use of satisfaction surveys. Such monitoring instruments provide feedback to policy makers, providers, and citizens on the extent to which care processes meet the needs of LTC users.

This chapter starts with an overview of LTC needs assessment in OECD countries, looking specifically at the extent to which there is standardisation in the process of measuring and assessing care needs. It then reviews how information from needs assessment is used to formulate care plans, and the extent to which clinical guidelines and protocols are incorporated in care planning process to drive good practices. The chapter concludes by reviewing care quality monitoring policies.

Using standardised assessment to plan appropriate care and allocate resources

All OECD countries use comprehensive (care) needs assessment to measure the level of disability of LTC recipients and determine eligibility for benefits (examples in Table 5.1; Colombo et al., 2011). Needs assessment can take place at different stages in the care episode and is an extremely useful tool to track changes in physical and cognitive conditions of LTC users. A growing number of OECD countries have adopted *standardised* assessment tools to better develop individual care plans. These tools are used by clinicians, registered nurses, trained LTC workers, or case managers to appraise the physical, cognitive and functional needs of LTC users and rank their level of impairment in scales and indices. They have several distinct advantages:

- Using needs assessment tools facilitates the normalisation of care processes and helps drive care processes towards desired benchmarks or levels of quality in an efficient manner, for example through the application of practice guidelines or protocols of good practice.

- Needs assessment tools can be effectively used to prepare tailored care plans (e.g., Spain, the United States (Medicaid), Japan and Canada) and highlight potential areas of concern and risk. Care plans specify appropriate care interventions, promote consistency in care and minimise variations in care provision. Care plans can also prevent adverse events, such as inappropriate prescription of medication for patients with multiple morbidities, and have been used to identify persons at risks and to track improvement in physical and cognitive conditions. Such plans are meant to ensure effective provision of care and can also help to collect data on the evolution of needs, thus supporting monitoring purposes.

- Standardisation of needs assessment also facilitates planning of continuity of care within a sector that is spread across different settings. For example, the RAI instruments (see this and the next chapter) have extended from nursing homes to home care, mental health, palliative care, and post-acute care.

- Needs assessments help governments identify care needs and can be better informed for targeted resource allocation.

- Standardised needs assessment tools have also made possible the collection of comparable data across providers.

- In sum, the use of standardised needs assessment tools has the potential to deliver better outcomes for LTC users and reduce inefficiencies, duplications, or care errors.

While at present there is no universal needs assessment tool, there are similarities between tools used in different countries. Functional capacities and needs of individuals are tested against a set of questionnaires in a number of specified areas. In some countries or settings, standardised instruments are used to assess nursing home residents, enabling the collection of basic physical, functional and psychosocial information about each LTC user.

For example, the Resident Assessment Instrument (RAI) has been utilised to assess LTC needs (in particular, in nursing homes) in Canada,[1] Finland, Iceland, Italy, the United States (Medicare and Medicaid), and Spain. France's AGGIR scale (Autonomie, Gérontologie, Groupe Iso-Ressourcaes), divides eligible individuals into six levels of dependency (Service-Public.fr, 2012; Da Roit and Le Bihan, 2010). Belgium uses two separate assessment tools (KATZ and RAI). Such examinations produce indices and scales that help care providers prepare care plans and can support co-ordination of care across settings. Care assessment is well developed for home-based care in Japan, Portugal, Germany and the United States (Cahill, 2012). Countries that employ RAI instruments have a set of standardised assessment criteria employed across different care settings, which can also be customised for specific setting such as home care. In addition to assessing clinical and cognitive functional needs of individuals, many countries incorporate questions related to social and quality of life aspects into needs assessment. For example, in Sweden, care managers and social workers take into consideration unique circumstances of individuals and consult with family and friends as well as LTC applicants themselves.

Assessments are usually carried out at the point of application to care and on a regular basis. In Canada, most jurisdictions require the assessment to be completed within 14 days of admission to a nursing home and then on a quarterly basis for the duration of the stay. Finland collects data for each resident in nursing home at admission, every six month, or

Table 5.1. **Standard assessment for eligibility and clinical guidelines**

	Standard assessment for eligibility and level of dependency	Clinical guidelines/protocols
Belgium	KATZ-evaluation (short evaluation)	
Denmark	They decide on a local level of help as a part of the local prioritising, and they make decisions regarding help to individuals based on concrete, individual assessments in each case, the assessments being prior to the local level of social services (EU peer review – Closing the gap, 2011-5662).	
Finland	No mandatory national standard assessment. Local municipalities are responsible for needs assessment and eligibility criteria. The RAI (LTCF and HC) instruments are used by many municipalities, covering appx 30% of LTC clients	The new Elderly Care Act will integrate assessment of health care methods (and medicines), clinical treatment guidelines and integrated work method
Iceland	RAI MDS 2.0	Based on RAI MDS 2.0 which incorporates clinical and care guidelines for care planning
Japan	Yes. Nationally Standardised system with 74 assessment criteria and results in 1-8 levels of dependency	Curriculums for everyday "medical care" such as suctioning of phlegm and tubal feeding in homes are newly added in the programme of Certified care worker and in the training course for other care workers. Certified care worker and other care workers who complete additional trainings for "medical care" can carry out the procedures. (Revision of the Certified Social Workers and Certified Care Workers Act)
Lithuania	Assessment of patient eligibility for nursing care is regulated by Nursing services in out-patient health care institutions and at home (Order of the Minister of Health No. V-1026, 2007)	
Malta		Standards of care have been drafted. Other clinical aspects and social care are regularly issued (e.g. Guidelines on protecting vulnerable elderly from the extremes of temperatures)
Portugal	Integrated instrument for bio-psychosocial evaluation of users	
Sweden	No national standards. Through a single entry system, assessment carried out by municipal social worker, a care manager. Municipalities decide entitlement to services (level, eligibility criteria, entitlement). Developing a care plan is mandatory.	National Guidelines in Care of Demented People (with focus on individual centred approach and multi-professional team based work, stroke care, diabetes care and adult dental care)

Source: OECD 2012 Questionnaire on Long-term Care Quality.

when conditions change. In the case of the United States, the data are collected as the core of a comprehensive assessment at start of care, at 60-day follow-up, and discharge; these data form a core part of the recipient's clinical record.

Professionals involved in needs assessments can be trained clinicians (e.g. Canada), a multidisciplinary team (e.g., Belgium, France, Germany and Portugal) or a trained social worker or care manager (e.g. Sweden and Finland). In Japan, assessment questionnaire results are electronically analysed and reviewed by a local independent committee of physicians, care managers, and academics (Campbell et al., 2010).

The results of need assessment tests are used to prepare tailored care plans. For example, in the United States, all nursing homes receiving payments from Medicare or Medicaid must develop a comprehensive care plan for each resident, which includes measurable objectives and timetables to meet a resident's medical, nursing and mental and psychosocial needs (CMS, 2011). RAI forms are used to monitor these care plans and help collect information of LTC users.

Assessment information can be linked to resource allocation plans. For example, RAI assessment instruments (see Chapter 3) are used to calculate Resource Utilisation Groups (RUG-III), which are used as a basis for nursing homes and home-care provider payments. Finland uses RAI data to calculate the price of services, although there is no obligation for data submission in order to obtain reimbursement. In the United States, the Outcome and Assessment Information Set (OASIS) uses data to develop home care resource groups and determine reimbursement for recipients with different levels of care needs (Mor, 2007; Mor, 2010).

Using assessment to derive quality information

Assessment tools enable the collection of basic physical, functional and psychosocial information about LTC users (Box 5.1).

Box 5.1. How quality data is collected and used in a selection of OECD countries

The **Canadian** Institute for Health Information (CIHI) has created and manages the Continuing Care Reporting System (CCRS) to capture demographic, clinical, functional and resource utilisation information on individuals receiving continuing care services in hospitals or long-term care homes in Canada. Participating organisations also provide information on facility characteristics to support comparative reporting and benchmarking. The clinical data standards for the CCRS were developed by interRAI, an international research network, and modified with its permission for Canadian use. The interRAI Resident Assessment Instrument Minimum Data Set (RAI-MDS 2.0)© is used to identify the preferences, needs and strengths of continuing care hospital patients or long-term care home residents. It also provides a snapshot of their services. The information, gathered electronically at the point of care, provides real-time decision support for front-line care planning and monitoring. The CCRS provides participating organisations with electronic reports, which include profiles of their populations, services and outcomes, including quality indicators. These reports are used by clinical quality champions, managers and policy makers for planning, quality improvement and accountability. The information is also made available publicly through CIHI's website, and in some provinces and territories (PTs) through their provincial quality organisations. Although the majority of PTs report to the CCRS, it is not universally implemented and thus indicators are not always comparable across geographical areas. Quality indicator information for depression, along with behaviour symptoms, pain, falls and pressure ulcers has been published with provincial comparisons in 2012 and an update report released in 2013 by CIHI for the first time (OECD 2012 Questionnaire on Long-Term Care Quality, 2012; CIHI, 2013).

The **Finnish** official service provision statistics are based on mandatory notifications on hospital care and residential care (including institutional care and 24 h sheltered housing facilities) and an annual cross-sectional data collection of regular home care clients. These data are collected and reported nationwide. They include indicators on use of restraints, antibiotics, psychotropic medications, pain; pressure ulcers, nutrition, and mobility. The most informative quality indicators are derived from a voluntary quality development network using the RAI assessment instruments in place since 2000. Some local authorities require RAI-based quality information as part of the service procurement contracts for residential care (JPHA, 2011; Leichsenring, 2010).

In **Sweden**, information is collected by the municipalities once per year, through a survey. The municipalities are obliged to provide information in order to receive national incentive grants for the development of elderly care services. A website, Elderly Guide, developed by the National Board of Health and Welfare, provides information to older people and their families about quality of care in all municipalities. It contains quality data for all municipalities as well as special housing, home-help services and day care services units. Thirty-six indicators are reported, including accessibility, user involvement, staffing, training and continuity of care

---

> **Box 5.1. How quality data is collected and used in a selection of OECD countries** (cont.)
>
> personnel, user independence, food, support for families giving care, physician involvement, preventative nursing care and services, management, follow-up and information availability (Leichsenring, 2010). The information in Elderly Guide is sourced mainly from special surveys and to a lesser extent processed from register data (Socialstyrelsen, 2009).
>
> In **Portugal**, to compliment the commencement of the National Network of Integrated Continuous Care (RNCCI) in 2007, which aims to provide all levels of integrated continuous care based on partnerships of public, private and third sector in care, a paper-free on-line web-based system of data management (GestCare CCI) was developed. This allows the continuous monitoring of assessments of recipients across transitory care and long-term care at provider, regional and national level. Each provider of care is attached to a contract that establishes standards (which specifies, among others, staff ratios, environment of facilities, safety of building, and inspection) that are monitored periodically by Local Co-ordination Teams and the information is transferred to GestCare CCI. Providers are required to collect and report data for a minimal data set. Needs assessment is an instrument that assists the monitoring process.

The RAI provides information on functional status and health conditions of residents on a number of clinical and social care areas (physical and clinical conditions, cognitive ability, psychological and social circumstances), measured both at admission and through periodical follow-ups. In the United States, the instrument is used to generate a Minimum Data Set, and the information is then collated into 24 quality indicators (Zimmerman, 2003), designed to help nursing home workers identify potential areas of concern and plan corrective interventions. The Center for Health Systems Research and Analysis produces quarterly reports providing results by facilities, adjusted for the residents' mix characteristics (Center for Health System Research & Analysis, 2013).

In Canada, data collected through assessment instruments are submitted to the Canadian Institute for Health Information's (CIHI) Continuing Care Reporting System. This is based on RAI MDS 2.0 and uses a system of electronic point-of-care collection giving immediate feedback to providers for care planning. Based on the data collected, CIHI produces reports and interactive web-based eReports. For example, CIHI provides facilities with comparative information every quarter to facilitate quality improvement over time and across facilities. Information is provided on volumes and pathways, demographics, outcome scales, quality indicators, and resource utilisation at provider level.

In Finland, data are transmitted every six months to the National Institute for Health and Welfare and results are publicly accessible. Portugal also publishes a report based on needs assessment every six months. Sweden, which does not use RAI instruments, has recently strengthened initiatives to report data on quality in long-term care by leveraging on the rich dataset derived from quality registers, and by colleting indicators from municipalities into a so-called "Elderly Guide".

Challenges and debates around using standardised assessment

A challenge for the future will be to modify assessment tools to reflect the complex needs of people with dementia, which involve assessment of cognitive impairment, and to encourage the use of assessment instruments for people with signs of dementia. Diagnosis is a critical element to ensure the appropriate intervention and development of good pathways for care of people with dementia. For example, France and Ireland use Mental State Examination to screen for cognitive impairment of older people. These individual testing tools encompass a set of questionnaires targeted to screen people for cognitive impairment only. Comprehensive standardised tests such as RAI also have a section to screen individuals for cognitive impairment.

Despite the existence of these tools, many people with dementia remain undiagnosed. In Ireland, only 54% of people over the age of 65 who had died on an acute medical ward had a Mini-Mental State Examination (MMSE) carried out during their hospital stay. In Norway, up to 50% of all residents in nursing homes with sure signs of dementia had not been diagnosed (Norwegian Ministry of Health and Care Services, 2006). Assessment for dementia is not always considered for older people attending accident and emergency department, even when there was frequent re-admission of patients and worrying signs such as falls, dehydration, self-neglect or a pattern of non-compliance with treatment (Cahill et al., 2012).

Another challenge surrounding the use of standardised instruments concerns the balance between standardisation of assessment and tailoring of care to individual needs and circumstances. To address this, many OECD countries using standardised assessment distinguish clearly between the process of assessment (which is standardised), and the process of drawing up a tailored care plan. In Japan, for example, the standardised needs assessment process is regarded as one of the strengths of the system. The evaluation is based on scores and does not take into account income/wealth or family conditions. Following assessment via a standardised questionnaire, a computer algorithm determines the duration (minutes) of the care needed and the amount of benefit a person will receive. Because of this scientific assessment, there is little room for arbitrariness or political pressure. The tailoring of services takes place only once decisions on eligibility have been made. The content of the care plan is decided "freely" by the user in collaboration with the care manager, but care managers are not involved in the assessment process.

Some countries that provide local authorities with significant autonomy in designing assessment tools are moving towards or considering some form of standardisation of assessment approaches. Under the 2007 Spanish LTC Law, a single three-scale instrument is now applied throughout the regions to evaluate the level of dependency (Herranz, 2007). England's 2012 White Paper "Caring for Our Future: Reforming Care and Support" has a plan to unify assessment to end so called "postal code lottery" in the level of benefits and packages. Municipalities have managed needs assessment in Sweden, but this has not been based on standardised guidelines. Recently, the government commissioned the National Board of Health and Welfare to develop an assessment tool to be used by the municipalities.

The use of clinical guidelines and protocols to standardise care processes is not yet widespread

Standardisation of needs assessment permits the consistent application of guidelines for care across users, and the development of protocols linked to care assessment processes. Where protocols, guidelines and expert standards are used, they provide useful recommendations for the management of users conditions (or multiple morbidities) and interdisciplinary teamwork, by putting together best practices in a specific area or condition.[2] Guidelines could be especially helpful for the care of the frail elderly because of the complexity of their needs and multiple vulnerabilities.

Providers that have used standardised assessment tools have the potential to compare the data gathered on their users to assess protocols, helping to identify areas of concern that may warrant intervention. However, while there is a tradition of development and use of clinical guidelines in medical care, there is comparatively less use of clinical guidelines to standardise *nursing care* in LTC settings. Guidelines are also typically framed in terms of recommendations to act, rather than recommendations about when to stop or not use treatments, or how to balance competing recommendations, for example on the use of pharmaceuticals (Guthrie et al., 2011). Thus far, few practice guidelines and care protocols that cut across care settings have been implemented.

Several countries have care guidelines that are not clinical. For example, Law 39/2006 in Spain encourages the development of "best practices" in nursing care homes. In France, best practices have been developed by national agencies such as ANESM (National Agency for Assessing LTC Organisations), ANSP (National Agency for Services to People), and CNSA (National Fund for Autonomy and Solidarity) (Naiditch and Com-Ruelle, 2011). In Japan, the development of practice guidelines is not mandatory, but each provider and organisation produce their own set of internal guidelines and monitor care workers' compliance. In other countries, good-practice guidelines encourage attention to user care needs and respect of minimum standards, although compliance is not mandatory. The National Institute of Health and Clinical Excellence (NICE) and Social Care Institute of Excellence (SCIE) under the NHS also publish national clinical guideline on dementia to assist GP diagnoses (Cahill et al., 2012). One specific area where clinical guidelines are starting to be developed is in dementia care (Box 5.2).

Box 5.2. **Guidelines for dementia care**

Dementia is a progressive and largely irreversible clinical syndrome that is characterised by a widespread impairment of mental function. Survey findings show that persons that develop symptoms of dementia are often not given sufficient explanation and lack a diagnosis. For example, only a third to a quarter of users living at home have custom-made living arrangements, and only 4% of those living at home receive a tailored day care offer in Norway. Belgium, Denmark, France, the Netherlands, Norway, Sweden, England, and Scotland have developed national dementia strategies that include directions on how care should be provided (Alzheimer Europe, 2011).

Guidelines specific for dementia care are emerging in countries. In Canada, the Coalition for Senior's Mental Health developed national, multidisciplinary guidelines on four key areas for the mental health of seniors, namely the assessment and treatment of delirium, depression, mood and behavioural symptoms in long-term care homes, and suicide risk and prevention of suicide (Conn et al., 2006). Others, such as NICE in the United Kingdom also give providers directions of how to manage information sharing with patients with dementia and their family (Cahill et al., 2012). Similarly, there are mental condition guidelines in France, Sweden, and Germany. The Swedish national dementia guideline points to the importance of forming multi-discipline professional teams, building capacity through training, and individualising care through person-centred care. The National Board of Health and Welfare, in co-operation with the Swedish Association of Local Authorities and Regions is tasked to develop and implement the guidelines in 2012-14. Recently, the United States also published a national Alzheimer's plan stressing the importance of specific care guidance for LTC providers.

Guidance targeted to professionals is considered influential for correctly directing dementia patients through the care pathway. This can range from assistance tools for correct diagnosis to proper guidance for different care options. Professional guidelines issued by national institutes, such as NICE in England, offer providers with a checklist on the type of information

---

> ### Box 5.2. **Guidelines for dementia care** (*cont.*)
>
> needs for dementia patients and their families. Post-diagnosis support and information, not only for families, but also for GPs, has been mentioned as key to national strategies to assist in the referral process, e.g. in Australia, England, Wales and Northern Ireland (Cahill et al., 2012). Ireland's National Dementia Education Project 2012 issued a guiding framework for education and awareness for person-centred dementia care in acute, residential, mental health and community care settings. The programme aims to assist staff working in dementia care to create an environment where people are cared for with dignity and a person-centred approach is fostered. It entails educational modules, resources such as an information booklet and a CD and for raising awareness of delirium (Health Service Executive, 2012). Another example is the Swedish Dementia Centre which, in co-operation with the National Board of Health and Welfare, has a website giving information related to national guidelines.

Monitoring of long-term care quality can take different forms

Tracking users' functional or cognitive outcomes, self-assessment reports, the use of satisfaction surveys, peer reviews and external evaluation of quality, are all tools for monitoring – on a more or less regular basis – that LTC quality does not deviate from set, agreed quality objectives or practice standards. Some OECD countries (Germany, Netherlands, some Canadian provinces) are also developing policies for measuring LTC user satisfaction. As quality of life is increasingly seen as an important metric to measure LTC quality, its objective monitoring becomes desirable.

As in the case of health care, tools for monitoring LTC quality can take different forms. These range from self-assessed reports by individual providers to external evaluations and public reporting:

- Self-assessment reports.
- Peer reviews.
- User experience and satisfaction surveys.
- External evaluation by external oversight (such as rating agencies and independent third-party agency) or government body.

Self-assessment is an internal evaluation that providers can make, often following instructions or guidelines specifying specific performance items (see also Chapter 7). This monitoring exercise gives providers much freedom regarding what information to monitor, and how to carry out the assessment. Self-assessment has been incorporated in accreditation procedures or information diffused in public reporting in Australia and Japan, however no country relies solely on self-assessed information in their quality monitoring process. For example, in Japan, providers can submit information on available services and management, while prefectural governors or contracted agencies, monitor other information from external reviews or inspections (JPHA, 2009). Self-assessment can cover issues such as occupational level and skill of personnel, the number of complaints received, national standards (protection, social activities, choice), and the results of care home residents interviews.

Peer reviews are quality monitoring methods that give an opportunity to providers to benchmark and compare services with other providers. The assessment is done by a peer, on the basis of commonly understood or internal criteria. Peer reviews can cover internal records, and may extend to monitoring whether providers' practice is in line with existing guidelines or protocols. Recommendations for improvements remain confidential and shared between peers. To date, there is relatively little evidence of the use of peer reviews among LTC workers.

Some OECD countries (Canada, Spain, Iceland, the Netherlands, Germany, England and the United States) have developed policies to monitor the *satisfaction or experience* of LTC users and their families, however only a few monitor regularly this aspect of care and results are not consistently published. These surveys record the view of LTC users on different aspects of care and facilitate the identification of problem areas, offering an opportunity for care recipients to voice their opinions. Information collected in surveys can range from quality of overall services to specific aspects on quality of life. Efforts to standardise the measurement of LTC users' experiences to overcome subjectivity biases give insightful, qualitative information regarding the process and outcomes of care from the perspective of the user. For example:

● In the Netherlands (in 2006), the Ministry of Health developed questionnaires for measuring the experiences of patients in different types of health care facilities, including nursing homes and homes for the elderly (so-called CQ Index; Winters et al., 2010). The survey is administered by an accredited, independent organisation. The institutions are ranked and the information is available to the public. The dimensions included in the CQ Index are: care plan and evaluation; shared decision making; treatment; information; body care; meals; professional competency; living comfort; atmosphere; living environment and privacy; activities; autonomy; mental wellbeing; security; availability of personnel.

● Germany has implemented three surveys of LTC users' satisfaction, covering both home care and institutional settings. The third report, published in 2012 shows an increase in the degree of satisfaction from 67% to 76% compared to the 2007 survey results published, although, on specific indicators, improvements have not been consistent.

● In Alberta (Canada), the Health Quality Council is mandated to report LTC residents' experience and satisfaction with the quality of services they receive. There were two surveys, one covering resident (2007/08), and one covering family experience (2007/08 and 2010/11). The former collected information on patient and respondent characteristics; reported family experience and perception of nursing home activities and services; family member rating of the care provided to the resident; willingness to recommend the nursing home; and suggestions on how care and services provided at the nursing home could be improved.

External evaluations are executed by evaluation agencies within the government (e.g. prefectures in Japan[3]) or by external bodies (e.g., the Care Quality Commission in England or the Aged Care Standards and Accreditation Agency in Australia), using a standardised assessment method or protocol. They are often used within licensing, accreditation and auditing processes. While this is by far the more expensive procedure, the evaluations provide an independent, objective assessment based on a set of evaluation criteria and standards. The Canadian Institute for Health Information has recently introduced new quality indicators such as the national standardised reporting system for LTC (so-called Continuing Care Reporting System) to which care organisations submit data.

Conclusions

This chapter started by reviewing the process of assessment of care needs of people with physical or cognitive limitations. While needs assessment processes seem to be well developed across OECD countries, this process is often used to facilitate decisions regarding the type of public benefits a person would be entitled to rather than to target care needs and guide care practices. Rather, across a growing number of OECD and EU countries, standardised tools and scales are used by clinicians to normalise the assessment of care needs and rank the level of physical, cognitive and functional needs and used to guide care decisions, resource allocation, or to support the development of quality indicators. Examples include RAI in the United States, Canada, Finland and Iceland; AGGIR in France; KATZ in Belgium or the Dutch national standard tool in the Netherlands. Such indexes help providers prepare care plans and can support co-ordination of care across settings.

While in some countries decisions about benefit entitlement take into account individual circumstances regarding a person's socio-economic status or family support, one of the strengths of these standardisation instruments is that there is little room for subjectivity in the process of assessing *nursing* needs. This means that standardised assessment instruments are not incompatible with tailoring of care services to the unique circumstances of LTC users or to regional differences.

Despite the potential of standardisation of needs assessment processes, they have not yet been employed to develop standards of practice. Rather, use of nursing guidelines and protocols is still quite limited. Possible reasons are that LTC workers have relatively low qualification levels, fewer peer-learning opportunities and low technical support for turning systematic assessment of care practices into guidelines. A further possible explanation is that clinical guidelines have often been developed around specific diseases, making it hard to adapt to multiple complex conditions of the frail elderly.

There is a need to develop better guidance for the care of people with complex neuro-degenerative conditions such as dementia. Assessment tools still do not address well the complex needs of people with dementia and the assessment of cognitive impairment remains therefore under-diagnosed. A positive development is the development of clinical guidelines around dementia care (Canada, France, Sweden, and Germany). Some national dementia strategies (e.g., Belgium, Denmark, France, the Netherlands, Norway, Sweden, England and Scotland) stress the importance of specific care guidance for LTC providers.

Traditional mechanisms for monitoring that care is safe and effective, such as self-assessment by care providers, are increasingly being accompanied by independent external appraisals, including as part of processes of auditing and accreditation. Among others, Germany, Netherlands, and some Canadian provinces are also developing policies for measuring LTC user experiences.

Notes

1. For instance, to date, eight Canadian provinces and territories have mandated the implementation of RAI assessment tools in nursing homes and hospital-based continuing care.

2. Guidelines are often produced based on evidence and promote standardised process in assessment, planning of care, treatment, and management (Conn et al., 2006). Guidelines are usually composed of step-by-step recommendations. Steps start from identifying individuals showing symptoms or at risks for screening and assessment, diagnostic criteria, treatment options by severity and assessment for referrals for psychiatric care, psychotherapies and psychosocial interventions, pharmacological treatment, monitoring of side effects and drug interactions, deciding duration of therapy and monitoring of after-treatment, and education and prevention

3. In Japan, there is no national external body responsible for quality assurance and oversight of LTC services.

References

Administration on Aging (2012), "Long-Term Care Ombudsman Program (OAA, Title VII, Chapter 2, Sections 711/712", Washington, DC, *www.aoa.gov/AoA_programs/Elder_Rights/Ombudsman/index.aspx,* accessed on 10 September 2012.

Agency for Healthcare Research & Quality (2008), "Spotlight Case: The Safety and Quality of Long-term Care", *Online Journal & Forum on Patient Safety and Health Care Quality.*

Alzheimer Europe (2011), "European National Dementia Strategies", *Dementia in Europe: The Alzheimer Europe Magazine,* Vol. 9, pp. 33-36, October.

Cacace, M. (2012), "Public Reporting on the Quality of Healthcare Providers: International Experience and Prospects", LSE Health and Social Care Formal Seminar Series, 9 May 2012, *http://www2.lse.ac.uk/LSEHealthAndSocialCare/pdf/LSE-Cacace_Public-reporting.pdf.*

Cahill, S., E. O'Shea and M. Pierce (2012), "Creating Excellence in Dementia Care: A Research Review for Ireland's National Dementia Strategy", Ireland.

Campbell, J.C. et al. (2010), "Lessons from Public Long-term Care Insurance in Germany and Japan", *Health Affairs,* Vol. 29, No. 1, pp. 87-95.

Castle, N.G. and J.C. Ferguson (2010), "What Is Nursing Home Quality and How Is It Measured?", *The Gerontologist,* pp. 426-442.

Center for Health Systems Research and Analysis (2013), *www.chsra.wisc.edu/,* accessed on 21 May, 2013.

CMS – Centers for Medicare and Medicaid Services (2011), "Ch 4: CAA Process and Care Planning of CMS's RAI Version 3.0 Manual", Centers for Medicare and Medicaid Services, October, Washington, DC.

CMS (2012), "Home Health Quality Initiative", *www.cms.gov/Medicare/Quality-Initiatives-Patient-Assessment-Instruments/HomeHealthQualityInits/index.html?redirect=/HomeHealthQualityInits/.*

Colombo, F. et al. (2011), "Help Wanted: Proving and Paying for Long-Term Care", *OECD Health Policy Studies,* OECD Publishing, Paris, *http://dx.doi.org/10.1787/9789264097759-en.*

Da Roit, B. and B. Le Bihan (2010), "Similar and Yet So Different: Cash-for-Care in Six Different European Countries' Long-Term Care Policies", *Milbank Quarterly,* Vol. 88, No. 3, pp. 286309.

Government of Alberta (2012), "Protection for Vulnerable Adults", Alberta, Canada, access on 10 September 2012, *www.seniors.alberta.ca/Protection/.*

Guthrie, B. et al. (2011), " Multimorbidity: The Impact on Health Systems and their Development", Chapter 6 of *Health Reform: Meeting the Challenge of Ageing and Multiple Morbidities,* OECD Publishing, Paris, *http://dx.doi.org/10.1787/9789264122314-en.*

Health Service Executive Elder Abuse Services (2009), "Open Your Eyes", Ireland.

Herranz, R. (2007), "Ley de Dependencia o el derecho a ser cuidado", Presentation, Tribuna Abierta, 15 October.

HIRA – Health Insurance Review & Assessment Service (2011), "Comprehensive Quality Report of National Health Insurance 2010, Korea".

Hugman, R. (1994), "Respect and Abuse in Book", Chapter 4 in R. Hugman (ed.), *Ageing and the Care of Older People in Europe,* Macmillan Press Ltd. New York, pp. 77-80.

JPHA – Japan National Council of Social Welfare (2009), *www.jpha.or.jp/sub/pdf/menu04_5_05_all.pdf,* Tokyo, accessed on 30 August 2012.

JPHA (2011), *www.kantei.go.jp/jp/singi/kinkyukoyou/suisinteam/TF/kaigo_dai4/sankou3.pdf,* Tokyo, accessed on 30 August 2012.

JPHA (2012), *www.shakyo-hyouka.net/index.html,* Tokyo, accessed on 10 September 2012.

Leichsenring, K. (2010), "Achieving Quality Long-term Care in Residential Facilities", *Discussion Paper for the Peer Review 2010, Germany, www.peer-review-social-inclusion.eu.*

Medicare (2012), *www.medicare.gov/HomeHealthCompare/search.aspx,* accessed on 10 September 2012.

Ministry of Health (2011), *www.umcci.min-saude.pt/SiteCollectionDocuments/Guia_RNCCI.pdf,* Lisbon, accessed on 31 August 2012.

Mor, V. (2007), "Defining and Measuring Quality Outcomes in Long-term Care", *Journal of the American Medical Association,* Vol. 8(3), Suppl. No. 2, pp. e129-137.

Mot, E. (2010), "The Dutch System of Long-term Care", *CPB Document*, No. 204, March.

Mukamel, D.B. et al. (2008), "Publication of Quality Report Cards and Trends in Reported Quality Measures in Nursing Homes", *Health Service Research*, Vol. 43, No. 4, August.

National Working Group on Restraint (2011), "Policy on the Use of Physical Restraints in Designated Residential Care Units for Older People", Health Service Executive, Ireland.

Norwegian Ministry of Health and Care Services (2006), "Subplan of Care Plan 2015: Dementia Plan 2015", Norwegian Ministry of Health and Care Services, Oslo.

Productivity Commission (2011), "Caring for Older Australians", Report No. 53, Final Inquiry Report, Commonwealth of Australia, Canberra.

Rodrigues, R. (2012), "Public Reporting within Europe: The Public Gets What the Public Wants?", unpublished document, European Centre, OECD Expert Meeting, OECD, Paris.

Schulz, E. (2012), "Quality Assurance Policies and Indicators for Long-term Care in the European Union – Country Report: Germany", *ENEPRI Research Report* No. 104, Work Package 5, February.

Service-Public.fr (2012), *http://vosdroits.service-public.fr/F1229.xhtml*, Paris, accessed on 8 September 2012.

Socialstyrelsen (2009), "Care of Older People in Sweden 2008", December, *www.socialstyrelsen.se/Lists/Artikelkatalog/Attachments/17857/2009-12-6.pdf*.

Sorenson, C. and E. Mossialos (2007), "Measuring Quality and Standards of Long-term Care for Older People", European Commission, Brussels.

Werner, E.S. and D. Polsky (2010), "Public Reporting Drove Quality Gains at Nursing Homes", *Health Affairs*, Vol. 29, No. 9, pp. 1706-1713, September.

Werner, R.M. et al. (2009), "Impact of Public Reporting on Unreported Quality of Care", *Health Services Research*, Vol. 44, No. 2, Part I, April.

WHO/Europe – World Health Organization Regional Office for Europe (2011), *European Report on Preventing Elder Maltreatment*, Copenhagen.

Wiener, J.M. et al. (2007), "Quality Assurance for Long-Term Care: The Experiences of England, Australia, Germany and Japan", AARP, Washington DC, February.

Winters, S. et al. (2010), "Determining the Interviewer Effect on CQ Index Outcomes: A Multilevel Approach", *BMC Medical Research Methodology*, Vol. 10, No. 75, downloaded from *www.biomedcentral.com/1471-2288/10/75*.

Wood, S. and M. Stephens (2003), "Vulnerability to Elder Abuse and Neglect in Assisted Living Facilities", *The Gerontologist*, Vol. 43, No. 5, pp. 753-757.

PART II

Chapter 6

Incentives for providers and choice for consumers

by

Yuki Murakami

and
Francesca Colombo,
OECD Health Division

Many OECD countries are looking at ways to change providers' and users' behaviours by strengthening incentives for quality improvement and creating a quality "culture". This chapter discusses the use of incentives to deliver responsive, safe, and effective care, addressing four main issues: 1) consumer-based initiatives such as those leveraging consumer choice and centredness; 2) the impact of performance incentives to encourage and reward providers to deliver higher quality care; 3) incentives to encourage care co-ordination and integration, the lack of which can have important consequences for safety, responsiveness and care effectiveness; and 4) the role of information technology in promoting outcome improvements and independent living.

Incentives to deliver quality care can be directed to consumer, providers or payers

Policies to drive LTC quality improvement are subject to increasing interest and experimentation. Regulatory processes are clearly important, but enforcement of regulation can be challenging and application to home care and assisted living settings lags behind efforts in the institutional care sector. Seeking ways to standardise care processes is desirable in many ways, but there are technical, informational and systematic barriers to overcome, as discussed in Chapter 5. Many OECD countries are now looking at ways to change providers' and users' behaviours by strengthening incentives for quality improvement and create a quality "culture". Such incentives can be internal, such as administrative and financial "stick and carrots"; or they can be linked to market-based approaches that provide greater users' choice and public recognition to high-performing providers.

This chapter discusses the use of incentives to deliver responsive, safe, and effective care, addressing three main issues. First, the chapter looks at consumer-based initiatives such as those leveraging consumer choice and centredness; it examines the impact of consumer-direction mechanisms, of LTC-providers performance rankings, and of approaches giving LTC recipients a greater "voice". Second, the chapter reviews the impact of performance incentives – such as pay for performance – to encourage and reward providers for delivering higher care quality. Third, the chapter looks at incentives to encourage care co-ordination and integration, the lack of which can have important consequences for safety, responsiveness and care effectiveness. There are different ways to encourage integration – for example integrating care, clinical pathways and information systems – and the chapter describes some of them. Finally, the chapter considers the role of information technology in promoting outcome improvements and independent living. Table 6.1 summaries such policies and initiatives in OECD and EU countries.

The evidence on impact of choice-based mechanisms on care effectiveness and safety is not robust

LTC users and their families increasingly demand freedom and autonomy in selecting and directing care, leading a number of countries to introduce mechanisms to improve person-centred care. Choice of care among different providers and care settings is the first and the most popular policy initiative that countries have taken to tailor care to consumer preferences. Many countries offer LTC recipients the possibility to receive a cash entitlement to buy care services (several European countries), or to choose among competing providers (e.g., Portugal, Spain, Japan, United States), or to choose between cash benefits and in-kind services (e.g., the Netherlands, Germany, the US Cash and Counselling programmes).

Without doubt, the possibility to choose care pathways and place the needs of care recipients at the centre of care processes is increasingly recognised as a fundamental dimension of care quality. Such policies also aim to support the development of competition in the care market to enhance quality and efficiency and contain costs (Arksey and Kemp, 2008; Da Roit and Le Bihan, 2010). However, well known market failures – including asymmetric

Table 6.1. **Cash for care, public reporting, provider incentive programmes, care co-ordination and ICT policies and initiatives**

	Cash for care	Public reporting	Provider incentive programmes	Avoidable hospitalisations and medical errors through care co-ordination	ICT programmes
Australia		Yes			
Austria	Federal cash benefits, respite care benefit, 24-hour care				
Belgium	At the federal level, the Allowance of the Elderly; at the regional level, care insurance			Nursing and ADL assistance are integrated into health coverage through INAMI	
Canada		Yes		The Ontario Government of Canada has a four-year Ageing at Home Strategy which focuses on the delivery of an integrated continuum of community-based services	
Czech Republic	Cash benefits are set based on an assessment of the persons health and social situation (similar to the ADL and IADL tests)				
Denmark	Availability varies according to municipality. BPA (Citizen Controlled Personal Assistance), Minimum 20 hours help per week needed, Calculated by type and duration of assistance by local council; no minimum or maximum, not for nursing care				
Finland	Care allowance for pensioners, disability allowance, and care subsidy for informal caregivers	Yes through InterRAI data collection for both residential and home care, quality of life is also measured, available on line, but not compulsory	Not national; several municipalities have adopted P4P-like contracts when procuring services	The new Elderly Care Act prescribes care co-ordination for clients with complex problems. National Database of Patient Summaries (incl. medications) is being developed by 2016. No direct surveillance data	National Database of Patient Summaries (incl. medications), and interoperability of electronic health records is being developed by 2016 Several local projects for use of communication technology and teleconsulting in home care
France	*Allocation Personalisée d'Autonomie* (APA), *Caisse Nationale de Solidarité pour l'Autonomie* (CNSA)			Health and social care services for home care have been integrated through so-called *Service Intégré de Soins à Domicile*	
Germany	Cash benefits also correspond to three care levels and amount to EUR 225 (level 1), EUR 430 (level 2) and EUR 685 (level 3) per month as of 2010	Reports online since 2010 for LTCI, quality report of medical service since 2012			
Iceland		In preparation for publication of findings of 20 outcome measures at aggregated level		In some localities, special service contracts have been made in order to integrate nursing and other services in the home	Most nursing home have movement sensors to help with monitoring of residents in risk of falls out of beds or chairs. Some nursing homes provide means to install phones but residents who wish to use a cell phone at their own expense do so. All residents in need of assistive devices for locomotion such as crutches, rollators or wheelchairs are provided with this free of charge by the nursing home. In some nursing home computers with Internet access are available for residents

Table 6.1. **Cash for care, public reporting, provider incentive programmes, care co-ordination and ICT policies and initiatives** (*cont.*)

	Cash for care	Public reporting	Provider incentive programmes	Avoidable hospitalisations and medical errors through care co-ordination	ICT programmes
Ireland	Constant attendance allowance, Domiciliary care allowance (half-rate), Carers allowance, Carer's benefit, Respite care grant	Yes			
Italy	INPS provides a national disability cash-benefit scheme, funded by the central government out of general taxation				
Japan	LTC leave: 40% of wage covered by unemployment insurance. Three months at maximum for one person	Yes	Financial rewards to good performing providers (mainly structure/input level, process level)	Care co-ordination by care manager (free of charge) under LTC insurance system	
Korea	Yes, National Programme: Care allowance, criteria for eligibility: live remote, unable or unsuitable to use LTC facilities, tax free	Yes, on line with five grades, biannually for LTCF annually for LTCH	Yes for LTCH (for the LTCH with less than lower 20% of total for both structure and process quality score, penalty is applied) and LTCF (5% of total payment per provider to the top 10%)		
Lithuania	Target compensations for nursing or attendance are granted according to the Law on State Social Assistance Benefits. This cash allowance are paid for person (family) to pay for a help of assistance. Cash allowance financed from the municipal budgets. LTC health services are provided for patients free of charge	Ministry of Social Security and Labour, municipalities, health care institutions, social care institutions, day care centres. The Department of Supervision of Social Services and other officials publish information in their websites		Integrated Help at Home Development Programme approved by the Minister of Social Security and Labour in 2012 (Order of the Minister of Social Security and Labour dated 20 July 2012, No. A1-353). The main goal of the programme is to ensure the accessibility (to expand social care services and include nurse care services) and variety of services of integrated help at home for elderly, disabled adults and children and for family members by consulting and involve informal carers (volunteers, neighbours and other) into process, etc.	Integrated Help at Home Development Programme (Order of the Minister of Social Security and Labour dated 20 July 2012, No. A1-353) is to enhance the technologies into disabled persons carers daily life. A special Internet portal eSenjoras (*www.esenjoras.lt*) has been established for senior citizens. It provides information on various campaigns and publishes relevant material.
Netherlands	Personal care budget – calculated depending on need for care, income, household situation and age, and for people with chronic illnesses, that is an LTC indication, a special cash benefit exists	Yes			
Norway	Basic benefit (*grunnstønad*) and Attendance benefit (*hjelpestønad*) from the general National Insurance Scheme (*folketrygden*)			Norway provides subsidy to municipalities who link their nursing homes to NOKLUS (Norwegian Quality Improvement of Primary Care Laboratories)	

Table 6.1. **Cash for care, public reporting, provider incentive programmes, care co-ordination and ICT policies and initiatives** (cont.)

	Cash for care	Public reporting	Provider incentive programmes	Avoidable hospitalisations and medical errors through care co-ordination	ICT programmes
Portugal		Yes		Programmes for continuous care, GestCare CCI integrated information system	
Slovenia	Cash benefits, provided by different Acts are paid directly to a person in need of a care. Insurance-based Assistance and Attendance Allowance is granted to pensionero				
Spain	Allowance for the care recipient to hire services, Allowance for the care recipient receiving informal care, Allowance for personal assistance				
Sweden		Yes	Remuneration for registry of each dementia patient in Dementia Registry and data on the prevalence of pressure ulcers, falls, and malnutrition in Senior Alert Registry Remuneration for health care authorities and municipalities for reducing hospital admissions, the use of inappropriate drugs, combination of drugs and psychotropic drugs among older people in institutional care	Piloted with an incentive programme 19 local demonstration or development projects aiming to stimulate the development of integrated care and innovative models of organising care. Less focus on building integrated care with primary care and institutional care	Technology for the elderly programme
Switzerland	Cash and in-kind benefit are complementary, "Helplessness" Allowance (*Allocation pour impotent*/API) of AVS/AI, Moderate or severe impairment, not eligible for Disability Allowance from Accident Insurance	Since 2009 there is a mandatory public reporting for health care providers based on national law. Quality indicators are in development	No		
United Kingdom	Informal carers may be eligible for Carer's Allowance	Yes on CQC website			Building Telecare, Telecare LIN, Whole Systems Demonstrator projects
United States	US Cash and Counselling programmes	Yes on Nursing Home Compare and Home Care Compare	In some states, value-based purchasing model	Yes	

Source: OECD 2012 Questionnaire on Long-Term Care Quality.

information, uncertainty that the provider is acting in the user's best interest and insufficient competition – pose challenges to using market-based mechanisms to assure quality in LTC services and high satisfaction of users or their families. Consumer direction mechanisms (such as the use of personal budgets, cash-for-care benefits or voucher systems), other tools for empowering frail elderly, public reporting and the use of star-rating systems are examples of initiatives to encourage consumers to self-direct care and protect their needs.

Consumer direction and vouchers

Consumer direction mechanisms empower care recipients and their families to make decisions on the care they need and value the most, and have now been introduced in nearly two-thirds of OECD countries. The use of cash-for care schemes and benefits is by far the most widespread among such mechanisms, especially in Europe. The choice usually takes place at the care entry points, typically at the end of needs assessment processes. Nordic countries – Finland, Sweden and Denmark – have encouraged the use of voucher systems that entitle care recipients to a subsidy to choose among competing providers (Colombo et al., 2011). The thrust is to allow users freedom of choice and incentivise providers to compete on quality and responsiveness.

Several studies have evaluated the impact of cash-for-care schemes (Nadash, 2012; Da Roit and Le Bihan, 2010; Lundsgaard, 2005; Colombo et al., 2011) and voucher systems (Colombo et al., 2011). Cash-for-care and vouchers are often associated with higher satisfaction among users. There is some evidence that the personal budgets pilot programme implemented in 2009 in England led to higher quality of life and sometimes favourable cost-effectiveness ratios (Carlson et al., 2007; Chinthapalli, 2012; Forder et al., 2012). If a choice is given, LTC recipients also prefer to choose cash instead of in-kind benefits (Nadash, 2011).

Little is known, however, about the impact of cash-for care on clinical outcomes of users and providers' quality strategies. An assessment of the impact of personal budgets in England found no impact on health status over 12 months of follow-up (Forder et al., 2012). Other studies point to a number of challenges in cash-for-care schemes. For example, there is important variation across countries and regions within a country regarding the extent of freedom of choice, range of benefit packages, and, ultimately, users' control over the care they receive (Nadash, 2012).

Having choice does not automatically empower LTC users to use benefits to maximise their outcomes without supervision and regulations. In fact, unregulated use of cash benefits can be counterproductive for quality of care – for example, when there is little oversight regarding the standards for the LTC workforce that can be paid for through such benefits, or regarding the modalities for using the cash benefits. A cash-benefit system with little regulation can discourage the formal LTC labour market and encourage a black or unregulated market to emerge (a main challenge in Italy and Austria). Critically, there is no robust evidence regarding the impact of consumer direction mechanisms on care effectiveness and safety. Most studies warn about undesirable outcomes and poor quality resulting from instances of poor or little regulation of consumer direction systems (Carlson et al., 2007; Genet et al., 2011; Meiners et al., 2002; Wiener, 2007). In voucher schemes, consumers rarely execute their right to switch providers. Many individuals are not aware of the available information, for example, 16% of Danish users were unaware of the opportunity to choose a provider (Colombo et al., 2011).

Empowering care recipients to improve quality of life

A widely employed concept when discussing quality of life and choice-based mechanisms is person-centred care. Several OECD countries are encouraging home-care like environments in residential settings (e.g., greater dining choices, flexible bathing time, self-determined schedules and care plans). Efforts have also focused on building close social contacts between LTC residents and carers.

In the United States, person-centred care and dementia mapping imply using staff to make systematic observation of symptoms associated with the wellbeing of people with dementia. Detailed observations and scoring of residents' wellbeing are fed back to care staff and managers to help planning, implementing and assessing person-centred care. Studies have reported a reduction in the prevalence of agitation or in the use of medication to suppress symptoms of agitation in nursing homes when these methods were applied (Chenoweth et al., 2009). Another tool employed to improve quality of life and care responsiveness in end-of-life care is the "advance directive", a communication tool which acts as a legal document to convey one's decisions and preferences about end-of-life care in advance (Allen et al., 2003). This aims to investigate upfront individuals' preferences over their treatment when they become cognitively and/or physically disabled. It seems to have lead to positive outcomes for nursing home residents needing palliative care (US Department of Health and Human Services, 2000).

Good information sharing and explicit guidance at different stages of the care process are necessary for delivering care that is responsive and person-centred (Mot, 2010). To give one example, Norway has handbooks directed at service recipients and their families, describing the rights and obligations according to the health and social services legislation, and providing practical instructions (such as applications, decisions and complaints) (Norwegian Ministry of Health and Care Services, 2006). Information sharing and guidance is especially important for family carers and in the case of people affected by dementia. In France, Medical Centres for Autonomy and Integration (MAIA) offer guidance regarding best care options; more than 100 such centres are expected to be established by the end of 2012 (Alzheimer Europe, 2011). A pilot programme in France offers information through a national dementia help-line that answers questions and directs people to their nearest local agency (Cahill et al., 2012). In the United Kingdom, Dementia Advisors have been appointed (across 22 nationwide locations); their remit is to help people with dementia and their families navigate the care and support system as their illness develops and help to ensure access to quality care, support and advice.

Another way to encourage care responsiveness and quality of life is through mechanisms to empower LTC users and their families against cases of abuse and complaints. Examples in countries include:

● Access points where people can report experiences of abuses as well as national-level campaigns. Ireland launched national media campaigns against elder abuses (Open Your Eyes) in 2008, targeted to those of aged 50 years old and over and focussed on disseminating information on protective and reporting services for cases of abuse. The US "Elder Abuse, Neglect and Exploitation Program" strengthens strategic planning and direction for programmes, activities, and research related to elder abuse awareness and prevention. In addition, the programme funds training for law-enforcement officers, and other professionals on recognising and respond to elder abuses and support outreach and education campaigns. Both are regarded as broadly successful.

● Education programmes for elderly and their families. These programmes teach providers and LTC recipients to recognise symptoms of elderly maltreatment, be aware of their rights, and provide training to professionals and social workers.

Public reporting on quality

While the systematic recording of quality measures in LTC is developing (Chapter 2), there has been large debate regarding the use of information on LTC providers' performance, staffing levels and auditing results to inform the public about what standards of care they can expect. The issue has become particularly relevant as OECD and EU countries implement policies to encourage choice across LTC providers, such as through the use of personal budgets or cash-for-care benefits and voucher systems described earlier. Public reporting responds to a need to reduce information gaps among consumers.

Public reporting provides purchasers of care (e.g. commissioners in the case of England), the general public and other relevant stakeholders with information on performance and audited results at a disaggregated level, i.e. provider or local level. The overall aim is to increase transparency and offer information to steer the choice of care recipients. It also aims to incentivise providers to implement improvements by appealing to their intrinsic motivation (e.g. professionalism) to safeguard their reputation (Cacace, 2012). A significant number of OECD countries make information on care providers available in the form of public reports at national level, such as inspections and audit reports, or governments' accountability reports (Australia, Canada, England, Finland, Germany, Iceland, Ireland, Japan, Korea, the Netherlands, Sweden, and the United States). There are also pilot projects in Austria and in Catalonia (Spain). Most of the countries collecting data on quality tend to make the results public. In England, the United States, Japan, the Netherlands, Germany and Sweden, reports are available at individual provider level.

Statutory requirements for public reporting differ from country to country (see also Box 6.1). Public reporting is mandatory in the United States, Japan, England, Germany, Portugal and the Netherlands, while it remains voluntary in Finland and Spain and in Austria's pilot projects. Inspection results highlighting deficits and history of non-compliance are provided internally in Finland, Spain and the Netherlands (Rodrigues, 2012). Reports can be accessed through the website of an independent regulator or review agency (e.g., England, Korea, Germany), a national agency (United States, Sweden), or local authorities (Japan). In the United States, *Nursing Home Compare* permits comparisons of information about every Medicare and Medicaid-certified nursing home. In Germany, the 2008 LTC insurance reform strengthened transparency agreements with providers, requiring inspection results to be posted at a visible location. In Australia, information is visible through the website of the Aged Care Standards and Accreditation Agency in Australia (Department of Health and Ageing, 2011). In Austria, Germany and the Netherlands, reports are accessible at each facility. The frequency of reporting varies between a few months (e.g., United States) and a year (e.g., Korea, Japan and Germany).

The degree of information provided varies from basic administrative information to information on quality by highlighting the results of inspections and quality indicators. The general trend is to move beyond structural inputs such as information on staffing and care environment (beds and services) and focus on patient centredness (e.g. meal choice, social activities) and clinical effectiveness (e.g. rate of falls).

Box 6.1. **Examples of public reporting systems in a selection of OECD countries**

In **Germany**, the Medical Advisory Boards of the Health Insurance Funds are responsible for the quality of nursing homes and home care services. The Local Residential Home Authorities (Heimaufsicht), a government agency, inspects and oversees nursing homes. The obligation to disclose audit results [section 115 (1a) SGB XI)] was introduced in 2008 (European Peer Review, 2009). The results of inspections of nursing homes and home care services have to be published and each nursing home and home care service needs to post the results in a highly visible area. More than 10 000 reports are now available online. In addition, providers are obliged to meet transparency agreements and report information for publication in transparency reports. The first transparency report was published in 2009 with the objective of giving people with care needs and their relatives the opportunity to be informed about the quality of care provided in residential facilities or home care services. The preparation of the audit reports and the publication of the transparency reports are two separate procedures. Transparency reports include not only inspections of the rooms, living areas and documentation on relevant activities, but also personal visits among the residents to verify their care status. Recommendations for improving quality are provided (European Review, 2009; Schulz, 2012).

In **Japan**, the 2009 LTC reform introduced an annual public reporting system on LTC services (JPHA, 2011). The system has three types of public reporting of LTC quality. The first is mandatory for all service providers; the second is mandatory for small-scale multifunctional home care, daily group care for seniors with dementia and community-based LTC prevention providers, while the last is a voluntary procedure for welfare facilities for the elderly. Municipalities are responsible for public reporting in the first two cases, while contracted agencies are responsible for voluntary reporting (JPHA, 2009). Under the mandatory reporting system, all service providers are required to submit information on staffing registration, vacancies, and a list of available services, as well as results of investigators' surveys. This information is available through each prefecture, and reporting criteria are standardised. Each prefecture can also require service providers to report on additional information, in which case each prefecture decides on criteria for evaluation and methodology. For community-based LTC services and prevention services, the reporting process starts with a collection of information from self-assessment and external assessment. The questions seek to examine the governance, management, community relationship, compliance with policies against abuse and human rights, training of staff, quality of life of users, and care management. The assessment is based on open-ended questions and no quality indicator is drawn, nor are providers ranked or graded. Rather, the information supports consumer decisions and helps provider self-improvement efforts. For welfare facilities for the elderly, the assessment process involves open-ended questions about the quality of services and a few items evaluating achievements (Shakyo-Hyouka, 2012). Each designated external agency sets their quality criteria. Assessment procedures are composed of a paper investigation and on-site visits. There is no quality indicator or rankings. The government has prepared national guidelines for evaluation. The process is annual or biannual. Because of its voluntary process, only 7.5% of the special nursing homes for the elderly and 3.2% of the total number of group homes for the elderly people with dementia underwent the assessment in 2011.

In **Korea**, monitoring and public reporting of LTC quality has been mandatory for all long-term care hospitals in Korea since 2008. All long-term care hospitals are subject to quality assessment and the results of assessment are published in an annual quality report and on the

---

Box 6.1. Examples of public reporting systems in a selection of OECD countries (*cont.*)

website of the Health Insurance Review and Assessment Services of Korea (HIRA). HIRA is an agency mandated under the National Health Insurance Act of 2000 to monitor and assess the quality of health care services to enhance the quality. Since 2009, HIRA has published an annual report on the results of quality assessment and the Comprehensive Quality Report of National Health. Long-term care hospitals have been one of the facilities where quality assessment is carried out. HIRA uses administrative data, including insurance claims, providers' operational data and medical records, which are matched with resident registration data and survey questionnaires to develop quality indicators that are directly communicated to providers and published. Data on inputs (medical service workforce, equipment), processes (mainly utilisation) and patient status are collected through hospital surveys and collated into 35 quality indicators, including 23 structural indicators and 12 treatment indicators. Patient assessment charts are also used (Health Insurance Review & Assessment Service, 2011).

In **Portugal**, every six months, a report is published to present data on number of beds and home care places, contracts with the different providers of care, number of referral teams (Hospital and Primary Care), referrals evaluation times by Local Co-ordination Teams, time for identification of provider and admission by Regional Co-ordination Teams, number of patients referred to RNCCI, number of patients referred that have criteria to admission, number of patients admitted related to those that have criteria to be admitted, number of patients waiting to be admitted, motives that lead to referrals, patients profile (age, sex, family status, previous health and social support), number of patients in RNCCI by region and type of care, motives of discharge from RNCCI and destination, occupation rates, evolution of physical autonomy, prevalence and incidence of pressure ulcers, falls, mortality rate, professional training (OECD 2012 Questionnaire on Long-Term Care Quality; UMCCI, 2012).

Some of the submitted data from Medicare and Medicaid certified nursing homes and home health agencies in the **United States** are posted on the website of the Centers for Medicare and Medicaid Services (CMS). The public is free to access the information and evaluation of each facility and provider (Mor, 2006). In November 2002, the CMS launched the Nursing Home Compare website, reporting information about agencies that provide Medicare skilled home health care (this does not include all home and community based services). Reporting dimensions include: ADL management, pain and pressure ulcer treatment; preventing harm and preventing unplanned hospital care. The site also reports individual nursing homes' scores on a set of quality measures and results of inspections. CMS collects quality performance information on services availability, outcome measures and gives ratings of how well these facilities and providers assist beneficiaries in regaining or maintaining their ability to function. There are also process measures which evaluate the rate of use by the home health agency of specific evidence-based processes of care (Medicare, 2012; Castle and Ferguson, 2010). NHC provides the following information by provider and facility: i) results of inspection by state government from a database containing survey information (OSCAR); ii) Results of fire and safety inspections; iii) Penalty history or any complaints or cases over the last three years. Nineteen quality measures, generated out of the Minimum Data Set (MDS), are used for public reporting, highlighting things such as ADL change, mobility change, high-risk pressure ulcers, long-term catheters, physical restraints, urinary tract infections, and pain. For short-stay nursing home users, NHC includes delirium, pain and pressure ulcers. The Centers for Medicare and Medicaid Services launched a website in fall 2003 that publishes 11 quality measures out of the OASIS data on outcomes

---

> **Box 6.1. Examples of public reporting systems in a selection of OECD countries** (*cont.*)
>
> in home health care (Home Health Compare on Medicare.gov). These publicly reported measures include outcome measures indicating how well home health agencies assist their patients in regaining or maintaining their ability to function and process measures which evaluate the rate of home health agency use of specific evidence-based processes of care. As to home care users, information about agencies that provide Medicare skilled home health care has been available on the CMS website as of fall 2003 (CMS, 2012). A subset of OASIS-based quality performance information is posted on the website (ADL management, pain and pressure ulcer treatment; preventing harms and preventing unplanned hospital care).

Among the countries known to collect quality data, Canada, England, Finland, Germany, Korea, the Netherlands, Portugal and the United States publish the findings of quality indicators along with other administrative data at a provider or aggregated level. On the contrary, fewer countries are able to report data on user experience. The Netherlands is one such country where user experience along with effectiveness and safety of care data are published. Iceland is also in the preparation phase to start publishing the outcomes of 20 quality indicators of residents. Averages and aggregate data of providers are available (e.g., Korea, Germany) but such aggregated data are not necessarily provided in public reports. Countries such as the United States, Japan and England provide information at provider level. To limit the risk of regional variation, Japan requires a set of national standardised criteria to be reported in each region, which include a checklist of standards satisfied by different providers (JPHA, 2009).

Public reporting is more likely to be implemented for residential care settings; only a few countries require home care providers and assisted living facilities and rehabilitation services to make information available. Although consumers are more likely to be in need of information on home care providers and other services related to cash-for-care schemes, there is generally less focus on providing such information.

Impact of public reporting on LTC recipients

The impact of public reporting on consumer behaviours can be measured in a number of ways at each stage of the decision process, starting from the awareness stage, and then through the knowledge stage, attitude stage and action (Cacace, 2012). It is hard to assess whether public reporting on care quality has had a positive impact on awareness and informed decision making by LTC users. Little or limited evidence supports such changes in consumers' behaviours. For example, evidence shows consumers do not recall receiving and seeing information of quality of providers. In the United Kingdom, only 15% of users are aware of the availability of publicly reported information with only 1% of users actually using information displayed (CSCI, 2009).

By contrast, referrals and family and friends tended to be the most used source of information used in decision making. One of the reasons is that information, in the way it is disseminated, is not easily accessible or understood among the older population. Older people still tend to rely more on paper-based sources rather than web-based information. Computer literacy is not high and even among those who use the Internet, only around 25% of older people between 65 and 74 years old access the Internet at least once a week across a number of European countries (Rodrigues, 2012). Even if they do access and understand the information, they may not use it to make choices.

In general, evidence tends to show that the public perception is more positive when the source of information is neutral and published by an independent third agency. For example, in England, the Care Quality Commission is an independent body responsible for public reporting, which makes information on care homes and care at home available online (Care Quality Commission, 2013; Marshall, 2004). There is encouraging evidence that the public reporting through Nursing Home Compare in the United States – which presents information on management, ombudsmen, and opinions of users – has led to more informed decision making among consumers (Sorenson and Mossialos, 2007).

Impact of public reporting on provider behaviour

Regarding changes in provider behaviour, a number of studies have investigated how LTC providers and stakeholders respond to the availability of public reporting. The rationale is that giving providers and the public information on providers' performance relative to their peers may encourage poor performers to undertake improvements efforts.

Some evidence points towards improvement in outcomes related to care, for example:

● Korea makes use of the information to inform providers and help steer quality improvements. Indicators related to the safety of facilities, adequacy of living environment, and workforce showed improvement since LTC indicators started to be collected in Korean LTC hospitals in 2009 (HIRA, 2011). Public reports are distributed to the public, to medical care institutions and to policy makers. Results of assessment are also shared with medical care institutions, highlighting problems, areas for improvement and distance from benchmarks. Problem areas are diagnosed through on-site counselling visits where solutions are discussed. Since 2007, the Korea Health Insurance Review Agency has also developed a quality improvement support programme to coach institutions. There are also competitions with prizes awarded to institutions showing outstanding results or examples of good practices.

● In the United States, reporting on performance of nursing homes and home care has led providers to make some quality improvement effort (Mukamel et al., 2008; Sorensen and Mossialos, 2007; Castle 2005). A survey of more than 1 500 facilities carried out after the launch of Nursing Home Compare in 2002 showed some evidence that nursing homes with quality scores below the 20th percentile initiated corrective actions, such as reorganising staff, changing management and reviewing protocols (Mukamel et al., 2007).

● Results published from subsequent user satisfaction surveys in Germany showed improvement in aspects such as communications and responsiveness following the last report published in 2007. For example, the proportion of institutions with a prospective development plan increased from 84.1% in 2007 to 93.6% in 2010, while 96.8% of outpatient services could ensure continuity of staff. However, the 2012 report showed that only 59.3% of residents in nursing home who were at risk of pressure ulcers received the necessary measures (such as rolling), and the rate of performance has not changed since 2007. For ambulatory care services, 36.5% of beneficiaries receiving home care services were at risk of pressure ulcers but only 40.5% of them received advice from care services and for only 18.2%, providers agreed to provide measure to prevent pressure ulcers. Pain management also shows no improvement from 2007 (MDS, 2012).

Despite these encouraging examples, the evidence on impact on clinical outcomes is still not conclusive. In the United States, a study looking at the impact of website reporting on post-acute care measures found only modest gains in pain control and no effects for delirium use and walking before and after the launch of Nursing Home Compare (Werner,

2010). Evaluations of the introduction of public reporting on nursing home quality measures suggest that there may have been an effect on both measured and unmeasured quality items, suggesting little impact of public reporting on quality (Werner et al., 2009).

A possible explanation for these results is that providers might be more sensitive to reports on some care quality indicators than to others. Data on experiencing pain and on the use of physical restraints tend to improve following public reports, although change might be one-offs (Mukamel et al., 2008). Another possible explanation is that providers might need a long time to correct deficiencies on some of the outcome measures. Consumer choice mechanisms might be less effective where there is a shortage of providers as providers see little reason or have little incentives to improve quality.

In theory, public reporting provides opportunities for providers to "signal" their good performance and high quality services to stakeholders (such as LTC users, families and friends and LTC workers) and potentially increases the number of people wishing to use their services. But if providers do not see the impact of public reporting on their practice, they cannot appreciate the importance of submitting data when participation is voluntary. Only one in five care homes in Germany adhered to voluntary public reporting and one in five have certified quality management in place in Austria. Interest in voluntarily strengthening the quality of reporting is low where sanctions against low performing providers is minimal or not enforced. Another weak factor is that the range of indicators covered in public reporting is still limited.

Concerns have also been expressed that public reporting on quality of care might lead to unintended or undesirable consequences. There is a fear that public reporting might incentivise provider gaming. For example, providers might focus only on the items measured in performance assessments or seek to game the system (such as by reducing opportunities for physical activity to lower the incidence of falls, or using a wheelchair rather than allowing people to walk (Mor, 2007; Poductivity Commission, 2011). Providers may also "up-code" users' profiles to pretend that they are serving beneficiaries with more complex care needs. They could select those care recipients who would best demonstrate measured improvements, so that the risk of performing poorly against particular outcome measures is minimised (Mor, 2007).

Quality grading systems

A handful of OECD countries publish reports on LTC providers along with a grading of their performance relative to their peers. This aims to highlight deficiencies and variations in care outcomes and empower LTC users to make informed choices, thereby overcoming asymmetric information between consumers and providers. Grading systems can help to increase accountability and transparency and provide incentives for competition (Castle, 2009; Mukamel et al., 2008; Castle, 2009; Sorensen and Mossialos, 2007; Mor, 2010; JPHA, 2009).

Of the countries that publish performance reports online, Germany, Korea and Sweden and the United States use ranking of care providers. Conversely, England has recently discontinued a star rating. Indicators on various quality dimensions form the basis for ranking, although rankings are calculated differently across countries. To make grading accessible and easy to understand, two approaches are principally used: i) employ an assessment system according to school grades, e.g. from "very good" to "poor" (Germany, for example) (Schulz, 2012; Bavarian State Ministry of Labour and Social Welfare, Family Affairs, Women and Health and Federal

Ministry of Health, 2010); and ii) provide star ranking the way hotels and travel advisory websites advertise best hotels and restaurants (Korea and the United States). For example, HIRA (Korea) applies a grading method to LTC hospitals and medical care institutions using grades from one to five. Box 6.2 explains US grading systems as used since 2008.

Box 6.2. **Star rating system in Nursing Home Compare in the United States**

Nursing Home Compare is a national, online nursing home report card providing information on every Medicare and Medicaid certified nursing home in each state. A five-star quality rating system (one star being the lowest and five stars the best) has been added since December 2008 as a new feature on the website with the objective of simplifying information found on the website, making it more user friendly and providing nursing home residents and their families with a mechanism to assess nursing home quality, enabling them to make distinctions between low and high performing nursing homes. The website allows individuals to search nursing homes by name, city, county, state, or zip code. Each nursing home is rated on a scale of one to five stars based on three components: health inspection results, quality measures for short-and long-term residents, and staffing levels. Each home also receives an overall quality rating. Nursing homes that receive a five star rating are considered to have above average quality compared to other nursing homes in that state. Conversely, homes with one star have a quality rating much below the state average. But, CMS notes that nursing homes receiving one star ratings are still certified and meet all minimum federal safety and health requirements.

- Health Inspections Rating: Facility ratings for the health inspection component are based on the number, scope and severity of deficiencies identified during the three most recent annual inspection surveys as well as substantiated findings from the most recent 36 months of complaint investigations. All deficiency findings are weighted by scope and severity.

- Staffing Information Rating: It is based on two measure i) RN hours per resident day; and ii) total staffing hours (RN + LPN + nursing aide hours). This information is derived from the CMS Certification and Survey Provider Enhanced Reporting (CASPER) system, and is casemix-adjusted based on the distribution of MDS 3.0 assessments by Resource Utilisation Groups (RUGS)-III group to account for differences in acuity, meaning a resident with a higher need of care would be expected to have more direct care staff than a resident with lower need.

- Quality Measures Rating: The quality measure rating assesses resident outcomes to determine the quality of care that residents receive in the nursing home. The rating is based on the three most recent quarters of data reported to CMS by the nursing home (see Chapter 2).

- Overall Quality Rating: In order to calculate a nursing home's overall quality rating, CMS begins with the nursing home's health inspection rating and adds one star if the home received a staffing rating of four or five stars; one star is subtracted if the home received a staffing rating of one star. If the nursing home received a quality measure rating of five stars, another star is added to its overall rating; one star is subtracted if the home received a quality measure rating of one star. A nursing home's overall quality rating is updated monthly. The three sub-ratings are reported and updated on different schedules. When the five-star rating system began on 18 December 2008, 23% of nursing homes received an overall rating of one star while 12% received a five-star rating.

> **Box 6.2. Star rating system in Nursing Home Compare in the United States** *(cont.)*
>
> Because of regional differences in terms of eligibility, benefits, costs, and quality enforcement policies within the country, health inspection ratings are based on the relative performance of facilities within a state where a nursing home is located. CMS acknowledges certain limitations with its rating system. For example: *i)* the health inspection rating does not account for state variation in different systems and governance of Medicaid programmes; *ii)* the staffing and quality measures ratings are based on self-reported data by nursing homes; *iii)* the quality measure ratings is based on only ten measures; and *iv)* the rating does not measure resident or family satisfaction.
>
> *Source:* CMS – Centers for Medicare and Medicaid Services (2012), "Design for Nursing Home Compare Five-Star Quality Rating System: Technical Users' Guide", CMS, July.

The main criticism of rating systems is that different aspects of quality receive the same weight, with the result that deficiencies in one aspect (e.g., wound care or the prevention of pressure ulcers) can be compensated by good rating in others (e.g., nice surroundings, nicely decorated rooms). Germany's transparency report has led to some criticism that the results were too positively portrayed and over-rated. Providers often complain that quality assessment and ranking pay more attention to documentation than evaluation of the care provided and the outcomes of care (Schulz, 2012).

Choice-based mechanisms must be tailored to the unique characteristics of care markets

To date, there is no robust evidence linking public reporting of quality measures and other choice mechanisms to clinical quality improvement, despite encouraging results on satisfaction and responsiveness.

To make choice more effective, it is important to point out that LTC users are not typical consumers, or buyers of differentiated and privately produced goods and services in the marketplace. LTC recipients have limited knowledge and time to access and understand the information provided. As for the supply market, LTC services are often offered by non-for-profit or semi-public entities, and financing mechanisms are dominated by public resources. Providers competitive incentives are lowered by regulation, and the amount and type of information displayed in public reporting may not correspond to what LTC recipients want to know. There is little emphasis on how regulators might use such information to work with providers to drive improvement.

Threat of reputational damage can become a strong driver for improvement (Cacace, 2012). As public reporting and choice mechanisms in LTC are developing, lessons may be learnt from implementation in the health care sector. Experience suggests that it is important to make reporting adjustable to patients' needs, for example, allowing them to choose their own weights and preferences if public reporting adopts a ratings and grading system. The selection of indicators is an important factor, and should include both clinical as well as patient responsiveness and centredness indicators. Because the development of public reporting mechanisms tend to be top-down rather than an all-inclusive or bottom-up approach, it is important to involve all stakeholders affected by public reporting in the process. Attitudes towards online-based information platforms are changing and a new pool of older people will be more familiar with Internet and social media making a wider dissemination of information possible.

Encouraging quality through provider payment incentives needs more evaluation

Payment mechanisms in long-term care (such as per-diem in institutions and salary or fee for service in home care settings) have been criticised for not providing sufficient incentives for higher care quality. Providers' payment schemes based on performance (P4P) have been introduced in health care, for example in France, the United Kingdom, and Korea (OECD and the European Observatory, forthcoming). These schemes aim to improve clinical quality of care, and encourage providers to improve processes that can lead to higher quality, such as generic prescription, improved care co-ordination, or electronic reporting of clinical information.

While performance payments seem to be gaining some attraction as a potential means to reward better performance and influence providers' practice, only a few countries have initiated pay-for-performance schemes to improve LTC quality (Colombo et al., 2011). Often, these schemes combine public reporting with financial incentives and emphasise competition among facilities to improve quality of care (Mor, 2010; Productivity Commission, 2011). Evidence of the impact on quality is sketchy.

One example of P4P in the LTC sector is in Korea. The Health Insurance Review and Assessment agency (HIRA) assesses the quality of care provided by LTC hospitals covered by the National Health Insurance, while the NHI Corporation examines LTC providers under the LTC insurance scheme. The incentive scheme – Value Incentive Programme (VIP) – for LTC hospitals links evaluation results to fee payment. Admission fees for LTC hospitals are based on a per diem depending on staffing level and the functional status of the recipient. Since 2010, the NHI corporation withdraws payment linked to staffing levels for underperforming hospitals. As of 2010, 718 LTC hospitals participated in the VIP, and 24 indicators were used, of which 20 structural indicators and four process and outcome indicators.[1] The assessment is performed once a year and a composite score is estimated to generate an overall score for each LTC hospital. Results are published on the HIRA website and hospitals are notified. In 2010, LTC hospitals whose (composite) scores on structural, process and outcome indicators (see Chapter 2 for details) were below the 20th percentile of the total LTC hospitals evaluated were not given the incentive payment for the following two quarters. Similarly, under the LTC insurance scheme, LTC facilities are subject to mandatory public reporting which provides scores on their performance. The performance of each facility is examined against a set of quality indicators linked to the operation of the institution, environment and safety, rights and duties, process of care and outcomes of care. Scores are calculated based on composite scores with a weight applied to each area. The total score is generated for every facility which is then graded into five groups. Since 2009, the top 10% best performing facilities has been given a financial reward of 5% of total payment by the LTC insurance scheme. There are plans to expand the list of indicators and reduce the financial incentive to 3%.

In the United States, some states (New York, Wisconsin and Arizona) have implemented a value-based purchasing model for nursing homes since 2009 (some states started earlier as an ad-hoc basis) (Weiner, 2009). Three states participate in a federal pilot study for Medicare and ten states have the programme in place for Medicaid. The programme was initiated to counter criticism that the existing system did not differentiate reimbursement between high and low-quality facilities. Nursing home providers and facilities are assessed and paid based on their performance and/or improvement on a selected number of quality measures. Assessment is expressed in scores and encompasses measures on staffing, appropriate hospitalisations, outcome measures taken from the Minimum Data Set, and inspection survey results (CMS, 2012). High-quality facilities receive extra reimbursement which is used for improvement among the participating facilities. There has been little evaluation of the state-led programmes and the existing preliminary evaluation of federal pilot studies found mixed results (Wiener, 2012).

In Japan, a financial incentive for high-performing LTC providers has been added to the fee-for-service payment since the 2009 fee-schedule revision. Each service is priced under the LTC insurance fee schedule and there are additional points paid to nursing homes if they exceed a certain threshold regarding the number of elderly people successfully discharged from institutions to home (JPHA, 2011). Additional points can be paid to community-based care services (*houmon-tsuusho-related-services*) when a certain proportion of users successfully have improved their physical functions.[2] Further, a bonus payment is granted to nursing homes that recruit certain staff with a particular expertise (such as nutritionists, staff trained in dementia care, work experience of staff, etc.), or have comprehensive care planning for cases of end-of-life care and rehabilitation.

Although it has not been systematically introduced and varies by municipalities, some municipalities in Finland have recently moved towards requiring evidence of performance with in-built incentives and sanctions for the procurement procedures of contracts to providers. However, there are no standards or systematic criteria on how this process could be effectively promoted. Another interesting examples is offered by Sweden and Denmark. In Sweden, municipalities are responsible for payment of patients whose medical treatment have been completed if no place in the community can be found, while in Denmark, municipalities share 20% of the cost of hospital treatment. Since 2009, the Swedish government has linked payment to municipalities to quality measures in long-term care such as avoidable hospitalisations for chronic conditions, palliative care, dementia care and prevention, based on the rich quality registers dataset described in Chapter 2.

A review of P4P programmes in health care suggests that there has been no systematic and robust evaluation of the schemes, and that for those which were evaluated, the results were not robust enough to indicate positive impacts on health outcomes of individuals receiving treatment (OECD and European Observatory on Health Systems and Policies, forthcoming). This summary evaluation seems valid also for performance payment in LTC. Evidence available to date does not support direct causality between the use of payment incentives such as P4P and outcome improvement. There is encouraging evidence, however, that payment incentives might have positive "side effects" such as in encouraging providers to deliver comprehensive assessment using standardised tools, report outcomes through electronic records and databases, and target specific well-defined areas of underperformance. All of these are important factors for enabling and supporting, perhaps in a second time, actual quality improvements.

Well co-ordinated health and care services can reduce hospitalisations and adverse events

Many older people express preference for staying at home even when they become frail. Age-in-place policies have allowed many individuals needing LTC to continue living at home as independently as possible while receiving necessary care. But as people with multiple chronic conditions live long enough to become frail, or develop conditions as part of an ageing process,[3] the availability of well-co-ordinated services cutting across health and social care and allowing regular monitoring by different health professionals settings becomes critical.

Yet good co-ordination is often lacking. LTC systems in some countries are based on social care models with an insufficient focus on health care. Conversely, lack of strong primary care systems with linkages back and forth to LTC may trigger the unnecessary admission of old people to acute care hospitals. Poor care co-ordination is a main cause of unsatisfactory quality and can lead to adverse events and preventable hospital re-admissions (see study by Avoidable Hospitalization Advisory Panel, 2011). Gaps in communication (e.g., transfer of LTC users' information on pain and medication) during care transitions from hospitals to LTC settings are problematic. For people with dementia, conditions are not always recorded or communicated to hospital staff on admission (Thompson et al., 2010) or only known to a part of hospital staff (Cahill, 2012) (Box 6.3). In hospital settings, flaws in communication, such as change in personnel shifts and patient transfer can account for 70% of all sentinel events (Alvarado et al., 2006; Weatherly et al., 2010). Poorly co-ordinated care may also result in inappropriate use of medications (OECD, 2012b). The following section highlights some of the policy initiatives from countries addressing gaps in the continuity of care.

Box 6.3. **People with dementia have special care co-ordination needs**

People with dementia are at risk for hospital admissions although many of them can be avoided if early diagnosis and appropriate care plans and provision are implemented. Instead, they are at a high risk for a broad range of adverse outcomes including higher morbidity and mortality rates, increased length of stay in hospital and increased risk of discharge to institutional care (Cahill et al., 2012). For example, poor balance in community-dwelling people with dementia is a significant risk factor and is associated with an increased risk for falls and hip fractures with a result of hospitalisation and institutionalisation (Cahill et al., 2012). The rate of hospitalisations of people with dementia is high. In England, as shown by Sampson et al. (2009), 42% of individuals aged 70 years and over and 48% of people aged 80 years and over among those admitted to an acute hospital had dementia. In Ireland, about 20% of acute beds are occupied by patients with persistent cognitive impairment including people with dementia. Evidence highlights that people with dementia once admitted to acute hospitals often have far worse outcomes than those without dementia.

A mix of integration approaches with different incentives for providers and payers is possible

There is a vast literature on care integration addressing these missing links and exemplifying policies. Some policies aim to realign current health care and social care delivery models (e.g. between home care and primary care, rehabilitation and residential care settings) while others focus on addressing issues caused by a lack of integration (such as avoidable admission and re-admissions). Overall, all of the policies target to achieve and ensure seamless transitions across care settings from home and community care to primary care, acute care, rehabilitation and residential care. Such harmonisation is not only important for good quality of life of LTC users, but it is also a necessity to minimise harm to patients and costs incurred to overall health and LTC financing.

There are at least three main goals that integrating care pathway aims to achieve: improve appropriateness and consistency across; enhance choice and flexibility in service delivery, and improve service efficiency and patient outcomes. Care integration can take different forms that have been extensively studied in health care. In this context, types of integration have been clustered into three groups listed below in order of growing complexity and degree of integration: integration of information, clinical and professional integration, functional and service integration, organisational and structural integration (see Box 6.4).

> ## Box 6.4. **Forms of integrated care**
>
> **Integrated health and care information systems.** Transitions in care are known to be particularly problematic because relevant information may not be communicated in a timely manner or different documentation systems between health and social care or between municipalities and counties, integrated information systems enable to monitor LTC users as they move around different care settings and care transitions, harmonising information sharing among providers. Challenge is also time, place and professionals. Examples include standardised assessment instrument integrated into information system.
>
> **Functional and service integration** refer to effective management of different services, and setting a function to manage integrated care, referrals, and care transitions across care settings, through improved co-ordination. Initiatives implemented in countries have aimed at enhancing hospital discharge practices and more effective management of care transitions. Re-admission rates and incidence of falls and pressure ulcers can be used to measure success. Examples include single entry, case management and discharge practices.
>
> **Clinical and professional integration** refers to standardised diagnostic and eligibility criteria. This can be encouraged through comprehensive single assessment and care planning systems, integrated clinical and care records, care guidelines and protocols cutting across health and social care, and multi-disciplinary teams. Uniform, comprehensive needs assessment reduces delays in providing appropriate care and reduce variations in care planning. The system has been utilised in many countries. Examples include care planning, multidisciplinary teams, and clinical and care guidelines.
>
> **Organisational and financial integration** addresses organisational barriers such as different channels of funding, difficulties in access to services, and geographical boundaries. Responsibilities for health and social care are integrated under a single management or a single payment system. A barrier to integration of acute and LTC is fragmentation in financing. This reduces incentives for providers to develop care packages that involve both acute and long-term care. Examples include bundling payment, building partnerships across providers, and merging health and care providers.

Integrated health and care information systems

Assessment instruments using integrated information systems can be found in countries with InterRAI systems (such as Canada, Belgium, Iceland, and the United States) or programmes for continuous care (i.e. Portugal). In Iceland, all nursing homes have a computerised system documenting RAI assessments which is connected to the central RAI database managed by the Directorate of Health. In Belgium, the pilot project, BelRAI, seeks to establish a better information flow and improve the quality of care by unifying needs assessment and care data from home care, residential care and acute care (BelRAI, 2012). BelRAI utilises the online platform eHealth to collect information on LTC recipients. This information is then made accessible to different providers (physicians, nurses, dentists, LTC workers, geriatricians, dieticians, and psychologists). The participating hospitals, nursing homes and care organisations[4] have access to the BelRAI web application. The project started officially in June 2010 and each region takes financial responsibility for database development and management.

Portugal's GestCare CCI integrated information system monitors LTC user, referrals, admissions, transitions, waiting times and outcomes of care. Portugal's on-line data management system (GestCare CCI) allows continuous results assessment at provider, regional and national level. The database covers all stages including admission, referrals, and care process. Hospital discharge management teams, primary health care centres, local co-ordination teams, regional co-ordination teams and national co-ordination all have access to the information. Referrals, admissions, transitions, waiting times and patients waiting to be admitted, as well as outcomes of care are recorded and made available through GestCare CCI to the network of providers. GestCare CCI has an integrated evaluation tool generating online reports on different parameters. This helps to identify possible bottlenecks and critical performance issues (de Abreu Nogueira et al., 2009). It also allowed for the use of online referrals, clinical registry development and benchmarking to drive care improvement.

Interoperable electronic health records and health information exchanges support efforts to achieve a continuum of care and better co-ordination by enabling medical records to be portable across care settings. There are two key ingredients for success. First, strong information technology infrastructures need to be available or developed; and second, data portability is essential. Unique patient identifiers, for example, enable continuous monitoring of each individuals moving from one care setting to another. A majority of countries, however, only collect results of needs assessment and such data are not transferable or integrated. In many countries, nursing homes do not use an electronic medical record system, nor are records kept of transfers to home care settings.

Functional and service integration

Single-entry systems offer one way to encourage service integration. These are one-stop-shop mechanisms where potential LTC users can be screened, assessed, advised, and directed to appropriate services. The availability of single-entry points is influenced by the way LTC services are governed. Some systems are available at sub-national/provincial level in Canada and the United States, or at local level in Japan and Nordic countries. Often a single-entry point is combined with a case management system, part of government efforts to standardise procedures.

Discharge practices manage transfers from acute-care to LTC services and are critical to good quality outcomes. Enhanced assessment for post-hospital needs, enhanced communication between patients and families, post-care follow-up are the most common tools used. Others tools include fostering improved self-management skills for community-based care. Studies evaluating these interventions in Ontario, Canada found a slightly lower hospitalisation rates among those who participated in these initiatives than control groups (Avoidable Hospitalization Advisory Panel, 2011). In Colorado (United States), Care Transition Coaching interventions that use a coach to encourage management of care transitions, self-care, and improve communication across care settings have shown encouraging reductions in rates of rehospitalisation by coaching frail elderly with chronic conditions and their caregivers to ensure that their needs are met during care transitions (Coleman et al., 2006).

Financial incentives to foster integration have been applied in several countries. England's Community Care Act 2003 requires local authorities to reimburse the National Health Service

Trust for each day an acute patient's discharge is delayed due to the sole responsibility of social services, either in making an assessment for services or provision of such services.

As primary care has a major responsibility for preventing frail elderly hospitalisations by detecting health risks and referring frail older people to appropriate care and treatment, interest in encouraging integration between primary long-term care has grown. Sweden for example launched initiatives to improve collaboration between the hospital, primary health care and social services by encouraging innovative models of care and seamless care co-ordination. National grants were awarded to 19 local demonstrative projects to develop models of organising integrated care with a particular focus on reducing or delaying hospital admissions among people in communities. A popular example is the use of mobile teams which provide proactive, early interventions, offering the necessary care at home. Another successful case is Lidköpin county, where hospitalisation rates decreased hugely (an estimated 90 per cent) after the implementation of a common political board across counties and municipalities to deliver coordinated care for older people. Other counties have strengthened case management services that are used to detect older people at risk in order to provide service and care at an early stage.

Another example is Norway. Norway provides subsidy to municipalities who link their nursing homes to NOKLUS (The Norwegian Quality Improvement of Primary Care Laboratories) in order to strengthen the quality of the medical offer that is available in nursing homes.

Integrating dementia social care models into health care is of particular importance. The provision of integrated community-based systems of support for people with dementia would almost certainly reduce demand on acute hospitals. The importance of a multi-disciplinary approach to the management of the person with dementia living in the community and the appointment of a case manager help to identify multiple needs and co-ordinate the provision of appropriate responses. Increased knowledge about dementia care and improved communication strategies from primary care providers can limit the risk of hospitalisation (Thompson et al., 2010).

Some countries have implemented policies to reduce unnecessary hospital admissions among people with dementia (Scotland, Sweden and Australia). Scotland has supported alternatives to hospital admission, such as the North East Fife (a jointly funded health and social work team). The team provides community assessment and short-term care to older people with dementia and other mental health difficulties. Outcomes include reduced inpatient utilisation, reduced length of hospital stay and reduced day hospital attendance (Weatherly et al., 2010; Cahill, 2012). An evaluation of the Dementia Rehabilitation at Home (DRAH) project in Australia, piloted under the Innovative Pool Dementia Pilot, revealed that outreach and community-based specialist dementia services reduce the use of hospitals by people with dementia, leading to improved patient outcomes (Hales et al., 2006).

Clinical and professional integration

Several tools can help to encourage clinical and professional integration:

● Care planning has the potential to promote continuity of care and co-ordination across different health and care settings by tailoring care to individual needs and improving follow-up during the care episode. In England and Japan, for example, gatekeepers or case managers have the responsibility for creating care plans and monitoring conditions, from assessment to referral and end of care. England's Single

Assessment Process is a tool to encourage user-centred car based on checklists, guidance, and single assessment and protocols. A challenge however is to ensure that care planners not only guide recipients through LTC care services and benefits systems, but also facilitate co-ordination for medical needs.

● Portugal's integrated instrument for bio-psychosocial evaluation has been developed within the integrated care model GastCare CCI for LTC and post acute care. Outcomes are registered on an on-line data repository that allows continuous real-time assessment a national, local, and unit level, making it possible to benchmark data. Standardised Assessment systems as the Resident Assessment Instrument (RAI), have a strong potential for facilitating care co-ordination because they include a set of core-assessment items (e.g., physical functions, cognition, pain, relevant clinical complexity) that can be used across care settings (see Chapter 3). Transferring the information generated through RAI into medical records, and vice versa would improve this instrument even more.

● Joint clinical and care guidelines can help co-ordinate care through different pathways and reduce avoidable medical and care variations; with the exception of dementia care guidelines, clinical guidelines often do not span to social care (see also Chapter 5).

● Interdisciplinary care delivered by a team integrating different clinical aspects and developing shared guidelines and protocols – a practice in clinical settings (Temkin-Greener et al., 2009) – has been recommended as a way to respond to needs of LTC recipients with complex conditions, particularly if teams are trained to assist with assessment, follow-ups and discharges. In France, the *Service Intégré de Soins à Domicile* co-ordinates the distribution of tasks among health and social care professionals for home care. In Iceland, doctors are on call for emergencies or visit nursing homes two to five times a week. Most nursing homes provide physiotherapy and some occupational therapy. In the United States, multidisciplinary team-based programmes have been piloted; for example, the Programme of All-Inclusive Care for the Elderly (PACE) aims to provide comprehensive care to people who are enrolled in both Medicaid and Medicare (Temkin-Greener et al., 2004). The establishment of multi-disciplinary teams is usually left to each provider and further monitoring of outcomes is needed (Temkin-Greener et al., 2009).

● Canada and Australia also have implemented selected clinical integration trails. In Quebec, the System for integrated care for old people (SIPA) involves multidisciplinary teams providing home care services with round the clock on call availability. The focus is on primary care, case management, and making staff responsible for integrating community health and social services, and for co-ordinating hospital and nursing home care. In South Australia, the Healthplus co-ordinated care trial uses a network of GPs and other health professionals to develop individualised treatment plans, use disease management guidelines, and care planning tools. Both have shown evidence of improved health benefits and quality of life for participating patients.

Organisational and financial integration

There are some examples of organisational integration merging health and care. In the United States, the already mentioned PACE programme focuses on providing integrated health and social care for poor elderly people with complex care needs, by integrating day care, prevention and support care under a unique platform. The programme uses proactive case management, and pays providers capitated payments for delivering primary and LTC

(Colombo et al., 2011). Similarly, so-called social HMOs are insurance models spanning primary that use capitated payments and active management of care (Thomas et al., 2010). While some outcomes are positive – such as reduced hospitalisation and lower risk of long-term institutionalisation, this programmes can have high set up cost.

Merging health and care providers is a more complex organisational change that facilitates sharing of financial risks. In Belgium, nursing and ADL assistance are integrated into health coverage through the social health insurer INAMI. Health and social care services for home care have been integrated through so-called *Service Intégré de Soins à Domicile* in Belgium (as well as in France). In the United States, the health reform (Affordable Care Act, 2011) introduced several demonstration projects aimed at improving care co-ordination among nursing home users receiving both Medicare and Medicaid services, including two financing options for states to consider: a capitated integration model and a fee-for-service integration model. Similarly, bundling payments that provide a payment for a whole episode or pathway of care are promising approaches to integrate care. Another form of integration is through partnerships across providers to jointly monitor spending and performance, although without pooled funding or joint financial responsibility, it can be more difficult to achieve results (Harriette et al., 2007).

The Ontario Government of Canada has a four-year Ageing at Home Strategy which focuses on the delivery of an integrated continuum of community-based services to help seniors remain healthy and maintain independent lives in their homes. The strategy focuses on expanding community living options through enhanced home care and community services. Belgium provides medical co-ordination to high and complex health needs among LTC recipients in residential settings but it is still in the preparatory phase to comprehensively implement it across residential care setting. Some localities in Iceland have drawn special service contracts to integrate nursing and other services in the home, with the aim of creating single service outlets. This strategy has made it easier to meet elderly people's requirements and streamlined administration and funding arrangements. It has also facilitated better utilisation of employees skills and securing standards and safety. This integration plan is set to continue in the coming years.

Features of successful initiatives

Evidence on the impact of integrated care shows improved quality of life and a reduction of institutionalisations and hospitalisations, although further research on the cost-effectiveness of different models would be desirable. Successful initiatives share some comment features, for example: i) when direct interactions among patients and staff is encouraged; ii) when proactive care management and multidisciplinary teams are employed; iii) when patients or recipients most at risk of hospitalisation and frailty are targeted; and iv) when financial incentives are aligned (e.g., through bundling or capitation). The integration of clinical and service components stands out as especially important; this can be facilitated by a number of tools, ranging from portable information systems and records to the used of shared guidelines across social and care settings and single entry assessment processes.

Outstanding challenges remain. Besides the lack of systematic evaluation of pilots or projects, it has proved difficult to scale up small pilot projects. An encouraging finding is that organisational or vertical integration involving wide systemic reforms that are difficult to push through are not strictly necessary. Rather, clinical and service integration appear to be the critical dimension. Important factors that might delay integration and would be worth tackling include strengthening ICTs and information transfer systems, along with measuring and reporting of outcomes that can be linked to targeted initiatives; a focus on piloting and experimenting with innovative incentives linking payment to shared health and social outcomes; and encouragement of the use of shared practice and care guidelines.

Using ICTs to promote independent living and improve outcomes

There is much interest in the potential for ICT to drive improvements in care provision and outcomes through better monitoring. Nearly all OECD countries have policies, regulations or incentives to help LTC beneficiaries stay at home and live independently (Colombo et al., 2011). ICTs have major applications in LTC that could help patients remain at home (Box 6.5). These can be categorised into four types:

- Electronic Medical/Health/Patient Records refer to systems that are used by healthcare professionals to store and manage patient health information and data, and include functionalities that support the care delivery process (e.g. e-prescribing, decision support). Under-diagnosis of people with dementia in acute care could be improved through incorporation of diagnosis into electronic health records (Cahill et al., 2012).

- Personal Health Records (PHRs) refers to systems that are used by patients to access and manage their health information.

- Health Information Exchange refers to the process of electronically transferring (or aggregating and enabling access to) patient health information and data. Exchange may take place between different types of entities – for example – e-messaging between patient and provider, e-transfer of patient data between ambulatory care providers, or e-transfer of data at the regional level.

- Tele-health/tele-medicine refers to the use of ICT to support care between patients and providers, or among providers, who are not co-located. This may include applications such as remote home monitoring of patients, tele-ICUs and teleradiology.

The potential for ICTs in care for the elderly has been highlighted in many reports (OECD, 2012a). Benefits include:

- *Improved quality of care*: ICTs can provide on-the-job support for care workers, helping them improve communication, management of transitions and recording of quality outcomes. Telecare and telemonitoring devices can also support training of carers and help formal and informal care givers react appropriately to changing health conditions and thus improve the quality of care (Mollenkopf et al., 2010). For informal caregivers, ICTs can support monitoring and connectivity with trained workers and service providers.

- *Improved co-ordination between health and social care that prevent avoidable hospitalisations and medication errors*. For instance, electronic health records and integrated information systems can be employed to collect and share information on people in need of care and facilitate better communication between different stakeholders and institutions involved in care provision. Electronic prescribing can also improve accuracy in information transfer and drive improvement in quality as medication errors tend to be prevalent among elderly people.

- *Enhanced independent living*, reduced health and safety risks through assistive technologies such as social alarm systems, video-monitoring and electronic sensors (Mollenkopf et al., 2010). Where LTC users live alone, assistive technologies can complement or substitute labour, as with robotics, biosensors, and ambient intelligence[5] that help with living at home and using transport. For nursing home recipients, rooms can be equipped with movement sensors to help with monitoring of recipients at risk of falling out of beds or chairs. People can be provided with assistive devices to help movement such as crutches, rollators (e.g. walkers) or wheelchairs. Security alarms are one of the most commonly used arrangements.

Despite a number of potential applications, the adoption of ICTs in LTC remains somewhat limited to pilot programmes and initiatives in many countries. The most common applications are telecare, alarm services and assistive devices to help mobility. Structural and functional barriers to adoption include:

- *Organisational constraints and system fragmentation.* While ICTs can often help link health and social care settings, electronic medical and nursing records are typically not transferred across settings, due to separate governance structures and poor interoperability.

- *Significant cost associated with investment*, maintenance and training, and no robust evidence of cost effectiveness to justify investment costs (Mollenkopf et al., 2010; Colombo et al., 2011). Many studies, mostly pilot projects, have been undertaken and published to support the use of ICT in LTC; yet findings are still inconclusive.

- *Skills mismatch.* Users' ICT literacy remains a challenge to wider dissemination. The share of older people using ICTs regularly is still limited. There is some reluctance as LTC recipients prefer face-to-face human contact with care providers – although suitable, non-intrusive telecare equipment, including mobile telephone, is often welcome (Yeandle and Fry, 2010).

- *Strong privacy concerns.* The possibility of data misuse delays the development of IT infrastructure and the transfer of information across care settings (OECD, 2012).

Box 6.5. **Examples of ICT products and services to improve independent living**

There are a number of nationally led examples of assistive technologies. The Swedish government, in co-ordination with the Swedish Institute of Assistive Technology, has implemented the "Technology for the Elderly" programme since 2007. Around one hundred projects were awarded support to develop products and services to assist older people in their everyday lives. As a form of home help, Sweden grants financial awards to more than 160 000 people to supply security alarm in their residences in 2011. British Columbia (Canada), recently announced plans to make after-hours access to palliative tele-nursing available (British Columbia Ministry of Health, 2012). Japan has started 24-hours regular visiting and on-demand services which combine with multi-disciplinary services, which make heavy use of ICTs. In Norway, the Ministry of Health and Care Services will set up a national helpline for the elderly who are exposed to violence.

In England, the Department of Health initiated in 2005 the so-called "Building Telecare in England". This was followed by policy initiatives including Telecare LIN (Learning and Improvement network), and Whole Systems Demonstrator projects. Telecare LIN is a national network supporting local services applying telecare and telehealth to assist social care services for older people. By 2009, the number of those using telecare has expanded to over 1.5 million people, however there is no concrete evidence demonstrating its significance in service delivery (Yeandle and Fry, 2010). In addition, £15 million had been invested to train unpaid carers from 2009 to 2011 in the Caring with Confidence Programme. This consists of a number of modules including finance, care management, accessing support and services to improve quality of care of unpaid carers. The programme is delivered through a mix of

---

> **Box 6.5. Examples of ICT products and services
> to improve independent living** (cont.)
>
> on-line and text books (Yeandle and Fry, 2010). For a specific condition, England launched in
> early 2010 an Internet-based education programme for health and social care professionals
> regarding end-of-life care.
>
> In home care, the most common ICT appliances are phones (cell phones included) and
> alarms. There are also a number of interesting devises that serve to assist LTC users. ICT
> support systems (such as webcams) can remind LTC users to take medication. Other
> applications include temperature monitoring system (for patients with Chronic Pulmonary
> Disease; COPD, for example) and life sensors that are motion-activated to check conditions
> of LTC users and monitor their movement and daily living activities.
>
> The industries are paying particular interest in the development of ICT devises to
> improve access and mobility. For example, in Sweden, wheeled walker has become the most
> common assistive device since its introduction in the early 1980's. Housing adaptation to
> improve accessibility, such as removing doorsteps and adjustments in the bathroom, are
> quite popular as many countries provide housing adaptation allowances.

Conclusions

Policy makers are interested in knowing how best to incentivise consumer, providers, or payers to deliver safer, more responsive, and effective care.

Using market-based approaches is an appealing option. Assuming LTC recipients can act as informed consumers, these approaches allow care recipients to searching for the care option that best fits their individual circumstances. Two-thirds of OECD countries primarily in Europe have implemented cash-for-care, voucher or consumer directed benefits. These schemes deliver high levels of satisfaction among LTC users although they may not make a difference in health or functional outcomes. Which specific institutional features of these schemes might affect outcomes should be futher explored.

Consumer-centred approaches – especially quality-rating systems – are based on assumptions that frail disabled people can make informed choices. The quality and simplicity of the information they receive for comparing options is a key factor affecting their ability to choose. However, there are questions regarding the methodology of ranking systems and about how to address lower-performing providers. While care recipient satisfaction can be high, it is not known for certain that rating and choice-based systems have led to real improvements in quality.

Another way to encourage quality improvement is by offering providers financial rewards for delivering good outcomes. Initiatives to pay for quality improvements in long-term care are limited to a handful of countries (e.g., Korea, the United States and Germany to some extent). These initiatives show potential – for example, changing behaviours around specific quality or outcome items, stimulating greater reporting of data and greater use of assessment systems – but evidence on improvement in quality is not robust enough as yet.

The need to address fragmentation of care and improve care co-ordination in order to drive quality of care is well understood. However, delivering greater LTC co-ordination has proven to be challenging. There is a continuum of approaches to integration, ranging from integration of information, to service integration, clinical integration, and organisational integration. While there is some agreement that more complex patients and conditions might require a higher degree of integration (multidisciplinary teams, organisational collaboration, joint care planning, etc.) than in the case of patients with simpler care needs, it has proven difficult to collect systematic country examples for evaluation. Good case management or primary-care co-ordinators, availability of integrated information system linking data through portable records, multidisciplinary assessments teams, and single-entry points have all been identified as potentially quality-enhancing.

A last issue that is receiving much interest is the potential for ICT to drive improvements in care quality monitoring and to facilitate care-recipients' independent living. While the potential of ICT is huge, barriers to use remain, including privacy concerns, interoperability, high-investment costs and the need for sound evaluation of cost effectiveness.

Notes

1. Outcome indicators include 1) physical function: proportion of patients with reduced ADL, 2) eliminative function: proportion of high risk patients with indwelling catheter, 3) eliminative function: proportion of low risk patients with indwelling catheter, and 4) skin condition: pressure ulcer prevalence in the high risk patients.

2. 15 points per day will be awarded against good outcome of care which is measured as more than 50% of residents who successfully recover and return home. Five point per day will be awarded if more than 30% of residents successfully recover and return home. Under health insurance fee schedule for rehabilitation patients in rehabilitation wards in hospitals, additional points are also awarded if more than 30% of hospitalised for rehabilitation recover and return home.

3. For example, about 70% of people aged 75 years old and over in Sweden have two or more chronic diseases simultaneously occurring. Statistics from Scotland show that 65% of people aged between 65 and 84 have an average of 2.6 chronic conditions per person (OECD, 2012b).

4. Four consortia (two from Dutch speaking and one French and another from Germany-speaking) are participating which consists of six hospitals, nice nursing homes and 16 organisations for domicile care.

5. Ambient intelligence is where electronic environment responds to the presence of person.

References

Allen, R.S. et al. (2003), "Advance Care Planning in Nursing Homes: Correlates of Capacity and Possession of Advance Directives", *The Gerontologist*, Vol. 42, No. 3, pp. 309-317.

Alvarado, K.L. et al. (2006), "Transfer of Accountability: Transforming Shift Handover to Enhance Patient Safety", *Healthcare Quarterly*, Vol. 9, pp. 75-79.

Alzheimer Europe (2011), "The Global Crisis of Alzheimer's Disease", *Dementia in Europe: The Alzheimer Europe Magazine*, Vol. 9, pp. 29-30, October.

Arksey, H. and P.A. Kemp (2008), "Dimensions of Choice: A Narrative Review of Cash-for-Care Schemes", *Working Paper No. DHP 2250*, Social Policy Research Unit, University of York, March.

Avoidable Hospitalization Advisory Panel (2011), "Enhancing the Continuum of Care", Ontario, Canada.

Bavarian State Ministry of Labour and Social Welfare, Family Affairs, Women and Health and Federal Ministry of Health (2010), "Achieving Quality Long-term Care in Residential Facilities, Germany", Host Country Report, *Peer review*, 18-19 October.

BelRAI (2012), *http://wiki.belrai.org/fr/Wiki.jsp?page=Lexique#section-Lexique-BelRAI*, accessed on 10 September 2012.

British Columbia Ministry of Health (2012), "Improving Care for B.C. Seniors: An Action Plan", *www.seniorsbc.ca/documents/pdf/SeniorsActionPlan.pdf*, accessed on 1 October 2012.

Cacace, M. (2012), "Public Reporting on the Quality of Healthcare Providers: International Experience and Prospects", *LSE Health and Social Care Formal Seminar Series*, 9 May 2012, *http://www2.lse.ac.uk/LSEHealthAndSocialCare/pdf/LSE-Cacace_Public-reporting.pdf*.

Cahill, S., E. O'Shea and M. Pierce (2012), "Creating Excellence in Dementia Care: A Research Review for Ireland's National Dementia Strategy", Ireland.

Capitman, J. et al. (2005), "Long-term Care quality: Historical Overview and Current Initiatives", Report for the National Commission for Quality Long-term Care, the National Commission for Quality Long-term Care, Washington, DC.

Care Quality Commission (2013), www.cqc.org.uk/, accessed on 21 March 2013.

Carlson, B.L. et al. (2007), "Effects of Cash and Counseling on Personal Care and Well-Being", Health Services Research, Vol. 42, No. 1, Part II, pp. 467-487.

Castle, N.G. (2009), "The Nursing Home Compare Report Card: Consumers' Use and Understanding", Journal of Aging and Social Policy, Vol. 21, pp. 187-208.

Castle, N.G. and J.C. Ferguson (2010), "What Is Nursing Home Quality and How Is It Measured?, The Gerontologist, Vol. 50, No. 4, pp. 426-442.

Chenoweth, L. et al. (2009), "Caring for Aged Dementia Care Resident Study (CADRES) of Person-centred Care, Dementia-care Mapping, and Usual Care in Dementia: A Cluster-randomised Trial", The Lancet Neurology, Vol. 8, pp. 317-325.

Chinthapalli, K. (2012), "Personal Health Budgets Will Be Rolled Out to Over 50 000 People", British Medical Journal, Vol. 345, 3 December.

CMS – Centers for Medicare and Medicaid Services (2012), "Design for Nursing Home Compare Five-Star Quality Rating System: Technical Users' Guide", CMS, July.

Coleman E.A., et al. (2006), "The care transitions intervention: results of a randomized controlled trial", Arch Intern Med. Vol. 166(17), pp. 1822-8.

Colombo, F. et al. (2011), "Help Wanted: Proving and Paying for Long-Term Care", OECD Publishing, Paris, http://dx.doi.org/10.1787/9789264097759-en.

CSCI – Commission for Social Care Inspection (2009), "Commission for Social Care Inspection Annual Report and Accounts 2008-09", Commission for Social Care Inspection.

Da Roit, B. and B. Le Bihan (2010), "Similar and Yet So Different: Cash-for-Care in Six European Countries' Long-Term Care Policies", Milbank Quarterly, Vol. 88, No. 3, pp. 286-309.

de Abreu Nogueira, J.M. (2009), "Cuidados Continuados Desafios, Unidade de Missparaos", UMCCI-Unidade de Missão para os Cuidados Continuados Integrados, Lisbon.

Department of Health and Ageing (2011), "Quality Reporting: Community Care Common Standards and Quality Reporting Documentation", Department of Health and Ageing, Australian Government, www.health.gov.au/internet/main/publishing.nsf/Content/ageing-commcare-qualrep-standards.htm, accessed on 26 October, 2012.

Forder, J. et al. (2012), "Evaluation of the Personal Health Budget Pilot Programme", Discussion Paper No. 2840-2, Department of Health, 30 November 2012, www.personalhealthbudgets.dh.gov.uk/_library/Resources/Personalhealthbudgets/2012/PHBE_personal_health_budgets_final_report_Nov_2012.pdf.

Fotaki, M. (2009), "Are All Consumers the Same? Choice in Health, Social Care and Education in England and Elsewhere", Public Money & Management, Vol. 29, No. 2, pp. 87-94.

Genet, N. et al. (2011), "Home Care in Europe: A Systematic Literature Review", BMC Health Services Research, pp. 1-14.

Hales, C. et al. (2006), "National Evaluation of the Aged Care Innovative Pool Dementia Pilot", Final Report, AIHW Cat. No. AGE 48, Australian Institute of Health and Welfare, Canberra.

Harriette, G.C. et al. (2007), "Eligibility Criteria of Randomized Controlled Trials Published in High-impact General Medical Journals: A Systematic Sampling Review", Journal of American Medical Association, Vol. 297, No. 11, pp. 1233-1240.

Health Research and Information Division (2010), "Activity in Acute Public Hospitals in Ireland, 2009 Annual Report", ESRI Survey and Statistical Report Series No. 34, Dublin.

Health Service Executive (2012), "A Guiding Framework for Education and Awareness in the Development of Person Centred Dementia Care", National Dementia Education Project 2012, Office of Nursing and Midwifery Service Director, Health Service Executive.

HIRA – Health Insurance Review & Assessment Service (2011), "Comprehensive Quality Report of National Health Insurance 2010, Korea".

JPHA – Japan Public Health Association (2009), *www.jpha.or.jp/sub/pdf/menu04_5_05_all.pdf*, Tokyo, accessed on 30 August 2012.

Lundsgaard, J. (2005), "Consumer Direction and Choice in Long-Term Care for Older Persons, Including Payments for Informal Care: How Can it Help Improve Care Outcomes, Employment and Fiscal Sustainability?", *OECD Health Working Papers* No. 20, OECD Publishing, Paris, *http://dx.doi. org/10.1787/616882407515*.

Marshall, M.N. (2004), "How Do We Maximize the Impact of the Public Reporting of Quality of Care?", *International Journal for Quality in Health Care*, Vol. 16, Suppl. No. 1, pp. i57-i63.

MDS – Medizinischer Dienst des Spitzenverbandes Bund der Krankenkassen e.V. (2012), „3. Bericht des MDS nach § 114a Abs. 6 SGB XI", Qualität in der ambulanten und stationären Pflege, April, Essen.

Meiners,M.R. et al. (2002), "Consumer Direction in Managed Long-Term Care: An Exploratory Survey of Practices and Perceptions", *The Gerontologist*, Vol. 42, No. 1, pp. 32-38.

Mollenkopf, H. et al. (2010), "The Potential of ICT in supporting Domiciliary Care in Germany", *JRC Scientific and Technical Reports, EUR 24274 EN*, Institute for Prospective Technological Studies, Joint Research Centre, European Commission, Seville, Spain.

Mor, V. (2006), "Defining and Measuring Quality Outcomes in Long-term Care", *Journal of the American Medical Directors Association*, Vol. 7, No. 8, October, pp. 532-540.

Mor, V. (2010), "Improving the Quality of Long-term Care", *CESifo DICE Report 2/2010*.

Mot, E. (2010), "The Dutch System of Long-term Care", *CPB Document* No. 204, March.

Mukamel, D.B. et al. (2008), "Publication of Quality Report Cards and Trends in Reported Quality Measures in Nursing Homes", *Health Service Research*, Vol. 43, No. 4, August.

Nadash, P. et al. (2011), "European Long-Term Care Programs: Lessons for Community Living Assistance Services and Supports?", *Health Services Research*, Vol. 47, No. 1, Part I, Februrary.

Norwegian Ministry of Health and Care Services (2006), "Care Plan 2015: Long-term Care – Future Challenges: Report No. 25 (2005–2006) o the Storting Chapters 1, 2 and 3".

OECD (2012a), *OECD Internet Economy Outlook 2012*, OECD Publishing, Paris; *http://dx.doi. org/10.1787/9789264086463-en*.

OECD (2012b), "Ageing, Non-Communicable Diseases (NCDs) and Emerging Models of Care", Fast-Track Paper, DELSA/HEA(37), OECD, Paris, October.

OECD and European Observatory on Health Systems and Policies (forthcoming), "Pay-for-Performance in Health Care: Implications for Health System Efficiency and Accountability", OECD Publishing, Paris.

Productivity Commission (2011), "Caring for Older Australians", *Report* No. 53, Final Inquiry Report, Commonwealth of Australia, Canberra.

Rodrigues, R. (2012), "Public Reporting within Europe: The Public Gets What the Public Wants?", Unpublished document, OECD Expert Meeting, European Centre, OECD, Paris.

Ronchi, E. (2012), "Benchmarking eHealth Use", DELSA/HEA (2012)17, OECD, Paris, 1 June 2012.

ScholarWorks at UMass Boston (2011), "Leaving Home Care: Decision Making, Risk Scenarios & Services Gaps in the Home Care System", *http://scholarworks.umb.edu/cgi/viewcontent.cgi?article=1067&context=gerontologyinstitute_pubs*.

Schulz, E. (2012), "Quality Assurance Policies and Indicators for Long-term Care in the European Union – Country Report: Germany", *ENEPRI Research Report* No. 104, Work package 5, February.

Sorenson, C. and E. Mossialos (2007), "Measuring Quality and Standards of Long-term Care for Older People", Research Note, European Commission, Brussels.

Temkin-Greener, H. et al. (2004), "Measuring Interdisciplinary Team Performance in a Long-term Care Setting", *Medical Care*, Vol. 42, No. 5, pp. 472-481, May.

Temkin-Greener, H. et al. (2009), "Daily Practice Teams in Nursing Homes: Evidence from New York State", *The Gerontologist*, Vol. 49, No. 1, pp. 68-80.

Thomas, K.E. et al. (2010), "Conversion Diversion: Participation in a Social HMO Reduces the Likelihood of Converting from Short-Stay to Long-Stay Nursing Facility Placement", *www.ncbi.nlm.nih.gov/pmc/articles/PMC2879400/*.

UMCCI – Office of Mission Units for Continuous Care (2012), "Relatório de monitorização do desenvolvimento e da atividade da Rede Nacional de Cuidados Continuados Integrados (RNCCI), 2011" (Monitoring report of the development and activity of continuous care), Cuidados Continuados, Lisbon, February.

US Department of Health and Human Services (2006), "Ensuring a Qualified Long-term Care Workforce: From Pre-employment Screens to On-the-Job Monitoring".

Vaughan, J.J. and N.M. Silverstein (2011), "Leaving Home Care: Decision Making, Risk Scenarios & Services Gaps in the Home Care System by 12-1-2011", University of Massachusetts, Boston.

Weatherly, H. et al. (2010), "Financial Integration Across Health and Social Care: Evidence Review", Scottish Government Social Research.

Werner, R.M., R.T. Konetzka and G.B. Kruse (2009), "Impact of Public Reporting on Unreported Quality of Care", *Health Services Research*, Vol. 44, No. 2.1, pp. 379-398.

Wiener, J.M. (2007), "Commentary: Cash and Counseling in an International Context", *Health Services Research*, Vol. 42, No. 1, Part II, February.

Wiener, J.M. (2012), "Quality Assurance for Long-Term Care: The Case of the United States", Presentation at the OECD Long-Term Care Quality Expert Meeting, OECD, Paris.

Yeandle, S. and G. Fry (2010), "The potential of ICT in Supporting the Provision of Domiciliary Care with Particular Attention to the Case of Immigrant Care Workers and Informal Carers – The Case of the England and the UK", Centre for International Research on Care, Labour and Equalities, University of Leeds, A Presentation at IPTS Seminar, European Commission, Brussels, 19th January 2010.

PART III

Case studies:
Europe and the United States

PART III

Chapter 7

Quality measurement and improvement in long-term care in Europe

by

Henk Nies, Vilans, Utrecht,
and VU University of Amsterdam

Roelf van der Veen,
Vilans, Utrecht

and

Kai Leichsenring,
European Centre for Social Welfare Policy and Research, Vienna

A large variety of approaches to reduce risks and improve performance can be observed in long-term care across and within countries, depending on the role of public, private for-profit and non-profit care providers, as well as on governance mechanisms at national, regional or local levels. The introduction of quasi-markets and public tendering has triggered the need to increase transparency of providers' service quality towards public purchasers and users. This led to new types of supervising institutions and related instruments, such as performance measurement, public reporting and quality certification. These instruments and their rationales are not always compatible and contribute to tensions between stakeholders involved, for example concerning individual needs related to quality of life, dignity and self-determination. It is argued that internal quality management within and across organisations providing care services needs to be supported by enabling policies and mechanisms at the systems level to trigger a process of continual improvement. This entails further development of indicators that should be informed by evidence from multiple perspectives, to measure not only quality of clinical care, but in particular quality of life across care pathways. Ill designed quality assurance systems may hamper improvement processes and lead to bureaucracy, high administrative burdens and feelings of alienation of care workers.

The aims of quality management in long-term care

This chapter describes and analyses different approaches to quality management, assurance and quality improvement in the long-term care (LTC) sector in selected European countries, namely Austria, Finland, France, Germany, Italy, Slovenia, Sweden, Switzerland, the Netherlands and the United Kingdom (England). This selection covers the main welfare regimes and related models of LTC delivery as well as inherent approaches to quality in Europe. Most information in this chapter is based on research on quality management in LTC, during which teams from the above countries gathered data and information within the EU FP7 project INTERLINKS on "Health systems and long-term care for older people" (Nies et al., 2010). Additional information has been gathered through literature and related EU projects, e.g. "Quality management by result-oriented indicators" (European Centre for Social Welfare Policy and Research, 2010) in which the authors were involved over the past few years.

It is argued that internal quality management within and across organisations providing LTC services needs to be supported by corresponding enabling policies and mechanisms at the systems level; this would trigger a process of continual improvement by means of organisational development and indicators that measure not only quality of clinical care, but also quality of life, and that are informed by evidence from multiple perspectives. The chapter deals in the first place with formal LTC facilities and services. Although informal care and the phenomenon of migrant caregivers as private assistants would call for urgent endeavors in terms of quality assurance, these issues are not addressed here (see Pasquinelli and Rusmini, 2010; Bednárik et al., 2013).

Following an introductory section on definitions, rationales and approaches to quality management in LTC, the second section will focus on related policies and legal measures that have been implemented in the selected countries. The third section will highlight some specific methods and instruments used for quality assurance by regulators and for quality management by provider organisations. Finally, key dilemmas and challenges will be discussed in relation to measuring, monitoring and improving quality in LTC.

Approaches to quality management in long-term care

The complexity of defining quality management in long-term care

This section deals with definitions of quality management in LTC and categorises different approaches to quality assurance by regulators of LTC systems.

In general, quality management is defined as the cyclic process to assess and improve appropriate service delivery within any organisational structure (see Box 7.1).

From a quality management perspective, quality has been defined pragmatically as the appropriate delivery of a mutually agreed service or product (*www.iso.org*; see also ISO, 2010; ISO, 2012). To assess the quality of a service or product, it is therefore necessary to agree upon structural and procedural standards, and upon expected outcomes within an acceptable range of costs and prices. This agreement should be made between all stakeholders involved. Referring to LTC, this would not only include service users as

---

Box 7.1. **Quality management to ensure and improve quality of care**

Quality management consists of various features ranging from quality assurance to quality development and continual improvement. Quality management focuses on desired outcomes that ideally derive from defined structures and processes of care. Furthermore, quality management may also entail the definition and the attainment of desired results or outcomes of LTC activities, while paying attention to how (by which processes and based on which structures) they are reached (Donabedian, 1980). It may focus on efficiency of delivery as a proxy for quality or it may focus on notions of excellence or rely on professional norms of quality performance based on evidence of good practice.

The term quality assurance is used for the purposes of this overview as the activity of third parties to ensure and certify defined quality criteria from an external perspective (Bauer et al., 2006).

---

clients of formal services, public purchasers or the different types of providers and professionals. It also affects informal caregivers (relatives) as well as the general population because LTC as an acknowledged social risk is to a large degree funded by public resources (Leichsenring, 2010b; Colombo et al., 2011). It is this vast range of stakeholders that renders the definition of quality in LTC particularly challenging as both clinical expertise and values of citizens who are also co-producers of these services have to be harmonised (Haverinen and Tabibian, 2005). While clinical outcomes may be measured and assessed by means of person level and aggregated data, this is much more demanding when it comes to value-laden factors such as user satisfaction and quality of life from the different perspectives of stakeholders.

Outcomes of quality of care in LTC can be conceived as care effectiveness and safety, responsiveness and care co-ordination (see Chapter 1). However, from a managerial perspective, structures, processes and outcomes need to be considered, incorporating the different perspectives of stakeholders. For instance, management, professionals, inspectors, purchasers, service users and their relatives may hold different views and norms on using physical restraints in residents of care homes who suffer from dementia, who have a tendency to restlessness and continuous wandering.

As a result, ambiguities and inconsistencies exist in views on quality of care and quality of life in LTC. Quality in LTC is therefore a normative concept and reflects societal, professional and personal norms and views. As LTC has only started to emerge as a wide array of differentiated services over the past few decades – contrary to the long tradition and differentiation of the health system – it has not yet fully developed as a comprehensive system with a genuine identity, defined processes, pathways and products, and respective structures, policies and resources (Leichsenring et al., 2013a). Various services, interventions and facilities have been established by providers, policy makers and other stakeholders relying on standards and practices from other areas such as acute health care. However, these standards and practices do not always meet the specific needs and norms of LTC users and their relatives. In particular, this holds for pathways of care for frail older people with multiple needs to be met by different services that are funded and organised across different social and health care domains.

For a more user-oriented quality assessment in LTC, it is necessary to define quality management in LTC as the process that involves all stakeholders in a systematic dialogue about expectations and potential interventions, including monitoring and improvement activities that are informed as much as possible by available empirical evidence. Such a dialogue on quality in LTC is therefore a political and ethical process at different governance levels, not least at the "shop-floor level" of services, to develop a shared view on the LTC system, its goals, missions and the conditions of access as well as on other rights and duties of the stakeholders involved. Without any doubt, such a process is demanding and presumes relevant knowledge by a wide range of professional and policy making groups as well as by users of LTC services and civil society, especially those whose voice may not usually be heard.

Various approaches to quality assurance have been developed

Public authorities in their role as regulators and purchasers have hitherto developed various approaches to quality assurance and improvement:

1. A first approach is to *legally define (minimum) standards* in terms of structural criteria such as the size of rooms or levels of staffing (see Box 7.2) that are regularly checked by inspection agencies. The tangible influence of such criteria and the extent to which they contribute to "good" quality as an outcome experienced by service users and their relatives remains difficult to assess. With the extension of market-oriented governance and "New Public Management" mechanisms (purchaser-provider split, public tendering), it has also become necessary to better describe the quality of LTC services that are subject to tendering or need an accreditation for accessing the "care market". Countries such as Germany, England, the Netherlands and Sweden have therefore taken a next, innovative step by introducing new regulatory frameworks that focus on processes and outcomes and, for instance, prescribe the implementation of quality management. However, officially accepted criteria and indicators often remain restricted to variables such as clinical standards derived from a medical paradigm of care. Until now, the need for instruments and indicators that operationalise quality of life and values such as dignity and independence as genuine outcomes of LTC services has been addressed in a very limited way (Nolan et al., 2006; Magee et al., 2008; Schalock et al., 2008).

2. A second approach to ensure quality of care is based on *professional norms and guidelines to steer the care delivery process*. This approach is well established in the acute health care sector, but less in long-term care, which is partly due to its much weaker scientific and professional basis and lower qualification levels of staff. Nevertheless, the methodological development of expert standards for personal care, food safety, medication delivery, wound care, pain management, pressure sore prevention etc. has been significantly extended over the past few years (Schiemann and Moers, 2007; Dijkstra et al., 2003; Kottner et al., 2010; Van Nie et al., 2011). Indeed, there is growing evidence that LTC can be considerably improved by involving and rewarding staff to work on improvements (Frerichs et al., 2003; De Prins and Henderickx, 2007; Bode and Dobrowolski, 2009). Working on improvement by employing clearly defined and easily applicable indicators helps staff and management understand that their work is meaningful and valued. In an area where the workforce is becoming scarce and payment is often poor, work itself should be rewarding and motivating, as staff's quality of working conditions has an impact on the quality of care. For example, from 2005 to 2011 nearly 900 teams worked on systematic improvement based on expert standards in hundreds of LTC organisations in the Netherlands. This effort resulted in quality gains of 30 to 50% with regard to individual indicators such as pressure sores, medication errors, use of restraints and behavioural problems (Minkman et al., 2011).

3. A third approach could be described as a bottom-up *process of "self-regulation"* and has emerged in the context of increasing competition between providers that have an interest in improving their image and in making their performance transparent to (potential) users and purchasers. Also groups of "enlightened" provider organisations and their federations, in

particular in residential care, have implemented quality management approaches to better steer their performance and to improve user-orientation and quality of life in residential care by involving staff, users and other stakeholders (Leichsenring, 2010a; Nolan et al., 2006).

4. Finally, as an important precondition for defining quality and mutually agreed performance of LTC services, there is also some movement concerning the *establishment of basic values, rights and responsibilities in this sector*. Some countries have started to address this challenge at the national level, e.g. Finland (Ministry of Social Affairs and Health, 2008), the Netherlands (Boot and Knapen, 2005) and England (Glasby, 2011). Also the German "Charter of Rights for People in Need of Long-term Care and Assistance" that was developed by the "Round Table Care" offers an example for such endeavors (Igl and Klie, 2007) that were eventually also received at the EU level with a similar "European Charter" that geared in the first place at preventing abuse of older people with LTC needs (AGE Platform Europe, 2010; European Partnership, 2012).

In the reality of the selected European countries most of these approaches have been implemented as a mixture of interventions at different governance levels. Responsibilities for LTC planning, organisation and funding are often assigned to regional or local levels of governance. Other factors that influence the quest for quality assurance have been the degree to which the "care market" had been opened to new types of providers and to new forms of strengthening the purchasing power of users, e.g. by means of attendance and care allowances or personal budgets. Policies for quality assurance in LTC are therefore intertwined with a number of related political and corporate policies (Leichsenring et al., 2013b).

Table 7.1 gives an overview of the selected countries' institutional infrastructure and related policies as well as applied instruments and methods for assessing, measuring and steering quality in LTC. The following section will describe and discuss the differences and commonalities within and between these policies.

Institutional infrastructure of quality assurance and related policies in Europe

Emerging LTC systems in Europe are widely struggling with developing appropriate steering mechanisms, infrastructures and genuine policies for defining and ensuring quality of services. Related endeavors at the systems level concern legislation at various government levels and governance mechanisms that are increasingly characterised by competitive market mechanisms, rather than by traditional social planning. This has resulted in new types of "welfare mixes" with respect to the role of public, private for-profit and non-profit as well as households' contributions to care as in particular the number and proportion of for-profit providers has grown steadily (Colombo et al., 2011). For instance, they have reached a market-share in LTC markets of about 15% in Sweden, of almost 80% in England and of about 38% in Germany (Leichsenring et al., 2010). This development has fuelled debates and policies to create equal access opportunities and regulations that apply likewise to all stakeholders within the quasimarket of LTC, whether they are public, private, for-profit or non-profit (see also Huber et al., 2008). The needs for a transparent definition of quality requirements and transparency in LTC have therefore increased in importance to create a level playing field for all providers. Apart from compulsory quality requirements imposed by law, this implies for policy makers to design incentives for establishing continual improvement processes and an institutional infrastructure for guidance and monitoring. This section will describe related legislative interventions and mechanisms of institution-building in selected countries.

The individual policy mix applied across European OECD countries is dependent on the political culture in general, welfare regimes, national idiosyncrasies of care provision and the level of centralisation or decentralisation of responsibilities (see Table 7.1).

Table 7.1. **An overview of the institutional infrastructure for quality assurance, related policies and methods in selected European countries**

Country	Quality assurance polities/policies (institutional context, responsibilities)	Instruments/methods of quality assurance applied
Austria	Federal level (consumer protection); Regional legislation, restricted access of providers (authorisation); supervision	Public authorities (national level): voluntary National Quality Certificate for care homes Public authorities (regional level): defined structural (input) criteria; inspection (undisclosed) Providers: self-regulation; voluntary quality management
France	National level: Ministry of Health and Social Affairs National Fund for Autonomy and Solidarity (CNSA): co-ordination National Agency for the Assessment of Nursing Home and Home Care Providers (ANESM) Regional level: Regional Councils	Accreditation based on self-assessed "minimum standards" (structures and processes), service charters, protocols and guidelines of good practice; inspection (every 4-7 years) Providers: quality management mainly based on the ANGELIQUE system
Finland	Ministry of Social Affairs and Health: framework legislation and targets National Institute for Health and Welfare: research and guidance	Public authorities and providers: RAI benchmarking
Germany	Federal level (Ministry of Health; long-term care insurance): open market access; supervision (Medical Board of Health Insurances – MDK) Regional governments: supervision	Public authorities (MDK): accreditation criteria (structures and processes); yearly inspection based on "transparency criteria'"(outcome-oriented) developed in co-operation with providers; public reporting Regional governments: inspection of structural criteria Providers: various types of internal quality management systems
Italy	National: Ministry of Health and Social Policy: framework legislation Regional governments: regulation and supervision	Public authorities (regions, regional agencies): authorisation and accreditation (structural and process indicators; clinical governance); service charter; inspection Providers: voluntary certification of quality
Netherlands	Ministry of Health, Welfare and Sport: framework legislation Health Inspectorate: regulation and supervision	Public authorities (Health Inspectorate): compulsory quality assessment and public reporting (*www.kiesbeter.nl*) based on Quality Framework for Responsible Care (QFRC) including Consumer Quality Index (CQI), developed with involvement of providers. Purchasers: quality indicators and measures as requirement for funding Providers: certification, various kinds of internal quality management systems
Spain	National: Consultative Committee as advisory body to the Ministry of Labour and Social Affairs: standards and quality issues Regional governments: standards for authorisation and accreditation of LTC service providers; updating database of existing resources and services Certification agencies	Public authorities: legislation, database, standards, accreditation, certification, sanctioning Providers: quality management/improvement, quality management systems on voluntary basis
Sweden	Ministry of Health and Social Affairs: framework legislation National Board of Health and Welfare: research and guidance; evaluation Local authorities: supervision; contracting	Public authorities: National guidelines (expert standards) National quality registries (clinical indicators) Äldreguiden: public reporting Providers: various quality management systems, e.g. EQ-5D
Switzerland	Federal government: overall strategy, legislation Cantons: responsible for policies of quality control; set standards, implementation of federal law Health care insurers: monitoring quality and efficiency	Public authorities: Inspection and monitoring instruments, quality standards, statistics Health care insurers: reimbursement, needs assessment instrument (e.g. RAI home care) Accreditation agencies carry out compulsory certification
United Kingdom (England)	Ministry of Health Care Quality Commission (CQC): accreditation, regulation and supervision Local authorities: purchasing, commissioning (description of quality criteria)	Public authorities (CQC): registration, compulsory self-assessment based on "Essential standards of quality and safety'"(28 "outcome indicators"); public reporting Providers: internal quality management systems

Source: Nies, H. et al. (2010), "Quality Management and Quality Assurance in Long-Term Care – European Overview Paper", Vilans/European Centre for Social Welfare Policy and Research (INTERLINKS Report #2 – *http://interlinks.euro.centre.org/project/reports*), Utrecht and Vienna.

Many federal states – such as Austria, Spain and Switzerland, but also Italy – show a variety of policy mixes even between regions, with differences in defining structural and procedural authorisation or accreditation criteria. The fact that LTC services and facilities are often regulated at regional or local levels has hence resulted in a variety of service levels and a wide range of different structural and process criteria and measures to define quality (see Box 7.2).

Box 7.2. Examples for structural and process requirements of care homes defined by legal regulations in selected countries

The legal frameworks defining "minimum standards" and requirements for running care homes or other LTC services are under national responsibility in Nordic countries, the Netherlands and the United Kingdom (England), but also in Germany (LTC insurance) and Italy. Still, in most countries it is up to the regional or local authorities to specify criteria and quality standards.

Austria. Given the responsibility for LTC of the nine regional governments, structural standards vary from region to region. For instance, the size of rooms in a care home must be 24 m^2 in Vorarlberg, 13.48 m^2 in Salzburg, 17-18 m^2 (entrance not included) in Upper Austria, and 18 m^2 plus a bathroom of 4.2 m^2 in Carinthia. Similarly staffing ratios and staffing structures are defined rather arbitrarily at one full-time equivalent for 2.4 residents in Carinthia, where 40% of staff must be registered nurses, 50% assistant nurses and 10% others (trainees). In other regions staffing depends on the level of care needs according to the Austrian LTC allowance scheme, e.g. in Vienna the staffing ratio for residents at level one (lowest care needs, usually not eligible for residential care) is 1:20; in level 3 it is 1:2 and in level 7 (highest) it is 1:1, with 40% registered nurses, 45% assistant nurses and 15% home helpers (Leichsenring, 2009).

Germany. In Germany, the Federal Care Home Act was replaced in 2006 by regional legislation on structural requirements for care homes, and some regional governments started to make the so-called "professional staff ratio" more flexible. This regulation stipulates that a minimum of 50% of staff in German nursing homes has to be "professional care staff" (registered nurses, geriatric nurses), which triggered intensive debates about its arbitrary determination. It is argued that such stipulations might indeed hamper the development of appropriate (new) job profiles and continuous training of staff to adapt to the current challenges in LTC services, e.g. to improve quality of life of users with psycho-geriatric problems (Wipp, 2011).

Italy. The Italian framework legislation concerning minimum standards for the authorisation and accreditation of care homes includes requirements such as accessibility, the employment of a co-ordinator and professional staff (specified by regional authorities in terms of staffing levels), individual care planning and the publication of a Service Charter. Regional variations are therefore inevitable but the intensive bureaucratic and legislative activities over the past decade by regional governments actually resulted in relatively similar regulations. As an example, in Emilia-Romagna staffing ratios were set at 1:3.5 in care homes and 1:2.2 in nursing homes, single rooms must have at least 12 m^2 (Dgr 564/2000).

Public authorities that are purchasing LTC services, e.g. by means of public tendering and ensuing contracting (in England better known as "commissioning"), often fall short of clearly defining quality criteria or simply do not dispose of methods to do so (Leichsenring et al., 2010). Some countries (Netherlands, Spain, Switzerland) have introduced, however, compulsory quality certification as a requirement for accreditation, participation in public tenders and purchasing.

The fragmentation of multi-level legal regulations contributes also to a fragmentation of quality criteria as they are tackled by disperse bylaws and decrees. Individual requirements for home care are separated from regulations for care homes, training and education are governed by special acts and some issues might be regulated by consumer protection laws, as for instance concerning physical restraints in Austria. Somewhat more centralised regulations can be observed in the Netherlands. For instance, the Quality Framework for Responsible Care (QFRC) was launched as a compulsory guideline in this country based on indicators that were mutually agreed between the service providers, professionals, service users, health insurers, the inspectorate for health care and the national government. The QFRC contains measurable indicators to assess if the organisation provides responsible care, mainly in terms of clinical care and users' experiences. Based on the results it is the task of management to translate identified shortcomings into improvements (Frijters, 2010). Also in Sweden, providers are obliged to implement national guidelines and to provide clinical data for a widely developed set of 70 National Quality Registries that serve to monitor individual risk factors such as falls, palliative care or dementia care (Ljunggren and Emilsson, 2011).

In all countries legislation in relation to quality in LTC shows a tendency towards enhancing user-orientation, for instance in care planning, complaints procedures or concerning informed consent. The rationale behind these principles is that choice and control of service users have are a major priority in LTC. This notion is enhanced by cash benefits including "personal budgets" or "direct payments" (Huber et al., 2008). The on-going shift towards purchasing power of people with LTC needs at all ages also implies a shift of responsibilities in relation to quality assurance (Leichsenring et al., 2010). Service users are increasingly gaining rights to participate in and influence the planning and implementation of their treatment and services (*www.wedo-partnership.eu*). This may be guaranteed even if service users are not able to make decisions about their care themselves any more (e.g. by means of user advocates, in England and the Netherlands). Furthermore, general mechanisms as complaints procedures are stipulated in most countries to ensure users' rights and user participation.

This section highlighted that over the past 15 years a range of legislative and regulatory efforts has contributed to novel framework conditions for public, private non-profit and commercial providers of LTC services. These policies to ensure quality in LTC targeted in particular the sector of residential care, where management and staff of provider organisations had to put up with newly defined standards and procedures. Even if it was sometimes the providers themselves that called for more legal certainty, they were often overwhelmed by new requirements that were not always reflected in, for instance, better tariffs or wages. Indeed, care home managers and staff were suddenly confronted with the need to implement quality management processes for which they were not prepared or trained. This led to a large degree to half-hearted quality management activities at the shop floor, where these activities were perceived as a bureaucratic exercise to please the regulators, rather than resulting in improvement processes in daily care work.

Box 7.3. **Institution building in quality assurance**

The intensive legislative activities in the context of quality assurance in LTC have triggered the establishment of new types of institutions to develop guidance, expertise and monitoring resources. Many countries such as the Netherlands, Italy, Germany, France or Sweden have set up new, independent governmental agencies or third parties for quality assurance.

● The Swedish Board for Health and Welfare supported the elaboration of National Quality Registers and is currently working on quality indicators for LTC.

● The French government has put efforts in the foundation of a special government agency, the National Agency for Assessing LTC Organisations (ANESM), responsible for staff recertification, accreditation of providers and criteria setting for best practice with the aim to further professionalise the LTC sector.

● In Germany the introduction of the German LTC Insurance (1994) gave rise to the establishment of the MDK (Medical Board of the Health Insurances) as a central body for needs assessment and quality assurance in LTC.

● In Italy regions and autonomous provinces have established regional agencies for quality assurance in health and LTC to comply with a national framework legislation, to administer accreditation of providers and to serve as a third party to assess quality in social and health services.

● In England, three different inspectorates (the Healthcare Commission, the Commission for Social Care Inspection and the Mental Health Act Commission) were merged in 2009 into the "Care Quality Commission" (CQC) to streamline and integrate inspection mechanisms and tools.

● In the Netherlands recently the National Quality Institute has been established, which co-ordinates the development of quality standards and is responsible for collecting and publishing quality data of service providers. A website (*www.kiesbeter.nl*) publishes quality data of service providers across the country.

● Finland has laid down responsibilities for training, data-collection and monitoring with the National Institute for Health and Welfare. This resulted in significant improvements in a number of quality areas relevant for LTC, in particular expressed by clinical care indicators (Finne-Soveri et al., 2010).

● While regional governments developed legislation for residential care and home care services in Austria between 1997 and 2009, the quality criteria defined in related laws remained scarce. At the same time, the Federation of Care Homes and the Federal Ministry of Labour, Social Affairs and Consumer Protection engaged in a voluntary National Quality Certificate (NQZ) that can be obtained by care homes, which have successfully implemented an accredited quality management system (Trukeschitz, 2010). In 2013, an independent NQZ organisation was established to administer and further develop the certification procedure, also in the area of community care.

Methods and instruments to enforce and enable quality development in long-term care in Europe

The manifold challenges for quality assurance in LTC triggered legislators and regulators to apply various types of methods and instruments in a tentative process. This has been accomplished by means of pilot projects or the adoption of existing tools derived from traditional quality management devices (e.g. ISO, EFQM) or quality management in health care, where these methods had been used already earlier. This section will highlight some of the methods and instruments that have been applied in selected European countries, namely *i*) external quality assurance ex ante (authorisation and accreditation) and *ex post* (inspection and certification) imposed by regulators, *ii*) indicators used to measure and benchmark in particular outcome quality, combined with *iii*) user satisfaction surveys and *iv*) public reporting. Furthermore, such instruments include *v*) expert standards, *vi*) the implementation of specific quality management systems for LTC organisations (quality management, self-assessments, professionalisation) as well as *v*) incentives for quality development and continual improvement.

As already mentioned, quality assurance gained particular importance when the introduction of quasi-markets and public tendering triggered the appearance of new stakeholders and organisations, e.g. commercial providers of care homes or new types of care (intermediate care, day-care, etc.). In many countries this process changed the general structure of public service provision including the delivery of LTC. To ensure the appropriateness of a service provider, regulators need to make sure that an organisation fulfills basic pre-conditions for operating in a specific field (quality assurance ex ante). This is guaranteed by *authorisation and accreditation* (see Box 7.4). Furthermore, regulators need to monitor performance, which is usually ensured by a public inspectorate or by an independent third party responsible for quality certification. Finally, to ensure further improvement mechanisms benchmarking processes may complement standards and guidelines.

Box 7.4. Key instruments for quality assurance by regulators of long-term care provision

Authorisation is a compulsory procedure to ensure whether providers meet basic requirements, be they public, private non-profit or private for-profit.

Accreditation is a voluntary or compulsory method to regulate the "market entry" of any service provider. Service requirements are defined by specific legal regulations and compliance is assessed by inspection. In many countries, accreditation is a precondition for public funding and/or reimbursement. In this context it is necessary to set up procedures for controlling whether the required regulations have been fulfilled.

Inspection can be viewed as the a posteriori counterpart of authorisation, and as such it is usually carried out by state agencies that visit provider organisations more or less regularly (e.g. once per year in Germany, once every four years in France) to check for compliance.

Certification is a voluntary method to certify the compliance with a specific quality management system, generally defined by the International Standards Organization (ISO 9000ff.; see *www.iso.org*) or the European Foundation for Quality Management (EFQM; *www.efqm.org*). This process is to regularly assess ex post whether an organisation complies with its defined quality standards, whereby certification is accomplished by a third party, usually an accredited certification agency. For instance, in Switzerland certification is compulsory for all care homes. In some countries, e.g. Italy, certified LTC organisations gain special credits during tendering procedures.

It is by no surprise that particularly in those countries, where the provision structure had been changed radically since the 1980s from a hitherto purely public provision to a more mixed system with more private providers (England, Sweden, Switzerland) accreditation and more intense *inspection procedures* became a higher priority. The same is true for Germany, where the introduction of the LTC insurance was connected with a radical opening of the "care market" that had been dominated before 1995 by large non-profit organisations only. An additional, important driver for more "quality awareness" in LTC was certainly the constant critique by media in connection with scandals in nursing homes.

The introduction of these new quality assurance mechanisms in LTC, however, made the lack of relevant *indicators* to measure and quantify quality of care and quality of life in LTC quite evident. In order to quantify the level of quality assessed by any quality system it would be necessary to agree upon indicators at the national or the regional level. Initiatives to improve the evidence- and knowledge-base of indicators have no long tradition in LTC, unless those derived from clinical health care (for some examples see: *www.interrai.org*; Wingenfeld et al., 2010; see also Chapters 2 and 3 in this book). Some projects and initiatives have responded to this shortcoming in the recent past (see Box 7.5).

Box 7.5. Quality management by result-oriented indicators

The lack of specific indicators to measure quality of care and quality of life in a broader LTC perspective was at the origins of the EU project "Quality management by result-oriented indicators" that identified and validated a range of indicators applied in care homes of selected countries [Austria, Germany, Netherlands, United Kingdom (England)] to measure outcomes of clinical care, quality of life, leadership, economic performance and context (European Centre, 2010). During this project that used Delphi methods and validation workshops with professionals, it became clear that collecting data and measuring quality of life is challenging for LTC organisations. Working with indicators that signal potential shortcomings and help to steer change implies systematic measuring, planning, data-collection, control and implementation of improvement processes. It is recommended to concentrate on a restricted number of issues and on the development of improvement processes by involving relevant stakeholders.

The handbook produced in this project contains definitions and methodological hints for working with performance indicators. 94 validated indicators, of which 24 for assessing quality of care, 46 for quality of life, 17 for leadership, 4 for economic performance and 3 for contextual issues are spelled out.

Nevertheless, in many countries regulators have started to define and use *indicators* as a tool for inspection and public reporting of organisations' quality ratings. For instance, in Germany (MDK, 2008; Büscher, 2010), until recently in the United Kingdom (England) and the Netherlands, criteria and indicators allowing for ratings (stars, marks) that are publicly reported through the Internet have been introduced over the past decade (Mor et al., 2013). Sweden also introduced a variety of regional and National Quality Registers that allow users and regulators to monitor the quality of care providers.

Though *public reporting* is primarily aimed at increasing information accessibility to service users, it is also used by professionals, for instance to choose an employer according to their quality rating. In the context of New Public Management governance, public reporting of quality ratings is also considered to create a sense of competition among professionals and organisations to enhance their performance (Allen et al., 2011). Still, these practices are heavily debated in LTC as the evidence-base as well as the role of users in assessment processes and their ability to choose are far from reaching a consensus between stakeholders (Hasseler et al., 2010). Apart from methodological problems already mentioned above, this practice can only be a very first step towards better transparency and quality reporting for users as, for instance, many older people still do not have Internet access so that a significant number of service users remain excluded from this information. However, this might change quickly with new generations of older people increasingly used to information technology.

An important precondition for the involvement of users in assessing the quality in LTC organisations from their perspective are *surveys* to assess the quality of life and quality of service as experienced by the users, but also by their relatives and staff. Respective client satisfaction surveys provide feedback from users and can be used to construct outcome indicators. Surveys are usually arranged within an organisation as part of its voluntary or mandatory quality management system, but surveys can also be organised on a national level. One of the few examples of a national survey was implemented in the Netherlands (Box 7.6).

Box 7.6. **The Quality Framework for Responsible Care (QFRC) and the Consumer Quality Index**

In the Netherlands, the Institute for Research in Healthcare (NIVEL) and several other organisations have developed the Consumer Quality Index (CQ Index) as a standardised system for measuring, analysing and reporting user experience in health care. The instrument is partly based on the American CAHPS-instrument (Consumer Assessment of Healthcare Providers and Systems). The respective questionnaires provide insight in what clients find important and how they rate their experience with care. Surveys are carried out by accredited external agencies in accordance with the standards and guidelines. By law, each healthcare and LTC organisation has to arrange a survey once every two years. Results can be used by clients to choose a health insurer or health services, by client organisations representing the interests of their members, by insurers to assess the quality of services purchased, by managers and professionals who want to improve their performance, and by public authorities and monitoring agencies.

The CQ Index is a substantial part of the Quality Framework for Responsible Care (QFRC) as it provides a range of measurable indicators that show whether health and LTC organisations provide responsible care. The results of the QFRC are publicly reported for each organisation on a website (*www.KiesBeter.nl*). The intention of presenting these results online is to provide transparency of data and to stimulate organisations to improve their performance (Leichsenring et al., 2013b). The QFRC has recently been criticised because of multiple objectives it needs to serve, the administrative burden and the limited applicability for quality improvement. A revision has been proposed by the National Health Care Inspectorate, LOC (the national association of users' councils in long-term care organisations) and *Zorgverzekeraars Nederland* (the umbrella organization of health care insurers).

Another more traditional instrument to develop quality and professionalism in LTC has been derived from the health care system *as expert standards and guidelines* for best practice have gained in importance also in LTC. Apart from specific guidelines for disease management, e.g. dementia care guidelines or diabetes care, such guidelines are particularly of interest where they try to improve care pathways, interdisciplinary and inter-organisational working, e.g. concerning hospital discharge. Such guidelines have been developed in a number of countries, e.g. in Germany, the Netherlands and Sweden (see Box 7.7). Indeed, defining and ensuring quality with respect to the *integration* of health and social care services and *co-operation* between different professionals is one of the most challenging issues in LTC. Case or care management, discharge and integrated care programmes, multidisciplinary team work, joint care planning and regional networking are being developed (Leichsenring and Alaszewski, 2004; Nies and Berman, 2004; Leichsenring et al., 2013a), but indicators to measure their quality and to enhance impact, costs and efficiency across different settings for different patient groups are still lacking. An interesting example in this context is Italy where a unique national framework legislation was adopted "to realise an integrated system of health and social care" (L. 328/2000). Among other things this resulted in a partnership of most Regions, which had to adopt and implement this regulation, to co-ordinate issues of quality and accreditation in social and health care, and in the development of criteria concerning the management of care paths, discharge management, training and quality assurance (Di Santo and Ceruzzi, 2009).

Box 7.7. **Selected examples for expert standards**

Germany

The German Network for Quality Development in Nursing (DNQP, 2011) developed seven evidence based expert standards on clinical long-term care conditions: prevention and care of pressure ulcers, falls prevention, urinary incontinence, care of people suffering from chronic wounds, adequate nutrition, discharge management, pain management. The network consists of experts who are working in practice as well as scientists. In project teams and conferences they strive towards consensus. The development of standards follows a stepwise methodology. Consequently, the standards are updated and implemented as a model. They provide a basis for interdisciplinary work, in addition to medical guidelines. Use of these nursing standards have obtained a legal, and thereby, mandatory basis. The Network operates in close collaboration with organisations and networks from abroad.

Netherlands

In the Netherlands, the so-called care standard for integrated dementia care was developed. The process was led by Alzheimer Netherlands and supported by Vilans, the National Centre of Expertise for Long-term Care. A large number of professionals and representatives of caregivers' and users' organisations agreed on the description of appropriate quality of dementia care across services: counseling, care and treatment, and the organisation of these components. The standard is widely based upon accepted guidelines. It provides clarity to service users of what they may expect and to professionals of how their multidisciplinary collaboration should be accomplished; tasks and responsibilities as well as efficient and effective processes are clarified. The standard addresses issues such as prevention, early detection, diagnostics of the disease and of the care needs, referrals, case management and co-ordination, treatment, counseling and support, services such as domestic care, activities, housing, respite care, crisis intervention, integration of services, end of life care, informed consent and various other issues. Also indicators of good practice are formulated. The draft is now to be authorised by the various stakeholders (Alzheimer Nederland and Vilans, 2012).

Sweden

The first Swedish guidelines regarding dementia care were published in 2010 by the National Board of Health and Welfare (NBHW). The guidelines present evidence based and evaluated treatments and methods within health care and social care regarding people with dementia and informal caregivers. They are directed to the municipalities (e.g. social care, home help etc.) and primary care managed by the county councils. The Guidelines provide support to decision makers within municipalities, county councils and regions, so they can govern the different organisations according to systematic priorities. They also address doctors, nurses and other health and social care professionals on a managerial level. By using the guidelines it is possible to overcome barriers between different organisational bodies, because the Guidelines put the patient in focus (Emilsson, 2011; Rodrigues and Nies, 2013).

Partly as a response to on-going changes in the national regulatory frameworks, and partly through an intrinsic desire to improve performance, LTC providers have started to gain interest in *quality management systems*. Many care homes and some home care providers have some kind of quality management system in place, but for instance in Germany, not even 50% of care homes have a certified quality management system (about 20% in Austria). General quality management systems (ISO 9000ff. or EFQM) have been adapted to the specificities of the LTC sector in order to ensure improvements of processes and structures. However, measures to enable authorities or mandated third parties to verify the implementation and to evaluate the effectiveness of the applied quality management systems are still scarce, in particular with respect to outcome indicators. The introduction of a quality management system is an additional investment for providers of LTC services and facilities: it includes training of staff, consultancy, documentation, working-time of staff involved, costs for third-party audits (certification) and improvement measures. Often however, only scanty information is available to evaluate its potential benefits and cost-effectiveness (Groenewoud, 2008). With a systematic utilisation of tools such as the *PDCA cycle* (plan – do – check – act), it is however likely that staff and other stakeholders can improve performance, if they are supported by management and enabled to implement improvement measures. This has been underlined by quality management systems and supportive measures that have been introduced in and across various countries (e.g. RAI in Finland, E-Qalin in Austria, Germany, Luxembourg and Slovenia), but in particular by a wide range of in-house quality management systems, in some cases combining classical quality management instruments with organisational development and adequate learning and training methods (Minkman et al., 2011). *Self-assessments* address aspects linked to clinical quality and outcomes for service users (including their experience) as well as to intra- (e.g. effectiveness, access, safety) and inter-organisational quality (e.g. care pathways, discharge protocols, multidisciplinary assessment methods). Although quality management is often lacking scientific evaluation it can be seen as the cornerstone and basis for any quality assurance and improvement at the organisational level.

In this context, skills for quality management are one additional area for which continued vocational education and skills development are needed, as managers and staff in LTC are usually not specially trained in quality management. At the same time, they are confronted with more and more legal regulations, standards to comply with, and budgetary restraints (Leichsenring, 2010b, p. 14). Regulations in Finland and other countries show evidence that investment in training can trigger better outcomes and enhancement of defined quality indicators (Hammar et al., 2011; Leichsenring, 2011). Also the organisational model of Buurtzorg ("Care in the Neighborhood") in the Netherlands with its small self-managing teams of a maximum of twelve professionals indicates a way forward towards *professionalisation* that includes systematic quality management, in this case by means of the "Omaha System" to assess clinical quality of home care (*www.omahasystem.org*) in connection with an efficient IT-support. Apart from providing care in the neighborhood by integrating with other local organisations and informal caregivers, the teams are also responsible for organising further training according to the teams' and the individual professionals' needs (Huijbers, 2011).

Some national and regional regulators have used funding opportunities as an *incentive* for training in quality management as an incentive for professionals and provider organisations to enhance quality awareness and quality management skills. For instance, participation in the national "Care for Better" project in the Netherlands was encouraged by health care insurers by offering better contractual terms and related funding to service providers. Other incentives include credits during tendering procedures, e.g. in Spain, for organisations with a certified quality management system (Leichsenring et al., 2010), but similar regulations can be found as compulsory requirements for accreditation in various countries or regions, e.g. in the Netherlands and Switzerland (see above Box 7.4).

This section outlined some of the most important methods and instruments to assess and improve quality in LTC organisations. It has become clear that most of these methods have started only recently to be used on a broader scale. Legislation is by and large limited to defining structural and, at best, procedural criteria that are controlled by one-off inspections. While enforcement measures are rather restricted and tend to be counter-productive, working in partnership between regulators and providers to enable quality development seems to be more rewarding. Indeed, there are first signs for collaboration in developing indicators for quality measurements that go beyond those that are mainly derived from knowledge on clinical care. A broader concept of LTC would call for an improvement of cross-organisational and multi-disciplinary quality management from a quality of life perspective (Nies and Leichsenring, 2012).

Dilemmas and challenges for measuring and managing quality in long-term care

This section summarises and discusses the issues at stake and the cleavages that are linked to the slow, but quite steady development of policies and methods for managing quality in LTC. Indeed, not only in LTC issues around quality are always connected to values and contrasting objectives that need to be considered. While quality management has much to do with standardisation, the area of LTC that tends to promote user-orientation and individual choice seems to be hesitant). LTC is therefore a latecomer not only in the general development of social security systems, but also in terms of methods to define and measure at least basic quality criteria, e.g. by means of acknowledged indicators and their presentation to purchasers and customers. A particular challenge in LTC consists in the fact that, while individual services are still struggling with the implementation of quality management, assessments and improvement would be necessary to be realised across organisational, professional and sector boundaries.

Contrasting objectives are difficult to integrate into quality management

Quality measurements serve multiple objectives in quality management and quality assurance. They provide information to support users in choosing a service. They serve as a means to demonstrate accountability to society for the performance of care providers. They allow inspectorates to monitor basic quality requirements. They are used in commissioning services by public authorities, insurers and users ("value for money") to describe the quality of services delivered and for which they pay. In particular local authorities and other public bodies need to ensure they serve the population appropriately (public accountability) by means of appropriate indicators. At the same time, measuring and managing quality serves to monitor and steer quality improvement within organisations. Managers and professionals in LTC organisations must know how they are performing and in what respect they can improve their work.

These multiple objectives are not always compatible and are seldom equally appropriate for all stakeholders involved, particularly if negative results have direct or indirect negative economic consequences for providers. If they are honestly intending to improve their services, they must feel safe to be transparent on both positive and negative outcomes in order to learn for improvement. Even if it cannot be withheld that inappropriate care is not always only due to ignorance, and also fraud and conscious abuse can be retrieved in LTC, trust in and reliance on professional ethics is an intrinsic part of care delivery. This implies, for instance, to report errors, to openly discuss potential remedies with colleagues and to improve identified structural or procedural issues. However, contrasting objectives and requirements, e.g. by inspection or commissioning agencies, may compromise such approaches for instance if an inspectorate may close down facilities in case of poor performance, unbiased reporting and (internal) discussion will be compromised. Although still rather uncommon in LTC, the same would hold true for the introduction of performance-related payment systems (for health care see Mullen et al., 2010). If poor performance is badly paid or otherwise negatively sanctioned, it is likely that staff and management will not be motivated to report errors, mistakes and incidents from which improvement could be derived (Nies and Leichsenring, 2012).

However attractive it may appear at first sight to integrate all objectives into one set of quality indicators, in practice it causes biases that complicate each of the objectives. In a quality management perspective, indicators and measurements should neither be over- nor underestimated, but they could be taken as signals that contribute to "learning from errors" and continual improvement.

Standardisation of services versus individual needs

LTC services and facilities serve a wide range of people with different needs and expectations. The challenge in managing personalised services is to describe expected results and outcomes ex ante on an aggregated level. In other words, the tension exists in formulating individual needs, as services have to deal with individual expectations related to quality of life, dignity and self-determination and to steer and measure performance of the organisation as such. Such values are difficult to define and measure, not least because they include predominantly subjective and individual views. The involvement of users, relatives and friends as well as of staff and management in the assessment of these "soft" factors is certainly a first step to respond to this challenge. This could also avoid defining standards and thresholds, including expert standards, which may hamper individualised or innovative approaches. This challenge has not yet been sufficiently resolved.

The need for instruments and indicators that operationalise dignity or quality of life as an outcome variable has been addressed in a very limited way, not least due to the methodological challenges related to the translation into an instrument for their assessment in daily practice. From a methodological point of view, no consensus on instruments has yet been achieved, in none of the countries.

Clinical care remains an area of LTC where standardisation and the application of up-to-date, evidence based techniques is paramount. Experiences from RAI and other methods (see Chapter 3) suggest that there is scope for defining and measuring progress, in particular if data-collection is not seen as an end in itself, but as a tool to reflect upon practices and factors that influence results within each individual organisation and across different settings.

Contested quality indicators and their consequences on public reporting and tendering

The lack of generally accepted indicators to measure quality of LTC is a challenge for both policy makers and practitioners. It has therefore been addressed in various ways in the selected countries, in any case triggering criticism from groups of stakeholders. First of all, there is a common approach by legislators to define structural and (not always) process indicators and to monitor compliance – providers often perceive both as rather arbitrary. Secondly, validated indicators have been defined for clinical care (MDS-RAI; see Chapter 3) but their collection is considered cumbersome by staff. Thirdly, attempts to measure quality of life and user satisfaction are facing serious methodological problems in LTC, in particular as a large number of users are suffering from psycho-geriatric problems and indicators are often not reflecting the issues that are of key importance to individual users. Moreover, corrections for casemix are not always accomplished or not feasible due to the lack of data. Fourthly, quality data that serve multiple purposes (for instance purchasing information, information for inspectors, information for improvement) are often considered to be insufficiently reliable. Fifthly, if feedback of benchmarked data from central databases is lagging behind, the data are considered to be outdated and therefore useless for improvement purposes.

With this particular state of LTC services in mind, quality indicators in this sector should be considered in a pragmatic way. They may indicate specific aspects, at best showing results that were produced by particular structures and processes. Comparisons over time or, even more challenging, those between different care homes are therefore always problematic even without considering the potential interest of a provider or a professional to manipulate data. However, indicators may support professionals and managers of LTC services to check whether particular interventions have resulted in improvements, whether specific processes have served to reach specific objectives or whether given structures need to be improved. Such indicators might also help improve the relationship with regulators and purchasers if they are used to mutually reflect upon framework conditions that are needed to improve performance. Again, this requires a supportive relationship between providers and purchasers or inspector, based on attitudes of organisational and mutual learning.

Given this state of the art it is surprising that public reporting of quality ratings has been introduced in some countries – as outlined above – in a relatively relaxed way, not least as a means to enhance quality performance in a context of "quasi-markets". Even if there is some evidence from the acute health sector that publication of ratings or outcomes may improve an organisation's functioning, it is still unsure whether it really affects users' choice (Hibbard et al., 2005). There are signs that public reporting is more influential on care professionals' choice of their employer, as they prefer to work in a well-performing organisation and are better able to interpret the technical specifications of reported quality indicators. The idea that quality plays an important role in driving the choice of users has also failed to be tested, as users are faced with lack of information as well as with financial and mobility constraints that often prevent them choosing providers exclusively on the basis of any quality criteria, however they may be defined (Downey, 2011). Still, in particular the "consumerist" critique around the issues of choice and independence, voiced by the "independent living movement" of people with disabilities, has pointed out that it should be the users to choose and shape the type of care they prefer (Morris, 2006). For older people in need of LTC, in particular people suffering from mental health problems, who are frail and vulnerable and whose choice is constrained by the extent of their care needs, this approach remains widely unresolved. Scarcity of services, which in fact implies no choice at all, aggravates these limited options.

The lack of defined quality indicators has also resulted in public purchasers taking decisions over public tenders and ensuing contracts with service providers mainly on price, rather than on quality criteria (INSSP, 2010). Indeed, only where partnership-working between public purchasers and private providers is practiced, positive results can be reported (Leichsenring et al., 2010), but evaluations of whether quasi-markets have triggered improvements in the quality of LTC services remain scarce and of limited evidence (Scourfield, 2007; Stolt et al., 2010). Comparisons over time are not feasible, and comparisons between, for instance, for-profit and non-profit providers are difficult, again, due to the lack of universally acknowledged indicators.

Quality assurance in individual organisations versus the quality of long-term care pathways

Contracting and quality assurance are generally limited to individual services rather than to a "chain of services" or integrated care pathways. It would be an important indicator for progress in shaping emerging LTC systems, if quality management and assurance mechanisms were developing across organisations, with respective indicators for structural, process and outcome at the interfaces between sectors. Indeed, more developed thinking in terms of "care chains" and care co-ordination is needed to respond to users' real needs – "care trusts", more joint training and financial incentives for co-ordination in care provision may help to bridge the divide between health and social care. This might also make it possible to address the "quality-cost chasm", that is created by the fact that quality criteria are often defined by a specialised agency, while funding issues, are decided by completely separated institutions. As a result, providers are confronted with double-bind situations, as they have to comply with both funding and quality requirements under conditions of fixed prices or rigorous caps on prices (Leichsenring et al., 2010).

The division between health and social care, the variety of stakeholders involved and the lack of appropriate methods and incentives still stand against comprehensive approaches of quality improvement within and across LTC organisations. Nevertheless, the integration of services is at the core of LTC as an immoveable requirement. Therefore, quality management that links organisational structures (such as case management, multidisciplinary teams, single points of access, respite services, chains of care) need further attention from policy makers and health services researchers. Quality systems for integrated service delivery are being developed and implemented, for instance in the Netherlands (Minkman, 2011). But questions such as who is in the end responsible for quality that is delivered by a variety of service providers in a competitive environment, remain to be resolved.

Conclusions

This chapter has highlighted the key challenges for policy and practice in managing and measuring quality in LTC. It argues that quality management within and across organisations need to be supported by enabling policies at the systems level to further a process of continuous improvement and organisational development. Conversely, without an appropriate internal quality management system, external quality assurance, e.g. by means of inspections, remains restricted to rather limited and selective observations that are unable to grasp the complexity of LTC organisations and their potential for improvement.

Quality in LTC is a normative concept and reflects as such societal, professional and personal norms and views not only related to quality of clinical care, but also on quality of life. Standards that are derived from other areas such as acute health care do not always meet the specific needs and norms of LTC users, including families and friends.

Notwithstanding many pro-active and appealing initiatives that have been taken over the past two decades by different stakeholders, many dilemmas remain unsolved and require further organisational and political processes to learn from experiences. Quality management and measurement in LTC requires partnership in a process that involves all stakeholders in a systematic dialogue about expectations and potential interventions, including monitoring and improvement activities.

The introduction of market-mechanisms in LTC gave rise to debates and policies to create an equal level playing field for public, private, for-profit or non-profit providers, based on transparent definitions of quality requirements. This also gave rise to institutional infrastructures and institution building for guidance and monitoring. However, the fragmentation of multi-level legal regulations contributes to a fragmentation of quality criteria and therefore quality management. This often leads to bureaucracy, a high administrative burden and feelings of alienation of workers in LTC. In that case means and outcomes are poorly balanced: too high investments lead to too low gains in quality. The cost-efficiency of quality management in LTC is only anecdotally addressed. In order to maximise the potential benefits of quality management, cost-efficiency should be on the agenda.

The on-going shift towards user empowerment and purchasing power of people with LTC needs implies a shift of responsibilities in relation to quality assurance. Service users are increasingly gaining rights to influence how their treatment and services are being met. In terms of user involvement and empowerment of users to select and assess the quality of services received in LTC for older people could learn a lot from services for people with disabilities at working age. For instance, the EQUASS Quality Assurance certification programme developed by the European Platform for Rehabilitation (*www.epr.eu*) puts the user perspective at the centre of quality assessment and improvement, based on the principles of the Voluntary European Quality Framework for Social Services (SPC, 2010) and training of quality managers. An interesting initiative in this context is also the German voluntary initiative "Heimverzeichnis.de" (*www.heimverzeichnis.de*) that had been set up by a users' association, supported by the Ministry of Consumer Protection. Providers are invited to have their quality assessed by trained volunteers, usually pensioners, in terms of participation, dignity and personal autonomy offered. Results of positively assessed care homes are published online. Up till now, about 10% of care homes adhered (Stiehr, 2011).

Managing quality in LTC means to systematically address the cyclical process of planning, implementing, monitoring and improving structures, processes and outcomes within LTC organisations and to extend related methods across the spectrum of settings in which LTC is being provided.

Measuring quality in LTC is a necessary precondition that still presents a number of caveats in terms of definitions and mutually agreed instruments. Indeed, progress has been made in the area of clinical care quality, but quality of life and other contextual factors remain being challenged. Related indicators should be conceived in a pragmatic way as signals from which further improvement may be derived by means of quality management.

The current state of the art would call for more heavy endeavors and investments in research and practice to improve the knowledge base so that purchasers (most often public authorities) and users would get a better description of what they are purchasing. Yet, public investments are scarce amidst a financial crisis with the need to implement important budget cuts. The question is, whether this is a "penny wise, pound foolish" policy. The challenge of LTC systems is to achieve the Triple Aim in a sustainable way: improving the users' experience of LTC, improving their health and wellbeing, and keeping costs per capita as low as possible.

With respect to the governance of quality development and continual improvement there is a general search for appropriate incentives for (collaborating) organisations to strive towards excellence or optimum performance. However, regulators as well as providers of LTC continue to consider quality development predominantly as reducing risks and as additional costs, rather than an opportunity to improvements that trigger cost-efficient delivery of care. While this applies to a majority of individual organisations, quality management and quality assurance across the spectrum of LTC will be an additional item to be put on the agenda.

Priorities for quality management and improvement have been identified, one of which will certainly consist in education and training to prepare for the challenges of ageing societies with their increasing needs of LTC. In the LTC sector, where in most European countries the level of education and professionalisation is still weak and needs enforcement, adequate training for quality management in LTC will be a necessary precondition to realise its potential. The role of professional organisations in developing specific norms or standards of good practice appears to be particularly influential. Compared to acute health care, protocols and standards must be fine-tuned in much more local and context-specific settings with a focus on the improvement of users' quality of life. This implies that "protocols" that can be perfectly applied and controlled in the acute sector, may not be sufficient in LTC.

Moreover, frailty and multi-morbidity in older people require appropriate standards of care. Flexibility, skillfulness and the autonomy of professionals are needed due to the various settings in which they are operating, where they encounter multiple challenges in the context sensitive area of LTC. The large variety of professionals, but also informal caregivers need to be involved in developing more appropriate job profiles and related education programmes.

Finally, it has become clear that partnership working and a social dialogue between stakeholders at various governance levels is needed to better define and monitor expectations, requirements and outcomes of integrated LTC provision between health and social care sectors as well as between formal and informal care. However, this is not merely a matter of those who are currently involved in LTC but a general societal concern. With the vast majority of LTC being provided by informal carers (relatives, friends, neighbours), changing social structures and weakening primary social networks, the contributions of local communities are gaining in importance. Yet, no satisfying instruments have been designed to monitor the quality of integrated home care services, not to speak of innovative developments in community involvement. The relatively short history of quality management and quality assurance in LTC therefore leaves a wide range of complex challenges to be tackled in the near future.

References

ActiZ et al. (2007), *Kwaliteitskader Verantwoorde zorg Verpleging, Verzorging en Zorg Thuis (langdurige en/of complexe zorg)*, available at *www.zorgvoorbeter.nl/docs/Kwaliteitskader_Verantwoorde_Zorg_VVT_2007. pdf*.

AGE Platform Europe (2010), "European Charter of the Rights and Responsibilities for People in Need of Long-term Care and Assistance", AGE Platform Europe, European Association for Directors of Residential Homes for the Elderly (EDE) et al., Brussels, available at *www.age-platform.eu*.

Allen, K., R. Bednárik, L. Campbell, A. Dieterich, E. Hirsch Durrett, T. Emilsson, J. Glasby, P. Gobet, G. Kagialaris, J. Klavus, S. Kümpers, K. Leichsenring, G. Ljunggren, T. Mastroyiannakis, S. Meriläinen, M. Naiditch, H. Nies, M. Repetti, K. Repkova, R. Rodrigues, K. Stiehr, R. van der Veen, L. Wagner and B. Weigl (2011), *Governance and Finance of Long-term Care Across Europe. Overview Report,* University of Birmingham/European Centre for Social Welfare Policy and Research (INTERLINKS Report #4), Birmingham and Vienna, *http://interlinks.euro.centre.org/project/reports.*

Alzheimer Nederland and Vilans (2012) *Zorgstandaard dementie. Definitief concept. Versie 1,* Bunnik, Utrecht, available at *www.alzheimer-nederland.nl/media/11405/Zorgstandaard%20Dementie%20PDF.pdf.*

Bauer, J.E., G.L. Duffy and R. Westcott (2006), *The Quality Improvement Handbook,* Quality Press, Milwaukee.

Bednárik, R., P. Di Santo and K. Leichsenring (2013), "The 'Care Gap' and Migrant Carers", in K. Leichsenring, J. Billings and H. Nies (eds.), *Long-term Care in Europe. Improving Policy and Practice,* Palgrave Macmillan, Basingstoke, pp. 213-231.

Bode, I. and A. Dobrowolski (2009), "'Governance-performance' bei gemeinnützigen Trägern der stationären Altenhilfe. Zwei Fallstudien und ihre Botschaften", Bergische Universität, Wuppertal, *www.3q.uni-wuppertal.de.*

Boot, J.M. and M.H. Knapen (2010), *De Nederlandse gezondheidszorg,* Bohn Stafleu van Loghum, Houten.

Büscher, A. (2010), "Public Reporting, Expert Standards and Indicators. Different Routes to Improve the Quality of German Long-term Care", *Eurohealth,* Vol. 16, No. 2, pp. 4-7.

Colombo, F. et al. (2011), *Help Wanted? Providing and Paying for Long-Term Care,* OECD Publishing, Paris, *http://dx.doi.org/10.1787/9789264097759-en.*

Delnoij, D.M.J. et al. (2006), "Made in the USA: The Import of American Consumer Assessment of Health Plan Surveys (CAHPS) into the Dutch Social Insurance System", *European Journal of Public Health,* Vol. 16, No. 6, pp. 652-659.

De Prins, P. and E. Henderickx (2007), "HRM Effectiveness in Older People's and Nursing Homes: The Search for Best (Quality) Practices", *Nonprofit and Voluntary Sector Quarterly,* Vol. 36, pp. 549-571.

Dijkstra, A., M. Coleman, C. Tomas, M. Valimaki and T. Dassen (2003), "Cross-cultural Psychometric Testing of the Care Dependency Scale with Data", *Journal of Advanced Nursing,* Vol. 43, No. 2, pp. 181-187.

Di Santo, P. and F. Ceruzzi (2009), "Quality in the Long Term Care system-Italy", Studio Come (INTERLINKS National Report), Rome, available at *http://interlinks.euro.centre.org.*

DNQP (2011), *Deutsches Netzwerk für Qualitätsentwicklung in der Pflege (DNQP),* Hochschule Osnabrück, Fakultät für Wirtschafts- und Sozialwissenschaften, Osnabrück.

Donabedian, A. (1980), "The Definition of Quality and Approaches to Its Assessment", Vol. 1: Explorations in Quality Assessment and Monitoring, Health Administration Press, Ann Arbor.

Downey, J. (2011), "Old Age and New Speak", *Journal of Care Services Management,* Vol. 5, No. 1, pp. 23-27.

Emilsson, T. (2011), "Dementia Guidelines and Informal Carers", available at *http://interlinks.euro.centre. org/framework.*

European Centre for Social Welfare Policy and Research et al. (ed.) (2010), *Measuring Progress: Indicators for Care Homes,* PROGRESS, The EU Programme for Employment and Social Solidarity 2007-2013.

European Partnership for the Wellbeing and Dignity of Older people – WeDO (2012), "European Quality Framework for Long-term Care Services", available at *www.wedo-partnership.eu/european-quality-framework-long-term-care-services.*

Finne-Soveri, H., T. Hammar and A. Noro (2010), "Measuring the Quality of Long-term Institutional Care in Finland", *Eurohealth,* Vol. 16, No. 2, pp. 8-10.

Frerichs, F., K. Leichsenring, G. Naegele, M. Reichert and M. Stadler (2003), *Qualität Sozialer Dienste in Deutschland und Österreich,* LIT Verlag, Münster.

Frijters, D.H.M. (2010), "Quality of Care Assurance in Long-term Care in the Netherlands", *Eurohealth,* Vol. 16, No. 2, pp. 11-13.

Glasby, J. (2011), "The 'Big Care Debate' – Public Engagement in LTC Funding", available at *http://interlinks.euro.centre.org/framework.*

Groenewoud, S. (2008), "It's Your Choice. A Study of Search and Selection Processes and the Use of Performance Indicators in Different Patient Groups", PhD Thesis, Erasmus University, Rotterdam.

Hammar, T., M. Niemi and H. Finne-Soveri (2011), "RAI-benchmarking: An Instrument for Leadership and Development", available at *http://interlinks.euro.centre.org/framework.*

Hasseler, M., K. Wolf-Ostermann, M. Nagel and S. Indefrey (2010), "Wissenschaftliche Evaluation zur Beurteilung der Pflege-Transparenzvereinbarungen für den ambulanten (PTVA) und stationären (PTVS) Bereich", GKV-Spitzenverband, Berlin, available at *www.pflegenoten.de/upload/Pflegenoten_Endbericht_Beirat_u__WB_2010_07_21_6961.pdf*.

Haverinen, R. and N. Tabibian (2005), "The Outcomes and Benefits of Integrated Care – In Search of the Service Users' and Carers' Point of View", in J. Billings and K. Leichsenring (eds.), *Integrating Health and Social Care Services for Older Persons – Evidence from Nine Countries*, Aldershot, Ashgate, pp. 193-214.

Hibbard, J.H., J. Stockard and M. Tusler (2005), "Hospital Performance Reports: Impact on Quality, Market Share, and Reputation", *Health Affairs*, Vol. 24, No. 4, pp. 1150-1160.

Huber, M., M. Maucher and B. Sak (2008), "Study on Social and Health Services of General Interest in the European Union: Final Synthesis Report", DG Employment, Social Affairs and Equal Opportunities, Brussels.

Huijbers, P. (2011), "Neighbourhood Care: Better Home Care at Reduced Cost", available at *http://interlinks.euro.centre.org/framework*.

Igl, G. and T. Klie (2007), "Charta der Rechte hilfe- und pflegebedürftiger Menschen", in G. Igl and T. Klie (eds.), *Das Recht der älteren Menschen*, Nomos Verlagsgesellschaft, Baden-Baden, pp. 34-36.

INSSP – Informal Network of Social Services Providers (2010), "Seminar 'Impact of EU Legislation on Social Services", Updated Report, INSSP, Brussels, 29 September 2009, *www.feantsa.org*.

ISO – International Organization for Standardization (2010a), *Quality Management Principles*, ISO, Geneva.

ISO (2010b), *Building Trust. The Conformity Assessment Toolbox*, ISO, Geneva.

Kottner, J., R.J.G. Halfens and T. Dassen (2010), "Interrater Reliability and Agreement of the Care Dependency Scale in the Home Care Setting in the Netherlands", *Scandinavian Journal of Caring Sciences*, Vol. 24, pp. 56-61.

Leichsenring, K. (2009), "Developing and Ensuring Quality in LTC in Austria", European Centre for Social Welfare Policy and Research (INTERLINKS National Report), Vienna, available at *http://interlinks.euro.centre.org*.

Leichsenring, K. (2010a), "Introducing Civicness in Steering and Managing Social Services. Cases from Long-term Care", in T. Brandsen, P. Dekker and A. Evers (eds.), *Civicness in the Governance and Delivery of Social Services*, Nomos, Baden-Baden, pp. 113-124.

Leichsenring, K. (2010b), "Achieving Quality Long-term Care in Residential Facilities", Discussion Paper for the Peer Review 2010 Germany, available at *www.peer-review-social-inclusion.eu*.

Leichsenring, K. (2011), "The E-Qalin Quality Management System", available at *http://interlinks.euro.centre.org/framework*.

Leichsenring, K. and A. Alaszewski (eds.) (2004), *Providing Integrated Health and Social Care for Older Persons. A European Overview of Issues and Stake*, Aldershot, Ashgate.

Leichsenring, K., S. Barnett and R. Rodrigues (2010), *Contracting for Quality*, ESN, Brighton.

Leichsenring, K., J. Billings and H. Nies (eds.) (2013a), *Long-term Care in Europe. Improving Policy and Practice*, Palgrave Macmillan, Basingstoke.

Leichsenring, K., H. Nies and R. van der Veen (2013b), "The Quest for Quality in Long-term Care", in K. Leichsenring, J. Billings and H. Nies (eds.), *Long-term Care in Europe. Improving Policy and Practice*, Palgrave Macmillan, Basingstoke, pp. 167-190.

Ljunggren, G. and T. Emilsson (2011), "Developing and Ensuring Quality in LTC in Sweden", Forum for Knowledge and Common Development (INTERLINKS National Report), Stockholm, available at *http://interlinks.euro.centre.org*.

Magee, H., S. Parsons and J. Askham (2008), *Measuring Dignity in Care for Older People. A Research Report*, Help the Aged/Picker Institute Europe, London.

Ministry of Social Affairs and Health and the Association of Finnish Local and Regional Authorities (2008), *The National Framework for High-quality Services for Older People*, Ministry of Social Affairs and Health Publications, Helsinki, *http://pre20090115.stm.fi/ka1212393066110/passthru.pdf*.

Minkman, M.M.N. (2011), *Developing Integrated Care. Towards a Development Model for Integrated Care*, Kluwer, Deventer.

Minkman, M.M.N., H. Balsters, J. Mast and M. Kuiper (eds.) (2011), *Blijvend zorgen voor beter (Sustainable improvement)*, Kluwer, Deventer.

Mor, V., T. Leone and A. Maresso (eds.) (2013), *The Challenges in Regulating Long-term Care Quality: An International Comparison,* Cambridge University Press (in print), Cambridge.

Morris, J. (2006), "Independent Living: The Role of the Disability Movement in the Development of Government Policy", in C. Glendinning and P.A. Kemp (eds.), *Cash and Care: Policy Challenges in the Welfare State,* The Policy Press, Bristol, pp. 235-248.

Mullen, K.J., R.G. Frank and M.B. Rosenthal (2010), "Can You Get What You Pay Gor? Pay-for-Performance and the Quality of Healthcare Providers", *The RAND Journal of Economics,* Vol. 41, No. 1, pp. 64-91.

Nies, H. and P. Berman (eds.) (2004), *Integrating Services for Older People: A Resource Book from European Experience.* European Health Management Association, Dublin.

Nies, H. and K. Leichsenring (2012), "Nine European Trends in Quality Management of Long-term Care for Older People", *Kwaliteit in zorg,* Vol. 3, pp. 24-271.

Nies, H., K. Leichsenring, R. van der Veen, R. Rodrigues, P. Gobet, L. Holdsworth, S. Mak, E. Hirsch Durrett, M. Repetti, M. Naiditch, T. Hammar, H. Mikkola, H. Finne-Soveri, T. Hujanen, S. Carretero, L. Cordero, M. Ferrando, T. Emilsson, G. Ljunggren, P. Di Santo, F. Ceruzzi and E. Turk (2010), "Quality Management and Quality Assurance in Long-Term Care – European Overview Paper", Vilans/ European Centre for Social Welfare Policy and Research (INTERLINKS Report #2 – *http://interlinks. euro.centre.org/project/reports*), Utrecht/Vienna.

Nolan, M., J. Brown, S. Davies, J. Nolan and J. Keady (2006), "The Senses Framework: Improving Care for Older People Through a Relationship-centred Approach", University of Sheffield, Sheffield.

Pasquinelli, S. and G. Rusmini (2010), "La regolarizzazione delle badanti", in Network Non Autosufficienza NNA (ed.), *Secondo rapporto sull'assistenza agli anziani non autosufficienti 2010,* Maggioli Editore, Santarcangelo, pp. 77-90.

PSIRU – Public Services International Research Unit (2011), "Private Care Homes in the UK: Bankruptcy, Torture, and Lack of Regulation", University of Greenwich (PSIRU Brief 13 June), London.

Rodrigues, R. and H. Nies (2013), "Making Sense of Differences – The Mixed Economy of Funding and Delivering Long-term Care", in K. Leichsenring, J. Billings and H. Nies (eds.), *Long-term Care in Europe. Improving Policy and Practice,* Palgrave Macmillan, Basingstoke, pp. 191-212.

Schalock, R.L., G.S. Bonham and M.A. Verdugo (2008), "The Conceptualization and Measurement of Quality of Life: Implications for Program Planning and Evaluation in the Field of Intellectual Disabilities", *Evaluation and Program Planning,* Vol. 31, pp. 181-190.

Schiemann, D. and M. Moers (2007), "Expert Standards in Nursing as an Instrument for Evidence-based Nursing Practice", *Journal of Nursing Care Quality,* Vol. 22, No. 2, pp. 172-179.

Scourfield, P. (2007), "Are There Reasons To Be Worried About the 'Caretelization' of Residential Care?", *Critical Social Policy,* Vol. 27, No. 2, pp. 155-180.

SPC – Social Protection Committee (2010), *A Voluntary European Quality Framework for Social Services,* European Commission (SPC/2010/10/8 final), Brussels.

Stiehr, K. (2011), "Certified Quality of Life in Nursing Homes", *www.Heimverzeichnis.de,* available at *http://interlinks.euro.centre.org/framework.*

Stolt, R., P. Blomqvist and U. Winblad (2010), "Privatization of Social Services: Quality Differences in Swedish Elderly Care", *Social Science & Medicine,* Vol. 72, No. 4, pp. 560-567.

Trukeschitz, B. (2010), "Safeguarding Good Quality in Longterm Care: The Austrian Approach", *Eurohealth,* Vol. 16, No. 2, pp. 17-20.

US DHHS – US Department of Health and Human Services (2008), "MDS 2.0 Public Quality Indicator and Resident Reports", available at *www.cms.hhs.gov/MDSPubQIandResRep/02_qmreport. asp?qtr=13&isSubmitted=qm2.*

Van Nie, N.C., J.M.M. Meijers, J.M.G.A. Schols, C. Lohrmann, S. Bartholomeyczik. and R.J.G. Halfens (2011), "Comparing Quality Care in Dutch and German Nursing Homes", *Journal of Clinical Nursing,* Vol. 20, No. 17-18, pp. 2501-2508.

Wingenfeld, K., T. Kleina, S. Franz, D. Engels, S. Mehlan and H. Engel (2010), "Entwicklung und Erprobung von Instrumenten zur Beurteilung der Ergebnisqualität in der Stationären Altenhilfe", Federal Ministry of Family Affairs, Senior Citizens, Women and Health, Berlin, available at *www.bagfw.de/ uploads/media/Abschlussbericht_Ergebnisqualitaet_Internet_31.5.11.pdf.*

Wipp, M. (2011), "Eine qualitative Fachkraftquote", *Altenheim,* Vol. 12, pp. 24-27.

PART III

Chapter 8

Long-term care quality assurance in the United States*

by
David Stevenson,
Harvard Medical School, Boston

and
Jeffrey Bramson,
Harvard Law School Class of 2012, Boston

The market for nursing home care and other long-term care services is one of the most heavily regulated sectors in the United States economy. The present quality assurance system boasts an extensive regulatory scheme, with a complex interplay of federal, state, and voluntary rules controlling and monitoring the quality of nursing homes and, to a lesser extent, other home and community-based service providers. This chapter describes the current approach to long-term care regulation in the United States focusing on three key areas: 1) the standards for provider participation; 2) the monitoring and enforcement of compliance; and 3) public reporting and other market-based approaches to improving quality. It focuses primarily on nursing home care, given the predominant focus of regulation and the surrounding literature on this sector. It concludes with a brief discussion of the current state and future of long-term care regulation as well as lessons based on the US experience.

* This chapter is based on "Regulation of Long-term Care in the United States", in V. Mor, T. Leone and A. Maresso (eds.), *Challenges in Regulating Long-term Care Quality: An International Comparison*, Cambridge University Press, in press.

Introduction

The market for nursing home (NH) care and other long-term care (LTC) services is one of the most heavily regulated sectors in the US economy. Although LTC regulations can serve secondary ends, such as controlling provider supply or regulating the price of services, the majority of these rules are designed to ensure the quality and appropriateness of services. There are different theories for the presence of regulations, but a standard explanation is that they exist to address some type of market failure, such as consumers' inability to assess, monitor, and respond to low-quality care. Thus, government regulation can assist uninformed consumers by developing quality standards, evaluating whether standards are met, and enforcing improvement when necessary.

While similar factors could apply to regulation of other industries, the large degree of public financing for LTC services in the United States further justifies extensive governmental oversight. Indeed, although the government itself owns few LTC facilities, the federal and state governments are the primary payers for services rendered in these settings. Medicare, a federal entitlement programme of health insurance coverage for the elderly and other protected classes, pays for the majority of post-acute rehabilitative care provided by NHs, home health agencies, and other providers. These services are complemented by Medicaid, a means-tested programme for certain categories of individuals, primarily regulated and financed by the federal government but administered by the individual states. Medicaid is the primary payer for long-term services and supports, including the large majority of chronic NH care, in the United States.

Historically, the bulk of public LTC funding and regulatory attention in the United States has gone to the NH sector (Kane et al., 1998). At present, there are around 16 500 NHs and 1.6 million NH beds in the United States (Harrington et al., 2010). Over the last two decades, a wider range of home- and community-based services has become available, partly supported with governmental dollars (Kaye et al., 2010). Relative to the NH sector, oversight mechanisms for home and community-based providers (e.g., assisted living facilities) are under-developed, despite some overlap in the services provided and populations served.

Governmental regulation of LTC services in the United States is partly a response to political pressures by both the general public and the LTC industry. Periodic scandals and revelations about the quality of care in NHs and other LTC settings have required the US Congress and regulatory agencies in the executive branch to reassess the stringency of the rules iteratively over time. Toward this end, LTC regulations serve two related quality assurance functions. First, they are supposed to deter future violations of quality standards – the government cannot identify and pursue every violation, so it instead relies on unannounced inspections and harsh potential penalties to deter lapses in quality. Second, the rules signal to the public that these services are safe to use, something that is important to the maintenance of public confidence in the industry. At the same time, some regulations can serve more political ends and reflect the political strength of the LTC industry at the state level. For instance, state certificate of need programmes focused on the supply of long-term care providers can protect existing facilities by limiting market entry of possible competitor facilities.

Whatever the ultimate motivation behind LTC regulations, the present system boasts a comprehensive regulatory scheme, with a complex interplay of federal, state, and voluntary rules controlling and monitoring the quality of NHs and, to a lesser extent, other providers. This chapter begins with a brief description of how LTC regulation developed in the United States before moving to a three-part explanation of the quality control mechanisms currently in place: 1) the standards for participation; 2) the monitoring and enforcement of compliance; and 3) public reporting and other market-based approaches to improving quality. It focuses primarily on regulation of NH care, given the predominant focus of regulation and the surrounding literature on this sector. It concludes with a brief discussion of the current state and future of LTC regulation as well as lessons based on the US experience.

Historical development of long-term care regulation in the United States

The history of LTC regulation in the United States consists of three main eras: 1) the paucity of regulations before Medicare and Medicaid were passed in 1965; 2) the unco-ordinated attempts to control quality between 1965 and 1987; and 3) the aftermath of the Omnibus Budget Reconciliation Act of 1987 (OBRA '87), which redefined LTC quality control in the United States. For more on this history, several sources provide additional detail (e.g., Mendelson, 1974; Vladeck, 1980; IOM, 1986; Binstock, 1996). Our focus is on OBRA '87 forward (Box 8.1).

Box 8.1. **Historical development before the passing of the Nursing Home Reform Act**

Before the passage of Medicare and Medicaid, government support for LTC primarily came in the form of welfare payments to elderly and disabled individuals receiving long-term services and supports and through various programmes to support construction of LTC facilities. By and large, the federal government did not promulgate extensive rules regarding LTC facilities during this time, and attempts to control quality were undertaken mostly by individual states and municipalities. The passage of Medicare and Medicaid in 1965 initially did little to affect the stringency of NH licensure and other quality control requirements, largely because few extant facilities met the newly established standards of care. Federal policy makers accommodated this reality, reflecting a reluctance to face the embarrassment of creating an empty entitlement promise and a response to intense lobbying from states and LTC providers who feared losing out on federal dollars (Moss and Halamandaris, 1977). Although there were efforts to strengthen NH standards and their enforcement over the subsequent two decades, progress remained slow, despite tremendous growth of the LTC industry fueled by expanded government reimbursement.

By the 1980s, significant evidence had emerged of LTC quality failures. Two events in particular compelled Congressional action. First, a federal court determined that the federal government had an administrative obligation to guarantee facilities receiving federal money satisfied legal requirements, including provision of high quality care (Smith v. Heckler 1984). Second, Congress directed the non-governmental Institute of Medicine (IOM) to complete an independent study of NH quality and make recommendations about what reforms were necessary. The 1986 IOM report, "Improving the Quality of Care in Nursing Homes", detailed widespread quality problems and recommended a drastic overhaul of LTC regulation. Concurrently, the Government Accountability Office (GAO), the auditing arm of the US Congress, issued its "Medicare and Medicaid: Stronger Enforcement of Nursing Home Requirements Needed" report, finding that a third of all NHs did not meet existing federal quality standards. Following these events, Congress was compelled to respond with the introduction of the Nursing Home Reform Act.

As part of OBRA '87, Congress passed the Nursing Home Reform Act (commonly referred to simply as "OBRA '87"). OBRA '87 significantly altered the responsibilities of LTC facilities and remains the primary source of statutory LTC requirements, along with the administrative regulations promulgated in accordance with the statute.

Although OBRA '87 realigned many priorities, the most significant high-level change was the shift toward resident-focused, outcome-oriented standards. Responding to the critique that previous standards focused too heavily on structural elements of quality, the new regulations focused on quality of care, residents' rights, and resident-reported quality of life and satisfaction. Importantly, OBRA '87 granted residents rights and quality-of-life standards a regulatory status equal to that of the quality of medical care, and it incorporated direct observation and interviews with residents and families into facility inspections. OBRA '87 established the conditions of participation for NH providers to receive Medicare and Medicaid reimbursement and is considered the foundation of modern-day NH regulation in the United States.

Within the context of OBRA '87, several factors could further alter NH oversight. Market-driven approaches such as federally mandated public reporting have been growing steadily, emphasizing a supervisory role for the federal government, as opposed to one of only regulation and direct oversight. Nonetheless, a vast majority of the public believes that *more* regulation of NHs is necessary to ensure a higher quality of care (Furrow et al., 2008), a view shared by the majority of specialists within the LTC research and policy communities as well (Mor et al., 2010). Moreover, the regulatory framework for non-NH LTC providers remains relatively undefined, despite government resources funding care at home and in other residential settings such as assisted living facilities.

Nursing home provider requirements

US NHs are currently subject to requirements through two primary mechanisms: 1) licensure requirements; and 2) quality conditions that must be met to remain eligible for federal reimbursement of services. Although these two functions are fundamentally related, they are distinct in the United States, with state governments responsible for licensing NH facilities and the federal government responsible for determining conditions for reimbursement. See Figure 8.1 for a graphical depiction of the interaction of federal and state governments in LTC regulation, including their relationship with the various entities described in this chapter. The figure shows the partnership that exists between states and the federal government in establishing standards, assessing compliance, and enforcing those standards. The figure primarily refers to nursing home quality assurance, with other long-term care settings primarily governed by state law.

Federal quality control

While OBRA '87 was designed to improve quality in all NHs, Congress elected to apply the certification requirements only to facilities that receive Medicare and Medicaid payments (around 95% of all licensed facilities). The participation requirements in OBRA '87 are quite extensive and cover everything from nurse staffing and residents' rights to the minimum scope of dental services required (Kapp, 2000, p. 712).

Among the most crucial of the OBRA '87 requirements from the perspective of quality assurance is the mandatory implementation of the Minimum Data Set (MDS). The MDS is a database of information compiled from the Resident Assessment Instrument (RAI),

Figure 8.1. **Graphical representation of entities involved in LTC regulation in the United States**

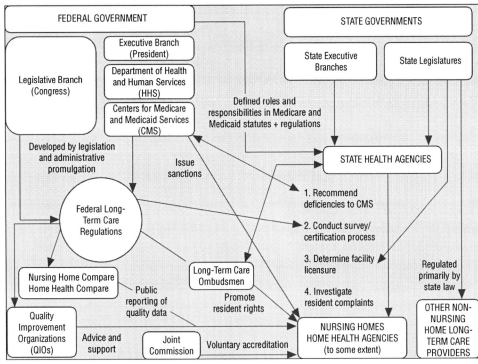

Source: Author for the OECD.

which monitors the care plans and quality outcomes for all residents in a given home. The requirement to collect and report these data has had broad consequences, despite the fact that the MDS itself does not have any performance benchmarks. First, following implementation of the MDS, there has been a marked improvement in many of the process measures in the MDS, including a decline in catheter and restraint use and increased use of advanced medical directives (Rantz et al., 1999). Second, there have been associated improvements in resident health, with lower incidences of many conditions often associated with poor-quality care, such as falls, pressure ulcers, and malnutrition (Kapp, 2000). Finally, the RAI has triggered more comprehensive discussions between residents and their care providers about individualised care planning, quality concerns, and end-of-life wishes.

The 2010 US Health Law – the Patient Protection and Affordable Care Act (PPACA) – leaves in place existing OBRA '87 standards, while adding some new requirements. Perhaps most notably, the new law includes provisions around transparency and disclosure of NH ownership structures (Furrow et al., 2010). In particular, facilities will be required to disclose information about entities with an ownership interest or managing control of their operations, in addition to reporting other entities involved in governance, administration, or operations.

State quality control

Participation conditions derive from federal statutory requirements and CMS-issued regulations, but the task of policing compliance with these standards falls on the states. Under OBRA '87, each state must create an agency to administer regulatory oversight, maintain health standards for LTC institutions, provide for regular review of each patient's needs within the NH, and otherwise comply with mandates. Although the states are afforded significant discretion in how to create and administer these agencies, some interstate uniformity is mandated. For example, the states are required to use federal forms and follow federal inspection protocols during the survey/certification process. CMS generally defers to state determinations of eligibility for reimbursement. However, statutes do allow the federal government to review state decisions and to overrule them if necessary. This prerogative, known as the "look behind" provision, guarantees that ultimate control is held by the federal government, at least formally.

Although the most important role of states in NH regulations is implementing federal standards, states that wish to increase the stringency of LTC regulation do have certain tools available to them. Many states, for instance, have staffing standards stricter than the federal guidelines (Harrington and Millman, 2001). The majority of states also have some sort of certificate-of-need (CON) requirement for entry into the NH industry (and, to a lesser extent, other LTC settings), mandating that new facilities address an unmet need and are consistent with a state's long-term health planning. Such programmes are controversial, however, given that they may unduly limit market competition (NCSL, 2011).

In addition to certifying that facilities are in compliance with federal and state participation requirements, states have primary responsibility for the initial licensure of providers, ostensibly giving them control over market entry and retention. Yet, state licensure requirements historically have excluded few facilities. Loss of license is considered a drastic remedy that is reserved for very serious breaches of patient safety and quality-of-care standards. Instead, the primary regulatory stringency exists in the federal conditions of participation (Furrow et al., 2008), which stem primarily from OBRA '87.

Voluntary quality control

NHs also may elect to undergo additional voluntary scrutiny. Chief among these programmes is accreditation from the Joint Commission, a non-profit standard-setting and accrediting entity financed through user fees from participating organisations. While the Joint Commission's determinations are deemed official for hospitals and some other institutions, they remain strictly voluntary for NHs. To date, there is no conclusive evidence that voluntary accreditation results in appreciable quality improvements, and replacement of the current NH regime with Joint Commission "deeming" is unlikely to occur.

Many NHs in the United States also take advantage of a range of related quality assurance and improvement activities. Almost half of all NHs in the United States., for instance, participate in the federally supported Advancing Excellence campaign, a programme that has engaged provider, advocacy, and policy stakeholders and is designed to assist NHs in working toward targeted, self-identified goals for quality improvement. Similarly, the federal Quality Improvement Organization (QIO) programme described below works with providers in a more consultative way than is allowed in the regulatory process. On the quality control side, NH providers, especially larger providers, may engage in internal quality assurance programmes that investigate adverse events, or utilisation review programmes to assess whether the services rendered to residents are medically appropriate (Kapp, 2000).

Non-nursing home settings

Regulations for home health agencies bear some similarities to NH regulations, with CMS establishing requirements and states administering them. However, the rules for these agencies are significantly less stringent than for NHs, and the regulations have focused more on cost and access to care than on quality (IOM, 2001). Furthermore, unlike NHs, home health agencies are deemed compliant with CMS if they are accredited by the non-governmental Joint Commission. This allowance could lessen the importance of the CMS requirements and have a deleterious effect if accreditation is too lenient (IOM, 2001).

Participation requirements for non-NH residential care facilities derive from state law. As such, there is wide variation in the nature of these regulations, including differences in how provider categories are defined, what services they may offer, and the licensure requirements themselves. There is also wide variability among states regarding the degree of government involvement as a payer and regulator, with some states clearly specifying the types of services that assisted living facilities can and cannot provide, and others giving providers broader flexibility to meet the needs of residents (Mollica et al., 2008).

Oversight of supportive or custodial home care and other HCBS services is generally performed by the states, again with wide variation. State agencies can define the scope and provision of these services as long as compliance with broad federal guidelines is maintained (CMS, 2011b). Federal requirements apply, however, when the services are provided through a home health agency.

Monitoring, compliance, and enforcement

Although provider conditions for participation largely derive from federal statutory requirements and regulations, the task of policing and enforcing compliance with these standards falls to individual states. This fragmentation of responsibility has been noted as a potential problem, as it increases bureaucracy without promoting federal-state co-operation and introduces state-level variation in the regulatory process. Perhaps reflecting this structural fragmentation, enforcement processes in the United States have suffered from recurring shortcomings, despite an increased range of available sanctions. To date, most regulatory and accountability efforts have focused on the individual provider or facility; however, some recent efforts have concentrated at the level of the parent company as well. In addition, through these and other activities, a greater emphasis on quality improvement has been introduced alongside quality assurance, and some activities have even sought to integrate the two endeavors.

Survey/certification and complaint processes

In accordance with federal regulations, state survey agencies conduct inspections or "surveys" of all NHs seeking reimbursement for Medicare or Medicaid services. These inspections take place every 9 to 15 months and are unannounced to the facilities, a feature aimed at preserving the element of surprise that compels NHs to remain vigilant for quality violations. State agencies then determine whether facilities merit a "certificate of compliance" or whether any deficiencies – where facilities are out of compliance – warrant citation. When found, each deficiency is categorised and rated by its scope and severity. Following inspection, recommendations are submitted to state and federal governing agencies for final certification (CMS, 2011a). Importantly, substantial cross-state variation exists in the percentage of facilities that receive deficiencies (ranging from 76-100%) and in the mean number of deficiencies per facility (ranging from 2.5-14.4) (OIG, 2008).

Beyond the standard survey process, residents may lodge complaints to state or federal regulatory agencies when they experience adverse events or are generally dissatisfied with the quality of care rendered by a facility, which are in turn investigated outside the standard survey process. The 2010 PPACA health reform law includes provisions to make filing complaints easier for residents by requiring state agencies to offer standardised complaint forms on their websites and to implement streamlined complaint resolution processes (Furrow et al., 2010). Consumer complaints data have historically been less widely available than deficiency data, although this has changed in recent years. Although complaints offer useful supplementary data in addition to survey inspections, around 80% of facilities did not have any substantiated complaints in 2007. As with deficiency data, consumer complaint rates vary substantially across states (Stevenson, 2006).

Available sanctions

Before OBRA '87, the only available sanction against non-compliant facilities was to terminate their eligibility to receive Medicare and/or Medicaid reimbursement. Although this extreme remedy might deter particularly egregious violations, it is a blunt tool that has been utilised infrequently. In 2006, for instance, the Office of the Inspector General (OIG) found that CMS declined to terminate participation in over half of the facilities that were sufficiently noncompliant to require that sanction (OIG, 2006b). Since the passage of OBRA '87, CMS has had access to a wider array of available sanctions against violating facilities. Upon a finding of a deficiency, the state (on behalf of CMS) categorises the seriousness of the violation based on its scope and severity and the facility's prior history of noncompliance. The remedies to address deficiencies range in seriousness from requiring a directed plan of correction, state monitoring of the facility, or directed in-service training (Category 1); to denial of payment for new admissions and civil monetary penalties – the latter of which are a relatively recent addition (1999) (Category 2); to further civil penalties, temporary management (receivership), and termination from the Medicare and Medicaid programmes (Category 3).

Another potential remedy focused at the level of the corporation rather than the individual facility is executing a Corporate Integrity Agreement (CIA), a contract that requires NH corporations with identified quality of care problems to consent to additional requirements in exchange for non-exclusion from the Medicare and Medicaid programmes. These requirements mandate that companies contract with an independent quality monitor authorised by OIG, providing the monitor with access to facilities, staff, residents, documents, and management staff. Companies also designate a compliance officer and appoint a corporate-level quality assurance committee to oversee clinical improvement and compliance issues throughout the corporation. CIAs, which generally last for 3-5 years, have been used increasingly by CMS in recent years, and there is some evidence that these contracts are capable of improving quality of care structures, processes, and outcomes (OIG, 2009).

The imposition of penalties is not limited to government; the courts are entitled to hold NHs liable for certain violations, an outlet that has grown in prominence since the late 1990s (Stevenson and Studdert, 2003). Residents have a private right of action against facilities for damages in tort and, in some cases, breaches of contract – such lawsuits resemble traditional medical malpractice cases. Although tort liability is commonly believed to increase incentives for delivering high-quality care, there is controversy about the authenticity of the link between such liability and care quality. In fact, existing evidence indicates that low-quality facilities are almost equally susceptible to tort claims as are higher-quality homes and that litigation does not have any positive impact on the subsequent quality of care that facilities provide (Studdert et al., 2011; Stevenson et al., 2013). It is unclear whether liability claims have an impact on the subsequent care that facilities provide.

Entirely separate from the statutes detailed above, the government may also hold facilities liable under fraud and abuse law, such as the federal False Claims Act. This law provides for severe sanctions against health providers that defraud the government either by billing CMS for services not actually rendered or, sometimes, for delivering services of such a low quality that they do not meet basic care standards. While this Act is infrequently used to police NH quality, it does serve as an additional protection against the most egregious violations.

Challenges

Monitoring and enforcing NH compliance is an imprecise exercise, particularly in a country as large and diverse as the US CMS and the state agencies face a number of challenges and shortcoming, some of which are addressed here.

Although administration of federal regulations should be consistent for both fairness and efficiency reasons, there is wide variation across and even within states as to the number of facilities cited for deficiencies, the threshold degree of violation necessary to trigger a deficiency citation, and the severity of conditions cited. Some of this variation can be explained by differences in facilities across states, but most appears to be inconsistency in how the same regulations are applied. There is considerable room for varied interpretations within the current regulations, and in the absence of clarification by federal authorities the outcome is a lack of uniformity (Miller and Mor, 2006).

Despite hundreds of CMS regulations and a broad range of available sanctions, studies have found state inspectors to be overly lenient in investigating and certifying nursing facilities, thereby undermining enforcement of existing standards. For instance, a 2003 Government Accountability Office (GAO) report concluded that surveys suffer from poor investigation methodologies and insufficient documentation, that many surveyors are too inexperienced to evaluate the severity of the deficiencies, that many states lack programmes to double-check the conclusions of the investigators, and that surveys are so predictable that most NHs are able to correct or conceal their grossest deficiencies shortly prior to the investigations (GAO, 2003). Other studies have reached similar conclusions (GAO, 2007; GAO, 2009), leading some to conclude that the survey and enforcement processes may need significant overhaul.

One of the achievements of OBRA '87 was the increased emphasis on outcome measures over the structural and process measures that had dominated regulations between 1965 and 1987 (e.g., resident functioning as opposed to a building's physical plant or documentation requirements). While such patient-focused and outcome-oriented measures more directly assess the quality of a NH, these measures can also be harder to determine, thus having the potential to undermine the effectiveness of the survey process (Stoil, 1994).

To address some of these limitations, the federal government launched a demonstration project in five states known as the Quality Indicator Survey (QIS) programme. This programme aimed to alter inspection methods to target the most serious deficiencies, increase accuracy, improve the usefulness and efficiency of state inspectors, and ultimately enhance NH quality. Although national rollout of the programme continues (26 states are currently in some phase of implementing the QIS), evaluation results have been mixed to date. A 2007 review by CMS found that the QIS is no more accurate than the traditional survey process and that it has failed to improve documentation or inspectors' speed and efficiency (CMS 2007). On the other hand, there was a marked increase in the number of deficiencies detected under the QIS, particularly in areas that have historically been under-cited.

Complaint investigation processes suffer from similar problems to the standard survey process. When the OIG evaluated the process in 2006, it concluded that state agencies failed to investigate many of the most serious alleged deficiencies, did a poor job of following up on complaints after the initial intake, and were insufficiently reviewed by CMS (OIG, 2006a). These findings echoed an earlier CMS-sponsored report (Zimmerman et al., 2003). These reports suggest that future quality assurance efforts in the United States should focus not only on the stringency of the regulations, but also on the implementation and enforcement of those regulations.

More generally, state inspectors currently function mostly in a policing role, looking for violations and issuing sanctions to NH facilities as punishment. The result is several-fold. First, NHs spend considerable time and resources attempting to correct the deficiencies that are most likely to be detected and sanctioned, rather than trying to improve overall quality. . Second, this approach can waste relevant expertise of inspectors, as they are able to serve only in a policing role and are restricted from offering information applicable to best practices or quality improvement. Third, when state agencies and CMS issue penalties against LTC facilities, the fines are generally paid to the government itself, siphoning money away from patient care in those homes that are already having quality difficulties (Miller and Mor, 2006).

The regulatory process need not of be adversarial to be functional, and coming years could see a further expansion of the government's role as an advisor or consultant for NHs. Indeed, the Medicare Quality Improvement Organization (QIO) programme discussed below is an ongoing effort to develop cooperation between regulators and providers. The resource-siphoning problem identified above has also been addressed by the recent PPACA law, which allows CMS to remit fines back to NHs generally (i.e., not directly to the deficient facility) for certain approved uses benefitting residents.

Alternate methods of quality monitoring and improvement

Governmental approaches to improving NH quality have not been limited to the traditional survey/certification/complaint methodology described above. Supplemental methods have been used to assure quality, a few of which are discussed below.

Medicare's federally funded QIO programme utilises private, non-profit contract entities at the state level to form a collaborative bridge between CMS and various health care institutions. Begun with an emphasis on controlling utilisation and identifying outlier providers, the QIO programme has moved over the last decade toward supporting health care decision making, measuring health outcomes, and providing technical assistance for improved quality of care. Concurrently, the programme has expanded from only acute care settings only to a broader range of providers, including NHs and home health agencies. Because QIOs do not function in a regulatory capacity, they may work with NHs in a consultative way. QIOs typically focus on clinical improvement and offer a range of assistance in both group and individual settings. For example, they may disseminate educational materials that highlight best practices and provide free technical assistance to individual homes through on-site visits. Although participation in the programme is voluntary, QIOs serve an important role not met by the federal/state regulatory structure, and CMS for the most part has been pleased with their ability to raise and address quality concerns (CMS, 2006). Nonetheless, the net effect of the QIO programme remains unknown, especially relative to the investment.

Authorised under the 1965 Older Americans Act and administered within state agencies by the Federal Administration on Aging, the LTC Ombudsman Programme serves an important extra-regulatory role in NH quality assurance. Though they lack legal authority, state ombudsmen are responsible for monitoring and promoting resident rights and for investigating and resolving complaints they receive from NH residents. These complaints and investigations are separate from the legally required complaints mechanism directed by the state regulatory agency, and they essentially constitute another set of eyes and ears to protect and advocate for residents. LTC Ombudsmen also serve as liaisons between the government and facilities by communicating best-practices information to NHs and informing public agencies of quality problems that require governmental attention (Kapp, 2000). Although there are no rigorous studies quantifying its impact, experience with the LTC Ombudsman Programme has been largely positive, especially given the modest investment of governmental resources.

Non-nursing home settings

As with NHs, other LTC providers are monitored by state agencies, and sanctions may be imposed by the state or by CMS, when appropriate. Both the state and federal governments traditionally have been lenient in their enforcement, however. CMS infrequently sanctions providers for providing low-quality care, and the states themselves have not taken an active role in identifying unlicensed providers and forcing them into compliance (IOM, 2001). So lax is the regulatory scheme that both the GAO and IOM have called for significantly greater state standard-setting, in order to address the consequences of weak governmental oversight (IOM, 2001).

Although these LTC providers are mostly immune from NH compliance regulations, some of the programmes and policies are similar. While only NHs must use the MDS system described above, home health agencies must develop patient care plans and track progress in the Outcome and Assessment Information Set (OASIS), which is a functional analogue to the MDS. The Medicare LTC Ombudsman Program, discussed above, is also utilised in all non-NH LTC settings that involve Medicare funds in order to promote patient advocacy and disseminate information about best-care practices.

Challenges

Little is known about quality in non-NH settings, and even less is known about the potential effectiveness of more stringent regulation in these sectors (Zimmerman et al., 2005). For instance, the paucity of information in the ALF area reflects a lack of uniform assessment data and uncertainty about the range of outcomes for which facilities should be held accountable. Moreover, care in ALFs has garnered relatively little attention from researchers and government officials, a feature that could change as more government resources are devoted to them. A recent survey of LTC specialists found that two-thirds of respondents favored adopting more stringent regulation of assisted living facilities along the lines of requirements for NHs (Mor et al., 2010), although assisted living providers themselves have strongly resisted such change.

Assessing the quality of care delivered in home settings and establishing an oversight strategy for home care presents a substantial challenge (IOM, 2001). While there is some evidence that the lesser regulatory stringency in these settings has come at the cost of lower care quality, more extensive research is required to pinpoint the drawbacks and to identify the appropriate areas for reform, in particular to ensure a continuation of the flexibility and consumer choice that are central to HCBS.

Market-based approaches

Given the limitations of the current regulatory approach described above, some have questioned whether NH care might benefit from a reformed view of regulation (Kapp, 2000; Walshe, 2001) and, more specifically, whether market-based strategies might be useful to consider. One paper by two leading long-term care researchers in the United States suggested that "the current regulatory approach to quality improvement in LTC should shift its emphasis to utilise a market-driven approach," with a focus on providing information to consumers about quality, effectiveness, and value (Kane and Kane, 2001). Such techniques rely on two related theories: 1) with enough information, NH residents and their advocates (as consumers) will select the highest-quality providers at a given cost; and 2) with the right incentives, NH providers (as suppliers) will compete on and improve quality in order to increase profits.

Public reporting

Designed to empower consumers in making informed choices and to stimulate provider competition on quality, NH public reporting began in 1998 with the Nursing Home Compare (NHC) website and received greater emphasis in the 2002 Nursing Home Quality Initiative (NHQI), both directed by the federal government. Under these initiatives, the federal government publishes quality information about all NHs eligible for Medicare or Medicaid reimbursement.

NHC initially included information on facility characteristics, resident characteristics, and state inspection reports. The initial, modest scope of NHC was bolstered subsequently by the introduction of the NHQI, first on a pilot basis in 2001 and then nationwide in 2002. The NHQI added to the reported measures a range of MDS-based assessment measures for short- and long-stay NH residents. The federal government has continued to modify the NHC website, most notably via the addition of the Five-Star rating system, through which providers receive star ratings based on their performance on composite measures. NHC has also added information about complaints, deficiencies, and enforcement actions against facilities. See Table 8.1 for a brief description of the quality indicators available on the NHC website.

Table 8.1. **Information available on the Nursing Home Compare public reporting website**

Five-star ratings	
Overall	Overall rating for the home, out of five stars.
Health Inspections	Also includes information on the number of health deficiencies and the most recent health inspection.
Nursing Home Staffing	Includes the number of residents, as well as the number of nursing hours per resident per day.
Quality Measures	Offers an extensive list of quality measures, broken down by long-stay and short-stay. These measures include items such as the percent of residents with pain, pressure ulcers, depressive symptoms, and who are physically restrained.
Other quality indicators	
Fire Safety Inspections	Includes information on fire safety systems, inspections, investigations, and deficiencies.
Penalties and Denials of Payment	Number of civil monetary penalties and payment denials against the nursing home.
Complaints and Incidents	Gives explanations and outcomes for any complaints by residents against the home, including information about the number of residents affected and the level of harm.
Nursing home characteristics	
Programme Participation	Medicare and/or Medicaid.
Certified Beds	Number of beds in the facility.
Type of Ownership	For-profit, non-profit, or government-owned.
Continuing Care Retirement Community	Does the home guarantee lifetime housing with tiered levels of care provision?
Resident & Family Councils	Types of resident feedback available.
Located in a hospital	Is the home associated with a hospital?

Source: Medicare.gov (2011), "Nursing Home Compare", available at *www.medicare.gov/nhcompare.*

Public reporting of health care quality information is designed to inform and shape behaviours of key stakeholders. For these efforts to succeed, decision makers must be aware of the reporting efforts; they must trust the validity of the information; and they must be able to access, understand, and act on the information in time to use it. Arguably, certain factors present a barrier to generating a sufficient consumer response to effect changes in provider behaviour (e.g., the level of cognitive impairment typical among NH residents and the time-pressured nature of the NH placement decision).

In terms of the consumer response to NHC, awareness of the website increased greatly after implementation of the NHQI, at least judging from the number of visits to the website and calls to a telephone assistance line (OIG, 2004). A recent study found that 31% of consumers use the Internet in choosing a NH, and 12% specifically recall using the NHC website (Castle, 2009). Another recent study found NHC impacted patient sorting on selected measures in response to public reporting, thus improving the match between high-risk patients and high-quality facilities (Werner, 2011). While these data points do not indicate universal seeking of quality information, they do suggest a role for public reporting in promoting consumer choice.

Nonetheless, it is unclear whether the factors underlying the quality indicators are consistent with those criteria most important to consumers. Quality indicators tend to focus on clinical process-based measures. Resident-centered assessments (such as patient satisfaction and quality of life) are generally absent from NHC, despite their frequent measurement and discussion in NH evaluation (Miller and Mor, 2006). Given the multidimensionality of NH quality (Mor et al., 2003), the lack of such indicators might preclude accurate determinations of which facilities are best for individuals (and undermine a primary purpose of public reporting) (Mor, 2005).

The wide range of services provided within NH settings further complicates public reporting. For example, those needing only short-term rehabilitative services in a NH require different care, and therefore different information, than those individuals needing long-term supportive services in the same setting. To date, there is little information about the ability of publicly available quality information to accommodate these diverse aims.

Evidence on the impact of NH public reporting on quality of care generally ranges from mixed to modestly positive. Several studies report that a large majority of homes examine their report cards, and many facilities actively use this information to address quality failures (Mukamel et al., 2008). Shortly after NHC was launched there was an improvement in certain quality measures, in particular those that most directly contributed to the report card rankings, such as pain treatment and restraint use (Konetzka et al., 2010). Other studies have used a range of methodological approaches to investigate reporting's impact on resident outcomes, with somewhat equivocal results to date (Mukamel et al., 2008; Werner et al., 2009; Grabowski and Town, 2011).

Pay-for-performance

Advances in NH payment, such as casemix adjustment and prospective payment, have improved the efficiency of provider payments. Still, most payment schemes in the United States provide little incentive to deliver high-quality care. Some have proposed altering NH reimbursement to link payments to performance outcomes, a system known as "pay-for-performance" (P4P). Such efforts can rely on bonuses for absolute quality outcomes (e.g., pressure ulcers below a specified target) and/or on bonuses for relative quality improvement over time. Although the basic motivations are similar in either method, the latter approach potentially incentivises (and rewards) mid- and lower-tier facilities.

Several state Medicaid agencies have already begun to implement performance-based compensation in their reimbursement of Medicaid-certified facilities. Moreover, to determine the prudence of applying P4P to Medicare-certified facilities, CMS directed the Nursing Home Value Based Purchasing (NHVBP) demonstration project (which subsequently may or may not be adopted program-wide) to test and measure the effect of the program's implementation in three states, starting in 2009 (Konetzka et al., 2010), the results of which are not yet available.

The efficacy of P4P in the United States is still unclear. States that have implemented P4P vary widely in system design and no standard approach has yet emerged (Arling, 2009). Although some investigations of state approaches to P4P are optimistic (Cooke et al., 2010), the only empirical evidence definitively in favour of the approach is a study from the 1980s in San Diego, California, in which researchers found that incentive payments in NHs had positive effects on discharge rates and residents' functional status (Briesacher et al., 2009).

Meanwhile, there exist concerns that P4P, if not carefully designed and overseen, could actually lead to negative consequences. If risk-adjustment is insufficient, for instance, providers may select only healthier, low-risk patients – a technique known as cream-skimming (Konetzka et al., 2010). Similarly, if only certain quality indicators are used in determining performance bonuses, providers may seek improvement in these measures at the expense of others. In short, while P4P is intended to align financial compensation with quality assurance goals, it also opens the door to gamesmanship and other quick fixes with potential harm to residents.

Non-nursing homes settings

Market-based approaches also play a role outside of the NH setting, primarily for home health agencies. The Home Health Compare tool provides detailed quality information on all certified home health agencies in the country, similar to the Nursing Home Compare website described earlier. While Home Health Compare does not use the Five-Star ranking system, it does offer numeric information about the track records of the agencies in assisting daily activities, managing pain and other symptoms, treating wounds and preventing sores, avoiding harm, and preventing unplanned hospital care. These numbers are then compared to state and national averages, allowing for quality comparison. The federal government also has sponsored the Home Health Value-Based Purchasing demonstration, similar to its NH analogue described earlier, testing a pay-for-performance approach to provider reimbursement.

Conclusions

This section draws together some lessons learned and considerations for the future. The regulatory schemes described in this chapter have had frustratingly mixed results, with some areas performing significantly better than others and with considerable uncertainty where evidence of effectiveness is lacking. LTC regulation in the United States has been relatively successful at improving quality in certain easily measured categories. For example, in the wake of OBRA '87, which emphasized outcome-oriented and patient-centred approaches to quality control, there has been a drastic decrease in the use of restraints and catheters, as well as drops in dehydration rates and pressure ulcers. Patient autonomy has also been bolstered, both by OBRA '87 and by other laws such as the Patient Self-Determination Act of 1990 (Kapp, 2000).

On the other hand, quality problems clearly persist in the NH sector in the United States, which suggests the existence of significant regulatory failures (GAO, 1987; GAO, 1998; GAO, 1999; OIG, 1999a; OIG, 1999b; GAO, 2002). The current regulatory system has struggled not only with actual quality control, but also with the detection and reporting of deficiencies. The GAO reported in 2008 that 70% of federal follow-up or "look behind" surveys (described above) uncovered at least one deficiency with the "potential for more than minimal harm" compared to initial state surveys, a figure that got worse over the decade (GAO, 2008). More seriously, 15% of these federal follow-up surveys identified state surveys that missed the most serious deficiencies: those that constitute immediate jeopardy or actual harm. Such under-reporting also makes it difficult to determine the true extent of quality problems.

The effectiveness of the regulatory scheme must be evaluated in the context of the costs of regulation, which can be very high. Although no single number encapsulates the total costs of regulating this industry, a 2001 study estimated the annual costs of the NH survey/certification process at USD 382 million, or USD 22 000 per home (Walshe, 2001). Allowing for inflation, growth of the market, increases in regulatory stringency, and the addition of the complaint, public reporting, and quality improvement features, the direct costs likely reach into the billions.

On top of these costs are expenditures by NHs to comply with federal and state standards. These costs include preparation for the surveys, data compilation, responding to complaints, and other such measures designed to promote compliance. These costs are difficult to measure, but a recent study calculated the marginal cost of correcting one deficiency in a NH at USD 3 608, and found that a one-standard-deviation increase in regulatory stringency was associated with a 1.1% increase in NH operations costs (Mukamel et al., 2011). Although this study was the first of its kind, this preliminary figure indicates that these indirect costs, in the aggregate, may be substantial (Mor, 2011).

Looking ahead

In recent decades, the US federal government has taken many steps to improve the LTC quality assurance process, especially for NHs. The current system is considerably improved relative to the insufficient and uneven regulation in place before 1987. Nonetheless, the current level of regulatory stringency in the United States has not consistently led to the safe, effective, patient-centred NH care that was envisioned by OBRA '87. In light of these results, some scholars and policy makers have argued for even tougher standards and better enforcement. Others have cited this outcome as evidence that the regulatory system is ineffective and should be replaced by simpler, less punitive measures (Walshe, 2001).

In conceptualising an approach to LTC regulation, there are several potential trade-offs to consider based on lessons from the US experience:

- The more decentralised that the monitoring and enforcement of regulatory standards are the more inefficient and inconsistent these processes are likely to be. Nonetheless, the federal-state arrangement reflects the nature of the US Medicaid programme and also has the potential advantage of state inspectors being more attuned to local conditions and practice norms.

- The transition of quality assurance from structure- and process-based quality measures to outcomes-based measures must be supported by a robust data infrastructure and clear, consistent guidance on how to apply existing regulatory standards. The development and implementation of the MDS resident assessment dataset and the more recent QIS quality assurance system provide useful guidance for similarly focused efforts.

- Completely separating quality monitoring and improvement activities comes at a cost. Although the threat of sanctions or closure for poor performance are important deterrents, using a regulatory approach that is exclusively punitive will be constrained in its ability to help struggling providers identify root causes of problems and to work effectively in addressing them. Quality improvement and quality assurance should be viewed as complementary tools that government can use to improve nursing home quality.

- Market-based strategies to improve LTC quality have an intuitive appeal, but their overall effectiveness in assuring or improving quality of care remains an open question. With P4P in particular, policy makers must balance the need to ensure sufficient financial incentives to spur desired behaviours while minimising the potential for unintended consequences.

- LTC quality assurance remains underdeveloped in home and community-based settings in the United States. As more public resources are devoted to care in these settings, one tension that will likely increase is the trade-off between allowing providers flexibility (e.g., in structuring housing and service options for consumers) and ensuring greater standardisation of care and access to services. Assisted living will likely be an important test case in the United States as these facilities continue to serve a more disabled clientele and as public dollars for residents in this setting likely increase.

Ultimately, it is hard to predict future regulatory changes in the United States, but given the current political climate and optimism about the effects of P4P and public reporting, a continued emphasis on market-based approaches is likely to endure. Other suggested reforms could gain traction in the future, including strengthening oversight and enforcement, considering a facility's past quality performance in setting the frequency of inspections, and allowing QIOs and survey agencies to work together in integrating quality assurance and quality improvement. However, LTC regulation is a politically charged topic with high stakes, features that entrench the status quo and make substantial reform difficult.

Perhaps the most important change in the future of LTC regulation will be a greater incorporation of consumer voice in how LTC is delivered, evaluated, and reported. In particular, quality measures and indicators could begin to integrate core issues of patient satisfaction, quality of life, and care experience. If this shift occurs, LTC in the United States may finally fulfill the vision of person-centred care and individual choice, dignity, and respect envisioned by OBRA '87.

References

Arling, G. (2009), "Medicaid Nursing Pay-for-Performance: Where Do We Stand?", *The Gerontologist*, Vol. 49, No. 5, pp. 587-595.

Binstock, R.H. et al. (1996), *The Future of Long-Term Care: Social and Policy Issues*, Johns Hopkins University Press, Baltimore.

Briesacher, B.A. et al. (2009), "Can Pay-for-Performance Take Nursing Home Care to the Next Level?", *Journal of the American Geriatrics Society*, Vol. 56, No. 10, pp. 1937-1939.

Castle, N.G. (2009), "The Nursing Home Compare Report Card: Consumers' Use and Understanding", *Journal of Aging and Social Policy*, Vol. 21, No. 2, pp. 187-208.

CMS – Centers for Medicare and Medicaid Services (2006), "Report to Congress on the Evaluation of the Quality Improvement Organization (QIO) Program for Medicare Beneficiaries for Fiscal Year 2006", available at *www.cms.gov/QualityImprovementOrgs/downloads/2006RtCQIO.pdf*.

CMS (2007), "Evaluation of the Quality Indicator Survey (QIS)", available at *www.cms.gov/CertificationandComplianc/Downloads/QISExecSummary.pdf*.

CMS (2011a), "Certification & Compliance: Nursing Homes", available at *www.cms.gov/CertificationandComplianc/12_NHs.asp*.

CMS (2011b), "HCBS Waivers – Section 1915(c)", available at *www.cms.gov/MedicaidStWaivProgDemoPGI/05_HCBSWaivers-Section1915%28c%29.asp*.

Cooke, V. et al. (2010), "Minnesota's Nursing Facility Performance-Based Incentive Payment Program: An Innovative Model for Promoting Care Quality", *The Gerontologist*, Vol. 50, No. 4, pp. 556-563.

Furrow, B.R. et al. (2008), *Health Law: Cases, Materials and Problems* (6th ed.), Thomson/West.

Furrow, B.R. et al. (2010), *Health Care Reform Supplement to Health Law: Cases, Materials and Problems*, Thomson/West.

GAO – Government Accountability Office (1987), "Medicare and Medicaid: Stronger Enforcement of Nursing Home Requirements Needed", available at *http://gao.justia.com/department-of-health-and-human-services/1987/7/medicare-and-medicaid-hrd-87-113/HRD-87-113-full-report.pdf*.

GAO (1998), "California Nursing Homes: Care Problems Persist Despite Federal and State Oversight", available at *www.gao.gov/archive/1998/he98202.pdf*.

GAO (1999), "Nursing Homes: Additional Steps Needed to Strengthen Enforcement of Federal Quality Standards", available at *www.gao.gov/archive/1999/he99046.pdf*.

GAO (2002), "Nursing Homes: More Can Be Done to Protect Residents from Abuse", available at: *www.gao.gov/new.items/d02312.pdf*.

GAO (2003), "Prevalence of Serious Problems, While Declining, Reinforces Importance of Enhanced Oversight", available at *www.gao.gov/new.items/d03561.pdf*.

GAO (2007), "Efforts to Strengthen Federal Enforcement Have Not Deterred Some Homes from Repeatedly Harming Residents", available at *www.gao.gov/new.items/d07241.pdf*.

GAO (2008), "Nursing Homes: Federal Monitoring Surveys Demonstrate Continued Understatement of Serious Care Problems and CMS Oversight Weaknesses", available at *www.gao.gov/new.items/ d08517.pdf*.

GAO (2009), "Medicare and Medicaid Participating Facilities: CMS Needs to Reexamine Its Approach for Funding State Oversight of Health Care Facilities", available at *www.gao.gov/new.items/d0964.pdf*.

Grabowski, D.C. and R.J. Town (2011), "Does Information Matter? Competition, Quality, and the Impact of Nursing Home Report Cards", *Health Services Research* [e-pub ahead of print].

Harrington, C. and M. Millman (2001), "Nursing Home Staffing Standards in State Statutes and Regulations", Henry J. Kaiser Family Foundation, University of California, San Francisco.

Harrington, C. et al. (2010), "Nursing, Facilities, Staffing, Residents, and Facility Deficiencies, 2004 Through 2009", Department of Social and Behavioral Sciences, University of California, San Francisco.

IOM – Institute of Medicine (1986), *Improving the Quality of Care in Nursing Homes,* National Academy Press, Washington.

IOM (2001), *Improving the Quality of Long-Term Care,* National Academy Press, Washington.

Kane, R.L. and R.A. Kane (2001), "What Older People Want from Long-Term Care, and How They Can Get It", *Health Affairs*, Vol. 20, No. 5, pp. 114-127.

Kane, R.A. et al. (1998), *The Heart of Long-Term Care,* Oxford University Press, New York.

Kapp, M.B. (2000), "Quality of Care and Quality of Life in Nursing Facilities: What's Regulation Got to Do With It?", *McGeorge Law Review*, Vol. 31, No. 3, pp. 707-731.

Kaye, H.S., C. Harrington and M.P. LaPlante (2010), "Long-term Care: Who Gets It, Who Provides It, Who Pays, And How Much?", *Health Affairs*, Vol. 29, No. 1, pp. 11-21.

Konetzka, R.T. et al. (2010), "Applying Market-Based Reforms to LTC", *Health Affairs*, Vol. 29, No. 1, pp. 74-80.

Medicare.gov (2011), "Nursing Home Compare", available at *www.medicare.gov/nhcompare*.

Mendelson, M.A. (1974), *Tender Loving Greed: How the Incredibly Lucrative Nursing Home 'Industry' is Exploiting America's Old People and Defrauding Us All,* 1st ed., Knopf, New York.

Miller, E.A. and V. Mor (2006), "Modernizing Regulation", Chapter 6 in *Out of the Shadows: Envisioning a Brighter Future for Long-Term Care in America,* Brown University.

Mollica, R., K. Sims-Kastelein and J. O'Keefe (2008), "Assisted Living and Residential Care Policy Compendium, 2007 Update", National Academy for State Health Policy, Portland, available at *http:// aspe.hhs.gov/daltcp/reports/2007/07alcom.htm*.

Mor, V. (2005), "Improving the Quality of Long-Term Care with Better Information", *Milbank Quarterly*, Vol. 83, No. 3, pp; 333-364.

Mor, V. (2011), "Cost of Nursing Home Regulation: Building a Research Agenda", *Medical Care*, Vol. 49, No. 6, pp. 525-536.

Mor, V. et al. (2003), "The Quality of Quality Measurement in U.S. Nursing Homes", *The Gerontologist*, Vol. 43, No. SII, pp. 37-46.

Mor, V. et al. (2010), "The Taste for Regulation in Long-term Care", *Medical Care Research and Review*, Vol. 67, No. 4 Suppl., pp. 38S-64S, August.

Moss, F.E. and V.J. Halamandaris (1977), *Too Old, Too Sick, Too Bad: Nursing Homes in America,* Aspen Systems Corporation, Germantown.

Mukamel, D.B. et al. (2007), "Nursing Homes' Response to the Nursing Home Compare Report Card", *Journals of Gerontology Series B: Psychological Sciences & Social Sciences*, Vol. 62B, No. 4, pp. S218–S225.

Mukamel, D.B. et al. (2008), "Publication of Quality Report Cards and Trends in Reported Quality Measures in Nursing Homes", *Health Services Research*, Vol. 43, No. 4, pp. 1244-1262.

Mukamel, D.B. et al. (2011), "Does State Regulation of Quality Impose Costs on Nursing Homes?", *Medical Care*, Vol. 49, No. 6, pp. 529-534.

NCSL – National Conference of State Legislatures (2011), "Certificate of Need: State Health Laws and Programs", available at *www.ncsl.org/IssuesResearch/Health/CONCertificateofNeedStateLaws/ tabid/14373/Default.aspx*.

OIG – Office of the Inspector General (1999a), "Nursing Home Survey and Certification: Overall Capacity", available at *http://oig.hhs.gov/oei/reports/oei-02-98-00330.pdf*.

OIG (1999b), "Quality of Care in Nursing Homes: An Overview", available at *http://oig.hhs.gov/oei/reports/oei-02-99-00060.pdf*.

OIG (2004), "Inspection Results on Nursing Home Compare: Completeness and Accuracy", available at *http://oig.hhs.gov/oei/reports/oei-01-03-00130.pdf*.

OIG (2006a), "Nursing Home Complaint Investigations", available at *http://oig.hhs.gov/oei/reports/oei-01-04-00340.pdf*.

OIG (2006b), "Nursing Home Enforcement: Application of Mandatory Remedies", available at *http://oig.hhs.gov/oei/reports/oei-06-03-00410.pdf*.

OIG (2008), "Memorandum Report: "Trends in Nursing Home Deficiencies and Complaints", available at *http://oig.hhs.gov/oei/reports/oei-02-08-00140.pdf*.

OIG (2009), "Nursing Home Corporations Under Quality of Care Corporate Integrity Agreements", available at *http://oig.hhs.gov/oei/reports/oei-06-06-00570.pdf*.

Rantz, M.J. et al. (1999), "Minimum Data Set and Resident Assessment Instrument: Can Using Standardized Assessment Improve Clinical Practice and Outcomes of Care?", *Journal of Gerontological Nursing*, Vol. 25, No. 6, pp. 35-43.

Smith, P. v. M. Heckler (1984), "In re the Estate of Michael Patrick Smith v. Heckler", 747 F.2d 583 (10th Cir. 1984), United States Court of Appeals, Tenth Circuit, 29 October.

Stevenson, D.G. (2006), "Nursing Home Consumer Complaints and Quality of Care – A National View", *Medical Care Research and Review*, Vol. 63, No. 3, pp. 347-368.

Stevenson, D.G. and D.C. Grabowski (2010), "Sizing up the Market for Assisted Living", *Health Affairs*, Vol. 29, No. 1, pp. 35-43.

Stevenson, D.G. and D.M. Studdert (2003), "The Rise of Nursing Home Litigation: Findings from a National Survey of Attorneys", *Health Affairs*, Vol. 22, No. 2, pp. 219-229.

Stevenson, D.G., M.J. Spittal and D.M. Studdert (2013), "Does Litigation Increase or Decrease Health Care Quality? A National Study of Negligence Claims Against Nursing Homes", *Medical Care*, Vol. 51, No. 5, pp. 430-436.

Stoil, M.J. (1994), "Surveyors Stymied by Survey Criteria, Researchers Find", *Nursing Homes*, Vol. 43, No. 4, p. 58.

Studdert, D.M. et al. (2011), "Relationship Between Quality of Care and Negligence Litigation in Nursing Homes", *New England Journal of Medicine*, Vol. 364, No. 13, pp. 1243-1250.

Vladeck, B.C. and Twentieth Century Fund (1980), *Unloving Care: The Nursing Home Tragedy*, Basic Books, New York.

Walshe, K. (2001), "Regulating U.S. Nursing Homes: Are We Learning from Experience?", *Health Affairs*, Vol. 20, No. 6, pp. 128-144.

Werner, R.M., R.T. Konetzka and G.B. Kruse (2009), "Impact of Public Reporting on Unreported Quality of Care", *Health Services Research*, Vol. 44, No. 2.1, pp. 379-398.

Werner, R.M. et al. (2011), "Changes in Patient Sorting to Nursing Homes Under Public Reporting: Improved Patient Matching or Provider Gaming?", *Health Services Research*, Vol. 46, No. 2, pp. 555-571.

Zimmerman, D. et al. (2003), *Nursing Home Complaint Investigation: Building the Model System*, CMS, Baltimore.

Zimmerman, S. et al. (2005), "How Good is Assisted Living? Findings and Implications from an Outcomes Study", *Journals of Gerontology, Series B: Psychological Science Sciences and Social Sciences*, Vol. 60, No. 4, pp. S195-S204.

ORGANISATION FOR ECONOMIC CO-OPERATION AND DEVELOPMENT

The OECD is a unique forum where governments work together to address the economic, social and environmental challenges of globalisation. The OECD is also at the forefront of efforts to understand and to help governments respond to new developments and concerns, such as corporate governance, the information economy and the challenges of an ageing population. The Organisation provides a setting where governments can compare policy experiences, seek answers to common problems, identify good practice and work to co-ordinate domestic and international policies.

The OECD member countries are: Australia, Austria, Belgium, Canada, Chile, the Czech Republic, Denmark, Estonia, Finland, France, Germany, Greece, Hungary, Iceland, Ireland, Israel, Italy, Japan, Korea, Luxembourg, Mexico, the Netherlands, New Zealand, Norway, Poland, Portugal, the Slovak Republic, Slovenia, Spain, Sweden, Switzerland, Turkey, the United Kingdom and the United States. The European Union takes part in the work of the OECD.

OECD Publishing disseminates widely the results of the Organisation's statistics gathering and research on economic, social and environmental issues, as well as the conventions, guidelines and standards agreed by its members.

THE EUROPEAN COMMISSION

The European Commission's Directorate General Employment, Social Affairs and Inclusion pursues policy, legislative and financial initiatives in order to create more and better jobs, combat poverty and social exclusion, promote social justice and protection, enable the free movement of workers, ensure labour mobility, promote workers' rights and solidarity between generations and contribute to the better functioning of labour markets, achievement of full employment, social progress and a highly competitive social market economy in the European Union within the context of the Europe 2020 Strategy.

OECD PUBLISHING, 2, rue André-Pascal, 75775 PARIS CEDEX 16
(81 2013 13 1 P) ISBN 978-92-64-19452-6 – No. 60643 2013-01